ALSO BY WILLIAM H. GOETZMANN

Army Exploration in the American West, 1803–1863 (1959)

Exploration and Empire (1966)

When the Eagle Screamed: The Romantic Horizon in American Diplomacy, 1800–1860 (1966)

Colonial Horizon: America in the Sixteenth and Seventeenth Centuries (1969)

A Guide to Computer-Assisted Historical Research in American Education, with Arthur Moehlmann, Gerald Everett, and David Van Tassel (1970)

THE AMERICAN HEGELIANS

THE AMERICAN HEGELIANS

An Intellectual Episode in the History of Western America

EDITED BY

WILLIAM H. GOETZMANN

With the assistance of DICKSON PRATT

ALFRED A. KNOPF   NEW YORK   1973

This is a BORZOI BOOK *published by* ALFRED A. KNOPF, INC.

Copyright © 1973 by William H. Goetzmann

All rights reserved under International and Pan-American Copyright Conventions. Published in the United States by Alfred A. Knopf, Inc., New York, and simultaneously in Canada by Random House of Canada Limited, Toronto. Distributed by Random House, Inc., New York.

Library of Congress Cataloging in Publication Data
Goetzmann, William H., comp.   The American Hegelians.
Bibliography: p.
1. Philosophy, American—19th century.
2. Hegel, Georg Wilhelm Friedrich, 1770–1831—Influence.
I. Title.
B893.G6   1973   191   72–11032
ISBN 0–394–48165–8

Manufactured in the United States of America

FIRST EDITION

For Norman Holmes Pearson

CONTENTS

PREFACE
AND ACKNOWLEDGMENTS

THIS anthology attempts to portray a different kind of Western America from that usually pictured in the sagas of the frontiersmen and the Indians. It is the story of an intellectual movement that was concentrated in the West and emanated outward through all America, markedly shaping civilization in the nineteenth century. But, contrary to the Turnerian myth, this intellectual movement was not derived from the wilderness experience of the frontier. It did not emerge "stark and strong from out of the forests." Rather, it was borrowed from Germany and brought west to Cincinnati, Chicago, and St. Louis, where it seemed to have its greatest social applicability, and where it seemed to fit the drama of the historical situation—the emergence of a great city on the very edge of the frontier. Thus, a close look at Hegelianism as it took root and developed in St. Louis and other parts of the West provides a clue to the character of the "Western Mind," that ever-present but elusive phenomenon which has been for so long obscured by frontier nature myths and Rousseauan images of buckskin-clad hunters and heroic men on horseback. It further makes clear that the West did indeed *have* a mind, of a complex and subtle order, that related more directly to its people and its institutions than to fashion, as indeed it does today, often to the surprise of first-time observers and careless image-makers.

Beyond this, to study the American Hegelians is to appreciate the grass-roots pluralistic society that was growing up in the West. Many of the chief figures in the movement were Germans and their story reflects the values, attitudes, and sometimes quaint preoccupations of newly arrived Americans. It clearly projects their grandiose dreams which arose out of hard realities and constant ideological clashes on both sides of the Atlantic. More than anything else, their story suggests that the American dream was a cosmopolitan dream shared by Europeans, immigrants, and the native-born alike in its larger features. They all believed in some variety of Hegel's faith that America was inevitably a "country of the future." In St. Louis, as the story of the Hegelians indicates, this took on the form of a highly emotional interconnection in the minds of the intellectuals between progress, civilization, and urbanism. To develop the great metropolis, whether in St. Louis or Cincinnati or Chicago with its "high buildings," was to develop civilization and hence the entire country. The same spirit could be detected in far-off San Francisco and in literally thousands of failed "booster towns" in between. This suggests that though mid-nineteenth-century America was overwhelmingly rural in population, it did not wish to remain so. The drive for urban development and "civilization" had a far greater velocity than did pastoralism, as the Populists found to their sorrow.

Thus the chronicle of the American Hegelians takes on more than regional significance. It constitutes an important episode in the social history of America. Led by its colorful and eccentric prophets—the philosophic Stallo, the revolutionary Willich, the ambitious Harris, the dreamy Snider, and the demonic Brokmeyer—American Hegelianism was an electric symbol of American dynamism in what Howard Mumford Jones has recently called "The Age of Energy."* Perhaps because, like the West itself, it succeeded too well and diffused itself through the whole culture, it has been largely neglected and forgotten. To remedy that neglect is the purpose of this anthology.

Much of the material pertaining to the American Hegelians now lies buried in depository or "book retirement" libraries, unused and for the most part unavailable to students. One researcher leafing through a volume of the *Journal of Speculative Philosophy* in 1972 noted that its pages "had not been turned for 101 years" and decided not to further disturb its condition. He turned to lager beer instead, perhaps inspired by German "culture," and so noted his course of action in the margin of the *Journal*. The present anthology is designed to bring the Hegelians out of the dusty book depository into the sober light of day where their ideas can be considered in more convenience and comfort, and, hopefully, in an atmosphere of genuine excitement.

I owe a special debt of gratitude to my student and research assistant, Mr. Dickson Pratt, who prowled through many libraries locating obscure volumes and articles, all the while mastering the art of the Xerox machine. At all points in this project, I have conferred with Mr. Pratt and have found his incisive comments on philosophy invaluable. I wish also to thank my students in a class on "Victorianism and Modernism," in particular Mr. Herbert Hovenkamp. Most of them became fascinated as I was with Hegelianism and idealism, and their creative observations helped me more than they know. Further, I would like to thank Marshall and Karen Kuykendall for their gracious hospitality and for many hours of stimulating philosophical conversation at the "Kuykendall Ranch."

* Howard Mumford Jones, *The Age of Energy* (New York: Viking Press, 1972).

I am likewise indebted to Professor Loyd Easton, whose own book, *Hegel's First American Followers*, is a major and pioneering work, for permission to reproduce his translations of the writings of August Willich. In like fashion, I am obliged to George P. Adams and William P. Montague for permission to reproduce John Dewey's "From Absolutism to Experimentalism," which appears in their excellent work, *Contemporary American Philosophers*. The Missouri Historical Society was most gracious in supplying me with Xerox material from Henry C. Brokmeyer's great unpublished manuscript translation of Hegel's *Larger Logic* which is printed here for the first time. For her help I especially wish to thank the Society's archivist, Mrs. Frances Stadtler. Mrs. Denton J. Snider granted me permission to publish selections from her husband's works, for which I am grateful. I would further like to thank the circulation and interlibrary loan departments of The University of Texas Library for their efforts on my behalf and most of all for their patience; and Barbara Marrs and Barbara Pickett, who typed the manuscript, for an equal measure of effort and patience. Casting bread upon the waters, the University of Texas Research Institute has supported me generously in the writing of an overall intellectual history of the United States. This anthology is an unexpected by-product of that support as well as of my own curiosity. I hope it will be regarded as the first installment in repayment of my colleagues' faith in research. And, finally, I wish to thank Mr. Alfred A. Knopf, my publisher, also a man of good faith, for his encouragement in the completion of this project.

WILLIAM H. GOETZMANN

Austin, Texas
June 1972

THE AMERICAN HEGELIANS

INTRODUCTION:
THE AMERICAN HEGELIANS

I

HAD anyone been observant enough on a winter night in 1858, he might have seen emerge, from the Old Mercantile Library Building in St. Louis, two men engaged in heated discussion, oblivious to the cold. One of them would be a cultured, dignified New Englander, currently employed in the river city as a teacher of shorthand. His name: William Torrey Harris. The other, a shabbily dressed, bewhiskered, and demonic-looking man with "the quick almost wild eye of the hunter," was sure to be Henry C. Brokmeyer, a German iron-molder. While the United States was suffering the trauma of "bleeding Kansas" and seemed destined for civil war, the two disputants had other things on their minds. That night and for many months afterwards they would argue the merits of Georg Wilhelm Friedrich Hegel as if the fate of the Union and even civilization itself depended upon their ideas.

If not that night, then on other nights they would argue their way through the streets of St. Louis until, eventually, they might find themselves before Brokmeyer's unpretentious lodging house. Repairing to his single, austere room, they would continue their debate as the gaslights of the city flickered out and the country moved one day closer to war. Usually, Harris stood his ground, as he had on the night they first met at the Kant Society meeting in the Old Library. He defended Victor Cousin and Immanuel Kant, while Brokmeyer deployed against him every formidable weapon in the arsenal of Hegel's *Larger Logic*. Eventually, before the year was out, Harris, Cousin, and even Kant were crushed beneath the onslaughts of Brokmeyer's arguments. In his diary for 1858, Harris wrote "Brokmeyer" and "Hegel" in capital letters, and the two men agreed that perhaps the most important and pressing mission in America at the time was to "make Hegel talk English." Only the logic of the great German philosopher could transcend the social and intellectual differences among peoples within America, which three years earlier Walt Whitman had called "a teeming nation of nations." In Hegel's works, especially the *Larger Logic*, lay the keys to the true achievement of freedom, individualism, and order that would be necessary for a

3

rapidly changing America symbolized by the burgeoning metropolis of St. Louis itself as it rested in the heart of the continent on the crossroads between North and South, East and West.[1]

History has taken relatively little notice of Brokmeyer and Harris, but their ideas nonetheless had consequences of importance to the future of America. These two became the founders of the St. Louis Movement in philosophy, the chief vehicle by which Hegel's ideas and those of virtually every other major post-Kantian German philosopher entered the mainstream of American thought. In this role, Brokmeyer and Harris not only stimulated the professionalization of philosophy in the United States, but, as they and their followers applied their ideas, wrought significant changes upon American institutional life. Their efforts insured that the great tradition of philosophic idealism that began with the Puritan Platonists lived on and played a vital role in American life well into the twentieth century.

Brokmeyer and Harris were not the first Americans to be exposed to Hegel's thought, nor were they the first American Hegelians. As early as 1820, George Bancroft, the prominent American historian, had attended Hegel's lectures in Berlin. Though he became the foremost exponent of transcendental history in America, Bancroft had found Hegel's lectures "unintelligible" and the man himself "sluggish." He soon stopped attending his lectures.[2] Little by little, however, as Boston intellectuals like Bancroft, George Ticknor, Edward Everett, and Frederick Henry Hedge absorbed German philosophy at firsthand through study in the country of its origin, and as German immigrants began arriving in America after 1830, the ideas of Hegel filtered into the United States. Some thinkers, like the radical transcendentalist Theodore Parker, became interested in Hegel because of his impact on the German "higher critics" of Christianity like David Friedrich Strauss. Strauss and others, under Hegel's influence, had critically examined the Gospels and the life of Christ from a modern historical standpoint, concluding that Christ was not God but a supremely good man whose moral imperatives deserved to be followed. Strauss's *Das Leben Jesu* (1835–36) carried this message, and it made a profound impact on the fiery Parker. The title of Parker's most famous sermon, "The Transient and the Permanent in Christianity," was taken from one of Strauss's own sermons.[3] As New England's freethinking Unitarians like William Ellery Channing, Theodore Parker, and Ralph Waldo Emerson turned more and more to German thought, Hegelianism, along with Kantianism and the theology of the "higher criticism," became loosely interrelated, and sometimes interchangeable, influences on their thought. In 1842, James Murdock published the first American overview of German thought, *Sketches of Modern Philosophy Among the Germans*. Hegel was included in this survey as "the most unintelligible writer" Murdock had ever read.[4] President Asa Mahan of Oberlin College in his *System of Intellectual Philosophy* (1845) followed the transcendentalist line in praising Kant, Coleridge, and Kant's French disciple, Cousin, but he roundly condemned Hegel as a pantheist.[5] Theologians, more than anyone else, dimly perceived that Hegel's thought had proceeded dangerously beyond that of Kant. Just as the rebel Unitarians began as liberals and were quickly carried into religious radicalism by Kantian, Schellingian, and Coleridgian thought, so too were the Kantians themselves in danger of being outflanked by Hegel and his adherents. Perhaps the key book of the period was Frederick Henry Hedge's anthology, *Prose Writers of Germany* (1847), which was intended to parade the glories of Kantian thought before the American intellectual public. However, Hedge, assisted in his translation work by Henry Boynton Smith, who had studied at Halle and Berlin and was friendly with Hegel's widow, also included selections from Hegel in the book.[6] This unfiltered exposure of Hegel's ideas bore unforeseen consequences. For one thing, it convinced Brokmeyer that Hegel's thought was all-important, and Hedge's work thus led to the founding of the St. Louis Movement.

While native Americans were absorbing German thought through study abroad and through books, German immigrants had begun to expound their ideas in America. Francis Lieber, an economist then living in Boston, wrote of Hegel in his *Encyclopedia Americana* (1829–33). More important, Frederick Augustus Rauch, an immigrant who became president of Marshall College in Mercersburg, Pennsylvania, published in 1840 *Psychology, A View of the Human Soul, Including Anthropology*, which, crude as it was, was the first Hegel-inspired book of American origin. His work went through several editions and was read by most of the transcendentalist rebels. Meanwhile, in Cincinnati, as the German population swelled during the 1830s, a number of thinkers had emerged who had begun to launch Hegel's ideas into the mainstream of American thought.[7] The most important of these were Johann B. Stallo, Peter Kaufmann, and August Willich, who were joined by Moncure Conway, a Virginian.

Stallo, a lawyer by profession, was to become widely regarded as the most significant philosopher of science in nineteenth-century America. His book *The Concepts and Theories of Modern Physics* (1881) largely overshadowed an earlier work that did much to promulgate the Hegelian gospel in America, *General Principles of the Philosophy of Nature, With an Outline of Some of Its Recent Developments Among the Germans, Embracing the Philosophical Systems of Schelling and Hegel and Oken's System of Nature* (1848).

Peter Kaufmann, a former ministerial student, Rappite teacher, and newspaperman, was a devotee of utopian experiments. He was fascinated by the veterans of the Rappite and Owenite communities and attempted to start a colony himself in Ohio called "The Society of United Germans at Teutonia." Josiah Warren's concept of a "time store" may have been derived from Kaufmann's "labor-for-labor" store which he first established in Philadelphia in the 1820s.[8] In *The Temple of Truth, or The Science of Ever-Progressing Knowledge* (1858), Kaufmann set forth his own pseudo-Hegelian philosophy which he called "perfectionism."

August Willich had been a captain in the Prussian Army. Disgusted with authoritarian and undemocratic rule, he resigned his commission and joined Karl Marx in his Rhineland campaigns against the state's oppression of workers. After he had performed gallantly in the workers' losing battle in Baden in 1849, assisted by Friedrich Engels as his adjutant, Willich settled for a time in London, where he worked as a carpenter. Then, in 1851, he came to America, eventually making his way to Cincinnati. During this period, he broke with Marx, but he never abandoned his socialist activism. As editor of the Cincinnati *Republikaner*, Willich published in 1859 and 1860 many articles reflecting a radical Hegelian point of view. When the Civil War broke out, he raised a regiment of Ohio German volunteers and later assumed command of a similar regiment of Indiana Germans. He rose to the rank of major general after having participated in such bitter campaigns as Chickamauga, Shiloh, Chattanooga, and Sherman's March to the Sea. Willich was one of four Marxists who rose to the rank of general in the Union Army during the war period. In this case, action was joined with thought, and Willich's ideas and behavior represent the way in which Hegel's thought did so much to inspire abolitionist and workingmen's causes in nineteenth-century America.

Moncure Conway, after ordination as a Methodist minister, migrated northward in the early 1850s to Harvard Divinity School. He subsequently came under the influence, not of his teachers at that school, but of Emerson and, especially, the radical Parker. He became devoted to Hegelianism through the new theology of Strauss, and to militant abolitionism through the influence of Parker and other Boston zealots. When, in 1856, he was dismissed from his first pulpit in Washington, D.C., for his abolitionist views, Conway moved west to Cincinnati where, as minister to the First Congregational Church, he found the atmosphere for a time more congenial. In this capacity, he helped to bring Hegel as well as abolitionism to Ohio.

Thus, by the 1850s, Hegel's ideas had been carried west to Ohio both from a seedbed in New England and directly from Germany. The same process, though with somewhat greater complexity, was consummated in St. Louis beginning on that wintry night in 1858 when Harris, the

New Englander, met Brokmeyer, the German. The latter had arrived in the United States in 1844 with no command of English and no money. Working as a hide-tanner, bootblack, shoemaker, or anything that would earn him a living, by 1850 he had amassed a comfortable fortune and turned to the life of the mind. After being disappointed with Georgetown College in Kentucky, he enrolled at Brown, where, while studying with Francis Wayland, he discovered Hegel in Hedge's anthology. This led him to further readings in Hegel and ultimately to the conviction that the Swabian philosopher held the key to all that was worthwhile in human life. In 1854, Brokmeyer abruptly left New England and, taking Hegel's works, went to live in a Thoreauvian hut in the wilds of Warren County, Missouri. He became, as it were, an intellectual Daniel Boone out on the "long hunt" for the meaning of thought and civilization. While on his lonely quest, Brokmeyer lost his fortune, and hence was forced to come in from his retreat to earn his living as an iron-moulder in St. Louis, where he met his destiny in the person of Harris.[9]

Harris came from North Killingly, Connecticut, and attended Yale College for two years, more out of custom than interest. His main attention had been directed toward spiritualism, mesmerism, and phrenology. Franz Gall and Johann Spurzheim and the Connecticut wizard Orsen Fowler were his gods. Then, one day, he made contact with German transcendentalism through a lecture delivered by Bronson Alcott. Soon he had waded through Parker's sermons, the writings of Goethe, Coleridge, Kant, and Cousin, and he was then a convert to transcendentalism. Along the way, he managed to learn German so that he could read the new philosophy in its original language. In a transcendentalist spirit of adventure, Harris left New England for frontier St. Louis. He had just arrived on his "errand into the wilderness" when he encountered Brokmeyer.[10]

The immediate consequences of the meeting of Brokmeyer and Harris were twofold: Harris became a member of a St. Louis philosophical circle which, among other thinkers, discussed Kant and later Hegel, and in which he was subsequently to use his great talents as an organizer in formalizing its activities; and he set Brokmeyer to work translating Hegel's *Larger Logic*, a task that occupied the latter for the rest of his life. As a result of Brokmeyer's genius and enthusiasm, and because it was inaccessible and hence mysterious. Hegel's *Larger Logic* became a magic book for the St. Louis intellectuals. It was the touchstone and ultimate authority for most of their philosophical discussions.[11]

In 1866, after Brokmeyer had served as a Union officer in the Civil War, the St. Louis intellectuals met again at Harris's instigation to found the St. Louis Philosophical Society, devoted, of course, primarily to the study of Hegel. The following spring, in 1867, because his article attacking Herbert Spencer had been rejected by the *North American Review*, Harris persuaded the Society to launch the *Journal of Speculative Philosophy*, which became the most important philosophical journal in America from 1867 to 1893.[12]

The men who comprised the fifty-one charter members of the St. Louis Philosophical Society represented a broad range of interests that reflected the frontier metropolis of St. Louis which was already calling itself "the future great city of the world" and competing furiously with thriving Chicago.[13] Perhaps the most outstanding member of this group was Denton J. Snider, a self-styled "writer of books" who was to accumulate some forty titles to his credit by the end of his long life—all published by himself in a fiercely independent spirit. Snider, who came to St. Louis from Oberlin in 1863, was the historian of the St. Louis Movement. It was he who recorded the striking personalities of Brokmeyer and Harris in incisive detail, recounting Brokmeyer's famous intellectual combats with Alcott and Emerson during their visits to St. Louis and Harris's perpetual consternation at his Prussian friend's aggressiveness at almost every meeting of the Society. Most important, Snider captured the subtle relationship between the everyday activities and ambience of St. Louis and the goals and pretensions of the Hegelians. To him, the bustling city with its overflowing German population and its bourgeois energy signified the working-out of Hegel's destiny for man. James Eads' great iron bridge, the first to cross the Mississippi, was then under construction, and it symbolized for Snider the "concrete universal" as it applied to America. Eads' bridge was "the solidest, purest, truest fact of the time. . . . God's thought creating the world . . . gossamer abstractions turning concrete and practical . . . Hegel's *Logic* with its intricate fine-spun web of Pure Essences realizing itself in yonder structure with all its turns, nodes, iron rods and braces. . . . I went to school to the Eads Bridge. . . ."[14]

And, in addition to his forty books ranging from a study of the pertinence of Hegel's thought to the history of the Civil War to treatises on psychology and psychosis, Snider was also a social activist. He promoted the Kindergarten Movement, worked with Jane Addams in Hull House, and founded "free universities" in St. Louis, Chicago, and Milwaukee. All his writings and activities suggest that Snider, deeply concerned with the emerging mass society of his day, was attempting, through the application of Hegel's teachings, to redefine traditional American individualism in an era of mass urban culture.

Other members of the Philosophical Society included George Holmes Howison, soon to become doyen of philosophy at the University of California; Judge J. Gabriel Woerner, eminent legal scholar and author of *The Rebel's Daughter*, perhaps the most insightful of all American

Civil War novels; Thomas Davidson, Aristotelian founder of a utopian colony in Keene, New York, as well as the Breadwinners' College in New York City; and Frank L. Soldan, next to Harris St. Louis' most famous public school educator. Auxiliary members of the Society included Amos Bronson Alcott; Ralph Waldo Emerson; General Ethan Allen Hitchcock; Johann B. Stallo; William Gilpin; Henry James, Sr.; the Scottish philosopher J. H. Stirling; the Prussian educator Karl Rosenkranz; Frederick Henry Hedge; James B. Eads; Joseph Pulitzer; and J. H. Fichte of Germany. The members' correspondence was extensive and so was their influence. Clubs devoted to German philosophy sprang up all over the Middle West, from Milwaukee and Chicago to such unlikely places as Peoria and Davenport. These built up enormous support for the Hegelian-oriented national education policies of William Torrey Harris, when he became the first United States Commissioner of Education in 1889.

Further, the *Journal of Speculative Philosophy* attracted articles and attention from most of the major American philosophers of the day such as George Sylvester Morris, Charles S. Peirce, William James, and John Dewey. It also introduced its readers to numerous translations of the works of Kant, Schelling, Hegel, and Fichte, while at the same time it allocated a great deal of space to Oriental philosophy, especially the *Bhagavad Gita*, which had begun to intrigue Americans. And since philosophy itself was viewed as a universal and fundamentally humanistic activity, every issue of the *Journal* contained sections discussing literature and the fine arts. Thus, it was a prime vehicle for the expansion of liberal humanism and emphasized the importance of such studies to the formation of a true civilization.

Gradually, as the nineteenth century wore on, Hegelianism and German philosophy in general spread from amateur societies such as the St. Louis Society into the colleges and universities. Morris preached its doctrines first at Michigan, then at Johns Hopkins. George Herbert Palmer, as chairman of the philosophy department at Harvard, enthusiastically taught Hegel and made a place for the German-trained idealist Josiah Royce in his department. Howison was virtually the only professional philosopher in California, and John Dewey, trained by Morris, and an early Hegelian, never quite abandoned the Swabian's theories as he carried pragmatism and American thought forward into the twentieth century.

In a sense, the story of Hegel's adventures in America is the story of the diffusion of a set of very complex ideas and attitudes from one culture through another. It reflects the way in which intellectual change came about in America as bombardments of European ideas were continually absorbed and then applied—or misapplied—to new situations.

Unlike Marx, who was generally scornful of New World possibilities, Hegel always viewed revolutionary America as the land of the future— the next major stage upon which the drama of freedom and progress would unfold. American civilization was a supreme example of what he called "the concrete universal" expressing itself in the very founding of a civilization in the wilderness. American Hegelians adopted much the same spirit. As they moved west, first to the Ohio frontier, then to St. Louis, and finally—in the person of George Holmes Howison—to California, they were convinced they were bringing with them a new and profound rationale for the free and yet orderly community that they would inevitably help to create. Thus, the Hegelians, like all people of the nineteenth-century American frontier, carried with them a particular concept of civilization as they moved into the wilderness. They did not find these ideas in nature. Rather, like everyone else in the march across the continent, they were "programmed" with ideas from an older culture that seemed to have their greatest applicability in the New World. The fact that many of the Hegelians were Germans rather than English-speaking people has tended to obscure their importance in the general frontier movement. It has also obscured the nationwide significance of their German-oriented culture in the face of interpretations of moving-frontier America that overemphasize the significance of English thought, customs, and institutions.[15] Actually, in nineteenth-century America, German culture was so pervasive as to be virtually dominant. The Romantic Movement, including transcendentalism and the major literary achievements of the American Renaissance, was fundamentally German in origin. Higher criticism of the Bible and the Christian religion, which liberalized American theology, was likewise German. The professionalization of all educational activity from kindergartens to graduate seminars and scholarly organizations such as the American Historical Association were Teutonically inspired. The development of science— geology, chemistry, physics, etc.—and the geographical exploration of the continent rested upon a basis of German science extending from Alexander von Humboldt to Ernst Mach. And along with the explorers went German scientists, German artists, and German cartographers who mapped and sketched America, while aspiring young painters like Albert Bierstadt went to Germany and brought the Düsseldorf style back home to dominate American art in the late nineteenth century. It would be difficult to examine any phase of American culture in the last century that was not influenced by German thought. The diffusion of Hegel's ideas through America is thus a symbolic component of the much larger history of pluralistic, cosmopolitan America.

Historically speaking, the Hegelian movement ultimately proved itself a victim of entropy. Its energies were so vastly diffused over America that its identity largely disintegrated. Led by Harris, the St. Louis Hegelians, except for the stubborn Brokmeyer, moved east to dominate for a time the Concord School of Philosophy—a chautauqua of the mind that lost itself in gross Genteel Traditionalism. Brokmeyer returned to the woods near Muskogee, Oklahoma, where, in a way quaintly reminiscent of Jonathan Edwards, he taught abstruse philosophy to the Indians and wrestled with his hopeless translation of Hegel's *Larger Logic* which was never published after all. Harris, meanwhile, went on to serve as United States Commissioner of Education, where his ideas were so sound and so pervasive that they seem like common sense today. Snider spun out his life with kindergartens, free universities, and writing books that now largely remain unread on library shelves. Johann B. Stallo specifically recanted his Hegelianism in *Theories and Concepts of Modern Physics,* but, as scholars have pointed out, Hegel's evolutionism nonetheless underlies Stallo's whole critique of nineteenth-century belief in static and unchanging science.[16] As regards social reform and even revolutionary ideology, Hegel retreated backstage, giving way to Marx, whose dialectical materialism in point of fact rested on Hegelian foundations and proceeded in the materialistic direction in which Hegel himself was heading at the end of his life. After August Willich, others such as Joseph Weydemeyer, Friedrich Sorge, Joseph Dietzgen, and Daniel De-Leon rounded out the nineteenth century as radical reformers in a Marxian and materialistic version of Hegelianism.[17] Twentieth-century Marxism, which pervaded America, continues to have Hegel as its intellectual ancestor. And, finally, John Dewey, the chief exponent of what is commonly assumed to be the most "American" of American philosophies, pragmatism, nonetheless owed his sense of philosophy as process, his sense of social conscience, and his sense of collective individualism to his early mentor, Hegel. Thus, in one view, Hegelianism can be seen as a kind of intellectual energy that diffused itself throughout nineteenth-century America. It was as powerful and as efficient as Henry Adams' celebrated dynamo which ushered in the Age of Electricity and now, perhaps deceptively so, seems just as commonplace and unobtrusive.

II

The source of the intellectual energy, described above, that pulsated through mid-nineteenth-century America was Georg Wilhelm Friedrich Hegel. Born in Stuttgart in 1770, he first attended the nearby University of Tübingen, where his closest friends were the philosopher Friedrich von Schelling and the poet Friedrich Hölderlin. After graduating with no great distinction, he became a tutor in Switzerland and Frankfurt. In

1800, he went to Jena, where he served as a teaching assistant to his friend Schelling, the professor of philosophy. At Jena in 1806, even while Napoleon's armies were engaging German troops in a great battle outside the city, Hegel managed to write his first important book, *Phenomenology of Mind* (1807). From 1808 to 1816 he was headmaster of a school at Nuremberg, during which time he married, and completed the two massive parts of his *Science of Logic* (the "Larger Logic" so greatly admired by Brokmeyer and the St. Louis Hegelians). For two years, from 1816 to 1818, he was professor of philosophy at Heidelberg. Then, in 1818, he assumed the chair of philosophy at Berlin, where for thirteen years he was the principal power in German philosophy and to some extent influential in the Prussian State. He died suddenly in a cholera epidemic in 1831, at the height of his fame.[18]

For the American Hegelians, the details of Hegel's life were less important than the problems which his philosophical analysis seemed to solve. Lockean and Scottish philosophy had served Enlightenment thinkers well with their appeal to empirical common-sense experience and simple reason. The criticisms of David Hume, however—particularly his demonstration that laws of cause and effect were not apparent in the data of sense experience—were disturbing, as was the idea, implicit even in Locke's philosophy, that somewhere in the human makeup was a nonrational mechanism, a conscience, that determined the priorities and choices that reason made. In the work of the Lockeans and Scottish common-sense philosophers, there thus obtained an inherent contradiction between the concepts of the *tabula rasa* or blank mind in the state of nature and the innate conscience. Immanuel Kant solved this problem for a time by positing two worlds dependent upon human perception. One was a noumenal world made up of the concrete objects of nature, of things in themselves. The other was a phenomenal world of things as they are experienced by the individual. Much of Kant's work was devoted to vigorous logical analysis of the forms of phenomenal experience from which he derived what he called "a priori" categories. In positing a mental world of the a priori, Kant made explicit the active role of the mind in the structuring of experience and thus wrought a revolution in philosophy. Those who followed him, such as Fichte and Schelling, gradually became most concerned with the world of the a priori in which resided innate ideas. Fichte saw the a priori world dominated by will as an expression of the individual moral ego. For him, the individual was delineated by a conscious imposition of his will upon the world around him. Schelling tended to see this world less rigorously and rationally than did Kant or Fichte, and to throw it open to innate ideas of intuitive and poetic fancy, which by their unique nature helped to define the specific individual.

For the most part, American romantics derived their insights into the epistemological problem from the English poet Samuel Taylor Coleridge, who freely borrowed from Kant and Schelling. In his *Aids to Reflection,* which became a bible to American romantics, Coleridge accepted the dual world of Kant, but with crucial Schellingian modifications which made nature *in itself* accessible to the poet. The work of Coleridge enabled romantics, particularly in the New World, to construct a new metaphysic and a new philosophy of perception. The whole world was idealist: it had the quality of mind and in most cases was conceived of as a reflection of the mind of God. God's mind revealed itself in all the appearances of nature from the minute and trivial to the grand and sublime, and all were interrelated. God also equipped man with the unique ability to perceive the cosmic significance of these forms. Each natural form was a symbol of a spiritual or poetic form—or a whole host of spiritual or poetic forms on the boundless horizon of God's imagination. If man viewed nature symbolically, he could thus cross over the threshold of the noumenal world and roam freely over the Elysian Fields of God's a priori world. In the words of Ralph Waldo Emerson, he could become "part or parcel of God." The role of the poet or artist was simply to focus men's minds sharply and intensively on particular symbols and thereby help them to penetrate the veil of nature, releasing their spirits to join the overarching mind or soul of God. In the context of its time, this was an extremely radical philosophical position because it freed every man from the common categories of experience and reason, it allowed him to express himself with extreme individuality, and it "blasphemed" in asserting that man could become God. It was a philosophy that placed a premium on individual intuition and expanded the soul, if not the ego.

But this philosophy, while generally satisfying to the majority of romantics, was hardly satisfying to Hegel. How could one know when he had truly expressed his individuality and become "part or parcel of God"? How did one know when he was truly a "self" or a "self-determined" being? And then what relationship did this "self" bear in any practical sense to all the other "selves" and to the total world of concrete experience? Hegel believed this view to be nothing more than another form of mysticism, which he detested. Thus he set out to define true self-hood and to relate the self to the world.[19] In so doing, he grappled directly with the fundamental social problem of all idealisms—the nature of the relationship of a set of abstract metaphysical ideas that defined the world as mind to the thousands of everyday concrete events that made up the experiential life of the individual or groups of individuals. Hegel's mission, then, was nothing less than rescuing philosophy from the twin disasters of mysticism or irrelevancy.

He began with the "self" and a paradox of experience. The self as pure being was nothing. Every experience was either a past event or a potential future consequence as an individual passed relentlessly through time. Thus the individual could define himself only through past experiences or future expectations, both of which were not the self here and now. He could characterize himself only in relation to other individuals or events and hence he took on his identity through a process of identification through the "other." Inevitably he reached out to more and more external experiences in an effort to define himself internally, for the individual could be defined only by his context and his relationships as they evolved through time. True freedom, then, and true self-definition came only from an ever-widening series of social and institutional relationships. The function of the world was to define the individual.

When he turned to the classic problems of philosophy, Hegel developed his dialectical logic, which was really a more rigorous expression of the fundamental paradox of human existence. The dialectic—thesis, antithesis, synthesis—made his tenets a philosophy of process, but one which, as it went on endlessly, implied a progressive unfolding or revelation of the mind of God in concrete experience rather than in mysterious and foggy sublimities. For the individual, every confrontation with reality could be formulated in terms of the dialectic—the "me," the "not me," the "larger and more complete me." And the larger and more complete the self, the greater one's self-knowledge and one's freedom. As this process continued through time, individuals became defined by institutions and cultures or stages of history called civilizations, each broader and more self-expressive than the last. Each new civilization contained within itself the experiences of the past and looked toward the future. This whole process Hegel called, in his paradoxical fashion, an expression of the "concrete universal." For, just as the self is known through the "other," or good is known through evil, or truth through error, so too was the universal world spirit of God known through the continual perception of the incompletenesses of his universe. But the concept of incompleteness, imperfection, non-universal, "not-God," implies its opposite, and hence Hegel's system becomes inevitably teleological and potentially complete. For him infinity becomes not the open-endedness of the mathematicians and the later pragmatists; rather it was finite, the complete unfolding or expression of the mind of God in concrete experience.

Clearly, none of the American Hegelians grasped Hegel's system in its entirety. *The System of Logic*, for example, was not even available in translation to those who could read only English until 1929, despite Brokmeyer's mighty labors on the project. But they did comprehend most of the essentials of the above outline of the German's thought and they relentlessly applied it to American situations. They rejected New England romanticism and declared themselves intent upon "transcending transcendentalism" to a higher stage of civilization. Thus they embraced the idea of the "concrete universal" and of philosophy as process which enabled them to give spiritual meaning to Darwinian evolution and to adapt to such major social changes as the development of the frontier, the industrial revolution, and the American Civil War. In the realm of religion, they could accept Strauss's doctrine of "Christ the good man" because as "not-God" he revealed God. Strauss put God to work in the practical realm of the religion of humanity and eventually in the social gospel which argued essentially that by doing honor to man, one does honor to God. In answer to charges that to see God as "the concrete universal" was to be a pantheist, American Hegelians generally fell back on Hegel's assertion that this in no way substituted nature worship for God because, in revealing himself through nature, God stood above and beyond it. The dialectics of the "self" and the "other" proved this.

American Hegelians saw the individual as being defined by his participation in the community which consisted of ever-enlarging groups from the family to the circle of friends, the work group, the church, the school, the city (St. Louis, "future great city of the world"), the political party, and the state. Thus the problem of the one and the many, the individual and the community, was easily solved for them—or at least the course of action, however difficult it may have been, was always clear. Whenever possible, the individual should join the community. Josiah Royce, though he professed himself to be not an Hegelian, gave perhaps the best expression to this idea in his philosophy of loyalty. He asserted that the moral imperative was always to maximize one's loyalty to the community, whether it be the raw mining town of Grass Valley, California, or the community of philosophers, or the world community of states. Ultimately, the rule was to be loyal to loyalty itself.[20]

Virtually every event in nineteenth-century America could be fitted into the ongoing dialectic and the unfolding process of the concrete universal. Denton J. Snider, for example, in his writings about the Civil War, saw it as a clash between principle (the North) and the law (the South) out of which would inevitably emerge a better America.[21] Likewise, one could apply this interpretation to the clash between ethnic groups, political parties, or economic interests. Hegelianism was a philosophy of unbounded optimism born out of a virtually infinite series of desperate situations, and it thrived on clashes and confrontations— the fierce contradictions of teeming, ever-changing life. Indeed, the primary mode of Hegelian thinking was first to locate the contradictions inherent in any situation and then to set about to resolve them. This meant translating them into the dialectic of thesis and antithesis and then looking for a larger, more inclusive resolution of the contradiction in a synthesis of the two. Such a thought process came naturally to Americans, who, from the time of the formulation of the Constitution onward, had habitually resorted to compromise by combination—the incorporation of as many divergent views as possible in a broad consensus—as the solution to most problems. By making a problem bigger, enlarging its scope or parameters, it could usually be resolved. This way of thinking was a kind of Manifest Destiny of the mind, aiming always towards the formation of the greater community.

As Marxism became one of the varieties of Hegelian experience, however, the accent fell more and more on the "concrete" rather than the "universal." That is, Marxists like August Willich, Joseph Weydemeyer, Friedrich Sorge, and Joseph Dietzgen espoused the doctrine of the dialectic, but they were less concerned with the unfolding of the world spirit. Their goals were more immediate in that they attempted to promote workingmen's movements and the proletarian class struggle. They were far less interested in achieving synthesis within the culture or in the American notion of the larger, greater community than they were in generating the clashes out of which gains for workingmen and total victory for the proletariat might come.[22] For them, Hegelian spiritualism gave way to dialectical materialism and atheism. The American Marxists no longer felt compelled to sustain what in their minds was the illusion that God and spiritual values were significant. In this sense, Hegelianism in America, as in Europe, became submerged in the tides of naturalism.

But whatever their particular persuasion might have been within the general scheme, virtually all the American Hegelians were absorbed with the concrete "stuff of life." Thus, they were perpetually curious about the analysis of institutions that would lead to greater self-realization of the individual, no matter what class or group defined his context. In their emphasis upon collective critical intelligence and the continual analysis of society's institutions, they did not stand far apart from John Dewey's matured version of pragmatism. However, theirs was a philosophy with an alternative method for attaining truth. Whereas the pragmatists essentially pursued the scientific method of induction, problem-formulation, hypothesis, and testing, the Hegelians worked upon the a priori or deductively derived plan of thesis, antithesis, and synthesis. For Dewey and the pragmatists, every problem was unique. For the Hegelians, every problem had to be recast into Hegel's triadic relationship before it could become meaningful. Every positive had to be considered in terms of its negative before true progress, i.e., synthesis, could result. The truth did not lie in between poles of opinion, but in a larger combination of them. Hegel's world, and hence that of the American

Hegelians, was characterized by all the comforts of mechanistic uniformity and a sense of the rationally determined result, yet it also allowed for change. Indeed, it swallowed up and co-opted change into its rationalistic system. In so doing, it made for renewed discipline over men and things while at the same time it generated excitement over inevitable progress and confidence in the future.

To the pragmatists, however, the Hegelians were too confident, too deterministic. They ignored the fact of the chance universe and the existence of genuine novelty. Really new possibilities could be institutionalized away in the interests of reason and discipline. For them, Hegelian freedom was not freedom. Individualism was collectivism and what seemed open-ended in the long run was really closed for each specific human being as he lived out the only lifetime he had. This was a price that the cosmic-minded Hegelians were willing to pay. The pragmatists who, in a sense, defined freedom in terms of chance and chaos, were not so willing. But the Hegelians realized that, in a world of potentially limited options, genuine choices that did not infringe upon one another's freedoms did not present themselves in terms of the easy "free play" assumed by the pragmatists. The latter's philosophy of method depended upon a relatively empty continent and a relatively empty globe where a great deal of innovation and eccentricity, if not extravagance of behavior, could be tolerated. As the globe and continent filled up and the world began to shrink in the mid-twentieth century, as the options became narrower, the margins for error less and less, the Hegelian tendency to generate unity out of opposing forces did not perhaps seem so quixotic and visionary as it once did to the men of the "confident" years in the first half of the twentieth century, when pragmatism had for a time replaced Hegelianism and was running at high tide.

[1] Harris first met Brokmeyer sometime in the winter of 1858 at a meeting of the Kant Society in the Old Mercantile Library in St. Louis, where they engaged in very animated debate over the respective merits of Kant, Cousin, and Hegel. They carried on their discussions for some time that year until Harris was converted to Hegel. My account of their meetings and debates is a reconstruction of the situation based on the following sources: Denton J. Snider, *A Writer of Books* (St. Louis: Sigma Publ. Co., n.d.), pp. 387–89, 393; Henry C. Brokmeyer, *A Mechanic's Diary* (Washington, D.C.: E. C. Brokmeyer Publisher, 1910), pp. 13–14, 230–33; William Torrey Harris, *Hegel's Logic* (Chicago: S. C. Griggs Co., 1890), pp. viii–ix; Kurt Leidecker, *Yankee Teacher* (New York: The Philosophical Library, 1946), p. 320.

[2] Loyd Easton, *Hegel's First American Followers* (Athens, Ohio: Ohio University Press, 1966), p. 4.

3 *Ibid.*, pp. 6–7.

4 *Ibid.*, pp. 12–13.

5 *Ibid.*, p. 13.

6 *Ibid.*, p. 14.

7 *Ibid.*, pp. 9–12 for Rauch. Easton's book focuses on the Ohio Hegelians and is the best overall study of their thought and activities. Most of the biographical data on the Ohio Hegelians in this introduction is derived from Easton.

8 *Ibid.*, p. 100. For Warren, see Madeleine B. Sterne, *The Pantarch* (Austin, Texas: University of Texas Press, 1968), p. 73, and Robert DeWeese, "Josiah Warren and the Making of a Scientific Individualism," unpublished paper, American Studies Program, University of Texas at Austin, 1972.

9 The best biographical sketch of Brokmeyer appears in Henry A. Pochmann, *German Culture in America* (Madison, Wis.: Univ. of Wisconsin Press, 1957), pp. 643–44. However, Pochmann, as does the writer in the *Dictionary of American Biography*, relies heavily on Brokmeyer's *A Mechanic's Diary*, which is sometimes erroneous. Further biographical material appears in Snider, *A Writer of Books*, pp. 294–398.

10 For biographical data on Harris, see Kurt F. Leidecker, *Yankee Teacher* (New York: The Philosophical Library, 1946).

11 Pochmann, *op. cit.*, p. 644.

12 Snider, *A Writer of Books*, pp. 326–27.

13 For members, see Pochmann, *op. cit.*, pp. 646–47. For the St. Louis attitude, see Denton J. Snider, *The St. Louis Movement in Philosophy, Literature, Education, Psychology, with Chapters of Autobiography* (St. Louis: Sigma Publ. Co., 1920), pp. 70–137. Logan Uriah Reavis, according to Snider, proclaimed St. Louis "the Future Great City of the World" and published a widely distributed pamphlet, *Removal of the Capital*, which called for transference of the United States capital from Washington, D.C., to St. Louis (*St. Louis Movement*, pp. 84–85).

14 *St. Louis Movement*, p. 108.

15 For an example of this, see Louis Wright, *Culture on the Moving Frontier* (New York: Harper & Row, Torchbooks, 1961; orig. pub. Bloomington, Ind.: Indiana University Press, 1955).

16 See Easton, *op. cit.*, pp. 84–87.

17 For a recent survey of these figures, see: David Herreshoff, *American Disciples of Marx from the Age of Jackson to the Progressive Era* (Detroit: Wayne State University Press, 1967). The most comprehensive work on American socialism is Donald Drew Egbert and Stow Persons, eds., *Socialism and American Life*, 2 vols. (Princeton, N.J.: Princeton University Press, 1952).

18 *Encyclopedia of Philosophy*, ed. Paul Edwards (New York and London: Macmillan, 1967).

19 *Ibid.* One of the clearest analyses of Hegel's thought, to which I am greatly indebted, appears in Josiah Royce, *The Spirit of Modern Philosophy* (Boston and New York: Houghton Mifflin, 1906), pp. 190–227.

20 See Josiah Royce, *The Philosophy of Loyalty* (New York: Macmillan, 1908).

21 See Denton J. Snider, *The American Ten Years War, 1855–1865* (St. Louis: Sigma Publishing Co., 1906).

22 See Herreshoff, *op. cit.*, *passim.*

PROLOGUE:

"AMERICA IS THEREFORE THE LAND OF THE FUTURE"

Georg Wilhelm Friedrich Hegel

Hegel viewed the relentless progress of freedom as a series of world-historical events whereby the "concrete universal" was revealed in broad stages of culture or civilization. In *Lectures on the Philosophy of History* (posthumously published in 1837), he turned his attention to North America, expressing a view of the United States quite similar to that of the Founding Fathers of the American Revolution. It was the "Land of the Future" where the next great civilization would emerge, one that could learn from and synthesize the experiences of earlier cultures originating in the Old World. At the time of Hegel's writing, however, America was still a vast frontier of abundance where sheer space and agricultural plenty precluded incorporation of the permanently established institutions characteristic of the Old World, along with the inevitable dialectical clashes between them, which Hegel saw as the hallmarks of matured civilization.

Georg W. F. Hegel, *Lectures on the Philosophy of History*, trans. J. Sibree (New York: Colonial Press, 1900), pp. 85–87.

. . . In North America the most unbounded license of imagination in religious matters prevails, and that religious unity is wanting which has been maintained in European States, where deviations are limited to a few confessions. As to the political condition of North America, the general object of the existence of this State is not yet fixed and determined, and the necessity for a firm combination does not yet exist; for a real State and a real Government arise only after a distinction of classes has arisen, when wealth and poverty become extreme, and when such a condition of things presents itself that a large portion of the people can no longer satisfy its necessities in the way in which it has been accustomed so to do. But America is hitherto exempt from this pressure, for it has the outlet of colonization constantly and widely open, and multitudes are continually streaming into the plains of the Mississippi. By this means the chief source of discontent is removed, and the continuation of the existing civil condition is guaranteed. A comparison of the United States of North America with European lands is therefore impossible; for in Europe, such a natural outlet for population, notwithstanding all the emigrations that take place, does not exist. Had the woods of Germany been in existence, the French Revolution would not have occurred. North America will be comparable with Europe only after the immeasurable space which that country presents to its inhabitants shall have been occupied, and the members of the political body shall have begun to be pressed back on each other. North America is still in the condition of having land to begin to cultivate. Only when, as in Europe, the direct increase of agriculturists is checked, will the inhabitants, instead of pressing outwards to occupy the fields, press inwards upon each other—pursuing town occupations, and trading with their fellow-citizens; and so form a compact system of civil society, and require an organized state. The North American Federation have no neighboring State (towards which they occupy a relation similar to that of European States to each other), one which they regard with mistrust, and against which they must keep up a standing army. Canada and Mexico are not objects of fear, and England has had fifty years' experience, that *free* America is more profitable to her than it was in a state of *dependence*. The militia of the North American Republic proved themselves quite as brave in the War of Independence, as the Dutch under Philip II; but generally, where Independence is not at stake, less power is displayed, and in the year 1814 the militia held out but indifferently against the English.

America is therefore the land of the future, where, in the ages that lie before us, the burden of the World's History shall reveal itself—perhaps in a contest between North and South America. It is a land of desire for all those who are weary of the historical lumberroom of old Europe. Napoleon is reported to have said: "*Cette vieille Europe m'ennuie.*" It is for America to abandon the ground on which hitherto the History of the World has developed itself. What *has* taken place in the New World up to the present time is only an echo of the Old World; and, as a Land of the Future, it has no interest for us here, for, as regards *History*, our concern must be with that which has been and that which is. In regard to *Philosophy*, on the other hand, we have to do with that which (strictly speaking) is neither past nor future, but with that which *is*, which has an eternal existence—with Reason; and this is quite sufficient to occupy us.

I

THE ST. LOUIS MOVEMENT

1

STARTING FROM ST. LOUIS

Denton J. Snider

The St. Louis Movement was officially initiated with the founding of the St. Louis Philosophical Society in January, 1866, as related here by Denton J. Snider, a founding member and the lifelong historian of the Movement. Actually, however, ground had been broken with the meeting of William Torrey Harris and Henry C. Brokmeyer in the winter of 1858. The Civil War intervened and Brokmeyer, the Movement's driving force, "put away his philosophy for a copy of Hardie's *Infantry Tactics*," serving, as did Snider, with the Union Army in the great conflict.

The selection below, from Snider's definitive history of the St. Louis Movement, recounts the formation of the Philosophical Society, the crucial roles played by Brokmeyer (who sometimes spelled his name "Brockmeyer"), Harris and Hegel's *Larger Logic*, the Society's "Book of Fate." It further lists some of the founding members and chronicles the everyday activities of the Society. But, perhaps most important, Snider has captured the exact relationship of the Philosophical Society to the cultural ambience of mid-nineteenth-century St. Louis, with its limitless western aspirations. Many St. Louisans felt that the West, and their city in particular, had been responsible for Union victory in the Civil War. The seizure of the arsenal at Camp Jackson in the city had been the first Union victory and had saved Missouri for the Union. To Snider, along with Brokmeyer a participant, this was a "world-historical deed." The West having played so mighty a role in the war, there was nothing to limit its boundless future expansion during the post-Civil War years. In the words of L. U. Reavis, an enthusiastic civic booster, St. Louis was destined to be "The Future Great City of the World." The St. Louis Hegelians were set on making certain that such "pre-destined" greatness would be firmly grounded in universal philosophical principles.

Snider himself lived for 84 years, from 1841 to 1925. He was the last surviving member of the Philosophical Society and certainly one of its

most productive. He published more than forty books at his own expense
and served for long periods of time as a public school teacher, roving
lecturer from Chicago to Concord, promoter of Hull House, the Kindergarten Movement, the Free University, and the Universal College. The
latter two were forerunners of the modern "university without walls,"
adult extension classes, and the Chicago "Great Books" program. He was
at all times the philosopher *engagé*, as were most of the St. Louis Hegelians. It was the essence of Hegel's philosophy itself to demand that all
universal principles be expressed in concrete activity—in the clash of
ideas and actions. These principles gleam through all Snider's writings,
as they did through his life.

Denton J. Snider, *The St. Louis Movement in Philosophy, Literature,
Education, Psychology, with Chapters of Autobiography* (St. Louis,
Sigma Publ. Co., 1920), pp. 5–15, 24–35.

FIFTY years and more have passed since the phrase *The St. Louis
Movement* began to be heard in certain limited circles over the
country, and occasionally to be used in brief printed reports of the
Public Press. To most people it only meant something started in St.
Louis for the fleeting moment, a little bubble of the time soon to
burst into lasting oblivion. Undoubtedly those who initiated it had
a vague feeling that they might be doing a germinal deed of permanent and ever-growing significance; but that was just what the future
alone could prove.

Now it so happens that the present writer is the sole survivor of
that early group of men for whose designation this special locution,
The St. Louis Movement, was first coined. And in one way or other
to him alone, in his solitary condition, this same designation is not
infrequently applied today. One inference at least may be made:
the name still persists in living, and with it the thing, or conception,
doubtless hazy enough in most cases. The subject keeps rising to the
surface, asked about, talked about, written about, thought about,
often very inaccurately and even mockingly; yet the old idea somehow will not die and get itself well buried for once and for all. Indeed
it seems to have a certain weird power of assuming new shapes, of
preserving itself through multiform stages of evolution, in fine the
uncanny gift of re-incarnation. So that Spirit, or ghost, or eidolon
long ago risen and named *The St. Louis Movement*, is still among
us and at work, even if under forms a good deal changed from its
pristine epiphany. . . .

The starting-point of the St. Louis Movement was the birth of the

St. Louis Philosophical Society which took place in January, 1866, after due preliminaries. About a dozen gentlemen assembled in a down-town law-office, according to agreement; out of this number two men stepped forth as the original founders and first members. One of them, the real originator, was chosen President of the Society —Henry C. Brockmeyer, then a practicing lawyer in the city; the other, the active organizer, became its Secretary—William T. Harris, then principal of one of the Public Schools. Each of them spoke briefly his inaugural, emphasizing with enthusiasm the prospects and purposes of the organization; both failed not to flash some prophetic lightning upon our unlit future.

These two men were not only the officers, but were in essence the Society, and remained such. They proved themselves the two philosophers of us all; they might be called Philosophy incarnate; it was their breath of life, but likewise their limit, as time revealed. They turned out very different from each other, not only in their lives but even in their philosophic gift; and yet, as to persistence they were quite alike, inasmuch as both clung to their favorite discipline and its one master till the light of their days went out. They both died, as it were, with their favorite philosopher's favorite book clutched in the still hand.

Moreover, from this time forward, I became more deeply associated with these two strongly pronounced personalities, in my practical career as well as in my spiritual evolution, than with any other living men. From the natal hour of this Philosophical Society, they were my friends and fellow-workers in the same general cause, which goes under the name of the St. Louis Movement. Each of them wrought in very different fields of external vocation; Brockmeyer became Missouri's Lieutenant Governor, and Harris rose to be the Nation's Educational Head; still, the enduring undercurrent of both their natures remained Philosophy to the last, and just the one Philosophy, indeed just the one Book of Philosophy. A single remark I may add here about myself: my life-stream persisted in cutting a distinct channel for its flood, though it kept inside the same St. Louis Movement.

With an affection, which hopes to be eternal, I write the last sentence of this prefatory note to dedicate the present history of our common labors as a monument to the memory of my life-long friends and associates:

HENRY C. BROCKMEYER
WILLIAM T. HARRIS

*　*　*　*

Thus the Philosophical Society was born into the world, and proceeded to its work under its two leaders, certainly minds of unusual gift in the line of thought. The formal Society has long since vanished, having been soon taken up into the larger and more lasting St. Louis Movement which became not merely a doctrine for the few, but a pervasive influence in the community, and had its followers throughout the country. It must be remembered that philosophy brought not revenue, but rather expense. Each of us had to make his living by some special vocation, which gave him bread, but not the bread of life. Two very different callings we had to practice, the economic and the spiritual, and this remained the discipline of a life-time.

Among the members seated in a little group about the officers, I was seemingly the youngest, having just passed a birth-day which tallied me twenty-five years old, on the preceding ninth of January of said year (1866). There is no doubt that strong pulsations of Hope burst up expressed by the leaders, or cowered down unexpressed in the hearts of the rank and file, among whom I took my position in the rear line, but always ready to step forward when the hour struck.

Such, then, was the open, explicit starting-point of the St. Louis Movement, though evidently it must have had earlier premonitory throbbings. The two officers of the Society before mentioned, Brockmeyer and Harris, took hold of their work as men already experienced. Indeed their first acquaintance dated back to 1858. I had met them informally at a small gathering in North St. Louis the preceding autumn of 1865, when I first heard them plan the Society. Still there had been no organization, probably no very definite purpose beyond the mutual benefit of conversation on favorite topics.

It may be mentioned here in advance that our two leaders were students and indeed well-disciplined followers of the German philosopher Hegel, and they naturally turned the rest of us in the same direction, though the Society laid no claim in its Constitution to the propagation of any single philosophic system. Thus it was in principle an open tournament for the best jouster. Moreover, Harris was a zealous missionary by nature, as well as a born teacher; especially in those early years his zeal was aflame for the one he deemed the philosophic master. He had all of Hegel's Works in the original, and he soon found out those of us who could muster a little German, and he formed the design of putting us into an inner group of pupils who might become agitators and promulgators. The first time I met him at his home in the fall of 1865, some months before the organization of the Society, he slipped into my hand one of

Hegel's volumes and set me at once to work on a lesson. He would even go around to our rooms and correct our translations. At that time only one volume of Hegel's Works had been done into English (Sibree's Translation of the Philosophy of History). Thus the first experience of mine was that I had become a pupil in a school for the study of Hegel. That was just what I needed at the moment, so I eagerly followed the hint of Providence.

The situation possibly for a year or so took this shape: I, and perhaps half a dozen others, became the free pupils of Harris as instructor, while Brockmeyer remained more in the background as a kind of overlord or higher scholarch. But in the fall of 1866, I, wishing to see and hear more of him, entered his law office, professedly as a student of Jurisprudence, but really as a pupil of the University Brockmeyer in person, for he had become to me a personal University whose curriculum I must take at least for a year, before anything else in this world was for me possible. Moreover I bought the entire set of Hegel's eighteen volumes in the original, and began making explorations in that philosophic ocean on my own account and at my own risk. Thus I began my mental circumnavigation, not of the globe only, but of the Universe.

It soon became manifest that there was one book of Hegel which uprose the lofty center round which all the other works of the philosopher, all our studies, in fact all the thought of the All itself gathered—that was Hegel's so-called *Larger Logic*. This was very different from Whately's text-book which I had studied at College, indeed it went quite the reverse of the whole line of treatises on Logic from Aristotle down to the present. This Logic was declared to be the movement of the pure essences of the world, stripped from their outer illusory vesture. Of course I rebounded from it at the start, but I always returned to it as the one fortress of thought to be assaulted and captured for dear life's sake, wherein I was helped often by quick flashes of Brockmeyer's lightning insight. This book has the reputation of being the hardest book in the world, the one least accessible to the ordinary human mind even when academically trained. My wrestle with it was long, intense, and not wholly victorious at the close; still after years of entanglement I pulled through its magic web of abstractions and obstructions, and left them behind me, not lost but transcended.

Now it so happened that an English translation had been made of this book by Brockmeyer about the year 1860, near the beginning of the Civil War. The volume was handed around in writing, copied, discussed, and to a greater or less extent appropriated spiritually. The strange fact is that it was not then printed, and still stays unborn in manuscript after nearly sixty years of waiting. Thus the creative book of the system was never put into English type, and has remained quite inaccessible to the English-speaking student. This to my mind has been the chief fatality in the propagation of the work and its doctrines, for it always has had and always will have its distinctive appeal to certain minds and even to certain times.

Indeed one is inclined to think that this translation of Hegel's Logic has had a peculiar doom hanging over it from the moment of its first written line. I have watched it more than half a century, now rising to the surface, then sinking out of sight as if under some curse of the malevolent years. Personally I never used it, never needed it, I had the original and could read it more easily than Brockmeyer's English, which on the whole was very literal—so literal that I often had to turn back to the German, in order to understand the English. Here was supposed to be the first duty of the Philosophical Society: to revise and pay for publishing this central work; still we never seriously started. Harris might have printed it in his Journal, but for some reason or other which to this day remains conjectural, he would not. I found Brockmeyer re-translating the original on his return from the Indians in the early nineties. And I saw him thumbing over the manuscript only a few days before his death in 1906. It was his one Supreme Book, his Bible; it meant to him more than any other human production, and was probably the source of his great spiritual transformation from social hostility and inner discord and even anarchism, to a recon-ciliation with his government and indeed with the World-Order, after his two maddened flights from civilization.

So our Philosophical Society, and after it the St. Louis Movement, had its weird Book of Fate interwoven through it from the first yet never fully realized at the last, in print or otherwise. And a similar lot befell our President Brockmeyer himself, who to my mind rep-resented Genius born but never fully realized in print or otherwise. And must not something of the kind be said of St. Louis herself? But that man and his sole volume, both of unwon destiny, will often peer out of this narrative for a moment, as the stream flows on toward the outlet. Our Secretary, Harris, had also his lifelong wrestle with this same elusive, if not illusive, Book of Fate, which caught and held him in its subtle labyrinthine texture of finest-spun metaphysic.

Undoubtedly we all partook of the character of our communal environment. My stay in St. Louis caused me to share in its inner-most life, and had the effect of making me believe that in it lurked a greater possibility than in any other city of the West, if not of the whole United States. This huge dreamy potentiality of civic grandeur we all believed to be quite on the point of pitching over into a colossal reality. Just that was the strongest, most pronounced trait of the town at this time: it clung to an unquestioning faith in its own indefeasible fortune. This was bound to come, and in a hurry; we did not even need to fight for our greatness, it would be forced upon us. And we did not seriously fight for it, but with calm resignation awaited the resistless downpour of riches, population, and life's other blessings from the fascinated Gods. Such was the divine belief which became a kind of St. Louis religion, and entered deeply into the character of the city, of the individual citizens, not sparing the philosophers whose special claim was to pierce to the Pure Essences underneath all lying Appearances. Certainly I was not an exempt. Hence when the prophet came voicing to our ears what lay already in our hearts: *Behold, St. Louis the Future Great City of the World,* we all accepted it as a divinely sent Gospel, as very Truth denuded of all her illusory drapery.

In my own case through this long deep participation in our city's most fateful experience, a bond of the spirit was formed which all my absences, defeats, disillusions have not wholly shattered. . . .

Alongside these four elements of St. Louis [the Roman Catholics, the New Englanders, the Southerners, and the Germans], all of which represent the realm of prescription as handed down from time immemorial, I am going to place the fifth element, also cultural, though very small in size and in voting power. But it was fresh, native to the soil, sprung of the place and the time. This new and renewing element was our St. Louis Movement, which arose on the spot whence it took its name, claiming to be original, autochthonous, like only unto itself—unless it, as before intimated, was the product of some influence far deeper and larger than itself, of which it was itself hardly aware.

There is no doubt that its members proposed to break with tradition, which dominated the intellect of the city; they were inclined to challenge the whole realm of prescription derived from Europe and from our own older Atlantic States, Northern and Southern. They did not say so, but they seemed animated with the spirit of the Camp Jackson deed, which marked a new turning-point, even if very local and minute, in the World's History. A vast hope lay in the time, in the city, and particularly in the Philosophical Society, which proposed to reconstruct the whole universe after some model now dimly evolving in St. Louis, and certainly not altogether transmitted from the Past.

Perhaps the majority of us were by vocation prescriptive teachers, but the traditional Higher Education was to be rounded out, though not supplanted, by the New University. And some such educative institution soon began to sprout up in the community outside of the regular schools and academic instruction. . . .

In like manner the traditional religion did not satisfy. Few of us went to church, though there was no open rupture with ecclesiastical organization. Some of the members doubtless kept up their old religious affiliations; but our officers, I know, held aloof, yet without antagonism. Still the most distinguished clergyman of St. Louis joined us somewhat later, for the sake of religion, he said. He was right in his statement. In fact, the St. Louis Movement was in the deepest sense religious, not as formal but as universal; we sought to win a fresh spiritual communion with the Divine Order and its Orderer, and to create for the same a new unworn expression. But to accomplish any such purpose we had to throw aside the old carcass of tradition (as Emerson calls it, perhaps too disparagingly) and to begin over.

So we deemed ourselves going back to the original underived fountain-head of young inspiration. And we did break loose from the four transmitted cultural elements of the city, as already narrated. But what could we do in our emergency? Whom did we grasp for as spiritual guide in the shoreless welter outside of all fixed landmarks of prescription? None other than a philosopher handed down to us from Europe, and the necessary product of European conditions [Hegel]. That is, we took a foreign traditional philosophy to countervail the tradition which had been already imported, planted, and taken root here at home. . . .

Accordingly the St. Louis Movement had its start from a philosophic motive, from a system of thought already formulated and organized which we were to master and to apply. Moreover it was a system of idealism, one that put stress upon Idea or Spirit as the primordial creative source of all things. It was a great and necessary discipline which trained us to see underneath the mighty phenomenal occurrences of the passing hour, and to probe to their original starting-point, to their creative essence.

The time was calling loudly for First Principles. The Civil War had just concluded, in which we all had in some way participated, and we were still overwhelmed, even dazed partially by the grand historic appearance. What does it all mean? was quite the universal question. Of course the answer varied in a thousand shapes; there was the political, the religious, the social, the economic, even the wholly selfish and sensual answer. Naturally our set sought in philosophy the solution, that is, in Hegel as taught by our leaders. A great world-historical deed had been done with enormous labor and outer panoramic pageantry. What lay in it for us and for the future? So we began to grope after the everlasting verities, the eternal principles, the pure Essences (*reine Wesenheiten*) as they are called by our philosophic authority. These transcendent energies of man and of the world were said to be collected and ordered in one book—Hegel's Logic. So the St. Louis Movement may be called a child of the period, a peculiar infant indeed, but nevertheless a legitimate birth of the time's spiritual struggle. And this infant seemed to be sent by the time to a world-school for its discipline. . . .

It was, accordingly, one of the spiritual offshoots of the Civil War, and belonged, I have to think, peculiarly to the West, of which during those years St. Louis was the central and most important, indeed the symptomatic city. For the West did the great positive act of preserving the Union, while the East, valiantly fighting for the same cause, did hardly more than keep its own line of separation, "the Fatal Line" it has been called, which at last could only mean division and secession. There was, accordingly, felt just in this city the spur to discover and to utter the soul of the Age's Great Deed, for it was peculiarly our own. "Find me the philosophy of that," said the Spirit of the Time to the philosophers now marshaling just on the spot. We took the best help accessible to us from the past, and made it our starting-point. . . .

So the fifth element we sought to introduce into the cultural life of St. Louis, and preached our new evangel with no little unction and keen-edged enthusiasm. We claimed to represent the original, indigenous, self-determined soul of the city as distinct from the one brought hither from the outside. We were in a revolt against the four imported elements, from the early French settlers to the last-come German Forty-Eighters, whom our President Brockmeyer, himself a German, branded as negative—hostile to all positive thought and its institutions. He was a good hater, altogether too good; still there is no doubt that the high-bred Latinists (*Lateiner*) from the German University were inclined to scoff at our philosophic master and at our Movement as something long since transcended over yonder in the old country.

Let that be as it may; still the reader is not to forget the secretly gnawing dualism which lurked in the St. Louis Movement, and which will keep driving it forward beyond itself till it reach a higher reconciling synthesis in a new world-view. This of course lies many years ahead, yet it has its first life-pulse in the present situation. But as I look back at the Movement now, it really lapsed into tradition in assailing tradition; it became prescriptive just in its denial of prescription; it took for granted what it never granted. I must have felt somewhat of this deeper dissonance from the start, for I never could quite bring myself to write and publish anything on philosophy proper. I deemed myself not yet a worthy initiate. Then I was already beginning to grow a peculiar literary conscience; whenever I took my soul's pen in hand, it was for my highest self-expression; otherwise I must wait, even if forever. Nevertheless I pursued desperately philosophy as the one present remedy, as the universal science; if its warring contradiction cannot in some way be pacified, then the universe is battle and becomes Ragnarok.

Of course I was at first unconscious of this deepest undercurrent in our St. Louis Movement, and only came to recognize it, not so much by thinking it out, as by living it out in my daily activities for decades, till the cycle of discipline might be finished. Meanwhile let it be held fast that this far-down underworld's struggle of the spirit is what gave strength and length of life to our St. Louis Movement. Indeed that antinomy of ours between tradition and non-tradition may be deemed the primal originative force or spring of all individual culture, as well as of civilization itself. . . .

As far as I now remember, the Society led not so much an active, practical life as a rather quiet, theoretical existence; chiefly it was the public means to show famous visitors certain formal attentions; for instance, when Mrs. Julia Ward Howe came to town and read a paper on Philosophy, the Society received her, listened to her lecture, and even indulged in some criticisms, to which she replied in veiled but sarcastic reproof of our philosophic egotism. In like manner it heard Emerson and invited Alcott, the famous Concord philosophers, with whom our Secretary, Mr. Harris, kept in friendly touch, for the sake of the future.

The real work of the St. Louis Movement was done individually, or in little groups and classes. I cannot now recollect that I ever read a paper before the Philosophical Society. The spirit of the Movement, as far as I shared it, I applied to Literature; Judge Woerner applied it to Jurisprudence, and it colors his legal work on Probate Law; Brockmeyer turned it into Legislation and Politics; Harris made best use of it in Education. The St. Louis Movement, accordingly, took the character of a subtle pervasive influence, rather than an organized propagandism. Its life pulsed in the small coteries which met usually in parlors or private rooms for the study of some special book or subject. In this fact lay its chief worth and its persistence.

It is true that a certain grouping or arrangement of persons and their philosophic doctrines took place, as we gathered to discuss some theme or to listen to some address, or even to read together some book. The situation was something of this kind:

I. The President or the Secretary, or both, were the central figures, ardent exponents and disciples of Hegel, and led the talk.

II. Then came the opposition, for usually in the early times we had some straggling dissidents who would object here and there. Of these I remember enough to set down three.

   1. Thomas Davidson, who usually upheld Aristotle as against Hegel, and even the Greek world against the Christian. A lively and ingenious Scotchman, who never seemed to me to have any particular persistent conviction. At that time he was certainly a jolly drifter and general free fighter, with much effervescence of erudition.

   2. Adolf E. Kroeger, a Fichtean, and translator of several of Fichte's works and of other German books; also an upholder of Kant against Hegel in many warm disputes. He belonged to the earlier set. I saw a letter in which Longfellow praised his English translations of early German poetry.

   3. Louis F. Soldan, later Superintendent of Schools, whose general attitude was neutral, belonging distinctly to no side or perhaps to all sides. He was a student of Spinoza and Dante, and later had literary classes in Faust.

III. Finally came what may be called the rank and file, varying a good deal with the years and the topics. Here I properly belonged. But we were eager learners and questioners, being generally sympathetic with the Hegelians, especially with the two leaders, who had really something positive to give, and produced the general atmosphere. Numbers of good people may be put here, such as Judge Woerner, Judge Jones, Principal Childs; the ladies, though not regular members, were best represented by Miss Mary Beedy and Miss Anna Brackett, both of the Public Schools.

This was the situation in the earlier times. Later came a group of excellent, but quite different people, such as Prof. Cook, Dr. Holland, Miss Blow, Miss Fruchte. And so the leaven kept working through various layers for many years, till at last the active spirit seemed to lapse into a state of quiescence.

Such is a brief sketch of the first general alignment of the Philosophical Society, as I recall it after some fifty years and more. All these first members have passed on, though a few out of the later groups still survive, no longer in the buoyancy of youth, yet active. I suppose that the interest of such a seemingly fortuitous society is that it unwittingly bears in its bosom something permanent, some living seeds destined to grow in the future and bear new fruit.

How long did the Movement last? In one sense it is going on still, as already indicated, though in a number of ways much changed. But that first impulse had its own life with rise, culmination and decline. Different participators would naturally chronologize the period differently, according to their experience; but to my vision it ran about twenty years (1865–1885), from my first electric shock at touching the live wire in the house of W. T. Harris one Sunday afternoon till I quit St. Louis on my wanderings, not to return with the spirit's renewal for quite another twenty years. The two leaders, Brockmeyer and Harris, had left the city some years before. The influence lingered still in the Public Schools, but without any decided official hold. Moreover the city itself seemed changed in character; it passed into that peculiar eclipse of hope and ambition, which lasted nearly a generation. It lost its leadership in the West— its commercial, and still more emphatically its intellectual leadership. . . .

2

A MECHANIC'S DIARY

Henry C. Brokmeyer

Henry C. Brokmeyer's *A Mechanic's Diary* is perhaps the strangest and most interesting of the writings left by the St. Louis Hegelians. It was not published until 1910, four years after Brokmeyer's death, and purports to be a record of his activities in the year 1856. And yet, in both large and small matters, the "diary" so departs from established fact as to suggest that Brokmeyer really intended it to be a utopian extension of his own experiences rather than a strictly historical account. Thus, to cite certain small but crucial points: Brokmeyer did not meet William Torrey Harris in 1856, but in 1858—yet he vividly describes their long philosophical conversations in the "diary." Likewise, Brokmeyer did not marry until 1861, while the "diary" for 1856 closes with his wedding. More importantly, Brokmeyer portrays himself as the founder of a large German immigrant colony where Belleville, Illinois, now stands, whereas his actual holdings consisted of a solitary hut on eighty acres of Warren County, Missouri, wilderness where he almost died of exposure until rescued by Harris in 1859. All this indicates that the "diary" is Brokmeyer's highly imaginative western version of Thoreau's *Walden*. But instead of describing a solitary retreat from society, Brokmeyer is intent upon portraying his entry into St. Louis society and the way in which his Hegelian principles could be put to work in shaping the destiny of the "Future Great City" and its surrounding countryside in the heartland of America.

Brokmeyer, the irascible, demonic driving force behind the St. Louis Hegelian Movement, was, indeed, very much involved in the life of St. Louis and the State of Missouri. He rapidly rose from iron-molder to the status of respected lawyer and public figure. During the Civil War, he became a Lieutenant Colonel and later served as Lieutenant Governor and, briefly, as Governor of Missouri. *A Mechanic's Diary* reflects his great concern for the specific, concrete processes of economic development in St. Louis. At the same time, Brokmeyer seizes every opportunity to show how Hegelian dialectical principles underlie and govern even the most commonplace actions of men. Whether it be in the shop among his fellow workers, out in the country among the immigrants, or in the solitude of his unpretentious room, Hegel is always at the front of Brokmeyer's mind as he seeks to apply his lessons to America.

The selections below represent a sampling of the "diary" selected in such a way as to designate something of his range of activities and interests as well as his deepest thoughts. They are reprinted from *A Mechanic's Diary* (Washington, D.C.: E. C. Brokmeyer Publisher, 1910), pp. 1, 11–12, 55–60, 73–74, 79–81, 121–23, 229–33. Throughout the narrative, "H—" is, of course, Harris. The concluding excerpt refers to the visit of Bronson Alcott to St. Louis in 1859, when the outspoken Brokmeyer did his best to publicly insult the Concord visionary, much to the embarrassment of Harris and the other more genteel Hegelians.

St. Louis, May 1, 1856

TO-DAY I bought this book, in which I intend to note down, from time to time, such happenings as may seem to have some meaning for the future. I do this because I find myself tempted to discredit my own memory now and then, when I recall the last twelve years of my life, with the ups and downs, the successes and failures, as they occurred.

The first thing that I will put down is the fact that I have to-day selected this city for my future home. I have traveled over the country from the state of Maine to the state of Louisiana, and from the Atlantic Ocean to the buffalo pastures upon the Eastern slopes of the Rocky Mountains, and if there is a center of population that has as fine a country tributary to it as the city of St. Louis—East, West, North and South—it has escaped my observation. Here if anywhere industry, economy and honest conduct must mean success—unless we have to believe that the world is but an annex of hell, as some people seem to think. I heard this expression for the first time to-day, in a crowd that had gathered in front of the banking house of P. B. & Co.: "The world is an annex of hell and St. Louis is located upon a choice quarter section!"

Well, the banking house has failed, and as I bought exchange on it in the East, in order not to carry any considerable amount of money about me on my trip out here, and failed to exercise due diligence in presenting my paper for payment—I can sympathize with the poor fellow. When, twelve years ago, I landed upon the wharf of the city of New York, after a seven weeks' voyage across the Atlantic, I was seventeen years old; had twenty-five cents cash in my pocket, and a knowledge of three words of the English language in my head. I had not relative, friend or acquaintance upon the continent. To-day I landed upon the wharf of the city of St. Louis. I have a full dollar left for every cent I had then. I know the language of the country, and a considerable portion of the country itself. I am master of three trades, with splendid health!

"Quarter section of hell!" Nonsense! The devil doesn't build cities, and this city is being built. The devil doesn't transform the wilderness into a home for civilized man. This is done by industry, economy and honesty. What the devil has the devil to do with that? I am fixed. Here I stay. This is my home. I have lost what I had. Well, I will try and not lose the loss—the lesson it has taught me. . . .

"My heart, sir, burned with the love of liberty, and that was the reason I sought this land of the free and the home of the brave!" exclaimed Mike upon the floor to the left of us, while discussing the cause of immigration of this country with Jake, who worked upon the floor to our right. Mike had straightened up; as he made the remark, he executed the appropriate gesture, or intended to do so, by bringing his right hand with a graceful movement in contact with the left side of his breast. Unfortunately for him, his hand touched his body a little too low down, and instantly Jake improved the opportunity.

"Nonsense, Mike! Nonsense! That is not your heart. That is your stomach! No doubt, something hurt you. But it was the craving of your stomach for grub, instead of your heart burning for liberty that brought you to this country. I leave it to the Doctor, here," pointing to Doc Hall, "whether that is not your stomach which you pointed out as the thing that hurt you."

A general peal of laughter, which fairly set the waves of dust floating upon the beams of yellow light that streamed through the grimy windows a dancing with mirth, was the answer of the shop. I enjoyed the hit. But the most amusing part was to watch the quirks and turns, the dodges resorted to by Mike, to obtain credence for his feigned motive. Honest hunger, the universal birthday present of nature to every son of man, was a motive too low in his estimation, a motive that has made him a good molder, and as such, a substantial acquisition to any community of sane beings, must be disowned, and in lieu of it, a motive is avowed which if true could only make him an acquisition to some community of Bedlamites. "No, sir; I will never consent that you shall think so low of me! I never did and never will entertain the true. What! Accuse me of being a true man!"

I need not to add that this was one of the bright days of the shop.

May 23, 1856

The humor continues.

"I say, Earless!"

"What! Is it Fritz?"

"How do you like him? Your name? How do you like to be Earless?"

"Well, to tell you the truth, Fritz, there are a few happenings in life but what I manage to squeeze some comfort out of them, and so it is with my new name. I would rather be called an earless Dutchman for a blunder I made myself than a lop-eared Dutchman, by the grace of an ignorant populace."

"And it is proud you are of your new name, is it?" said Mike.

"I really don't see why not, Mike. The fact is, I do not recall any occasion when the actual loss of ears would have been a great inconvenience since I have been in the shop, except on one occasion, and that was yesterday, when you told us, with that burning eloquence, what brought you to this country."

"Hurrah for our Earless Berkshire!" hallooed Jake.

"Well, Jake, I will tell you in confidence; of course, I don't care of its going any farther, that your Berkshire did not lose his ears by the teeth of a yellow cur." (Jake being a light sorrel.)

"Next," cried the Doctor.

"I move you, sirs, that the Berkshire have the privilege of treating the shop, and hereafter the rights of a regular apprentice," cried Mike.

"Second the motion," cried Fritz.

"So do I," echoed Jake.

The motion carried unanimously, and I stood bilked out of a keg of beer, which was drunk to-night, it is not necessary to add, with the best of humor. When they got through, I said: "Gentlemen, as this was a treat of the shop, intending to intimate that it was a forced contribution, I claim the privilege of inviting you to another keg, to be drunk Monday night, on my account."

"That was a poser, Henry," said the Doctor, on our way home. "That keg of beer for Monday night knocks the wind out of the last grumbler in the shop."

"Well, I propose to earn some money in that shop, and one way or another they could make it disagreeable for me. The good will of the humblest is not to be despised. And then, I was betrayed, on the spur of the moment, to say a thing wholly unbecoming for me, and it is but right that I should pay some smart money for the smart-aleckism which I was weak enough to display. There is an unconscious appreciation of propriety of conduct in an assembly of men, which will influence them in their action in a manner they themselves do not know, and the fact should not be lost sight of by him who has to deal with them."

Another Sunday. The discovery of Jake that hunger is the cause of European emigration to this country will not let go of me— sticks to me. Hunger, physical want, want of nurture, a mere priva- tive, a negative to produce an affirmative result. "There is nothing in the effect that is not in the cause," they say in metaphysics. But here there is a cause with an effect precisely the opposite of the cause. Hunger seeks, produces food, and is thus cause. But food, the effect, gratifies, annuls hunger, its own cause. The annul- ling of its own cause, however, can only result in an annulling of itself, and the process of nurture starts anew—or rather continues its self-perpetuating round. Want spurs exertion to create means. The means supply want, annul it, but in so doing they exhaust themselves, and want reappears. This is the economic process— not a mere restatement, in more general terms, of the process of nurture, as it may appear to be at first glance, but an elevation of that process into the domain of intelligence. For it is intelligence that generalizes hunger into want; recognizes it as a negative, a need; converts exertion into labor, by directing it to produce the greatest amount of means with the least outlay of exertion. In this the law of economy, intelligence minimizes the negative, the need, the power of necessity, to its lowest terms. It claims the world for its home, and directs that there, where the natural conditions are the most favorable, that there, and there alone, does it recognize exertion as labor rationally applied. From this it is plain that emi- gration is an economic necessity, a part of the process by which rational intelligence elevates itself above the necessity of physical nature.

Well, hunger brought me here, whatever agency it may have had in bringing other people. Nay, for that matter, to what else but hunger have I to account for my presence, not merely here, but in the world itself? I came into it hungry. The only reality about me, when born, was hunger; all else was mere possibility, that might and might not become real. But hunger was a bawling reality. Whence then did this reality come, if nature had no need of swallowing itself, no need to digest itself into intelligence? Nature furnished eyes that saw not; ears that heard not; a palate that tasted not; a nose that smelled not—the whole a living unit of sensitivity that was nothing and wanted everything. To see I had to learn and thus earn it; to use my ears, nose, palate I had to do the same. I had to do this and without me it could not be done. Hunger alone was without me, without my causation; came of itself, naturally, that is—by nature.

But upon what does this hunger, thus caused by nature, feed if not upon nature? Nature then is both in one the appetite and the bread the appetite feeds upon; and the result of this self-digestion of nature, of this process, is the ideality. It is the hunger of nature for ideality, the want, the need thereof, that brought me here.

But that which constitutes the want, the need of another is that upon which the other depends. It can not do or be without it. This is the very meaning of need. It follows then that nature, the real, depends upon the ideal, its own product; and while I am here, the product of the processes of nature, these processes are not without me.

But I, as a product of nature am not ideality. I was born an individual, a bawling want, and ideality does not bawl! I was born an individual, the mere possibility of ideality, and it is real, absolute ideality that nature wants, that nature depends upon. To realize this possibility, to elaborate my individuality into true ideality, into universality, into harmony with that which constitutes the want, the need of nature, that upon which nature depends, this is the problem of life before me. . . .

July 11, 1856

I have recommenced my annual course in Hegel's "Logic." It is a strange book and attractive to me, on account of its noiselessness. Whenever the world within or without commences to brawl so loudly that I cannot hear my own voice, I take a journey into the realm of this primeval solitude. I sometimes think it is a great pity that the man did not live to-day, or at least at a time when the railroad facilities were far enough developed to show him what a book ought to be for man when he travels by steam. As it is, I don't know of a single chapter, page or paragraph that can be read and understood in passing by it at the moderate rate of speed of, say, forty miles an hour, no matter how large the letters might be made, or how long the fence to give room for their display. Yet, even in his day, it was known that a book should be written in such a manner "that he who runs may read," and the circumstance that we do our study, not while running, but while rushing along, leaves us necessarily in a condition the more seriously to regret that he did not comply with the canons of his art, as calculated for his own day and generation. Had he done so, there can be no doubt, when the superior sagacity of ourselves is duly considered, that the increased speed, the haste at which we have arrived, would have been no detriment to the general usefulness of the book. As it is, I fear it never will be of much value as a source of popular entertainment.

I have heard it said that it is owing to the theme, the subject treated, that the work is so obscure; that there are subjects, like the integral and differential calculus, for example, that refuse to be treated in such a way as to become popular reading—or to give up their information to the general public at first glance. As to that, of course, I do not pretend to judge. But it does seem to me that if there is a theme in nature, art or science that ought to be popular, that ought to be thoroughly familiar to everybody, it is the one treated in this book; for it treats of nothing but human knowing—knowing, the peculiarity that distinguishes man from the brute. That is the only subject it touches upon, and it treats of that, not in its idiosyncracies, not as it is developed in this or that individual, but as this universal characteristic, as the very essence of all men, as that which makes man what he is—man.

Why, then, is this not the most popular of themes—seeing that each one of us has within himself the entire material treated of?

Or, is it true that we live habitually out of doors and are strangers nowhere so much as in our own house?

The knowing, thought, reason may be occupied with a variety of objects—with objects derived from the senses, from the emotions or from reflection; but in logic it deals with itself, with its own products alone, and the knowing that results, free from all foreign content, is therefore called a "pure" knowing. The products of thought which it investigates, while at first glance they may appear formal and empty, are nevertheless in their totality the ultimate presupposition of every mental operation. They are the products of the human mind, as contradistinguished from the individual mind—of the human mind in its universality. They form the ground work, the foundation of all communication, association and co-operation of man with man; and all the achievements in science and art, whether applied or ideal, are but the tangible and visible results of those invisible powers. They give continuity to human endeavor, and enable the present to strike its roots deep into the spiritual alluvium of the past. To investigate them in their simplicity; to define each in its sphere; to exhibit the law of their genesis, and thus reveal their self-consistent totality—this is the object which the author sought to attain.

July 12, 1856

I was thinking to-day about the importance of the object mentioned in my last note, but upon looking around, I see nothing to compare it with. It either has all the importance there is, or none. Then it occurred to me that it might be wise to consider whether it was possible of attainment. But to find out something about the knowing, without knowing, would be to know without knowledge— a trick too difficult for me. I do not know how it might be with "Dogberry, of the watch," but as for me I can not turn it.

"Man know thyself" was at one time regarded as a divine command. But for man to know all about himself except the knowing would be to know all about himself as a beast, not as man—if the knowing is that which distinguishes him from the beast. For the knowing to know itself must therefore be regarded as the only adequate compliance with this mandate.

If I reflect upon this theme several propositions that never occurred to me before become at once self-evident. If the knowing investigates itself, its own products and their genesis, it is evident that in so doing it relates itself to itself; for it investigates itself, not some other objects. Again, it is also evident that in this occupation the knowing determines itself, as there is no other than itself to affect its activity. It subpoenas before it the universal products of the human mind, and by virtue of its own inherent universality, recognizes them as its own. In determining this content it therefore determines itself, not as this or that individual, whose intelligence is clouded by this or that interest, passion or presupposition, but as vital humanity—the individual dominated by his inherent universality, the individual as man; for it is only in this attitude that he participates in the thought of the race, the results of which he proposes to investigate.

Again, the results obtained will sustain a different relation to the objects investigated than the results from mental operations where the object is any other than the knowing—as, for example, in simple consciousness. In that sphere of knowing it is sufficient that the result, the mental determination, correspond with the object, in order that it may have the value of truth, but here it must necessarily be identical with its object before it can have any value or validity; for it is the knowing that investigates the knowing. The result can therefore only be true when the knowing knows itself—

is identical with itself. Then, in the sensuous consciousness the mental operation cannot be corrected. There is no facility for comparing the sense determination with the object, and thus [to] ascertain their correspondence beyond a doubt. The results are therefore affected with more or less relativity. But here the object itself, the knowing, is the ever present critic, to determine the sufficiency of its own expression or embodiment, and the results, therefore, are capable of being ascertained with absolute certainty.

Then again, the criterion of truth for simple consciousness fails to certify to the truth of existence. Coming down the street I see a hump-backed, knockkneed dwarf; behind him, a splendid specimen of manhood, with the fully developed form of an Apollo. Now, which is the man and which is the dwarf? My mental determination of the one is as perfect as of the other, and therefore, according to this criterion, for all that it can tell me, the one is as true an existence as the other.

But, the question grants the correctness of the mental determinations involved, and asks, is the object presented by them true? It is the truth of the existence itself, whether it is a true embodiment of the idea, of the intelligence, that is presented by the sensuous consciousness—it is this, the truth which enables us to distinguish between the abortions of nature and art and the true embodiments of either, that the question seeks to ascertain. But this cannot be answered by the sensuous consciousness repeating, "The object is as represented!" To answer this question the consciousness elevates itself to a higher plane. The intelligence interviews itself, its own determinations of the object, and by comparing with them the given presentation of sense, it determines whether the latter is a true embodiment or an abortion. But, even in this occupation, the highest phase of the knowing in practical life and general literature, it is not in simple relation with itself. It is still occupied with an object derived, partly at least, from without. It compares its own products with another, and although it determines this other, through its own products as criterion, still the result can only be a correspondence and not identity. But in the investigation under consideration the knowing considers these its criterion, its own products, in their ultimate elements, separate and apart from the others; these principles, through which it determines the other, themselves are the objects of investigation and identity and not mere correspondence is the criterion of the validity of the results.

Again, if in this investigation the knowing relates itself to itself, then the mediation involved, and such there must be, if the genesis of the results is to be rendered apparent, must necessarily be self-mediation—the knowing, mediating itself, with and through itself; for it has no other from whom or from which it can derive its own products.

But mediation, in the prevailing logic, means the mental process involved by which it is rendered apparent that from a given proposition some other proposition follows. The last proposition is derived from another, through another, the mental operation; and self-mediation is specifically excluded as vicious, as reasoning in a circle. According to this view, then, our investigation can only result in conclusions destitute of validity.

But it must be remembered that the prevailing logic is itself the product of the knowing determining itself, of self-mediation. Aristotle did not investigate sticks and stones in order to discover the rules of syllogistic reasoning, as it is called, but the knowing as it presented itself in his day, and especially from its discursive side. Nor did he employ aught else but his own knowing in the investigation. Hence the result of that investigation, the prevailing logic, is itself the product of self-mediation, and any conclusions drawn from its rules against the validity of the self-mediation of thought invalidate them themselves. Such conclusions only indicate that the science that purports to give the laws of the activity which results in knowing is itself incomplete.

This view is strengthened if we look at other spheres of knowing. In the investigations of what is usually called inorganic nature, or the material world, mediation still means, in accordance with this logic, the antecedent phase of the process which produces the event or thing to be explained—that is to say, the derivation of the event or thing from another through another. As a result of this knowing we have "inorganic nature"—that is to say, our knowledge of nature is inorganic. But self-mediation means the derivation of the object from itself through itself. Applied to nature, it means the process of organization and disintegration, through which it or any one of its organic systems perpetuates itself. Under this view the isolated event or thing is not explained by being derived from another event or thing, but only when comprehended as a necessary phase, part or member of the totality to which it belongs. The knowing, which derives the thing from another, while perfectly legitimate, as simplifying the problem, is therefore but a partial compliance with the demand of reason, which refuses to recognize the knowing as complete, as possessed of validity and value, unless it has penetrated its object so as to see that object as a self-mediated totality—as it has done, for example, in the case of the mechanical process of the solar system.

Another peculiarity of the results of this investigation is that they are not results, in the usual sense of that term—not at least insofar as the mind associates with that term the meaning of finality. For in this knowing, if it has to penetrate its object, which is itself, so as to see it as a self-mediated totality, each step in that mediation must be a result and premise at the same time—result, conclusion from a preceding, and premise for a succeeding result; and while distinct from both it also contains both; the preceding explicitly, the succeeding implicitly; the preceding in its fully developed form as result, revealed and present to the knowing, and therefore extant for it; the succeeding implicitly, that is to say, potentially, but not as yet extant in fully developed form for the knowing.

Thus the knowing to be investigated possesses within it, in itself, potentially, all the results which the investigation will develop, but it does not possess them as results. As such it will possess them only at the end of the investigation, when it will be conscious of them, and thus self-conscious knowing, self-conscious intelligence. And thus, what the knowing is in itself at the beginning will be extant and for it at the end, through it, through its own mediation, the investigation. Thus the knowing, the immediate consciousness by virtue of its own inherent, its potential self-consciousness, realizes itself through the investigation as self-conscious intelligence. . . .

July 14, 1856

Read over my note on the study of logic and see nothing in it to change, even if it was to be read by everybody. For what does it amount to but this, that if the knowing investigates itself, it in so doing relates itself to itself, it mediates and finally determines itself. Nobody can deny that. Then, as to the knowing being at the bottom of all human affairs and achievements, I don't think that anybody can question that either; certainly not, if he has ever done as much as to mold a skillet, or raise a hill of potatoes, or a row of beans. From these, ordinarily regarded as very humble undertakings, up to the founding and building up of an empire, which we as a people are doing to-day, there is not a move made, not a finger or foot stirred in the right direction, but is and must be guided by intelligence. Every worker in his place must know how to do his part, before the work can succeed.

While this is quite obvious, it is also true that the kind of knowing involved in these affairs differs in some respects from the knowing referred to in my note of yesterday—that is to say, from the knowing that will result from an investigation of the knowing; for this will be a knowing of the knowing, a knowing conscious of itself, a self-conscious knowing; while the knowing investigated is the simple knowing of immediate consciousness. As the latter directs the hand how to do, so the former directs the immediate consciousness how to know. It is this peculiarity of self-conscious intelligence that withdraws it largely from the public eye, and covers up its workings from the scrutiny of journalistic review and supervision.

But what are the inevitable conditions under which the one is transformed into the other? What are the conditions under which the simple, the immediate knowing of consciousness is transformed into self-conscious intelligence? What is the law that governs this transformation, the investigation under consideration?

To become conscious of an object, the knowing must determine that object; to determine means, first of all, that it must distinguish the object from the mind itself and from every other object. Without this condition having been complied with, there is no object, no distinct object before the mind, the knowing or the consciousness. There is no evading of this condition. It is inherent; it is absolute. Hence, if the mind is to become conscious of itself, the knowing a knowing of itself, the simple consciousness self-conscious intelligence, it must determine itself the same as any other object—that is, it must distinguish itself from itself and from every other object. This is the first step in the process—a compliance with the first condition.

The next step is, that in cognizing this object, thus determined, the knowing cancels this determination; for it cognizes the object as itself—that is, as not distinguished from itself. These are the inevitable conditions of self-conscious activity, and the fountain, the source of all determination; the primitive diremption no less than the final return into identity with itself, of the energy of the pure knowing.

To become self-conscious, therefore, means for the consciousness to become an object to itself. To do this the consciousness must dirempt itself and determine the results of this diremption, the one from the other. The activity of diremption and the determining of the results by which this relation is established are one act, which when viewed in its effect upon the preceding entirety or oneness of consciousness, is negation, in that it negates that oneness. Again, the consciousness before the diremption is universal totality, and the dirempting together with the determining thereof, the negation of this totality, are its own act. Hence consciousness as totality is universal negativity, while in self-consciousness we have universal negativity relating itself to itself.

It contains both consciousness and the determinations thereof;

but the latter, not as yet consciously; for self-consciousness is not as yet self-conscious intelligence. To become such it must SEE that it contains consciousness and its determinations. For self-consciousness to see that it contains both means not merely that it includes them, but this seeing is itself the comprehending activity which sees and includes at one and the same time. This activity of seeing is the process of mediation through which the simple consciousness, that knows that there ARE things, elevates itself through self-consciousness into self-conscious intelligence, into reason, that comprehends what consciousness knows.

The main steps, phases or elements in the process through which self-conscious intelligence realizes itself are:

First, the diremption, the diremption of itself by consciousness. This is the first determination. The simple negation of its oneness, of the wholeness of consciousness, of its immediateness.

Second, the process of mediation posited by this negation, which results in the negating of the negation, through the perfect interpenetration of its elements by the intelligence, identifying them as or with itself by comprehending them, and thus restoring itself to self-consistent oneness not as consciousness, with an object other than itself, but as self-conscious intelligence that is and comprehends itself as its own object.

Thus pure immediateness by negating itself posits mediation; and mediation by negating this negation posits immediateness—but immediateness as result. This result is the knowing that comprehends itself—pure self-conscious intelligence. The process, our investigation, is the becoming of this result, the realization of this knowing; and consciously followed, that is, subjected to the conditions adduced, it is the method of Hegel—the mode of action of self-consciousness itself in its activity of realizing itself as self-conscious intelligence.

July 15, 1856

In summing up my note of yesterday I have self-relation, self-mediation, self-determination, together with the conditions that govern the mediation, all derived from a mere cursory glance at the nature of the work which the author proposes to himself. But these are the elements that constitute the roots of both, the terminology and the method which he employs in the solution of the problem. The terminology is derived from the theme and the method is the embodiment of the law that governs self-conscious intelligence in its activity of self-realization.

It is not the fault of Mr. Hegel, or anybody in particular, that in

order for self-consciousness to realize itself into self-conscious intelligence, the knowing into a knowing of itself, into reason, it must
become self-related, self-mediated, self-determined; that it must be
in itself before it can become extant—before it can be for itself;
that it must negate itself as being in itself in order to become extant,
to become for others, and that it must negate this negation, this
being extant and for others, before it can become for itself pure
self-conscious knowing. These are the inherent, the inevitable conditions of the problem itself, and not the gratuitous vagaries of the
author. The knowing can not evade them. To question them shows
a want of reflection upon the problem.

Suppose the knowing, say I myself undertake to discuss the least
one of the questions involved—the question of "what is and what is
not?" Some simple-minded fellow, wholly oblivious of the ridiculous,
asks me:

"What do you mean by 'IS'?"

Having defined what everybody knows, or supposes he knows,
the simpleton requests further a definition of the terms of the definition. These too having been given, he renews his request, as each
successive definition of necessity involves new and undefined terms.
I can not evade his questions, for a special law says I must answer;
and not until I arrive at the self-defined totality of the content of
the knowing will I have complied with the request, to define the
terms of my definition. Nay, I will not see the end of this demand
unless I remember that it is the knowing defining itself—that it is
self-relation, self-mediation, self-determination, which to be true
and exhaustive must comply with its own inherent nature, with the
law that governs its activity. Silence therefore upon these questions,
or a cheerful compliance with this law is the only alternative for
me.

Have examined Plato and find that this law underlies what they
call his dialectics—that is, the part that treats of the pure categories; for these categories are themselves results and being of self-
conscious intelligence, are at once the product and embodiment of
its nature. Hence, when thought makes them objects of its activity,
and thus vitalizes them, they define themselves as their own opposites; and thus generate and elaborate the elements of a higher
synthesis, a more perfect expression, a more complete embodiment
of the intelligence. Plato, unconscious of this law, failed to see their
genesis, and failing of that, he failed of the logical sequence that
dominates their totality.

It is also this law that underlies the antinomies of Kant; and a
want of its appreciation that dictated the remarkable account which

that author gives of the content of reason. It is the recognition of this law, and its conscious application to the general content of the knowing, that distinguishes Hegel from the philosophers of the world, and if we understand by that application the derivation of that content from the knowing through its own activity consciously subjected to this law, we have Hegel's "Logic," the work that I am studying.

Plato and some of his predecessors had discovered the peculiar, the dialectical nature of the categories—such as being, nothing, one, many, motion, rest, becoming, ceasing, change, permanence, with the rest—and recognized them under the names of ideas, as the essence of things. Aristotle, clearer and more comprehensive, had shown that self-determined intelligence was the only adequate principle for the explanation of the objects that present themselves to our knowing, if for no other reason than that it alone is adequate to explain itself. The Neoplatonist, Proclus, added the insight that the views of Plato and Aristotle were complementary and not antagonistic, as the latter supposed. But neither had inquired into the law that governs self-conscious knowing in its activity, and thus exhibited the necessity of the results of that activity; nor had any of their successors and repeaters deemed it necessary to push the inquiry in this direction.

It is this principle, however, which in its historic development and embodiment has become the power that to-day wields the sovereignty of the earth, and demands obedience from me, either in accordance with, or despite my conviction. To exhibit this principle as a necessary result is to remove from its embodiment the appearance of arbitrariness and to restore to me my freedom through my conviction: for it exhibits that principle and its embodiment as the result of my own rational nature. But when I remember that the embodiment of that principle, the world of institutions, the family, civil society, state and church, the world of mediation, has been created by self-conscious intelligence, and that as such it rests for its vital power upon human conviction; that it performs its function effectually and fully only so far as it is the embodiment of the free conviction of the living as well as of the dead—if I remember this, then the work stands before me in its true signification.

July 16, 1856

There is a matter in regard to the note on the study of logic that has been haunting me all day. I have looked at it since I came home and see that where I touch upon the necessary conditions under which self-conscious intelligence realizes itself, I define consciousness to myself as universal negativity, in that it dirempts itself and thus negates its immediate oneness or totality. But as this is the final source of all self-determination, it follows that all self-determinations are negations. It also follows that self-consciousness, as it is the relation of consciousness to itself, is universal negativity relating itself to itself and therefore in its results, absolute affirmation; for it is universal negativity relating itself to itself, not to another—and that, too, actively. It is a process of mediation, of cognizing, through which the primitive negation of consciousness is negated. It is through this activity, through which self-consciousness realizes itself into self-conscious intelligence, that the originally negative is transformed into an affirmative result, and the principle becomes evident that all negation is not negative.

Mr. Hegel illustrates this by the familiar example—not that "two negatives make an affirmative," for that is not true—but, that to negate a negation is affirmation. This, itself abstract illustration, may be further illustrated by observing that ignorance is a determination, a negation. But to negate this negation through the process of culture the result is affirmative-intelligence; a process that ought to be familiar to the pedagogical fraternity; and it will not have escaped their penetration that even the first negation is not in itself reprehensible. The child that comes to them is not punished because it is ignorant. If it were not ignorant, it would not come, and the process of education, of culture, would not exist. It is the nature of this negation to be a deprivitive—to be a part, a fraction, not a whole. As such it does not comprehend itself, but it is still a part of the affirmative, and as such contains or is the process of mediation, the activity which negates it, which turns it into an affirmative result—back into the self-consistent totality. This renders itself tangibly certain to every teacher on pay day, nor is it necessary to trace the result, his pay, back again through the family relation, which it maintains, into the reproduction of the inception of the process, and thus illustrate its perpetuity and the principle as a phase of the process of the universe.

Again, vice is a determination, a negation; but to negate this negation through the process of moral reformation, the result is affirmative—virtue.

Thus individuality, individualism, is a determination, a negation; but to negate this negation through the process of life into rational universality, both on the side of intelligence and on the side of the will, the result is affirmative—a free, rational being.

Nay, the world itself is a determination, a negation; but the negation of this negation through the processes of nature, life and intelligence, the result is affirmative—the in and for itself existing self-conscious intelligence.

But it is not merely this side, the return into self-consistency, into harmony with itself, it is also the other side, the diremption, the self-determination of consciousness, the becoming no less than the return, that is revealed in the law. It is the simultaneous operation of both of these sides that gives us the self-perpetuating process of the universe. . . .

August 10, 1856

Sent the figures on the cost of railroad transportation to Mr. F—— this morning. I obtained them from a work on railroad construction, which appeared recently in London. It gives the results of special experiments, and also the general experience collected from practical operations. He soon called over and wanted to know where I got "those figures." I told him.

"And you believe them reliable?" he asked.

"I know they are—only they are not likely to remain so long."

"What do you mean?"

"They will be superseded by lower ones."

"Of course, there you are again. It's a mystery to me, Henry, that a man like you, with good common sense on every subject of ordinary interest, should allow himself to be carried away the moment he is called upon to look at anything that points to the future and its development. There seems to be no limit to your belief as to its possibilities, and yet you are no visionary fool!"

"I tell you, Mr. F——, the cause of this mystery. It is such men as you who teach me the faith I entertain as to the future. You have within the last ten years revolutionized the kitchen by furnishing it with new implements. Mr. McCormick only the other day discharged every reaper from all the harvest fields of all the world, and every mower from all the meadows, to keep them company. Mr. Singer and Mr. —— have discharged all the tailors and sewing girls, or increased their productive capacity from fifty to a hundred fold. Do you think this will stop with what has been accomplished? How long will it be that the shoemakers, the harnessmakers, the saddler's awl will be where the tailor's needle is today? How long before every implement used upon the farm, in the mill, in the mine, in the shop, in short—every implement of human industry, will be superseded, replaced by more effective ones, and the world be born anew?

"And whence is this? Around me I see a people, drawn as it were, by lot of destiny from all the nations of the earth. The only condition attached for the individual to become incorporated is that he possess the courage to forsake the old and adopt the new—to forsake the old, his home, the use and wont of his fathers, dare a perilous voyage and not tremble in the untrodden gloom of the wilderness. There is not a man or woman upon this continent whose blood is not freighted with this courage. They could not be fathers and mothers here without it. This people did not inherit a home; they built it; wrought it out with their own toil. It is new! They are furnishing it with new furniture—new implements. The same audacity that bore them beyond the wont and use of their father's house, that caused them to claim a continent for their home, and the world for their enterprise, causes them to call in question every method, every implement transmitted from the past—because it is transmitted.

"Now, look at the natural resources upon the watershed of the Mississippi alone, awaiting the energy of this people, armed anew from day to day." . . .

August 20, 1856

Met Jochen, with my dear one, according to appointment, at the usual time and place, and on the way home I related to him my trip to —— County a week ago, and also told him the amount of land I bought and entered. He whistled, muttered to himself and gave every indication of being highly gratified with what he learned, but said not a word—as is his custom when driving his colts. Now and then he ejaculated: "Narren tant"—that is, "fool's folly," as near as it can be rendered into English—but he said this only to himself. On reaching the gate we found little Yetta and Henry awaiting us with great impatience, and had to listen to a long complaint from Yetta, addressed to Uncle, that "Papa stole away and did not take her with him; and it was Sunday, too; and that she had a great mind of being mad at him."

Mrs. Hanse-Peter also came to receive us at the gate, with her usual cordial smile, but she was not as bright this morning as customary; she was suffering from a headache. While eating breakfast Jochen ordered the horses to be changed.

"You see, Henry," said Jochen, "you and me will drive over to the church. There is preaching to-day on the ridge, and the women folks can keep house by themselves. Feeka has one of her headaches and Miss Elizabeth can stay with her, and Henry—she can't understand our preaching nohow."

This arrangement, although at first demurred to by the ladies, and in a special manner by the children, was finally acquiesced in, which Jochen accepted in a kind of matter of course manner. As soon as breakfast was over we started, and when we got beyond the last gate he remarked:

"See, Henry, I took these horses because I can drive and talk at the same time; but I can't do that and I ought not to do it with the colts.

"Now, that land you bought—that is a great matter. I know it. I worked for old man Pheyety during one whole harvest. He lives only eight miles, as the crow flies, from Krome, our old neighbor from Doerren. The great thing is that wood land. Mr. Pheyety, somehow, always allowed it to be understood that he owned it, and there is not a stick of timber cut on it but by him, and he touched it very lightly—always saving it like, intending to buy it, no doubt. Well, sonny, this is all right. There isn't a finer location between here and Cairo. It's good enough for a prince. But, sonny, you must promise me one thing."

"What is that, Jochen?"

"You promise me that you will never sell a foot of it! Yes, you promise me that! You see, sonny, people grow; but land don't. Folks here think there is no end to it; but you and me know better. We have seen your father pay eighteen hundred dollars an acre for land that can't produce half the crops with manure that it produces without."

"But what in the world can I do with it? I can not farm myself; and then I have all that vacant property in the city that must be improved in order to bring in money."

"What property in the city?"

I explained to him the extent of my acquisition.

"All the better for that, Henry; all the better for that. Now, that is something like. That begins to look like you. 'Narren tant'—I told you they didn't get you when they got your money. But come now, you promise me that you will never sell that land, and I will show you what we can do with it. Give me your hand, sonny, that you will never sell that land as long as it does not bring you the whole money that them fellows stole from you."

I gave him my hand and made him the promise.

"Now, sonny, you see, that is the reason we are going to church to-day. 'Fresh eggs, good eggs,' as your father used to say. God's blessing is always worth picking up; and our Mr. Pastor has inquired about you, and I have had to explain and to explain why you didn't come to church. Now, he is a good man and he has several blessings about him that we may as well pick up.

"He has been after us for some time, the older settlers, I mean, who are beginning to get along in the world, to pick up a little for a rainy day—to put a sum of money together for him to buy land with. He wants to rent it out to newcomers and new beginners among our people; to give them a chance to earn a home for themselves. Do you see anything now, sonny?"

"No, I do not. I am not familiar with the situation. But let me hear further."

"You see, we go to church and after service I tell him that I have found something for him. Then I explain that you have a thousand acres of land—you see, sonny, you must buy the forty acres to make it a round thousand—a thousand acres, where he can settle twenty families on, if he wants to. Forty acres is enough for a beginner; Witte and Krome had no more. We give them a five-year lease, the first three years free of rent, on condition that they put up the necessary buildings and fences; and put the land under cultivation. The fourth and fifth year they pay you seventy-five cents an acre a year rent. After that your farms are complete and the people will want to buy them, and they will have something to pay for them with, in part at least, if not entirely.

"You see we will divide it into four farms, three eighties or two hundred and forty acres to the farm. That makes it a quarter of a mile wide and a mile and a half long—not as close together as might be, but other things make up for that. The houses are built in front of the timber, on the north line of the farming land, where they are sheltered from the north wind in the winter and have a free draft of air in the summer. That is a great matter for both man and beast. They will also be convenient to water—but you and me have to go out and locate the building places. These four farms can be cut up into as many pieces as they please, for the present. That is a matter for them to consider. Next year, this time, there shan't be a tuft of prairie grass on the land, if we live and have our health."

We arrived in sight of the church before we got through building air castles; and yet there was nothing very extravagant or impracticable in his scheme, when I came to examine it during service. This proved a little tedious to me. The trouble is that I learned the principles and doctrines in the form in which they are presented from the pulpit to-day when I was a child at school, where the Bible was our only reader. At fourteen years of age I could correct from memory any misquotation from its pages. The inner meaning of the Christian creed, its profound theory of the universe, breathed into its conceptive forms by the fathers of the church, from the works of the ancients, from Plato, Aristotle, Plotinus, Proclus and the rest, and which the course of the world in its progress only serves to verify more and more clearly to thought, is as much a mystery to the preacher as it is to the congregation. He treats the conceptive forms of poetry and representative thought, the technique of poetry, as dry, sober prose, and leads what germs of thought are awakened here and there among his hearers into endless difficulties. They look for help but find none, for he has nothing but the formal logic, which itself is helpless, without flat assumptions. It serves, however, to clean their minds of rubbish, to sweep the granary of the soul clean of whatever chaff presents itself to sight, but in this process the grain beneath and not in sight is liable to go with it. This gives us the rhetorical inanity of the press, literature, forum and pulpit.

"There is no holy of holies in man and no priesthood to attend its altar" is the well-founded assurance of the thought of the day.

After the close of the service, the minister shook me by the hand with a special fervor of welcome, and as soon as the opportunity was offered, the crowd having retired, Mr. Hanse-Peter broached the subject nearest his heart. But he had hardly begun when Mr. Witte came up and insisted that we go home with him for dinner, this being pastor's day at his house—that is, when the minister dines with him. This being the case, we took the preacher in our wagon with us and drove down. On the way Jochen opened the matter to him, in detail. But all he said in response was: "Ah, the good God, he still lives. We of little faith!" When we arose from the table, however, he launched out into a regular sermon, directed at Witte and Jochen. He showed them how the Almighty Father of all was not dependent upon the good will of any special set of any of his children, but that when he wanted to accomplish a good work, he could find the means where man least expected it. Here he, the minister, had been laboring for more than a year to get the means to help those who could not help themselves. And when he was well nigh discouraged, not because of the hard-heartedness, but because of the hard, the close-fistedness of his children, the good God sent him help from an entirely unlooked for quarter. Yes, he raised up friends that assisted Mr. B——— to his own, and then gave him light to see far enough to help his fellow men while he was helping himself—God's hand was as clear as the noonday sun in the whole matter.

At first I did not see his drift, but it soon appeared. It was nothing less than to inform his two friends that he confidently relied on them to set a good example to the rest of the brethren, in furnishing teams and implements to assist those he intended to settle on the land.

He then turned to me and wanted to know the terms on which the land could be had. I told him I would leave that to Messrs. Witte and Hanse-Peter, as they were more familiar with what was customary, and that I asked no more. They soon agreed upon the conditions, which Jochen had detailed to me, as fair to all parties. This proved satisfactory to Mr. Pastor and we agreed that I should make out leases to four persons, to be recommended by the minister, for two hundred and forty acres each; that they should have the privilege of subletting to such persons as Mr. Pastor might recommend— themselves being responsible for the fulfillment of the conditions of the lease.

With these arrangements fairly understood we said "good-bye," and Jochen felt a foot taller, at least.

"Yes, yes; see, sonny! He is a good man. He helps the people to help themselves. We will have to furnish the teams and plows to break the land, but not for nothing. They have to pay us in work. He will see to that. He will see to that. The man or woman that will not work when he or she can is not a member of his church. He would not know them.

"But now, sonny, we must run over to the land not later than next Monday. We will start Saturday morning and be back Monday night. We will go to Krome; take him with us; show him the building sites; and he can attend to everything for us. He speaks the language and can understand our people. Then, Sunday, we drive over to Mr. Pheyety and stop with him over night. Now, you make yourself ready for this."

I agreed to do so and then spoke about the details of the leases— the conditions, etc.

"That is not necessary," said he.

"You don't need a scratch of the pen. We tell Mr. Pastor what we want and he will attend to the rest. You need not to think, sonny, he is a fool; he knows his people. A man that don't do as he tells him don't get any help from him. And then, you know, he sends the black fellow (the devil) after them, and that helps—helps better than to send the constable or sheriff. A member of his church that goes to court is no friend of his."

"That's all very well, Jochen, but then you know there is such a thing as death in the world; and I have adopted the practice, ever since I met with that loss, to do business simply on business principles, as far as the legal side of it is concerned. That does not imply any distrust, but it means that mankind in their experience of more than a thousand years have found it profitable and safest to adopt and follow these rules. It is for the protection of all parties concerned. It does not reach the essence, or the meaning of the contract. In that we can be as liberal as we choose, but the form, it should be legally perfect. That places it above the contingencies of life and death, and beyond the whims and changes of purpose, to which we all are subject."

"Nay, as to that, Henry, you are right. A man who knows these things himself, he is a fool, if he depends upon somebody else. I only meant as long as Mr. Pastor is alive, we will have no trouble."

"But did you notice, sonny, how he threw for the ham with the sausage?" (A great saying among these people. It means that a person concedes a small to gain a greater point or thing.)

"How the good God got you friends to help you to get back a part of what was stolen from you."

He forgot to say that the same good God permitted the stealing first.

"Jochen, we can not expect that he should remember everything. He, at least, accomplishes good purposes, and whether his theory is correct or not, if it helps him to do that, or if he believes that it helps him, and so makes his task easier, why should we quarrel over it? His theory may have many flaws, but his actions have none. They help us to transform a wilderness into a home for civilized men; and it occurs to me that that is more than the most beautifully consistent theory about abstract truth ever did or ever will do."

"That may be so, Henry, but then you know he ought not to think that he is talking to children all the time. When I plant my crops at the proper time on land well prepared, 'tend them right, take care of my stock well, and see to it that I am not swindled out of my earnings by sharpers—in all this, I do and only obey the will of God Almighty and His blessings follow my obedience. And when Mr. Pastor says so, I believe him. But when he comes with long rigmaroles about this and about that, and about the other, and all to get me to put money into things that I know nothing about, you see, Henry, I can't see God's will in that. I believe God wants me to keep what I earn. In that I can see His blessing, and I am not going any further than I can see."

With this peculiar confession of faith, we reached home with everybody happy at our return. . . .

September 22, 1856

Saw Mr. O. D. F——— and the more I see of him the more I admire the man. While talking with him to-day in his office shop, I noticed that he kept looking through the glass partition which cuts it off from the store. Finally he called one of his salesmen, who was busy waiting on a customer.

"Antwine!"

The man stepped into the office.

"You tell Mr. Nickolls, the man you're waiting on, to make his bill as small to-day as he can. Tin has come down and we have not had time yet to mark down the goods. He will not do himself right by buying a large bill to-day."

He then turned round to me and went on with the conversation. He is very much opposed to slavery. It seems to be repugnant to his entire moral nature. I told him that I had read the last few days the travels of a man by the name of Humboldt, in the valleys of the upper Orinoco and the Amazon; and that the author gave a description of the peculiar method adopted by the monks to Christianize the natives; that they simply organized armed forays, captured what they did not kill and confined the captives at what they called the missions, until they were tame—not unlike [the way] our people capture and tame bear cubs and other wild beasts and train them to do tricks.

"And does he justify such conduct?" he asked.

"No; he denounces these forays as in violation of the laws of both God and man, although he does not use that expression—he says 'church' and 'state'; and as utterly subversive of the natural freedom of the native population, of which he is a great champion. Indeed, when science demands to examine the headwaters of the Orinoco, through the eyes of the author, and this could not be done without his ascending the falls of the Maypures, and the Indian navigators who render this possible showed signs of availing themselves of their natural freedom and some of them were put in the stocks over night to prevent them from doing so; and one, who is caught in the act, gets a terrible flogging with raw hide on the bare back—the author takes special occasion to rehearse his confession of faith, according to Jean Jacques Rousseau. He declares 'that all men are born free and equal.' He recites this before he rides, while they row —row against the double current, the current of the river and the current of their own inclinations.

"An article of faith of this kind is a great thing; its rehearsal, upon proper occasions, a wonderful solace! It withdraws the mind from the incongruous facts presented, and centers its attention upon its own self-consistent harmony, so beautiful to contemplate!

"He also relates how some thirty thousand of these 'beautiful people'—Caribs, almost as good as no cannibals at all—I use his language literally—only eating those they have killed, have been deprived by these outrageous armed forays of their 'natural freedom,' and are living at the missions; while some ten thousand of the same tribe are still enjoying their natural liberty, of eating their enemies, the Cabrees, or being eaten by them, as the exigencies of this 'natural freedom' may determine."

"And you do not believe in the great principle that all men are born free and equal?"

"Of course I do; but it doesn't apply to me. I know that I was born the equal of any man in helplessness. I know that I was born in abject helplessness, in utter dependence. But to my mind dependence and freedom are incompatible conditions. To say that I was born free is not true—however it may be with other men. I was born destitute, even of the capacity to utter my wants, my dependence, except by an inarticulate bawl! The measure of freedom which I enjoy I have to achieve, and this achieving is the task of my life. According to my reading and observation, this also is the task of all men; and their achievements in the accomplishing of this task are mine, if I possess myself of them.

"To do so I must obey the conditions under which this alone is possible. These conditions are not of my originating, and yet I must obey them, whether I will or not. I am the ignorant, helpless, dependent thing I was born until I do obey these conditions, and in accordance with them acquire the facilities that lift me above that helpless ignorance and dependence.

"I must articulate that senseless bawl; not in accordance with my own sweet will, but in accordance with forms of utterances involving pronunciation and arrangement of words into grammatical relations. At the same time I must acquire the meaning, the content of these words, the human elements that fill these utterances—not as I may dictate, but as they exist, before my mind enters the community of mind, wherever it is met. In all this, the mere A. B. C's of my rational self, the exercise of my will was and is that I conclude to obey, that I will acquire—because I do not possess—that I will achieve the implements of freedom, because I was not born with them."

"But, did you not have the choice, Henry, to remain as you were born if you wanted to—to learn these things or not, as you saw fit? Were you not born with that freedom?"

"No, I was not. I could not remain as I was born, for I could not remain at all. But for the help of others I would not have remained an hour. The word 'acquired' was not only furnished by my race, but the opportunity to acquire it. The food and raiment—nurture, amusement and culture—all were from another, not from myself. That is the condition in which nature abandoned me. What she did for Mr. Rousseau, Mr. Humboldt and all the rest who talk about their endowments by nature, endowments of rights, of freedom and the like, I don't know. I only speak for myself. She left me with a mass of dying organic matter dangling from my body, which alone was enough to remand me back to the elements in short order, but for the interference of a human being other than myself."

"But did she not provide within the breast of the woman who gave you birth an endowment that compensated for your helplessness?"

"Precisely, as she had done within the breasts of all the individuals of the genus mammal at large, only perhaps not as effectually in the human specie as in some of the rest for, I notice, there are statutes upon the books of the civilized world against infanticide, and this would suggest that the endowment alone was found insufficient in this case to protect bare existence even. But suppose that it was sufficient, what has that to do with me? Did that make me free, what was in the breast of another? Could I do as I pleased because another could not do as she pleased? But you say that she was compelled by nature to do as I pleased—that is to say, nature subjected her natural freedom to my caprice. But I thought that the phrase—'all men are born free'—included woman, too, as if it read, 'all men and women are born free.'

"The truth is, Mr. F———, I found myself utterly destitute and the fact even that I found myself at all I owe to others and not to myself. But the other to whom I owe this is my own race, to them who had preceded me, and who welcomed me with the resources which they had wrought out against the necessities of nature. These resources they placed at my feet for my acceptance; and the glory of the age is that they are free for all—free for all alike, under the same conditions of acceptance.

"But these conditions are the reverse of those implied in the abstraction quoted. For these resources are the results of human achievements and not the products of nature. As such results they must be achieved by me, for this alone gives them perpetuity and myself freedom. Nature cannot confer them, for she does not possess them. I must achieve them, or they are not for me. I must achieve them, or the freedom which they confer is not for me. Each and every generation must achieve them, or they vanish from the face of the earth, for they are human achievements. Nature does not produce, nature does not perpetuate them. Let one generation of the civilized world cease from acquiring, from vitalizing these achievements; cease from subjecting its caprice to the immutable conditions of acceptance of these resources, and the world of man is back where Mr. Humboldt found it on the plains and in the jungles of the Orinoco and the Amazon; with natural freedom presiding over the feast, when Carib eats Cabree and Cabree eats Carib, as nature may determine."

"But, Henry, you seem to use the word freedom in a different sense from what we usually attach to it. We ordinarily use it in relation to the political affairs of man."

"That may be, for to me a free being is a self-determined, self-dependent being; and this I am not by nature but by attainment. Man as man is free; not through nature, not through another, but through himself; and I, the individual, can only attain the freedom of my race by making its purposes my own. Under this view I need the religious, the educational, the social, the economic resources of the race, no less than the political; for I am speaking of freedom as a reality and not as an abstraction. I need all the resources; all are sacred because essential to my purpose.

"Of course, Mr. F———, if a man is free by nature, he needs nothing. At the outside, perhaps, temporarily he may need something in the shape of a fence to keep the runty pigs and breechy cattle out of his field, out of his sphere of industry; something to protect life and property—of course, only temporarily, whilst this, our Gospel, is taking possession of the hearts of man. In the meantime, that government is best that governs least? Certainly. And no government at all is the best government of all; for is not man free by nature? What need has he for instrumentalities to attain what he has?

"But the freedom secured by such a political organization for the individual happens to be only a possibility, not a reality, an abstraction and not a concrete fact. This possibility may eventuate for him in the four walls of a prison, or in a dangle from the gallows, or in the presidential chair. It is because of this peculiar circumstance that I deem it of no concern to me, and suit my thoughts and words to the concrete fact. I accept such an organization for what it is, a guaranty for the possibility of freedom, but to render that possibility real is the task of my life, in the performance of which I need all the resources I have mentioned. To mistake this possibility for the reality, to strut about talking of natural freedom, of natural rights, it is this that I mistrust. It is this strutting, this riding of the possible and claiming it to be real—it is this claim, that I own by nature what can only be mine by the most earnest, patient and persevering exertion, that nauseates me; this claim which takes from life its rational purpose and end and fills the air with self-pitying sobs at the terrible, the horrible outrage that condemns a free being to be self-dependent. It perverts every situation and condition in life. The honest toil by which I achieve my physical independence is 'degrading drudgery!' Of course, to a man free by nature! The skill and art that render that toil less exacting are the attainments of 'a mere mechanic!' The rules of conduct that render co-operation between man and man possible, and thus reduce toil to its minimum, are extremely irksome 'sacrifices of a part of the natural freedom'—and therefore to be deprecated under all circumstances.

"Indeed, this would seem the only rational aim left in life, to see to it that this deprecation be thorough. To swing on the gate and eat sugar 'lasses will, of course, be the splendid avocation of all—men, women and children—the great mass. But as for us, it is our special province, peculiarly gifted as we are for that purpose, to see to it that this 'freeman by nature,' this free being, dependent upon another than himself, be not imposed upon in this universe.

"This perversion of the entire significance of life permeates everything. Take the case before us.

"Mr. Humboldt desires to determine the geography of the upper Orinoco, and to make such meteorological, astronomical, geological, mineralogical, botanical and other observations as the opportunity may afford. To carry out this purpose he requires the local knowledge, skill and endurance of natives who are compelled to render this service by those who have obtained control over them. They render this service at the risk of their lives on more than one occasion. Now, this service was as essential to the accomplishment of the purpose of the journey as that which was rendered by Mr. Humboldt. He could no more stem the current and surmount the cataracts of the Orinoco than they could express for us in the technique of science the results of the journey—although the most important parts of these results had been known to them and their fathers for generations.

"But who were these men to whose hard toil, skill and courage—they jumped over-board whenever necessary, where Humboldt and his companion did not dare touch the water for fear of crocodiles and Carib fish—I say, who were these men to whom science is as much indebted as to Mr. Humboldt for whatever benefit it has received from the journey? Nobody! They were mere laborers. Their services did not even entitle them to have their names mentioned in the chronicle of the achievement. Certainly not! But didn't we deprecate the sacrifice they were compelled to make of their natural freedom? Of course, we deprecated merely! We accepted the fruit of the sacrifice and then we deprecated!" . . .

Lost all the evening listening to Mr. Alcott. No, it was not a clear loss, for the man is clean—in the sense that he avoids the mud. "A remarkable case of reversion," said I, on the way to my room, to the eager questions of Mr. H————.

"What do you mean, is he not original?"

"Yes, if the re-appearance of Ammonius Saccas, that is, Ammonius the sack carrier, the peddler, as we would say now, can be called original."

"But, who is Ammonius Saccas?"

"An Egyptian, founder of the Neoplatonic philosophy, who lived in the second and third century of our era, died in the year 243. He loafed around Alexandria, like the great Grecian assumption hunter, Socrates, had loafed about Athens, some five or six hundred years before, and talked with people that had nothing else to do but gas and listen to others gassing. It was a favorite way of communication between man and man, almost the only way at the time, for, while they had a written language, it was only written; they had no printing press to render the printed word accessible to all. It is appropriate that Mr. A———— should revive, or attempt to revive, this infantile method, because of the matter he has to communicate! This itself is as old as the method and as capable of meeting the wants of the day."

"And you mean to say that Mr. Alcott is not original, in both thought and action?" Mr. H———— asked, as we entered my room.

"He is simply odd in both, and original in neither. Egyptian mummy wrappage is not a new invention, and the walking of the streets of Boston or Concord, habited in such toggery, may attract attention, but is hardly calculated to set a new fashion. The thing of interest is the appearance of the man, when and where he lived, and whence he came. If you reflect upon that, it will indicate how utterly the spirit, the meaning has been lost, out of the forms employed to transmit it. Remember this man is no idle visionary, nor a frivolous notoriety hunter. He is simply a sincere and earnest man, who has found the solutions of life's mysteries, propounded to him in the sacred places, unsatisfactory; and is striving to find and utter what his soul craves. He was told, as we were, that God made the world, in the first six days of the year one, according to Moses; that, in doing so, He meant well, but that somehow the things did not run exactly to suit Him, and He sent His only Son to straighten matters out. That His Son found a hard job of it, and had finally to submit to an ignominious death, in order to accomplish His mission, and that, even then, it amounted only to a saving of a very small per cent of the investment. Now, this answer was no answer to him, any more than it is to you or to me; and he has burrowed 'round until he hit upon some fraction of the works of Iamblichus, or even Plotinus, perhaps. The latter was a pupil of Ammonius Saccas, and the former a disciple of Plotinus; and from them he has picked up a part of the philosophical idea concerning the universe, as it was subsequently developed into much more concrete form by Proclus. Thus, in attempting to deal with the question—how is multiplicity, the multiplicity of objects that present themselves to our intelligence, derived from unity—the subject of his discourse to-night—he adopts the theory of emanation, which we find in these authors— that is to say, in Plotinus, as opposed to the theory of evolution, held by others, who start from what they suppose to be the diametrically opposite pole."

"How is that?"

"The emanationists commence with the One, which they call God, but wholly inscrutable, wholly unknown and unknowable. They proceed, however, to describe, and every description ends with 'but He is more than this.' From this unsayable, unknowable, they predicate, conceptively, of course, that is, by figures of speech or imagination, as the very term 'emanate' shows—a resultant, an effect, very nearly identical with the One, not quite, but very nearly so—as you heard to-night. From this second, a third is derived, in the same way, and of the same character—that is, a little lower, not quite up to the excellence of its cause, the second, and so down, from God-head to atom.

"The opposite theory, or what takes itself for such, also starts with unity, and evolves thence the multiplicity. They call it matter, however, and are quite certain that their first is the very opposite of the first of the emanationists. With them the wholly formless eventuates in a cell, the cell in a bunch of cells, and so on up to man."

"But, what is the difficulty of the view presented by Mr. Alcott?"

"There is no difficulty about it except when you commence to think of it; and then it amounts to nothing, as you can see for yourself. They start with the One, unknowable, inscrutable. Of course, consistently they ought to stop right there, for what can be deduced from the unknown? But, they proceed to regard it as the cause of a second, a little, a very little, less than the first. It is important to make the difference as small as possible, or the student might gag at it, and the theorist would not have an opportunity to get in his graduation, observable in the multiplicity presented for explanation. You see, in deference to the old assumption, that like begets like, the two, first and second, ought to resemble each other like two peas from the same pod; indeed, the more they are alike the better—as we heard to-night. The difficulty, however, is they differ by the full diameter of the universe—are as unlike as difference and identity themselves. For, we are told that one is self-existent, primordial being, and the other is created, derived being; their resemblance, therefore, is like the resemblance between independence and dependence; the resemblance that differs by all the difference there is. With one bound we whiz down from God-head, the uncreated and self-existent, to atom, the derived, the created; and our beautiful fabric of gods, demi-gods, angels, men, down to mud, vanishes in thin air—and that is what we got for our evening's time. For, Mr. Alcott has not even read the man whose opinions he tries to peddle about; that is to say, he has not mastered the thought of the period in its entirety. He has picked up the weak side, the conceptive forms by which those thinkers endeavor to bridge over the chasm between unity and multiplicity, for which Plotinus, for example, uses among others the image of a spring, the source of rivers, itself undiminished—in all their crudities and is utterly lost in the mazes of their fancies. Had he applied himself and swept the deck, as we say in steamboat phrase, got to the bottom of the thought of the school he has stumbled on, seized that thought in its matured forms, as expressed in Proclus, he would have recognized the shaft where the fathers of Christian theology dug the gold for their forms of 'God, Father, Son and Holy Ghost.' But, instead of that, he revels in the miraculous theology of Iamblichus, as we see it in the life of Pythagoras by that author."

"But what about the other theory, evolution. It doesn't present any difficulty, does it?"

"Oh, no! It only begets something from nothing! That's all. Matter, the formless, eventuates in mind, absolute forms, of course, by degrees; like the other arrives from absolute form at the formless. Both are theories in an eminent degree. They account for a circle by drawing a straight line. Whence this water? From the river. Whence the river? From the spring, away up yonder! You see, it is the nature of water to run down hill; now, away up yonder there is a spring, and out of that the water boils, and then runs down hill all the way until it passes your door. How long has it been running down hill? Oh, nobody can tell. Always! Always, that is a long time! I wonder why it has not got all down by this time?

"We live in Asia, and see a mighty stream boiling out of the earth. We follow down its course, and the farther we go the less it becomes, until it is utterly lost in the sand. But, our neighbors live in Europe. They too see a river born, only it is a mere brooklet. But, following down its course, they observe it is increased by additions from without. The farther it flows the larger it grows, until the brook becomes a stream, and the stream a mighty river, with the commerce of nations on its bosom.

"Both see the mighty stream of things of Heraclitus, and each applies to it the images which he has picked up from his surroundings. But, do they answer the question? The stream runs down hill, but why has it not got there by this time? How does it happen that it keeps on running?

"Ah, I see. The water, some while running down and some after it gets down is etherealized, arises in the form of vapor, and is lost in air. In this form it envelopes the globe, and, by what we call the meteorological process, it, from time to time, that is constantly, now here, now there, changes back again into water. Of course, I see now why it keeps on running down hill, because I see how it gets up there, and this too answers the first question, whence the water. I see it, as a factor, result, consequence, or whatever name I apply to it, of a process, an integral of a whole, of a circular activity, in which it is both cause and effect, ground and consequence, end and means! It was in this sense that the thinkers of Alexandria—not its miracle mongers, who thought, because they heard their masters teach that the Divine is within man, that therefore they must endow their masters with all the fabulous performances which the imagination is so fond of attributing to the Divine —stood by the stream of events and change, as seen by Heraclitus. They used the picture of the stream, of emanation, of radiation even, for the transition from unity to multiplicity, it is true, but they were far from stopping there. They were masters of the thought that had preceded them, from the One, the being of Parmenides, to the One, of self-conscious thought—the thought that thinks itself, of Aristotle. To them the stream of events was not the squirt from a box-elder instrument, in the hands of a big boy, but a section of the self-dependent, self-sustaining process of the universe. All the dialectic of Plato is at their command, and with significance such as even Plato himself never saw in it. They were in possession of every element of the idea, its resolution from ideality into reality, and from reality back into ideality; what they did not have was its logical form—the form through which it alone seizes and compels conviction. If Mr. Alcott had penetrated to this thought, he would not be peddling emanation theories with Pythagorean dietary notions, and cut up shines, such as are reported of him, as a member of society and a citizen of the State. I do not mean to say that he is reported even as a bad man—but as one who does not see his place in the institutional world of man, and denies that there is one for him— he, such an extraordinary reversion! He would have seen—"

"What? I am curious to know. Don't stop."

"No, I only wanted to find a note which I penciled down some years ago, when I studied these authors! Oh, here it is. Shall I read it?"

"By all means, if it is pertinent to the subject."

"You can judge of that, after you hear it. It says: 'Philo, the Jew, was born twenty years before Christ, and outlived the latter. He was distinguished for his knowledge of the Platonic philosophy, and his method of interpreting the Old Testament, that is, the sacred book of the Jews, by allegoricalizing the text as a vehicle for Platonic thought. This method was subsequently followed by the fathers of the church, in regard to the life and thoughts of Christ, as recorded in the New Testament. Instead of Platonic, however, they drew the thought from Neoplatonic sources, chiefly from Plotinus and Proclus. They precipitated events into thought, and thus made the latter typical of human life, the thought they obtained as stated, and fitted the events to it. It was in this way that the one obtained reality, and the other significance, commensurate with the highest development of the race. The process up to that time had been for thought to create its own events, through the life of specially chosen disciples. But now the life of all human life as such became the content, and the thought of the race its exposition and guidance. The one life of Galilee, in its birth, renunciation, death and ascension, at first typifies and then becomes the process of the universe: First, in its self-determination, diremption, negation, signifying the birth, the eternally begot Son; secondly, the negation of this negation, the renunciation and death of this Son; third, the absolute affirmation— the ascension into spiritual existence of the Son.

"This viewed as the life and being of the Son of Man, the second Adam; Adam Kadmon—that is, man as such—man generically, and we have human life in its significance as a factor of the process.

"This life begins in an off nature, the unconscious, the external, the spacial, the side by side, the outside of itself, the other as such, the negative of spirit. Its function in the process is to invert this, to negate this negation. From unconscious to transform it into conscious, and thence through self-consciousness into spiritual being, into pure knowing; to turn the external into the internal, the spacial into ideality, the negative of spirit back into spirit. Hence, the doctrine of total depravity, that man is not by nature as he should be; of redemption through Christ, of a triune god—all these are mere correlation of the philosophical idea, which the fathers of the church derived from the Neoplatonic philosophy, and interpreted into the New Testament Scriptures, as Philo interpreted Platonic ideas into the Old."

"Who says this? From whom are you reading?"

"Who says this, in so many words? Nobody, that I know of—in thought and fact every history of human thought, if it deserves the name, will furnish you the data, from which you will have to say it. From whom am I reading? From myself; from memoranda which I made when I was studying the development of thought in the world. It was my habit to drive down stakes, here and there, into the ground, in order not to lose myself in the subterranean workings of this mole, whose hills are visible enough on the surface, for they constitute what are called the events of history, but whose workings are not quite so readily followed."

"And you think Mr. Alcott would have seen this?"

"How could he have helped but see it? And not only this, but he would have seen that the world as then existing—the world into which the idea was born—the Roman despotism, was doomed. Nay, beyond that, he must have seen how this idea created could not help but create its own world out of and upon the ruins which it caused, and the barbarism which it found; its own world into which, he, Mr. Alcott was born—a world called by those who furnished the ground plan 'The Kingdom of Heaven,' by way of contrasting it with what then was the Roman world. Had he possessed himself of the whole thought, instead of the defective expressions of one phase of it, he would have recognized in the triplicity of function established by the constitution of his own world, the executive, legislative and judicial, quite a recognizable feature of the idea, even if only in an external way, and in the instrument itself something else than 'a league with the devil and a covenant with hell.' Just imagine a Caligula in the audience, how he would have shouted 'and damnation' in redundant emendation of the phrase! And yet we could not have blamed the big boy with the squirt gun; he was the embodiment of squirt gun theories, and what else is the idea to him but damnation, utter and dire damnation! He would also have seen—I mean Mr. Alcott, not Mr. Caligula—in civil society something more than a mere fortuitous agglomerate created by 'an innate tendency to truck,' as Adam Smith has it—he would have seen a rational organization, through which the individual becomes generalized, through his own act and deed—his single insignificance into the significance, his poverty into the resources, his caprice into the freedom of the race. He would have seen each work for all and all work for each, without riding antediluvian, communistic abstractions!"

"How do you make that out?"

"I mold my skillet. In doing this I am taskmaster and employer of the tailor who cuts and sews my garments, the spinner and weaver who furnishes the cloth, the collector and producer of the fiber, the raw material that enters the cloth. I also employ the shoemaker who makes my foot gear, the tanner and finisher who furnishes the leather, and the producer of the hide, of the tan bark, lime, hen guano, oil, tallow, lampblack, used in converting it into leather. The farmer sows, plants and harvests for me—whether in Asia, Africa, Europe, Illinois, or Missouri; whether he raises corn, wheat, rye, barley, oats, potatoes, beans, peas, pumpkins, water or musk-melons; or cotton, sugar, coffee or tea; lemons, oranges, pine or other apples, pears or plums. The common carrier transports, the huckster peddles, the banker makes exchange, the builder builds, the butcher butchers, the baker bakes, the cook cooks for me—of course, just for the present, I do this latter myself.

"Then, I have another set of employes, busy inventorying for me what there is to be found upon, within, under and above the earth. And another set to weigh and measure what is found. Still another set to look into earth, air, fire and water, to see what they are made of. Then, the artists to show what they were intended to be."

"Stop, man! If all these are your employes, how do you manage to keep them to their task?"

"In the simplest way in the world—even by attending to my own well. For, while I am taskmaster for all of these, for productive industry as a whole, I am such only in so far as they are taskmasters for me; now, if I fail to attend to my own task well, they will not buy my ware, and I stand discharged, both as employe and employer. But, as long as I do, as long as I produce not what I want, but am governed by the common, the general purpose, I have them. They take my ware, they employ me, and, in turn, I step into the market and pass sentence by choosing or rejecting as suits my wants, am employer in my own person. In this way, and for this reason, the thing is self-sustaining, a rational whole, in which each member is both end and means; and every unit is permeated by the common purpose—self-perpetuation.

"Now, how could a man, with a mind not occupied with squirt gun theories, or 'innate' nonsense, look at such an existence, when it is in actual being—when he himself lives, moves and has his being in, through and by virtue of it, without recognizing in it a realization of the idea; the idea which human thought has found, as underlying, or creating every organic existence, and the universe first of all? You will observe how busy the thing is throughout! Each unit attending to its own affairs, and the whole to nobody else's. Then, the completeness of the thing—no overseer, no outside interference, automatic accuracy throughout."

"But, what about that big fellow, with the sword, the Government?"

"Don't you see the legend he keeps pointing out with that sword—'Here you reap what you sow!' That is it. That is the bodily presence of the common purpose. Yonder, it is present in each unit only—they are all actuated by this purpose, and in that sense it is the general purpose. Each seeks to perpetuate himself, but himself only! Now, this common purpose, as such, as common, as the purpose of the community, realized into independent actuality, is the Government—your fellow with the sword, pointing to that legend, 'Here you reap what you sow!' All of it, no less, no more.

"You observe, this helps wonderfully. It guarantees to me the result of my endeavor, and clears the way between me and my purpose of perpetuating myself by my endeavor. You also observe that he, the big fellow, has no purpose of his own to carry into effect, is only the purpose of the community; and that is the reason I said, no outside interference, no overseer, but guard only. The embodiment of the purpose of the community, he always says 'We,' in mediating the individual with the general purpose. It is a chain, the one—many, made of many links—not the string on which pearls are strung, that requires the heart of the jewel to be pierced. Take away the links and there is no continuity left!"

"Good-night, Henry. We will tackle this again; I must to the office now. You know I am harnessed, and not roaming at large. I will be over to-morrow afternoon, to study for an hour or two. Good-night."

3

HARRIS'S
INTELLECTUAL ODYSSEY

William Torrey Harris

The following is an extract from William Torrey Harris's preface to his critique of Hegel's *Logic* published in 1890. The selection chronicles the development of Harris's thought from that of a Kantian disciple of New England transcendentalism to that of a convinced, but not uncritical, Hegelian. Such intellectual progress is fairly typical of most of the Hegelians who invariably began, as did Hegel, with Kant.

William Torrey Harris, *Hegel's Logic* (Chicago: S. C. Griggs and Co., 1890), pp. viii–xv.

I MUST ask the reader to indulge me in further autobiographical reminiscences with the purpose of explaining what I have set forth as strictures on the Hegelian system.

As early as 1858 I obtained my first insight into this philosophy, in studying Kant's *Critique of Pure Reason*. I saw that time and space presuppose reason as their logical condition and that they are themselves the logical condition of what is in the world. Man, in so far as he is conscious reason, therefore transcends the world of time and space and is an immortal being, and possesses transcendental freedom also inasmuch as he is not conditioned essentially by the world—not essentially, but only in the expression or manifestation of his will, which expression he may altogether withhold. I saw also the necessity of the logical inference that the unity of time and space presupposes one absolute Reason. God, freedom, and immortality have therefore seemed to me to be demonstrable ever since the December evening in 1858 when I obtained my insight into the true inference from Kant's *Transcendental Æsthetic*. In 1859 I worked out my refutation of Sir William Hamilton's *Law of the Conditioned,* by proving the infinitude of space and showing that the supposed antinomy rests on confounding mental pictures with pure thought. The unpicturability of infinite space does not contradict its infinitude, but confirms it. In 1863 I arrived at the insight which Hegel has expressed in his *Für-sich-sein* or Being-for-itself, which I called, and still call "independent being." I did not obtain this insight by study of Hegel's logic, however, but rather by following out the lines of thought begun in 1858. This insight I supposed at the time to be specially that of Hegel, though I had not as yet read one-tenth of his logic. But I discovered afterwards that it is the most important insight of Plato, and that Aristotle uses it as the foundation of his philosophy. It has in one form or another furnished the light for all philosophy worthy of the name since Plato first saw it. St. Thomas Aquinas presents it in the beginning of his *Summa Theologica.* Leibnitz states it as the basis of his *Monadology.* But each thinker may claim originality, not only for his statement of it but also for the insight itself. For it cannot be borrowed from another, it is itself an original insight, because it is and must be a seeing at first hand of the necessity of all existence of whatever character to be grounded in self-determined being. All dependent being is a part of independent being; and all independent being is self-determined being.

The absolute is not, therefore, an empty absolute, an indeterminate being, but it is determined. It is not determined through another, but through itself. If there is no independent being there is no dependent being. If there is not self-determined being there is no being whatever.

It was a year or two later that I came upon a distinction between the true actual as totality, and the changeable real, which is partly actual and partly potential—in the process of change I saw that the full actuality is involved, partly affirmative as giving what reality there is to the phenomena, and partly negative as producing the change which negates the present real and actualizes in its place a new phase of potentiality.

It was in 1864 that I obtained an insight into the logical subordination of fate to freedom—the totality of conditions cannot have a fate outside it, but must be spontaneous in itself, and self-determined—hence all fate and all changes not spontaneous must be secondary and derivative from a higher source that is free. In 1866 I arrived at the first insight that is distinctively Hegelian and the most important aperçu of Hegel's logic. I wrote this out in a letter to my friend Adolph E. Kroeger, an ardent Fichtean, whom I had discovered and was endeavoring to proselyte for Hegel. I called it the distinction between comprehension (or *Begriff*), and Idea (*Idee*). It should really be the distinction that Hegel makes between negative unity or substantiality and *Begriff* or *Idee*. It is undoubtedly Hegel's highest thought. It is the insight into the nature of true being to be altruistic and to exist in the self-activity of others. It is the thought that lies at the basis of the doctrine of the Trinity, though rather as a logical implication than as a conscious idea. It is also the highest goal of the Platonic-Aristotelian system—indicated in the assertion that God is without envy (*The Timaeus* and *The Metaphysics*), also in the doctrine of the Good as the highest category.

This thought is not reached in its pure form by Plato or Aristotle, but rather in its ethical form—as it is the very fountain source of Ethics. Hegel's originality consists in seeing for the first time the pure-thought form of this doctrine. He names it *Idee*, to honor Plato as its first discoverer. For doubtless Hegel read into the Platonic doctrine of Ideas this pure thought. It must certainly be admitted that the attribution of the thought to Plato is correct, though with him it is not to be found stated adequately in its pure-thought form.

In 1866 I for the first time read through Hegel's larger logic, reading it in the English translation that had been made for myself and two other friends (George Stedman and J. H. Watters), by Henry C. Brockmeyer, in 1859 and 1860. I copied the work entire from the manuscript and am sure I read every word of it. But I am equally sure that I did not understand at the most anything beyond the first part of the first volume and could not follow any of the discussions in the second and third volumes, or even remember the words from one page to another. It was all over my head, so to speak. I had of course made myself acquainted with the categories and sub-categories of the work years before through histories of philosophy, and was gradually learning to think something into them; but I could make little of Hegel's deductions or discussions of them. This experience of my own, which lasted for years, is I presume the experience of other students of Hegel and also of students of any other system of deep philosophy. One has first to seize its general thought, its trend as a whole, and gradually descend to its details.

The translation which I copied out still exists, but has never been printed, any portion of it. Mr. Brockmeyer, whose acquaintance I had made in 1858, is, and was even at that time, a thinker of the same order of mind as Hegel, and before reading Hegel, except the few pages in Hedge's *German Prose Writers*, had divined Hegel's chief ideas and the position of his system, and informed me on my first acquaintance with him in 1858 that Hegel was the great man among modern philosophers, and that his large logic was the work to get. I sent immediately to Germany for it and it arrived late in the year. Mr. Brockmeyer's deep insights and his poetic power of setting them forth with symbols and imagery furnished me and my friends of those early years all of our outside stimulus in the study of German philosophy. He impressed us with the practicality of philosophy, inasmuch as he could flash into the questions of the day, or even into the questions of the moment, the highest insight of philosophy and solve their problems. Even the hunting of wild turkeys or squirrels was the occasion for the use of philosophy. Philosophy came to mean with us, therefore, the most practical of all species of knowledge. We used it to solve all problems connected with school-teaching and school management. We studied the "dialectic" of politics and political parties and understood how measures and men might be combined by its light. But our chief application of philosophy was to literature and art. Mr. Denton J. Snider, who entered our circle in 1866, has published his studies on Shakespeare, Goethe and Homer, and Mr. Brockmeyer has printed in the *Journal of Speculative Philosophy* his *Letters on Goethe's Faust*, and these will show sufficiently the spirit and methods of our studies in literature.

In 1873 I discovered the substantial identity of all East Indian doctrines. As early as 1856 I had begun to read oriental literature, but had not seized its essential spirit. I had looked for the same diversity of points of view that I was accustomed to in modern philosophy. Cousin's analysis of the oriental systems, as well as other histories of philosophy, had confirmed me in this mistaken path. But I undertook a thorough study of the *Bhagavad Gita* in 1872 and for the first time saw that the differences of systems were superficial, and that the First Principle pre-supposed and even explicitly stated by the Sanscrit writers was everywhere the same, and that this is the principle of Pure Being as the negative unity of all things. In this I came to see Hegel's deep discernment which early in this century, in the dawn of oriental study, had enabled him to penetrate the true essence of Hindoo thought even in the Western wrappages in which the European first discoverers had brought it away. Hegel could perceive the genuine oriental thinking through the English and French translations which interpreted the same into modern ways of philosophizing. Hegel's greatest aperçu is the difference between the oriental and occidental spirit of thinking and doing.

It was in 1879 that I came to my final and present standpoint in regard to the true outcome of the Hegelian system, but it was six years later that I began to see that Hegel himself has not deduced the logical consequences of his system in the matter of the relation of Nature to the Absolute Idea. I have explained . . . in many places this divergence of his system from the true doctrine of the Absolute Idea. But the wrong explanation of the use of Nature, strange to say, does not vitiate Hegel's theory of human life and of the Christian church. His doctrine of the Trinity makes the Second Person, or Logos, to be Nature, whereas it should make the Logos to be eternally a Person like the First, and Nature should be the *Processio* of the Holy Spirit. But he rightly interprets the doctrine of the invisible Church as the body whose spirit is the Holy Spirit.

This defect in interpreting the Absolute Idea gives rise to a species of pantheism which says that the Absolute is real only in the process of Nature, and his personality actual only in historical persons. This is not Hegel's precise doctrine but it may be inferred from that part of it which makes Nature to be the Second Person of the Trinity.

This criticism on the system of Hegel, so far as I am aware, is a new one, and I am confident of its truth.

II

THE ATTACK ON
MATERIALISM

Though Hegelian thought, with its emphasis on the "concrete universal" and institutional behavior, affected every aspect of American life from education to economics, its main thrust was as the spearhead of an attack on materialism. In the early nineteenth century, "materialism" conveyed a particular philosophical meaning. It referred to a galaxy of thought which pictured the universe as composed of irreducible particles held together according to Newton's laws in a familiar pattern termed "nature." The details and the laws of nature were hard facts which man, following an empirical epistemology, could know only through his senses. Born with Locke's *tabula rasa* or blank mind and an innate capacity to reason, man acquired all his knowledge through sense experience. His reason—a gift from an absentee God—allowed him to order his learned sense data according to God's prescribed laws of the universe, much as Newton had penetrated to the overarching truth of God's unchanging laws of the spheres. Metaphysically, nature was a machine operated according to strict and perfect mechanical principles whose permanent parts or atoms were the irreducible facts of nature. Such was materialism. Locke, following in a tradition initiated earlier by Bacon, was its chief inspiration. But the Scottish philosophers —David Hume, Thomas Reid, Dugald Stewart, and others—followed in his footsteps with an empirically grounded philosophy called "Common Sense Realism." This was the dominant philosophy of the early American Republic which had been thoroughly anglicized by the time of the Revolution.

German thinkers, however, took their point of departure from that other giant of the Enlightenment, Immanuel Kant, who perceived that man could know nothing about matter per se. He could only know about the "phenomena" or his conceptions of matter. This greatly exalted the role of man's mind, and also God's mind, of which it was a reflection or perhaps a part. The whole known universe possessed the quality of mind and to analyze precisely the workings of that mind was not only to gain familiarity with the secrets of the universe, but also to reintroduce something akin to spirituality (now much better understood) into a cold and lifeless world. Hegel's thought, as described in the general introduction to this volume, eliminated the dualism between mind and matter entirely; introduced motion or evolution into the world picture, as God's mind or the concrete universe unfolded; forged a new logic of the dialectic to describe this process; and, in a seemingly practical way, infused everything with universal spiritual significance and hence morality. As American intellectuals returned home from travel and study in Germany and as German refugee intellectuals poured into America, they brought with them the Continental philosophies of Kant, Schelling, Fichte, Jacobi, and Hegel. Armed with these intellectual weapons, they waged a war against the materialistic, "corpse-cold," philosophy of the day. The rise of New England transcendentalism marked the opening battle of this philosophical struggle which lasted throughout the century. The American Hegelians derived inspiration and encouragement from the Concord sages—Emerson, Alcott, Hedge, Ripley, and Fuller—but they regarded their assault on materialism as one in which the contest was carried on at higher spiritual and philosophical levels and with more sophistication. They were more "professional" and hence, they believed, more effective in the long run. Actually, both the transcendentalists and the Hegelians were merely the philosophical wing of a greater movement which included the sentimental and romantic artists, the nationalistic masses who had begun to believe somewhat mystically in their own folk cultures, and the evangelicals or pietists in religion who exalted emotion over pure reason. All this struck rich soil in America where for nearly two hundred years, since the Puritan Platonists first landed, the people had been accustomed in some fashion to reading spiritual meaning into nature. The selections that follow represent something of the variety of the American Hegelians' reflections on the struggle with materialism as it evolved through the nineteenth century.

4

UNDERSTANDING HEGEL

Johann B. Stallo

The best and most thoughtful treatise on Hegel published by an American in the first half of the nineteenth century was Johann B. Stallo's *The General Principles of the Philosophy of Nature, With an Outline of Some of Its Recent Developments Among the Germans, Embracing the Philosophical Systems of Schelling and Hegel and Oken's System of Nature* (1848). It was an ambitious book that lucidly expounded the work of the avant-garde German philosophers and at the same time offered some original contributions by the author himself. Though the author later disavowed it, the *General Principles* was one of the most sophisticated American philosophical studies written in the first half of the century.

Johann Bernard Stallo was born in Oldenburg, Germany, in 1823, and emigrated to Cincinnati when he was sixteen. There he became a schoolmaster, as well as a student of chemistry and physics at Xavier College. By 1844, he had mastered these subjects sufficiently to be appointed a professor of science at St. John's College, Fordham, New York. While teaching in New York, he wrote *The General Principles of the Philosophy of Nature*. Like almost all the idealists, he was attempting to account for science and the rapid progress of scientific (and hence materialistic) knowledge. His strategy was to undercut science and seek out the universal principles that formed its foundations and defined the true nature of scientific knowledge. Hegel's philosophy seemed to provide the answer.

J. B. Stallo, *The General Principles of the Philosophy of Nature, With an Outline of Some of Its Recent Developments Among the Germans, Embracing the Philosophical Systems of Schelling and Hegel and Oken's System of Nature* (Boston: Crosby and Nichols, 1848), pp. 351–70.

HEGEL

NATURE had now been recognized, by Schelling and his followers, in history, and history in nature; the eternal mind, the innermost spiritual being of man, in the material world, and the activities of the material world in the mind. If Locke had annihilated the mind, in beholding there nothing but the shadowy projections of external realities upon a primitive blank, and, as if to avenge it, Fichte had again made these external forms mere evanescent projections from the depths of the mind, it was now understood that the mind only expanded itself, evolved its faculties, in concentrating outward existences, that its exterioration was simultaneously an introversion, a descent into the depths of its being. This then led to the expiration of absolute idealism, with its independent, innate spiritualities, on the one hand, and of absolute materialism, with its gross actualities, on the other. For the energies of the mind are called into existence by material objectivity, and the external world attains to its true reality in the intelligence of the mind. The world exists not in its truth, unless it be thought by its organized intelligence, man, who is, as it were, the eye with which it surveys itself.

This higher unity of mind and nature was the grand *"apperçu"* of the Schellingian philosophy, but it was from its nature intuitive, and its only authentication depended upon the genial intelligence of the philosopher and the poet.* The question arose,—What is it that prompts the incessant evolution of the Eternal, the Deity, the Absolute? Why is the Spiritual a history, and nature a generation? Why is the infinite intensity of *mind* brought to light in the infinite extension of *matter?* What forces the idea to become a form, the "word to turn flesh," and the form again to resolve itself into an idea?—The answer to this question is the philosophy of Hegel. Hegel demonstrated that the great motive principle in the Absolute is its inherent self-opposition. The Absolute, in which all things live, is not, as with Schelling, the abstract identity of two spheres; it is the eternal *spirit, thinking itself* in nature and history. Its being is

---

* The host of ideas, anticipations, analogies, &c., which every new and original aspect brings with it, engendered, in Schelling and his disciples, a confidence in their genial intelligence, through which the eternal identity revealed itself, as they thought, spontaneously. This became, in time, the height of arrogance with many, who imagined, according to a just observation, that they had simply to seat themselves on the philosophical tripod in order to speak oracles. Their dogmatical asseverations and their everlasting rhodomontades, dealt out *ex cathedra*, are often disgusting.—I do not, of course, speak of the truly genial Schellingians, as Steffens, Troxler, Wagner, Klein, &c.

a process; but, since it is the absolute substance, a process which has itself both for its material and for its object or result. In dualizing itself, it yet remains in its eternal identity. Figuratively speaking, the fundamental ether of the Deity is *not repose, but activity,*— moreover, activity *within* itself, which must therefore distinguish itself as the acting subject and the passive object,—and, finally, activity *for itself,* which produces, evolves, but the intensity of its own inner nature. *Activity in and for itself is thought.* The unit discedes, enters into self-opposition, but only for the purpose of self-recognition,—in order, therefore, to reëstablish its unity, not *after,* but *in,* the discession. If we reflect upon the expression, "a *living* unit," we shall perhaps be less disposed to smile at the idea of a unity *in* the opposition, a unity that requires and *contains* the antithesis.

Nature is thus a product of thought, and in this all the objections of the philosophy of Kant are met at once. Hegel made it evident that the difficulty in the results of the Kantian "Critique," the inevitable opposition between the objective reality and the subjective idea, depended upon a misconception rooting in the old philosophical dualism. The reality, the truth of things, is, in the admission of everyone, that which bodies itself forth in the series of phenomenal variations; and Hegel proved that this "constant" is the result of the dialectic process of thought. The uncertainty of our agnition of external objects obviously arose from the assumption that those objects had a real existence independently of thought; that they might *be* different from what they were *thought.* The proof, then, *that their being lay in thought,* which is given in the "Phenomenology of the Mind," bridged over the chasm.

I foresee that the stubborn rigor of the dialectical procedure, to which I must needs adhere in following Hegel through the series of his logical reductions and deductions, will weary my readers. We shall have to reason our way up, sometimes perhaps tediously, from the Individual to the General, in the retrogressive individualization of which we shall again experience (if we may be pardoned the expression) all the toil of creation. The philosophical poet enchants us by revealing the mysteries of existence in adducing a number of phenomenal analogies all pointing to the same centre; he conjures up the spirit of nature from groups, where it would not be seen in individuals; he converts things into images, and, in all cases, causes the idea to flash upon us, so as, for a moment, to illumine our inmost being, where we see that idea written in its full identity, and thus gain an instinctive certainty of truth. Such comprehensive ideas, the offspring of genial perception, of which we at once behold the verification in and around ourselves,—which with a single breath infuse life into a thousand individual forms, and link the most distant phenomena and occurrences,—which at a word summon before us the past and conjure up the future,—are endowed with a charm which does not adorn the path of toilsome reasoning. It may be pardonable, on this account, to give a prospective glimpse of the goal, in advance of our serious investigation, which will bring us thither,—to state what are the leading ideas in the philosophy of Hegel, in contradistinction, 1st, to those views which pervade our ordinary reasonings, and, 2d, to the philosophical principles of some of his noted predecessors, with whom he has been often compared, and not unfrequently confounded.

First, then, as to the peculiarities of Hegel's philosophy, such as they appear when contrasted with views prevalent in our days, it is shown by Hegel, that existing things are not quiescent, permanent in their existence, and cannot be anywise comprehended as such in their nature, but that they are essentially *living processes*. Very vaguely speaking, this might be thus expressed: things are not, even for an instant, *stationary*; they are *fluxional*, and subject to incessant change. Their apparent quietude is but the quietude of commotion. This is, indeed, nothing new; Heraclitus had already said: Πάντα ῥεῖ, and it seems a very trivial, "every-day" enunciation; —we all know that finite things are coexisting with other finite things, subject, therefore, to their modifying influence, and, consequently, to change. But Hegel further shows, that this change is not merely an accident superinduced from without, but that it is prompted by the very nature, the "definition," of the thing within; that finite things are, from an *inherent* necessity, not only coexistent with other things, but driven to *self-negation*. Why we do not use the word "*self-annihilation*" will hereafter appear.

Pursuing this idea farther, let us see to what it leads. Change is a transition from one thing to another; for, when a thing has changed its state, it is really a different thing. The changing thing, inasmuch as the change is urged by its own nature, must, in consequence, at once *contain* and *exclude* the thing into which it changes; it implies a contradiction, by reason of its indwelling activity. In general, all activity, all life, is the unity of a contradiction. Let the reader, who finds difficulty in "realizing" (to use an Americanism) this apparent paradox, reflect upon an *act*. *In* the act that which originates thereby (and something always originates in an act, or something is after the act, which was not before it) *is* and *is not*.

In the same manner, the Deity is not, as usually taken, absolute, eternal rest. Ordinarily, though life, thought, activity, &c., are predicated of the Deity, they are appended thereto rather than deduced from it, which latter, even if attempted, would in fact prove impossible. "The eternal, infinite cause of all things is the Deity," is the general enunciation; "all other things are but effects of this cause." A *formal* connection between cause and effect is thus, indeed, established; but how the one necessarily belongs to the other remains incomprehensible. Hegel showed (or, if this be not granted, at least *endeavoured* to show) that the Absolute is to be conceived as distinguishing, "stating" (positing) itself as cause *and* effect, preserving, however, in this distinction its unity. The Absolute is, then, its own cause; it distinguishes itself as effect, but in the latter sees only its own identity, is therefore reflected into itself, and the unity *resulting* from this self-reflection is the true unity of the Absolute,—not the mere *simple* unity without process and discession. Let the reader look at this under any aspect he chooses; let him say, e. g., God thinks Himself,—God is essentially active,—God is a *spirit*, &c.; the only thing indispensable here is, to conceive the idea of a *living unit,*—a unit indeed, since it is without any external relations, since it relates only to itself,—a living process of self-distinction. Here lies the sense of so many propositions of Hegel, which have been decried as blasphemous, or ridiculed as nonsensical; as, for instance: The Absolute, the Deity, is a reconciled contradiction; the Deity is to be apprehended not only as a rigid, inactive *substance*, but likewise as an internally active, thinking, self-distinguishing subject; the Deity is self-origination, a circle, which *presupposes* the result as its own object and end,—proceeds from and returns to itself. Truth, it is said elsewhere by Hegel, is the *Whole,*—but the whole is only being which completes itself in its own development. The Absolute is essentially a result; not till the end of its process is it *itself*; in its nature it is *subject,*—self-exterioration, self-evolution. The Deity is only through *mediation,* which mediation is the moving self-equality, self-reflection, or, taking it abstractly, simple origination, the abstract "fieri." The pure self-agnition in its absolute exterioration, this ether as such, is the foundation of all science.

In the current philosophical systems, a quiescent substance, absolute quantity, is the material from which all qualitative differences are elaborated; in Hegel's philosophy, absolute difference, absolute quality, forms the beginning, from which quantity proceeds. Hegel does not attempt to evolve concrete forms from an abstraction; his "Absolute" is essentially concrete.—The reason for so many anomalies (as they are termed) in the philosophy of Hegel will now be apparent. Since truth is apprehended, not as something reposing in the bosom of its own being, but as the "Whole in its development," as the Absolute, not abstractly taken, but also in its phenomenal existence, in its individual exterioration, the system of metaphysics, which formerly consisted of nothing but formalities, must encroach upon the domain of all science. Instead of an establishment of certain forms, merely for construing the various material, form and material now stand in necessary relation; the material—nature, &c.—enter as essentially into metaphysical reasoning as the old formulas. It cannot, therefore, be startling to see that the natural sciences, history, &c., are an integral part of metaphysics. "The true form in which truth exists," says Hegel, "is its scientific system alone." Formerly, all the realities of life were excluded from philosophical speculation; they were beneath the level of thought; in the *Logic*, &c., of Hegel, the idealities are exhibited as producing themselves in and through these realities.

It will be borne in mind that, in the philosophy of Kant, an *original* duality of principles was presumed,—the principle of *mind*, of *intelligence*, on the one hand, and that of the *material*, on the other. The former only was hitherto (I speak, of course, of the systems whose influence is now felt, and which yet give to our textbooks of logic, &c., their tone) the subject of logic and metaphysics; and we have seen how fatal this proved to philosophical certainty. With Hegel, on the contrary, the absolute intelligence or mind, the Absolute, is in itself both the *infinite substance* (material) of all natural and spiritual life, and the *infinite form*, the active exterioration of this substance. It is not a bare formality, which would feign subject matter, but, on account of its impotence, remains a mere Ideal; it is at once an unlimited form, a ceaseless activity, and the material upon which it operates. . . .

HEGEL'S PHENOMENOLOGY OF THE MIND

Consciousness

I THE CERTAINTY OF THE SENSES

In the "Phenomenology," Hegel begins by showing that truth does not lie in the immediate data furnished by perception, but that universally the truth of any object involves mediation.—An object is before me, and for the certainty of this I have the vouching of the senses. Now this immediate certainty arises not from the circumstance, that my consciousness has unfolded itself in the perception, and that my thoughts have been set into flow,—nor from the multiplicity of relations in the object itself, and of the object to other objects; I simply possess the assurance: the object *is*. I, *this* particular consciousness, become sensible of *this* individual object.

This perception, then, presents the difference between the conscious "I" and the present object. Neither of them is absolutely immediate; I have the certainty of myself in and through the object, and the object is certain for and through the "I." Yet the truth seems to rest with the object; as to its existence, it appears to be a matter of indifference whether or not it be known by the "I." It remains therefore to be seen whether the "being" of that object is really such as the perception of sense exhibits it. What is the "this" before me? It is the "now" and the "here"; upon these two data my certainty of it depends.* Is this "now" any thing directly given? The "now" is night, for instance; but the truth of this vanishes;—if I write it down, it no longer holds good, as every truth should, for truth is permanent. I find, in looking at it again, that the "now" is morning. Nevertheless it is still "now"; it is neither night nor morning, and still it is nothing without them; it is therefore at once night, morning, &c. It is the particular "this" of perception, and likewise not "this." The truth arising from this negation of the Particular, which Particular is, in spite of its necessary negation, indispensable for its existence, is the universal "now."—Similarly, the "here" of the senses is, e.g., a tree. I simply turn around, and the "here" is now, according to the same senses, a house. The simple "here," which remains, is evidently the result of mediation. Mere abstract, general *being*, but being depending upon negation and mediation, therefore remains as the foundation for the certainty of the senses; and the truth beyond this generality of being attaches itself only to *my* opinion, to *my* knowing of the object. The relation between the object and my knowledge of it has now been inverted. The object, which was originally asserted to be the only thing essential to the certainty, has at present resolved itself into a bare generality; its truth as *this* object now lies in my knowing of it. I behold, hear, &c., this object; the "now" is day, because I see it; the "here" is a tree for the same reason. "I, this particular 'I,' assert the tree to be the 'here'; another 'I,' however, sees the house, and asserts *that* to be the 'here.' Both are attested by the same immediateness of sight, and yet the one vanishes in the other."† The only thing which does not

* There is question here merely of a certainty of the object as *being*, which is, in fact, all the senses pretend to furnish; not of the certainty respecting the qualitative *nature* of the object.

† Compare the "Phänomenologie des Geistes," pp. 75, 76.

vanish is the generality of the "I," whose seeing is neither a sight of the house, nor of the tree, but simply seeing, which, notwithstanding all this, again depends upon the mediating negation of *this* house, &c.,—in short, of the Particular. The seeing "I" is therefore as general as the "now," "here," or "this," and it is as impossible to say what is meant by the "I" as what is understood by "here" and "this." We are thus forced to place the nature of the certainty of the senses neither in the object nor in the "I," but in the totality of the two, such as it is immediately given. It is to be seen, then, what is immediately given.

The "now" is pointed out; this "now." In being pointed out it has already ceased to be; the actual "now" is no longer that pointed out, —it *has been*. Its truth therefore is, that it *has been*; but what *has been, is not*. The immediate presentation of an object is essentially a *movement*. First the "now" is pointed out and asserted as the truth; but next it is pointed out only as *having been*,—the first truth, its *being*, is revoked; thirdly, what *has been, is not*,—the revocation is revoked, the negation denied, and I return to the original truth as general: the "now" is. This movement exhibits the truth of the "now," namely, a "now" reflected into itself, a *general* "now," a multiplicity of "nows" comprised in a unity.

In an analogous manner the "here" pointed out is first and "above"; but next it is not an "above," but a "below," and so on. The one "here" vanishes in the other; what remains is nothing more than a negative "here," a simple complex of many "heres."

The dialectics of the certainty of sense thus consist simply in the history of its own movement, in its own experience, and are nothing forcibly superadded; nay, the certainty of the senses is nothing but this movement.

II OBSERVATION

There is consequently no truth in the so-called individualities of sense; the truth is the Universal, which is not *perceived* (by the senses), but *observed* (*wahregenommen*). Universality (generality) is the principle of observation; its immediate constituents, the "I" and the object, are both general. Simultaneously with the principle of generality these constituents have originated; the subjective observation is simply the movement in which the object is exhibited, and the object the same movement as a *unity*. The object is essentially the same as the subjective movement; the latter the development and separation of the items, the former their unital comprehension. For us, then, *generality as a principle* is the essence of observation; the subject observing and the object observed are not essential. But each of these separately is a generality; since they are opposed to each other, we are forced again to inquire to which of the two the essentiality belongs. Now the subjective movement of observation, being inconstant, is unessential, and the essence must lie in the comprehensive unity, in the object. The principle of this object, generality, is a *mediated*, not an *immediate* unity; it is simple only from the comprehensiveness of the movement of which it is the result. This, then, must appear as a feature in its nature; the object is one of many qualities. But quality is determination; determination depends upon negation; the "this" is consequently stated at the same time as "*not-this*."

The different qualities are independent of each other, and only meet, interpenetrate without interference, in the simple generality of the object, in the "here" and "now,"—the abstract medium of the many qualities. But these qualities themselves are simple generalities; this salt, for example, is a simple "here," but it is at the same time white, *and* acrid, *and* cubical, *and* of definite specific gravity, &c. These different qualities interpenetrate in the simple "here" without affecting each other. They are, however, *definite* qualities; they refer, therefore, not to themselves alone, but also to other qualities opposed to them. This negation of the opposite qualities does not take place in the simple medium, in the mere "*and*"; this medium is, consequently, likewise exclusive in its nature; it is a *unit*.

The object as the truth of observation, when complete, is therefore (*a*) indifferent, passive generality, the "*and*" of the many qualities, or, rather, materials; (*b*) the simple negation, the exclusion of other qualities; and (*c*) the many qualities themselves, and the two preceding momenta referred to each other: the negation relating to the indifferent medium. In so far as the differences belong to the indifferent medium, they are general, relate to themselves alone, and do not affect each other; but in so far as they belong to the negative unit, they are exclusive. The generality of observation becomes a *quality* only by developing out of itself, distinguishing and uniting, *exclusive unity* and *pure generality*.

By this object, then, as it now stands, consciousness is determined as an observing subject. It is sensible of the possibility of an illusion: for, though it immediately faces the "without," this is annulled as immediate, since generality has become the principle. The criterion for the truth of the object, then, is self-equality. We are therefore to inquire what is the experience of consciousness in its observation.

The observed object presents itself as absolutely *one, individ-*

ual; but it is observed also as a *quality*, which is general, and thus goes beyond individuality. My first observation, in which I took the object as individual, was therefore incorrect; the generality of the quality forces me to take the object likewise as a generality. Again: the quality is *definite*,—opposed to another quality and excluding it. I am consequently again compelled to abandon the generality, and to state the object as an exclusive *one*. There being, however, many qualities in the exclusive unity which do not mutually affect each other, the object is to be apprehended as a general medium, in which different qualities separately exist as generalities of sense, and yet as exclusive, since they are definite. The simple object is therefore observed as an individual quality, which again is *not* a quality, since it does not belong to an individual unity, nor definite, since it does not refer to other qualities. It is therefore the mere *being of sense*, and we have thus returned to the point whence we started. Consciousness in its observation of truth is reflected into itself, just as before in the certainty of sense; with this difference, however, that in the latter instance it appeared to contain the truth of the object, whereas now it contains the untruth. Of this, however, it is aware, and in this manner the object is maintained in its purity.—The object is first observed as a unit; then it ceases to be such, and presents the difference of qualities only to *my consciousness*. "This object is indeed white to *my* eye, acid to *my* tongue, cubic to *my* touch; I am therefore the general medium in which this separation of qualities takes place."

But the object, though a unit, is a determinate one, and determination depends upon contrast, upon exclusion. Thereby the qualities *as different* again become attributes *of the object*; the object is white, *and* acid, *and* cubical, &c.,—the simultaneous and independent existence of the different qualities. Their compenetration occurs in my consciousness. This gives me again a reversal of the relation; formerly consciousness attributed to itself the *multiplicity* of qualities in the object; now it makes itself responsible for their *unity*. The result of its experience, then, is that the duplicity is inherent in the object. The object by itself is a unity, equal to itself; but it is likewise for others, depending upon a difference from them. *Immediately* the objects do not differ from themselves, but simply from each other; this relation, however, is mutual, and each object is necessarily affected with the difference. Properly, then, it contains a twofold difference: first, the difference of its various qualities (the salt, e.g., being white inasmuch as it is not cubical, and *vice versa*, &c.), and, secondly, the difference from its counter object. Nevertheless, the latter only of these differences is essential to the object, conferring upon it a distinct individuality. But this latter difference is a relation to other objects; in virtue of this, the independent existence of the object is annulled; *as determined*, the individual object is nothing more than the relation to other objects. The very relation, then, which was said to be essential to the existence of the object, proves to be *the negation* of its self-existence; the object perishes through its essential quality.

III FORCE AND UNDERSTANDING.—PHENOMENAL
AND SUPERSENSUAL WORLD

We thus become the sport of a series of contradictions: of an individuality, which is at the same time a generality,—of an essence, which is unessential,—of an unessentiality, which is yet necessary; and we see that these contradictions are incident to the object. Our consciousness is in this manner forced to abandon its particular ideas, and to take the object as the unconditionally General, since that alone is lasting, invariable; having been informed, moreover, that *being for itself* and *being for other objects* are identical.—This absolute generality, moreover, precludes the difference between form and substance; for, were the substance something distinct from the form, it must be a *particular mode* of being for itself and being for other objects; but being for itself and being for other objects *abstractly* constitute the true nature of the object, the unconditionally General. Yet, in considering the object as one of our consciousness, or in its existence independent of our consciousness, we distinguish between form and substance. In the latter view we behold the object, first, as the general medium of several independent qualities, and, again, as a unit reflected into itself, in which that independence is annihilated. In the one case, the object is taken in its being for other objects, in its passivity, where self-existence is destroyed; in the other case, it is assumed in its being for itself. As to the former, each of the independent qualities is a medium; the generality of the object is essentially a multiplicity of generalities. These generalities, however, compenetrate, and thereby again annul their separation, thus returning to the unital medium. This movement, by which the unity effuses itself into multiplicity, and the multiplicity resumes itself in unity, is called *force*, which appears as twofold: first in its exterioration, as the independent qualities in their being, and again as reintroversion, or as *force* properly so termed.

Some readers will find this transition to force odd and perchance unintelligible. Hegel has shown that the intimate nature of the object is unity and multiplicity. If I take the object as one, this very unity *forces* itself into multiplicity, and conversely.

The understanding only makes this distinction and induces the duplicity, which does not subsist in the absolute being; exterioration and self-introversion are utterly inseparable. For the understanding, this duality of the force is not only necessary, but even substantial; it is, on the one hand, the mere introverted unital intensity, *being for itself*, and, on the other, the unfolded multiplicity of the different qualities; both of them, however, in necessary mutual transition. The unity of the force excludes the existence of the multiple qualities; yet it is the nature of that unity to be these qualities; it therefore unfolds itself into them, gives itself form. It seems, then, as if the form had been solicited from without; but this "without" is the object's own exterioration, the form itself, and the object now exists as the medium of the unfolded qualities. Still its nature is equally unital, and therefore the non-existence of the different qualities; this unity in its turn becomes the "without" of its present existence, soliciting it to self-introversion.

We have now an insight into this virtual duplication of the force; we have two forces, whose existence, however, is such a movement, that the being of each is a mere statement, a mere position in and by means of its counterpart. The one exists only by dint of its transition into the other; the two are not independent extremes connected by an intervening medium, but they exist solely in and through this medium.

"Through the medium of this play of the forces, then, we look into the background of things."* This medium, the being and simultaneous evanescence of the force, which co-includes the two extremes of its inner unity, and the outer multiplicity of the understanding, is the *phenomenon*. Our object has thus become a syllogistic trinity, whose extremes, the inner unital nature of things, on the one hand, and the multiplicity of the understanding, on the other, coalesce in their phenomenal medium. We look into the interior of things only through the phenomenon; the interior itself is transcendental, a "beyond," for our consciousness. This transcendental interior, however, reveals nothing whatever to consciousness; no more, to use Hegel's own simile, than *pure* darkness or *pure* light reveals any thing to the gaze. But the supersensual "beyond" results from mediation; it proceeds from the phenomenon,

---

* Phänomenologie des Geistes, p. 105.

and the phenomenon is its reality. The Supersensual is but the Sensual* taken in its truth, taken as a phenomenon, and not as a permanent reality, which it has amply proved itself not to be. We behold the play of the forces, a continual shifting of determinate appearances, whose truth consists merely in the *law* which manifests itself there. The law is the permanent image of the fleeting phenomenon. The supersensual world is a quiet realm of laws, indeed beyond the world of observation, since this exhibits the law only in continuous change; but it is nevertheless *present* in the world of observation, and its immediate type.

Yet the law thus present in the phenomenon realizes itself differently under different circumstances; it is a *determinate* law. This leads at once again to a multiplicity of laws, which multiplicity in turn contradicts our consciousness of a unital interior. The various laws must consequently reduce to *one* law, in which the determination is simply omitted, without an actual identification of the individual, determinate laws. These in their determination are then phenomenal, and the determination disappears in the reduction. But even in this general law we meet with a duplicity, since in it the internal difference (between its intense, introverted unity, and the exterior, unfolded multiplicity) is immediately apprehended, whereby the two momenta are at once stated as absolutely subsisting. Now according to the above, these differences must return into the simple unity of the interior; and thus we have the law, first, as the expression of the subsisting integrants or momenta, and, next, as their return into unity, which may again be termed *force*. To use the instance adduced by Hegel: electricity as simple is force; as dually existing, as positive and negative, it is law. In the capacity of a simple principle, electricity is indifferent as to its duality; yet when it exteriorates, manifests itself, it is necessarily as positive and negative.—The force, as such, then, is indifferent to its discession in the law, in its exterioration. Moreover, the integrants in that exterioration are indifferent with respect to each other. E.g., motion, as a law, divides itself into time and space,—into distance and velocity. But time and space, distance and velocity, in themselves, do not express their origin in this motion; they are conceived without it and without each other. Now the definition of motion cannot be that of a simple principle of simple being; division, duality, is necessary to it, and yet there is no necessity of the

---

* I use the word "Sensual" in preference to the word "Sensuous" introduced by Coleridge and others, because the former is more idiomatic, and not here liable to become ambiguous.

resultant parts (time and space) for each other. The necessity is, then, simply an illusory one, belonging to the understanding only. The understanding, therefore, is drawn into the same movement as that exhibited in the play of forces; a difference is stated, which is at the same time no difference, and hence revoked. It thus experiences that this absolute movement is the law of the interior; that the force decomposes itself into two factors, and again, that these factors recompose themselves into a unity; in other words, that, in the nature of objects, "there is necessary self-repulsion of the Homonymous, and necessary attraction of the Heteronymous. The force, the Homonymous, places itself in a self-opposition, which appears as an absolute difference; but this difference is really none, since the Homonymous repels *itself,* and, being identical with itself, necessarily re-attracts itself."*

By this principle the quiet domain of the laws, the immediate image of the observed world, becomes its own counterpart. We have therein a second supersensual world, "an inverted world," in the words of Hegel, in which the difference or internal discession of the interior becomes an immanent one. This supersensual world is an absolute self-antithesis, pure contradiction. As Hegel himself expresses it,—"This internal difference is to be apprehended as the self-repulsion of the Homonymous, and its reversal, the equality of the Unequal *as* the Unequal,—re-attraction of the Heteronymous. In aspiring to the truth of objects, we must apprehend *abstract change*, pure contradiction. The contradictory is not one of two,— for then it would be independent being,—but the contradictory of a contradictory. Though I place the one contradictory (one term) here and the other there, still, as I have the contradictory *as such*, each is its own antithesis, the '*alterum*' of itself."†

In short, we are inevitably driven to a unity *in* the opposition, to an identity *in* the difference,—in other words, to an infinitude *in* the Finite. Through this infinitude we see the law completed to a necessity in itself, i.e. we understand the transition of its unity into external variety, and conversely; and all the momenta, the phases of the phenomenon, are received in, reconciled with, the unity of the Interior. The simple unity of the law is infinitude, i.e., according to what has been said, 1st, it is self-equality, and nevertheless absolute internal difference,—the Homogeneous repelling itself, the simple force becoming a duality; 2d, the factors of this duality appear as self-existing, independent, truly different; 3d, since they

* Phänomenologie des Geistes, p. 107.
† Phänomenologie des Geistes, p. 121.

exist only as essentially different, as the contradictory of a contradictory, vitalized mutually as + and −, their nature is again unity and their duality annuls itself.

"This simple infinitude is the simple being of life, the soul of the world, the universal blood, which in its omnipresence is not disturbed by any contradiction, which comprises in its being all contradictions and their solution, which pulsates in itself without movement, and vibrates without disturbance."

We have now arrived at the point where the *system* of Hegel takes its root,—at this simple being, which is internally differential. The reader has a sufficient idea of Hegel's objective dialectics, which force every phase, meeting us at the first blush as permanent, into its very reverse, a palpable verification that it is *but* a phase, and affected with its own negation, with its counterpart. In the ensuing portions of the Phenomenology, Hegel, with the most trenchant acumen, dissolves the whole sphere of objectivity in this manner, so that the Phenomenology is, as it were, his Philosophy inverted. These investigations are of no immediate interest to us, because the same categories emerge in the body of the system itself.

HEGEL'S LOGIC

A. Quality

I. BEING, NAUGHT, AND ORIGINATION

The system of all science must germinate in the absolutely Immediate, upon which all thought and existence are ultimately based. This first principle, the utterly Indeterminate, from which all determinations proceed, is *pure being*. But pure, abstract, indeterminate being is identical with pure *naught*. Let those who demur at this endeavor to say in what the difference between pure being and pure naught consists. If there be difference, there is peculiarity, determination; and both are devoid of determination.

Being and naught are identical; nevertheless, in order to think them, we must keep them separate. We have here the first instance already of the identity supposing the difference, which appeared as the result of the Phenomenology. The identity of being and naught consists in their absolute transition into, their necessary evanescence in, each other; and this transition, their higher unity, is their truth.

Being and naught in mutual transition—*origination* and *evanescence*—form *existence*. Existence contains both (being and naught); it is *being with a determination, quality.*— Origination is the unity of being and naught; but not a unity which *abstracts from*, but which *comprises* them both. Inasmuch, however, as being and naught are in the embrace of each other, neither of them *is as such*; i.e., being is not as being, and naught is not as naught. Selecting a familiar instance to illustrate this: a salt consists of an acid and a base; but in the salt the acid exists not as acid, nor the base as basic. They *are* in this unity, but as *annulled*, as *momenta*. From their conceived independence they degenerate, as it were, into mutual complements.

II. EXISTENCE

Taking being and naught according to their difference, each exists as a unity with the other. Origination contains them as two such unities,—the one as immediate *being referred to naught*, the other as *naught referred to being.*

Naught received into being, so that the concrete whole is formally immediate, constitutes pure *determination*. This determination thus isolated is *quality*; and it is obviously twofold,—determination in *the form of being, reality*, and determination in *the form of naught, negation*, which latter further determines itself as *limit*.

Existence, therefore, presents the twofold aspect of *reality* and *negation*. These are different from each other, and yet they are in identical unity; existence as such a unit constitutes *the existing thing*. In the existing thing the simple self-relation is restored; it is *a negation of the negation*, a mediation with itself. The reality of existence identified itself with negation, hence *became* negation; but this negation is nothing without its reference to the reality, without its *re-annulment*, without a second negation; and the unity in this process is the existing thing.

Something *is*; it, moreover, *exists* and includes the process of origination. It is a transition, whose stages themselves exist; hence it *alters*. Maintaining itself, on the one hand, in its simple relation to itself, it is an existing thing as such; its negation likewise sustaining itself, on the other, it is its counterpart, its "*alterum*." Every existing thing is consequently affected with this inherent antithesis: *being in itself* (*per se,—an sich*), and *being for others*, for the "without." It *is*, and is *determinate*.

Viewing this relation more closely, we find the thing and its counterpart, its "alterum," coexisting; each acts as the negation of the other. Being for others is the negation of being in itself; but

this negation of the latter is possible only if it be immanent therein;* the determination therefore also pertains to being in itself, constituting its peculiar quality, its *limit*.

Pure being, the pure relation to itself, then, forms the being per
se in the existing thing; but not as an immediate self-equality, such
as we conceive pure being, but as the not-being of its alterum, as
existence reflected into itself. It is therefore, first, negative relation
to its alterum; but, secondly, it is affected by this alterum,—the
not-being of the same. In like manner, the alterum is first the negation of simple, self-related being; but it is not this negation as
pure naught, but a negation *necessarily referring to* being in itself,
as its own being reflected into itself.

Every existing thing necessarily refers to an alterum, to a
counter-existing thing, as to its negation; but this negation is not
an absolute one, but a negation of *something*; the negation *asserts*
the something, therefore, in denying it.—Being in itself, therefore,
depends for its whole existence upon its being for others, the existing thing upon its alterum; and, conversely, the alterum owes its
whole existence to its primary counterpart. *The existing thing and
its alterum are consequently identical.* Each is thoroughly and essentially affected and determined by the other. Being in itself is
inherently affected with its alterum, and herein lies its *definition*,
which is distinct from its determination. In the words of Hegel,—
"Definition is the affirmative determination as being in itself, to
which a thing remains adequate in its existence in opposition to its
complication with other things determining it,—in virtue of which
it maintains itself in its self-equality, even in its being for others."

In the sphere of the Qualitative, the differences maintain themselves even in their annulment; hence the repletion of the existing
thing with determination is distinct from that determination itself,
which appears only as being for others, and exhibits itself as
property. The properties of a thing depend upon its implication with
other things. This implication, which at first sight seems accidental,
is the necessary attribute of all finitudes.

The existing thing is the limit of the alterum, its negation, and
thereby its own affirmation. This negation of the first negation is
the being per se of the existing thing. The existing thing is the
"cessation of the alterum in it"; in other words, it is the limit to
every thing without. It *is*, then, in its limit; at the same time, how-

* This relation must be clearly seen. One thing limits another, not merely
in virtue of its extraneous coexistence with it, but because it was already in
the nature of the other thing *to be limited*. The *craving* for the limiting thing
was inherent in the limited one.

ever, the limit is that where and what the thing *is not*. The limit, therefore, is the mediation through which a thing *is* and *is not*. Something *is* in its limit: it is the cessation of the alterum in it; it *is not* in the limit: it *ceases itself* in the alterum.

The quality of every existing thing which constitutes its limit determines the thing and makes it finite. Finite things exist only in virtue of their *negative* relation to themselves; "they are, but the truth of this being is their end." They pass away, not from any adventitious, external necessity, but from the laws of their own being. The nature of finite things is to contain the germ of destruction as their inmost being; "the hour of their birth is the hour of their death." Yet this evanescence is not absolute; their negation is a relative one; they vanish into a higher reality.

It has been said above that existing things, simply because their existence implies a negation, are finite in a twofold sense: they are *limited*, and subject to *alteration*. An acid, for instance, exists as an acid only by the negation of its opposite base; but the base is the negation of the acid. Obviously, then, the existence of the acid depends upon the negation of its own negation. It is thus, first, limited, and secondly, it is forced to destroy the relative finitude of its existence by combination with the base. Existing things, therefore, because their being is a necessary relation to their limit, are forced beyond themselves, beyond their limit, beyond their finitude. Their definition (as in the case cited, the acidity) consequently becomes at the same time their destination,—that of transcending their finitude, of ultimately becoming infinite. The definition of the Infinite is already implied in the foregoing results. The Infinite is,—

(1) The absolutely Affirmative as the negation of the Finite; but since

(2) It *proceeds* from the negation of the Finite, it enters into mutual relation with this, and as such is the abstract, defective Infinite;

(3) The self-annulment of the Finite and Infinite as *one* process is the true Infinite.

(a) We have seen that the Finite contains in its nature a contradiction, which forces it to a negation of its own limits. The Finite is being with a negation; the negation of this negation is the Infinite, which latter is not therefore to be assumed, as in the usual views, as of *coordinate* existence with the Finite, without reference to it. The Infinite, on the contrary, is absolute being, which, after having limited itself in the

Finite, restores itself from that limitation. It does not for this reason arise in an *abstraction* from every thing finite, but the true nature of the Finite is its infinitude, its absolutely affirmative determination.

(b) The relation between the Infinite and the Finite is the following: the Infinite, being the negation of the Finite, is opposed to it as to its alterum, and the latter stands as the real existence of the former. As finite, however, this alterum contains the limit with the craving, the destination, to become infinite; and this craving satisfied *is* the Infinite. The two, then, are inseparable; the Finite is but the immediate origination of the Infinite, and *vice versa*. The transition from the one to the other, from the Infinite to the Finite, and from the Finite to the Infinite, gives the so-called *infinite progress*. The connection between them is necessary, but appears as merely external in this progress.

(c) Taking this union of the Infinite and Finite in its truth, we have the Infinite properly so called. The Finite is in its nature its own negation, and therefore includes the Infinite; the Infinite, conversely, is not as immediate, but as the negation of the Finite, and consequently also affected by the latter. *Both, then, are the movement of returning to themselves through their negation*; they are both results, and in this movement identical. In this identity consists the true Infinite. Once more I insist upon the precaution, not to confound identity in its ordinary acceptation, in which the supposed difference, upon close inquiry, proves to have been only an apparent one, with this identity, which includes the difference. This will ever remain a mystery to those who have not seized upon the fundamental apperception, that a contradiction of the momenta pointed out by the understanding pervades all existences. Everyone is prepared to admit, in case of necessity, that the Finite exists not without mediation; but to predicate this mediation of the Infinite, likewise, runs counter to all our habitual ideas. The *exclusion* of all mediation is usually considered as the very criterion of the Infinite; and this is a prejudice of which we must divest ourselves. The Infinite is not without the Finite; it is, indeed, the negation of the Finite, but in this negation the Finite is indispensably expressed and contained.

5

HERBERT SPENCER
STRIKES SPARKS

William Torrey Harris

By mid-century, the British philosopher Herbert Spencer had become the foremost exponent in England and America of the materialist philosophy. Beginning with the Lamarckian-inspired *Social Statics* in 1851, and continuing through the massive *Principles of Sociology* (1876–96), he expounded a world view that offered a "scientistic" or rigidly mechanical and empirical explanation for everything. When Darwin's *On the Origin of Species* was published in 1859, Spencer, without correctly understanding the implications of Darwin's description of chance mutation, eagerly co-opted the new scientific revelation and tried to make it the basis of his interpretation of the evolving universe. Indeed, devoted to science, he incorporated virtually every scientific discovery of the day into his work, from the laws of conservation of energy to Von Baer's studies in embryology. And yet, ignoring the essentially metaphysical neutrality of modern scientific work, Spencer was a teleologist. For him, nature clanked monotonously and relentlessly onward toward some far-off potential completeness which he called "equilibration."

The simplistic and mechanistic quality of Spencer's thought prompted a strong reaction from William Torrey Harris in St. Louis. His first serious article was an attack on Spencer which the *North American Review* refused to publish. Irked by this rejection, Harris founded in 1867 the *Journal of Speculative Philosophy*, which became the chief organ of the American Hegelians and the most important American philosophical journal of its time. Harris's article on Spencer was the first article in the first issue of the *Journal.*

William Torrey Harris, "Herbert Spencer," *Journal of Speculative Philosophy* I (1867): 6–9. Hereafter referred to as *JSP*.

THE CRISIS IN NATURAL SCIENCE

DURING the past twenty years a revolution has been working in physical science. Within the last ten it has come to the surface, and is now rapidly spreading into all departments of mental activity.

Although its centre is to be found in the doctrine of the "Correlation of Forces," it would be a narrow view that counted only the expounders of this doctrine, numerous as they are; the spirit of this movement inspires a heterogeneous multitude—Carpenter, Grove, Mayer, Faraday, Thompson, Tyndall and Helmholtz; Herbert Spencer, Stuart Mill, Buckle, Draper, Lewes, Lecky, Max Müller, Marsh, Liebig, Darwin and Agassiz; these names, selected at random, are suggested on account of the extensive circulation of their books. Every day the press announces some new name in this field of research.

What is the character of the old which is displaced, and of the new which gets established?

By way of preliminary, it must be remarked that there are observable in modern times three general phases of culture, more or less historic.

The first phase is thoroughly dogmatic: it accepts as of like validity, metaphysical abstractions, and empirical observations. It has not arrived at such a degree of clearness as to perceive contradictions between form and content. For the most part, it is characterized by a reverence for external authority. With the revival of learning commences the protest of spirit against this phase. Descartes and Lord Bacon begin the contest, and are followed by the many— Locke, Newton, Leibnitz, Clarke, and the rest. All are animated with the spirit of that time—to come to the matter in hand without so much mediation. Thought wishes to rid itself of its fetters; religious sentiment, to get rid of forms. This reaction against the former stage, which has been called by Hegel the metaphysical, finds a kind of climax in the intellectual movement just preceding the French revolution. Thought no longer is contented to say, "Cogito, ergo sum," abstractly, but applies the doctrine in all directions, "I think; in that deed, I am." "I am a man only in so far as I think. In so far as I think, I am an essence. What I get from others is not mine. What I can comprehend, or dissolve in my reason, that is mine." It looks around and spies institutions—"clothes of spirit," as Herr Teufelsdroeck calls them. "What are you doing here, you sniveling priest?" says Voltaire; "you are imposing delusions upon society for your own aggrandizement. *I* had no part or lot in making the church; *cogito, ergo sum*; I will only have over me what I put there!"

"I see that all these complications of society are artificial," adds Rousseau; "man has made them; they are not good, and let us tear them down and make anew." These utterances echo all over France and Europe. "The state is merely a machine by which the few exploit the many"—"off with crowns!" Thereupon they snatch off the crown of poor Louis, and his head follows with it. "Reason" is enthroned and dethroned. Thirty years of war satiates at length this negative second period, and the third phase begins. Its characteristic is to be constructive, not to accept the heritage of the past with passivity, nor wantonly to destroy, but to realize itself in the world of objectivity—the world of laws and institutions.

The first appearance of the second phase of consciousness is characterized by the grossest inconsistencies. It says in general (see D'Holbach's "Système de la Nature"): "The immediate, only, is true; what we know by our senses, alone has reality; all is matter and force." But in this utterance it is unconscious that matter and force are purely general concepts, and not objects of immediate consciousness. What we see and feel is not matter or force in general, but only some special form. The self-refutation of this phase may be exhibited as follows:

1. "What is known is known through the senses: it is matter and force."

2. But by the senses, the particular only is perceived, and this can never be *matter*, but merely a *form*. The general is a mediated result, and not an object of the senses.

3. Hence, in positing matter and force as the content of sensuous knowing, they unwittingly assert mediation to be the content of immediateness.

The decline of this period of science results from the perception of the contradiction involved. Kant was the first to show this; his labors in this field may be summed up thus:

The universal and necessary is not an empirical result. (General laws can not be sensuously perceived.) The constitution of the mind itself, furnishes the ground for it:—first, we have an *a priori* basis (time and space) necessarily presupposed as the condition of all sensuous perception; and then we have categories presupposed as the basis of every generalization whatever. Utter any general proposition: for example, the one above quoted—"all is matter and force" —and you merely posit two categories—inherence and causality— as objectively valid. In all universal and necessary propositions we announce only the subjective conditions of experience, and not any-thing in and for itself true (i.e., applicable to things in themselves).

At once the popular side of this doctrine began to take effect. "We know only phenomena; the true object in itself we do not know."

This doctrine of phenomenal knowing was outgrown in Germany at the commencement of the present century. In 1791—ten years after the publication of the Critique of Pure Reason—the deep spirit of Fichte began to generalize Kant's labors, and soon he announced the legitimate results of the doctrine. Schelling and Hegel com-pleted the work of transforming what Kant had left in a negative state into an affirmative system of truth. The following is an outline of the refutation of Kantian skepticism:

1. Kant reduces all objective knowledge to phenomenal: we furnish the form of knowing, and hence whatever we announce in general concerning it—and all that we call science has, of course, the form of generality—is merely our subjective forms, and does not belong to the thing in itself.

2. This granted, say the later philosophers, it follows that the subjective swallows up all and becomes itself the universal (subject and object of itself), and hence Reason is the true substance of the universe. Spinoza's *substance* is thus seen to become *subject*. We partake of God as intellectually seeing, and we see only God as object, which Malebranche and Berkeley held with other Platonists.

   (a) The categories (e.g., Unity, Reality, Causality, Existence, etc.) being merely subjective, or given by the constitution of the mind itself—for such universals are presupposed by all experience, and hence not derived from it—it follows:

   (b) If we abstract what we know to be subjective, we abstract all possibility of a thing in itself, too. For "existence" is a category, and hence, if subjective, we may reasonably con-clude that nothing objective can have existence.

   (c) Hence, since one category has no preference over another, and we can not give one of them objectivity without granting it to all others, it follows that there can be no talk of *noumena*, or of things in themselves, *existing* beyond the reach of the mind, for such talk merely applies what it pronounces to be subjective categories (existence) while at the same time it denies the validity of their application.

3. But since we remove the supposed "*noumena*," the so-called phenomena are not opposed any longer to a correlate beyond the intelligence, and the *noumenon* proves to be *mind itself*.

An obvious corollary from this is, that by the self-determination of mind in pure thinking we shall find the fundamental laws of all phenomena.

Though the Kantian doctrine soon gave place in Germany to deeper insights, it found its way slowly to other countries. Comte and Sir Wm. Hamilton have made the negative results very widely known—the former, in natural science; the latter, in literature and philosophy. Most of the writers named at the beginning are more or less imbued with Comte's doctrines, while a few follow Hamilton. For rhetorical purposes, the Hamiltonian statement is far superior to all others; for practical purposes, the Comtian. The physicist, wishing to give his undivided attention to empirical observation, desires an excuse for neglecting pure thinking; he therefore refers to the well-known result of philosophy, that we cannot know anything of ultimate causes—we are limited to phenomena and laws. Although it must be conceded that this consolation is somewhat similar to that of the ostrich, who cunningly conceals his head in the sand when annoyed by the hunters, yet great benefit has thereby accrued to science through the undivided zeal of the investigators thus consoled.

When, however, a sufficiently large collection has been made, and the laws are sought for in the chaotic mass of observations, then *thought* must be had. Thought is the only crucible capable of dissolving "the many into the one." Tycho Brahe served a good purpose in collecting observations, but a Kepler was required to discern the celestial harmony involved therein.

This discovery of laws and relations, or of relative unities, proceeds to the final stage of science, which is that of the *absolute comprehension*.

Thus modern science, commencing with the close of the metaphysical epoch, has three stages or phases:

1. The first rests on mere isolated facts of experience; accepts the first phase of things, or that which comes directly before it, and hence may be termed the stage of *immediateness*.

2. The second relates its thoughts to one another and compares them; it develops inequalities; tests one through another, and discovers dependencies everywhere; since it learns that the first phase of objects is phenomenal, and depends upon somewhat lying beyond it; since it denies truth to the immediate, it may be termed the stage of *mediation*.

3. A final stage, which considers a phenomenon in its totality, and thus seizes it in its *noumenon*, and is the stage of the *comprehension*.

To resume: the *first* is that of sensuous knowing; the *second*, that of reflection (the understanding); the *third*, that of the reason (or the speculative stage).

In the sensuous knowing, we have crude, undigested masses all co-ordinated; each is in and for itself, and perfectly valid without the others. But as soon as reflection enters, dissolution is at work. Each is thought in sharp contrast with the rest; contradictions arise on every hand. The third stage finds its way out of these quarrelsome abstractions, and arrives at a synthetic unity, at a system, wherein the antagonisms are seen to form an organism.

The first stage of the development closes with attempts on all hands to put the results in an encyclopaedical form. Humboldt's Cosmos is a good example of this tendency, manifested so widely. Matter, masses, and *functions* are the subjects of investigation.

Reflection investigates *functions* and seizes the abstract category of force, and straightway we are in the second stage. Matter, as such, loses its interest, and "correlation of forces" absorbs all attention.

Force is an arrogant category and will not be co-ordinated with matter: if admitted, we are led to a pure dynamism. This will become evident as follows:

1. Force implies confinement (to give it direction); it demands, likewise, an "occasion," or soliciting force to call it into activity.

2. But it cannot be confined except by force; its occasion must be a force likewise.

3. Thus, since its confinement and "occasion" are forces, force can only act upon forces—upon matter only in so far as that is a force. Its nature requires confinement in order to manifest it, and hence it cannot act or exist except in unity with other forces which likewise have the same dependence upon it that it has upon them. *Hence a force has no independent subsistence, but is only an element of a combination of opposed forces*, which combination is a unity existing in an opposed manner (or composed of forces in a state of tension). This deeper unity which we come upon as the ground of force is properly named *law*.

From this, two corollaries are to be drawn: (a) That matter is merely a name for various forces, as resistance, attraction and repulsion, etc. (b) That force is no ultimate category, but, upon reflection, is seen to rest upon law as a deeper category (not law as a mere similarity of phenomena, but as a true unity underlying phenomenal multiplicity).

From the nature of the category of force we see that whoever adopts it as the ultimate embarks on an ocean of dualism, and instead of "seeing everywhere the one and all" as did Xenophanes, he will see everywhere the self opposed, the contradictory.

The crisis which science has now reached is of this nature. The second stage is at its commencement with the great bulk of scientific men.

To illustrate the self-nugatory character ascribed to this stage we shall adduce some of the most prominent positions of Herbert Spencer, whom we regard as the ablest exponent of this movement. These contradictions are not to be deprecated, as though they indicated a decline of thought; on the contrary, they show an increased activity (though in the stage of mere reflection) and give us good omens for the future. The era of stupid mechanical thinkers is over, and we have entered upon the active, *chemical* stage of thought, wherein the thinker is trained to consciousness concerning his abstract categories, which, as Hegel says, "drive him around in their whirling circle."

Now that the body of scientific men are turned in this direction, we behold a vast upheaval towards philosophic thought; and this is entirely unlike the isolated phenomenon (hitherto observed in history) of a single group of men lifted above the surrounding darkness of their age into clearness. We do not have such a phenomenon in our time; it is the spirit of the nineteenth century to move by masses. . . .

6

A PHILOSOPHICAL PRIMER

William Torrey Harris

In the first volumes of the *Journal of Speculative Philosophy*, Harris also contributed an extensive "Introduction to Philosophy" which was a Hegelian interpretation of thought. The "spirit universal" is the capstone of all reality for Harris, as it was for Hegel. By this time, thanks to Brokmeyer's influence, he had transcended Kant.

This extract includes Harris's discussion of the universal and a capsule summary of his whole treatise, as taken from *JSP* 2 (1868): 176–181.

THE UNIVERSAL

THOSE who know of no other universal than that obtained by abstracting differences, and seizing the common marks of objects, have no philosophical conception of the universal. It is to be regretted that in the English language the word "general," which is the best word for the purpose, has sunk into a synonym of "common," and has a merely discursive use. From its root, GEN, we could expect a suggestiveness in it of the creative significance of the "universal." In such words as *genius, generous, genial,* we have the meaning referred to, and *general* was used by the spirit of our language (*Sprach-Geist*) to express the true idea of that which is "all-common" and at the same time the creative essence. In German we have *Algemein* and *Gattung* to express the two meanings.

In this chapter we hope to make clear how the *common* and *creative* have the same root, and to show in what sense the Universal or Generic may be said to be the only true existence.

THE PARTICULAR

Seize upon the world of reality as it offers itself and it breaks up into an infinite concourse of individuals,—side by side in space and succeeding each other in time. Each one seems to be peculiar and distinct from all the rest, and it is as impossible for us to find any two objects exactly alike as it was for the ladies of the Court at which Leibnitz resided, to find any two leaves of the forest exactly alike, though they searched with care. If we look upon each object as absolutely determined, fixed in its being, and at the same time attribute to it independent validity and real existence—this is the "common sense" view, and is held by those who are most opposed to idealism. Over against the particular it holds the *common* or *general*.

Experience is always engaged in discovering resemblances. What is *common* to *different* objects is funded, and the process called generalization. The common or general element is looked upon as more or less accidental or contingent; perhaps even regarded as subjective, and a mere reflection, made by the spectator.

Words stand for the common elements, and, the differences being abstracted, of course it follows that the general concepts for which words stand correspond to nothing real, but are merely figments of the mind, and are either arbitrary or the product of mental laws.

Such, in substance, is the view of those who never rise above the stages of sense and reflection. But in reflection arises a side which results finally in overthrowing this view;—it is the *dynamic* view, wherein all is treated as

THE RELATIVE

If we seize the particular, and demand of it what it is that gives it distinctness or separation from others, we are at once engaged in noting its complication with other particulars. We find that what constitutes it a *particular individual* is to be stated as a series of defects and potentialities which manifest themselves as we pursue our investigation. . . . Through these lacks or wants or deficiencies it is related to and dependent upon an outlying sphere of existence, which needs to be added to it to complete it. The particular, in short, exhibits its whole series of phases as a tendency to lose its distinguishing characteristics in attaining to a completer realization of the entire compass of its existence. That which is partial is so far forth affected with a mortal malady, and the wholeness of its universality is the healthy (whole-some) state which it needs.

The particular can only be seized by transcending it. Its own existence, too, is a self-transcending, for it has its *properties* through its relation to the Beyond. It *is* therefore only in the total compass or sphere that includes it, as a mere complemental part thereof.

The particular things in time and space are all self-transcendent:

each is heavy, i.e. is attracted to a body outside of it, and thus is a part of the unity formed by this relation. Earth and Moon and Sun make a system together, of which neither is independent. So, too, the Solar systems make a system, and this is a part of another system. The individual in space and time is what it is through its relation, and relation is a transcending of the individual. Since what it is, is through its relation, it is an embodied contradiction—it is its own negation. And hence what *is*, is

THE UNIVERSAL

For if we analyze the content of this phenomenal relativity we shall discover two sides which belong to the same essence: *1st*, the deficiency, want or lack manifested in its relativity, is the activity of the including totality or "negative unity"; *2d*, itself is negative to its including totality, for it loses its separate independence if the latter has full sway. Both these factors are actively united in what is called a *phenomenon*. It would not be phenomenal, i.e. transient, unless the negative unity of the including total annulled the real and caused the potential to become real. . . . Therefore in the activity which constitutes a phenomenon we have a manifestation of the including totality in its entire compass. Here we find the GENERIC. The Constant under the Variable is the *generic*, and *it,* we see, is the only true individual, for it alone abides and does not pass over into another, as the particular of space and time does continually. Hence words as expressing the *generic*, express the only actuality or the only *Being for itself.* That the Universal is that which preserves its identity, amid the changing and variable, is the principle which gives a basis to Realism as opposed to Nominalism. It is a strange spectacle to witness the very men who hold to the doctrine of the *Correlation of forces* take the position of Nominalists. They, in effect, say: All change or phenomenality is the play of forces which have no permanent individuality, for they are in perpetual transition, one force never retaining for a single instant its own identity, but always in process of becoming another different force. From this it results that there is no individuality either in given material shapes—for these are dependent on the play of forces —nor in the given forces, *heat, electricity,* etc., for these are ceaselessly changing their forms. Hence the Correlationist must and *does* hold that the *generic* entity of force is the only abiding, and hence the only true individual. Stated in the terms we have been using in these chapters: The *negative unity*, which is only one of the moments of the comprehension, . . . is named *force*, and the Correlationist does not rise to the standpoint of IDEA, and hence does not get beyond an abstract Pantheism, wherein all finite existence suffers birth and decay, and even intelligence is regarded as a finite when brought before this abstract Force. What he omits to consider is the fact that such abstract force, when thus elevated to the Universal, is necessarily spontaneous, i.e. self-determining or self-originating. For if force moves to restore the destroyed equilibrium of a given entire system—and no other concept of it will suffice—then, to have a continual or abiding force, we must have a continual destruction of that equilibrium. This restoring and destroying of an equilibrium is the realization of the pure potentiality and the return to the same, and is the Universal in its actuality as *Ego*, or the *Generic*, which is the root of consciousness.

When the "Positivists," and all others in that stage of knowing which deals with THE RELATIVE, come to perceive this other side and ascend to its comprehension, they will have attained the *aperçu* of Aristotle and Hegel, and become Theistic.

INSTITUTIONS OF SPIRIT

The embodied realization of the Universal or GENERIC, in its immediate form, is the EGO, as above intimated. But its embodiment in the individual has this difficulty: that the EGO is not completely possessed of itself until it frees itself from Nature, i.e. from the senses and from the reflective intellect. Its means of retaining itself as universal while in these lower stages are the INSTITUTIONS OF SPIRIT. Among the lowest forms of these is *fashion*—the commonness of humanity indicated by the prevailing fashion, and the difference thereof, indicated by the same. Then habits and customs, moral and ethical, constitute a deeper community of spirit. The FAMILY, next after the individual, is his first realization of the *universal*. In the family, the *tension of sex*, wherein the highest stage of Nature is reached, is cancelled. Nature never gets beyond this *tension of opposites* in any individual form; when we come to consciousness only, do we find a series of stages wherein this tension is solved and the two sides collapse into one-ness, just as the Ego knows itself, and this act is its fundamental characteristic. Man as *animal* is male and female, but as spirit he is his own object, and therefore celebrates this fact in the first institution of spirit—marriage, wherein he lays the basis of all culture and civilization. The individual longing, i.e., desire, which makes it a finite and dependent being is here annulled by being joined to the object of its desire, which object again reflects back the same dependence upon the first. Thus instead of a simple finite existence commencing with a given individual and ceasing with the same, we have by means of the family a realized universality, which receives the individual at birth and cares for him, and also lives on beyond him, and performs the last offices for him.

In CIVIL SOCIETY we have a higher realization of universality, wherein each man, through division of labor, is enabled to concentrate all his faculties on a speciality, and yet be sure of a supply of all the other specialities from the other individuals engaged like himself, only on different specialities; so that it is the whole *community*, only, that furnishes the complete outfit for each individual, and hence it acts as one organism, and each individual, through this act of transcending himself and making himself *for* all, receives in turn the service *of* all; and thus all are for him, and he is *for himself* through the reciprocal relation thus established. Hence civil society is an organism which serves the purpose of making Man universal in so far as the life in time and space is concerned; it makes all for and through each, and each for and through all. The relation begins from the individual and goes out to the many, but returns through them back to the individual.

Property is a realized universality of the individual will—nature transformed into a spiritual somewhat by being forced into the service of the spiritual. Again, property has a universal solvent—*money*,—wherein all property becomes fluid and transferable, thus making it completely the instrument of Society. Thus each is made free and self-dependent; for in so far as he energizes and relates himself to the community, just so far does the community relate itself back to him, and he gets the fruit of his own deed.

But civil society is not thus complete as an instrument of realization of the universal without an obverse side—THE STATE. It is the State which holds the wheels of civil society in their places and renders all permanent and secure. Were there only positive or useful deeds—productive deeds—possible from the individual, then government would not be necessary, for civil society could go on by itself. But in that case, moreover, the institutions of spirit would not be for the genesis and nurture of spirit, for that presupposes rudimentary or germ forms of spirit wherein the complete consciousness has not yet been reached. Institutions are to take the undeveloped individual (whether infant or criminal) and guide him to self-guidance (i.e. negate his negativity). But no self-determination can begin without negating its own determinations, and hence its first acts must be EVIL; for its own determinations, those of nature, and of the moral organization in which it exists, are in and for themselves right. But it—the individual will—has the right to be self-determined, and hence to cancel these limits as imposed upon it from without, through education, etc. But the first acts of the will are mere "self-will" and the opposite of the rational will, *and must necessarily be so*. Hence the State is absolutely indispensable as the highest institution of spirit (so long, at least, as the state of childhood exists), and its functions are obviously these: it makes the individual's deed his own, whether positive or negative. If he negates the rational organism of civil society or the family, the state interposes and adds the link which brings his deed home to him, and he finds himself negating himself and suffering the consequences. Thus he learns to will rational deeds, i.e. deeds which have a universal content, and will not hurt the doer when they come back to him. The doer is made universal by the state in the fact, that whatever the doer does, he does to himself, and is a complete circle. The state protects each from all and all from each, and each from himself, by this function it exercises of universalizing each deed: the individual reaping the result of his own deed from the beginning, finds that evil deeds negate his power of doing at all. By the mediation of the prison and the gallows, his deed, if evil, hurts him alone and saves every other individual of the community from injury. By the completeness of the mediation each deed recoils soon enough to prevent an accumulation great enough to annihilate the individual by its return stroke. This function of universalizing man as free-doer (which belongs to the state) is not an exceptional one, but the very means by which all arrive at a rational will—a will that does not forever contradict itself, as caprice does. If now and then a man grows up uncorrected and murders or steals, it is evidence of the imperfection of the realization of the universalizing power, but it is also a warning example of what we *all* should be, were there *no* state.

While the state stands for the highest realization of the universal on the practical side, there are spheres above it in which this is achieved in a far more adequate manner. In Art there is a subordination of the natural into the rank of a mere symbol for spirit. In this, spirit realizes its universality in being able to remove all alien *appearance to the senses*.

In Religion spirit recognizes its unity with the supersensuous essence that it has attained to by thought. It places the Universal before itself as its ideal.

In Philosophy, spirit, the Universal is to be reached as the form of Speculative Insight, and this is the highest form of spirit. . . .

Thus Art symbolizes the Universal in material forms; Religion makes it an object of conception, while Philosophy comprehends it concretely.

CONCLUSION

With the consideration of the Universal our Introduction may conclude. If anyone seizes the Universal as we have attempted to characterize it here, he will have seized the key to all thinking and Being, and will be prepared to accompany us through a consideration of the different systems of Philosophy that have prevailed and now prevail.

But this series would not be complete without giving a hasty review of our progress from Chapter I to Chapter X, and showing that each *aperçu* was a phase of the Universal, and luminous for that very reason. We may sum up, therefore, our results as follows:

CHAPTER I

Time and Space are *a priori,* and yet the logical conditions of the world; hence Mind, which is the source of what is *a priori* (and hence, for the reason mentioned, is the logical condition of the world in Time and Space), must be the Universal and a solvent of all that exists.

CHAPTER II

The Finite and Infinite distinguished: the Finite, "that which is limited by something other than itself"; and the Infinite, that which is its own "other" or limit, and hence, instead of *limiting* itself, *continues* itself, and is thus universal.

CHAPTER III

Categories, or general predicates, are the means by which we cognize, and as instruments must be presupposed by all knowing. Thus generalized, we must find a primitive category at the root or starting-point of our Knowing; and this is the category of Being. This category is the simple act of the mind in judgments—the "is"-ing— and hence we see that the primitive category is the Ego itself in its simplest form posited objectively, and hence the fundamental act of knowing is an act of distinguishing the self and identifying it with the self. All further knowing is the same process repeated, and hence it is the realization of the Universality of the Ego as intelligence. The Ego can have no other than itself as object for it.

CHAPTER IV

Being is dependent or independent—determined through itself or through another.—In all cases, dependent Being or Being through another is a *moment* (*or complemental element*) of a complex whole which is, as such, independent and self-determined.—Hence the Self-determined is the Basis of all Being, and it is hence the Universal or all-present form. Besides, since it is *self*-determined it is spontaneous and originating, creative of the special and destructive of the same. It is thus *Generic*.

This is the most easy ascent to the fountain-idea of Speculative Philosophy that I know of. It is the most elementary form of the *conscious* apprehensions of the Universal. It is the key to all great *aperçus* of Speculative Philosophy, and should be seized fully by the one who wishes to make anything out of the works of Genius.

The self-determined, if seized more clearly, proves to be dual—subject and object—and a unity constituting the individual. From which, if carefully considered, there follows conscious personality as the Supreme principle of the Universe; this and all other spiritual truths ray out from this great central point of speculation.

CHAPTER V

"Necessity and Chance" lead us to consider the subject of determination more fully.* An example of the *dialectic* is afforded in the

* The doctrine of the Universal is the cure for that form of fatalism now current in literature as a species of "Positivism." An example in point will be found in the "Atlantic Monthly" for September, 1868, entitled "The Impossibility of Chance," wherein the externality of all determination is insisted upon to the exclusion of all spontaneity. It requires only the tracing out of the train of thought there started, to its ultimate consequences, to see how unwarrantable are the inferences there drawn:

Facts are not absolute, individual, and definite existences; they are relative syntheses. The shallowest thinker seizes the merest unessential phase as the "fact" for him. The deeper the thinker, the wider and more comprehensive the synthesis included in his "fact." Newton thought the whole celestial mechanism in the fact of the fall of an apple. It depends on how far back one traces the causes, or how widely the "totality of conditions"; for each fact implies the whole Universe as the totality of its conditions. But this doctrine frees us completely from the tyranny of *immediate sensuous* facts, for it is evident that what the senses can perceive of a fact is a very small portion of the immense orbit which it fills. The "Negative Unity" which is arrived at by this degree of reflection is elevated above the *things* of sense, and can be apprehended only by thought.

But, in order to reach the Universal, one step more is requisite. The totality of conditions must be posited by itself since it has no externality conditioning *it* again. If we now inquire for the source of the determinations which arise in it, we have no resource but to acknowledge their spontaneity. Reflection is here "cornered," for it cannot go outside of the "All." If externality of conditioning rests ultimately on self-determination, the latter must be set up as the supreme principle and the former as a derivative one, or one that forms a mere phase of the latter. Hence "the impossibility of necessity" would be as rational a title as the one above alluded to. Chance is to be applied to the immediate form of spontaneity, and Necessity is the mediate form of the same, while Freedom is the same in its entirety.

treatment given in this chapter. Assuming, first, the standpoint of fatalism—all is determined from without by external causes—we see if this is thought as universal, that the all or Total must be without (or outside of) itself, and thus, at all events, self-determined. Hence Necessity must presuppose self-determination, and can apply only to the part and not to the whole or totality, which is universal and free.

CHAPTER VI

A more general form of treating the same subject (i.e. determination) is given in the chapter on Mediation.

The Immediate—that which is out of relation; the Mediate, that which is only in relation. Made Universal, we have Absolute Mediation—Self-relation—Self-determination, or the Universal again.

(*a*) The Immediate cannot be a determined somewhat, and is naught; (*b*) the Mediate is determined, and thus dependent or finite; (*c*) the Absolute Mediate is the self-relation, which is the Independent and True.

N. B.—The True and Universal is not a stuff, or material, or thing, or rigid substance; but is a relation to itself which can subsist only in activity, or in a process. Hence the Universal is not a simple Immediate nor a simple Mediate, but both in one, and the Active is the permanent substance.* The Universal, moreover, as a multiplicity in unity, is a system, an *organic* whole.

CHAPTER VII

We now trace further the insight into the nature of the Universal as a system. As *comprehension* it is the "negative unity" together with the "moments," and this is not the Absolute Universal which the IDEA is. It must be not merely a totality, but a totality of totalities, in order to be the Idea,† which is the highest thought of Philosophy.

---

* The Active is the ground of all Being. This doctrine distinguishes all Speculative Philosophy from its opposite. Plato, Aristotle, Heraclitus, Proclus, Plotinus, Hegel, Leibnitz, and others, hold this doctrine in some one of its various forms.

This is one of the first points for the student of Philosophy to direct his attention to. Until he can see *in his own way* this important doctrine, he can have at best only a historical knowledge of the various systems, and they will pass for mere opinions.

† Idea is used in this sense by Hegel alone. But it signifies the standpoint of Aristotle, and it is the speculative basis of the Christian Theology, especially as relating to the dogma of the Trinity. Leibnitz founded his Monadology on that *aperçu*. So, too, the national form of government of the United States is a realization of it. Recognition and Tolerance are the accompaniments of its realization.

In this connection, the doctrine of pure Theism, in contradistinction to Pantheism or Atheism, gets established.

All mere limitation from without vanishes in the sphere of the Idea, and instead of it we find *Recognition* as its form of relation to the "other-being."

CHAPTER VIII

In the "Idea" we found the true system which the Universal is, as the Absolute Mediation; in this chapter we have the Universal as the Actual. The moments of the Actual are *reality* and *potentiality*— a process of reciprocal action wherein the total is involved, and in which it maintains itself as absolute mediation or self-determination, or as the Universal. The "Form of Eternity" is the world's essence and actuality. The Phenomenal, seen from this standpoint, is an exhibition of the validity of the Eternal which abides in the activity (the "wrath of the wicked" turned into "praise," and all finitude in a state of being annulled by its own imperfections). The Finite is thus only a field for the display of the Idea.

CHAPTER IX

Finally, we approach the Universal from the standpoint of Pure Thought, and consider the question of *distinction* and *identity* in the most general form. Here again, as in Chapter V, we have an example of the dialectic.* The method which distinguishes Pure Thought is this: it places the subject treated of under the form of the Universal (the "form of Eternity") and considers the result. In such a crucible all baser metals give way and vanish, and leave the pure gold. To speak without metaphor: all categories when tried by this standard show their deficiency, or what they lack in order to give them independent Being. Thus *Identity*, if not simple immediateness or vacuity, is a self-relation, and involves distinction, and hence is Universal; self-distinction is thus the basis of identity. That negation of negation is the form of all Being or identity is here made manifest. This chapter may be called The Genesis of the Comprehension of the Universal.

* The ascent from the part to the whole is a dialectical process. A part taken as a whole shows its deficiencies as its presuppositions. It cannot be a part without presupposing the whole. But the dialectic is only a kind of ladder for the novice and for the preliminary stage of comprehension, and the speculative knowing uses the Idea, or the "knowing by wholes," as Thomas Taylor calls it. To see the necessary unity of independent totalities is the highest and most difficult step to attain; but the philosopher must not rest satisfied until he has attained this insight.

CHAPTER X

In the last chapter we recognize the soul of the method that has hovered before us in so many different shapes. The Universal is the creative source of principles, the solvent of all multiplicity, the criterion of truth, the abiding essence under the Phenomenal, the root of conscious identity. It is the Philosopher's stone, and by its alchemy the base dross of mere opinion may be converted into the pure gold of science.

7

THE HEAVENLY CITY OF NINETEENTH-CENTURY PHILOSOPHY

William Torrey Harris

Looking backwards in 1881, Harris presented a paper at the Kant Centennial Symposium held in Saratoga, New York. Entitled "Kant and Hegel in the History of Philosophy," this was his mature analysis of the way in which Hegel had superseded Kant. It was an excellent short review of the history of philosophy as well as a reflection of Harris's own intellectual autobiography.

William Torrey Harris, "Kant and Hegel in the History of Philosophy," *JSP* 15 (1881): 241–52.

Read at Saratoga, N.Y., July 7th, and at Concord, Mass., August 2d, 1881, by William T. Harris

THAT Immanuel Kant is the greatest figure in modern philosophy there can be no doubt. One would say, in the same sense, that Socrates is the greatest figure in ancient philosophy. Not that the ideas of Socrates were not very immature compared with those of Plato and Aristotle, but that Socrates alone gives the immense impulse and the true direction, and the method which Plato and Aristotle elaborate and make fruitful. So Aristotle comes *after* Plato in greatness if we regard this matter of original discovery of ideas— but Aristotle towers much higher in the perspective of time as we look back down the ages of human thought. All scientific thinking in our Christian civilization is Aristotelian, and Aristotle is "The father of all those who know," as Dante says in his "Inferno."

So it is with Kant. We should not find in him the world-historical personage that we do if he had not been the impulse to raise up widely differing schools of thought, and carry philosophy far above and beyond the limits of the system which he presented to us in person. Socrates, according to the trustworthy portraiture of Xeno-phon, only practised *dialectic*, and sought to bring to consciousness the wide distinction between universal and particular cognitions and show the substantiality of what is universal. His endeavor was for the most part negative—a breaking down of the conceited wisdom of the Athenian professors. Plato made this arrival at general ideas something positive—an arrival at the eternal forms of created things—a reaching of the Divine.

Aristotle seized the standpoint which Plato reached in a few of his writings as his highest thought—that of the creative Intellect and Will—the identity of the Good and the Pure Thought, and with it, as his principle, consistently explained the worlds of Nature and Man as they presented themselves in the fourth century before our era to the Greek consciousness. Kant's significance in the world arises from the discoveries which he made in the realm of Psychol-ogy, especially as regards the antithesis of Subject and Object in consciousness and their mutual limitations and interpenetrations. The importance of this investigation on the part of Kant depends upon the fact that modern consciousness is a movement, as a whole, towards inwardness and subjectivity, and, accordingly, modern philosophy is bound first of all to ask itself: "What is the criterion of certitude?" The Greek asked: "What is Truth?" If he could find the abiding, it was sufficient. Thales, for example, set up the principle that water or moisture is the fundamental abiding whence all originates and whither all goes. Anaxagoras set up Noῦς—Rea-son—or the principle of the universal—as this abiding somewhat. The psychology of Plato and Aristotle is a sort of objective affair, treating the mind like the world, and finding within it what is transitory and fleeting and what is abiding. Aristotle discovers that the eternal substance of mind, its true form, is Noῦς Ποιητικός—Self-active Reason.

Aristotle and Plato both classify correctly the various powers or faculties of the soul, and leave us correct statements of the scope of those faculties. Sense-perception, opinion, discursive reasoning, the-oretical insight by aid of pure ideas—the "Seeing by totalities" (as Plato calls it)—these are expounded and their limits defined.

Aristotle's great distinction of the phases of life or soul into vege-tative, feeling and rational is the solid basis of all that has been thought on the subject.

But the problem of certitude could not be a problem to the ancient mind, though ancient philosophy gave the impulse that developed into this subjectivity in consciousness which now needs to enquire for the criterion of certainty. The Christian religion moves the soul in the same direction towards the learning to know the constitution of the soul as *subject*.

This subjective tendency of thought, which is the characteristic of modern times, leads to a peculiar species of scepticism—a scepticism based on a partial insight into method. Method is the form of activity. The modern tendency seeks to know the form of the mind's activity—all faculties of mind exist only as active. Hence the problem of certitude arises only when the mind is directed upon its own method or form of activity. If the insight into method is partial it cannot be sure of the results of mental activity. All wrong views of method lead to wrong philosophical views.

Not to dwell upon this position, but assuming it as granted, let us define the position of the work of Immanuel Kant as the Columbus in the voyage of discovery into the realm of method, using "method," in the largest sense of the term, as the form of all mental activity— the will, the intellect, and the heart, or emotional nature. Understanding the importance of method, and the fact that any glimpse into the forms of activity will give a basis of scepticism that no amount of objective philosophizing can remove, we see at once the significance of that philosophy which will explore method in its entire extent—map out the provinces of all mental activity. The Critique of Pure Reason attempts this work as regards the intellectual faculties, and accomplishes a vast result. The Critique of Practical Reason defines the forms of the Will, and the Critique of Judgment one of the functions of the emotional nature.

This insight into method, which is the want and necessity of the modern mind, is the object which Kant successfully pursues. It relates essentially to the antithesis already named—the subjective and objective—what pertains to the ego and constitutes its forms, and what pertains to the object as object. It regards all cognition as composed of two factors, and it investigates and defines them. The ancient thinking also had two factors to investigate in cognition, but it did not regard the one as subjective and the other objective. It defined one factor as the universal and the other as the particular; hence arose the structure of formal logic of Aristotle as the chief contribution on the part of ancient philosophy to the world's science.

All modern philosophy has sought to bring together in some way these two antitheses—(Subjective *versus* Objective, and Particular *versus* Universal)—and show their relation. The movement of modern philosophy developed negative results at first. The distinction of subjective *versus* objective seemed to destroy that of particular *versus* universal, and to reduce the universal to an arbitrary aggregate, or to a mere *flatus vocis*. The war between Realism and

Nominalism has this great meaning in the history of philosophy and in Christian Theology—it is the first attempt to assert subjective *versus* objective against the Greek particular *versus* universal which tradition had brought down to the Middle Ages as the heirloom of speculative science. This accounts also for the great place which Aristotle's *De Anima* held in the controversy. The great Arabian commentators taught that the human mind is essentially Νοῦς Παθητικός, and hence not immortal, as individual human soul of John or James. That which differentiates—that which belongs to the particular—is perishable; the species lives, but the individual dies. Aristotle had shown how an individual may become an entelechy—that is to say, how a particular may unite within itself the attributes of the universal as a totality. Change and perishability happen because the particular is not adequate to the universal—the universal has *many* particular attributes or phases, while the special individual realizes only one, or at best some, of those phases. The process of the universal—and all true universals are active processes—annuls some of the particulars and realizes others; this changes the individuality, and it perishes or becomes another. Aristotle's entelechy is an individual that has realized within itself all of the potentialities, or phases, of the universal, and hence it possesses self-identity; its change does not change it; its activity is only the continuance of its function—a circular movement—what Hegel calls "a return into itself." The "first entelechy" possesses this immortal individuality, and yet has not realized the universal within itself by self-development. The acorn possesses individuality—the universality or *species* of the oak is in it, but only potentially. When the acorn grows, it realizes *all* the phases of the oak that were potential in the acorn and becomes a "*second* entelechy" or species realized in the individual, so far as this can take place in the vegetable realm, or, as Aristotle calls it, in the "Nutritive Soul." Such ascent from "first entelechy" to "second entelechy" is not as a fact possible except to the human soul, although the vegetable and animal souls manifest a *semblance* of it—a mere appearance of it in a sort of mimetic spectacle—the dramatic play simulating the ascent of the individual into the species—which is, however, only a *play*, and does not constitute an immortal individual as in the case of man. The great scholastic "fathers," commencing with Albertus Magnus and Thomas Aquinas, gained this insight of Aristotle, and were able to defend Christianity against the Moslem pantheism which denied true universality to human personality, or, in other words, denied that man as a subjective being could be essentially universal, and hence an immortal individual. The distinction of subject *versus* object had

appeared only in the obscure form of nominalism at that early
period. With the close of that period of the history of thought nominalism seems to have gained the ascendancy, and William of
Occam marks its triumph. He also marks the utter eclipse of the
great insight of Aristotle in theology, and a divorce of faith and
reason.

It is one of the most mysterious phases in the history of Philosophy, this triumph of nominalism at the close of a most wonderful
and most triumphant career of profound thinking—realistic thinking. Christian theology had been almost completed. Very little has
been added, or is likely to be added, to the wonderful system left
us by Thomas Aquinas—familiar to more people through Dante's
Divina Commedia than through St. Thomas's *Summa.* The mystery
clears up when we consider the momentous importance of seizing
in its entire compass this antithesis of subjective *versus* objective,
in philosophy. We discern the providential purpose in what seems
to us at first dark and inscrutable. Christianity, alone among world-
religions, makes the individual man worthy of immortal life in a
continued *human* existence of growth in intellect, will, and love.
For Christianity holds that God himself is Divine-Human. Hence the
human being need not lose his humanity in approaching the absolute, or when he is placed "under the form of eternity"—*Sub specie
eternitatis*—as Spinoza describes it.

If the human form is divine—the human mind being the image
of the divine mind—it follows that to know the nature of the mind
is to know in some sense the nature of God. In the two worlds—
the world of man and the world of nature—we may find a revelation of God. In man—in our minds—we may find the adequate
revelation in each individual—but not in each individual of nature;
there it is found only in species and genera. The Christian doctrine
of the infinite importance of each human soul and of the transcendence of the soul over all merely natural existences, through the
fact of its immortal destiny, generates the impulse towards subjectivity as already asserted. It sets human consciousness over
against nature: I am above and beyond nature—a soul belonging
to the supernatural order of existences. This leads to the perpetual
recurrence of the antithesis of subjective *versus* objective, and by
and by to the unfolding of all its negative phases. Nominalism, or
the denial of the existence of universals, is the complete sum of all
that is negative and sceptical in philosophy. It makes all that
possesses abiding in the form of genera and species a product of
the subjective synthesis of thought—a classification only for convenience. The reality consists of isolated individuals, each valid

over against the other. The result of this is atomism, and the principle that "composition does not affect the parts or atoms of which things are composed." When once reached it is impossible to explain anything by atomism without inducting a principle from the outside, a directing, arranging, combining intelligence which produces all that we find in the two worlds of nature and man. The atoms become pure simples—without properties in their isolation—and thus everything is transferred to the other factor in the world—to the ordering intelligence. Then the atoms become an empty fiction, utterly useless.

The only thing positive about nominalism is its attribution of all universality—of all abiding and substantial being to the subjective mind. It implies a great deal, but does not itself become aware of this wonderful endowment which it claims for the subjective mind.

It is wonderful to see how the most negative phases, the scepticisms, the heretical doctrines, the most revolutionary phases in history, all proceed from the same great principle of thought as the most positive and conservative doctrines, and that all of these negative things are destructive only in their undeveloped state and when partially seized. By and by they are drawn within the great positive movement, and we see how useful they are become. Through these negative and sceptical tendencies, arising from this great antithetic object of thought, the subjective *versus* the objective, we ascend into a knowledge of self-determining activity as it is in Mind, and this knowledge is far in advance of the old objective view of mind such as the world has inherited it from the Greeks. It is a proximate insight into the nature of the divine creative process itself. We ascend through a philosophic mastery of the relation between the modern and ancient antitheses—subject *versus* object and universal *versus* particular—to the plane that is above all scepticism. Scepticism is directed only against method—this is its essential nature. With the sceptics of old, as Hegel points out, the doubt was objective, and touched the method (or transition) between the particular objects of sense and the universals cognized by reason. Modern scepticism touches the method (or transition) between subjectivity and objectivity. The ancient sceptic doubted or despaired of the truth of the objects of sense-perception. It seemed that they wore out and perished in the course of their process. They were all in a flux, becoming each moment something else, presenting new phases of their universals (or their total processes). Modern sceptics doubt the truth of the objects of reason—the universals—species and genera—and are unwilling to accord real being to aught but the objects of sense-perception—to the very objects which ancient scepticism doubted. A strange inversion of standpoints within the history of scepticism!

But the cause of this is the turning of the mind in upon itself for the truth—a partial movement in this direction producing doctrines in which there is utter disharmony between the two antitheses, respectively the objects of ancient and modern thought. It is a movement that justifies and will justify the doctrine of a Providence in History—a true Theodicy.

Up to the time of David Hume the outlook might have been dubious enough to the realistic thinker. Nominalism had begun to see the ultimate consequences of its subjective point of view. There is no causality in the world, so far as we know—only sequence in time. "All our knowledge consists of impressions of the senses, and the faint images of these impressions called up in memory and in thinking." Even the Ego is only a subjective notion—a unity of the series of impressions called "myself." This is the subjectivity *of* subjectivity.

This is the point in the development of modern philosophy at which Kant rises and offers his more complete sketch of our subjective nature as an explanation of the world of man, and the world in Time and Space.

His sketch of the nature of mind has become familiar to all persons who make a pretence of cultivating philosophy.

The Subjectivity of man, as Will, Emotion, or Intellect, has native forms of its own—forms not derived from experience or from anything external. These forms make up the constitution of the mind itself. If we wish to know the truth we must be aware of the subjective factor in knowledge and make due allowance for it. Things-in-themselves are modified (in our cognition of them) through the constitution of the mental faculties that know them. What we actually know of things-in-themselves will be ascertained only after we eliminate from our cognitions the subjective element due to our mental forms.

All this was so simple and in accordance with the spirit of the subjective scepticism of the pre-Kantian period that it would have recommended itself at once as the best of good sense.

But who can paint the amazement of subjective scepticism when it first begins to comprehend the Critique of Pure Reason! It looks over the inventory of the possessions of our Subjectivity—"the forms of our mind"—and sees:

Time, Space, Quantity, Quality, Relation, Modality, God, Freedom, Immortality, the Beautiful, the Just, and the True! It takes away one's breath to see such things written down in the inventory of what is our subjective constitution. How rich we are!! "Ah, but all these are only subjective." "They do not apply to any object in itself, whatever; not even to the Ego-in-itself." "You cannot think your Ego as an object-in-itself because you cannot think it except in these categories. These categories apply to objects thought, but not to the subject thinking, as a thing-in-itself."

Well, we reply, what of that? What is the net result when we take all this into account?

To take this into account it was necessary to recall the great insight of Aristotle, and review ancient philosophy in the light of this Kantian discovery of the nature of subjectivity. After Socrates, came first Plato and then Aristotle; the third philosopher could *use* the philosophical insight which the first and second had jointly discovered and elaborated. So it was this time. Fichte and Schelling developed respectively the practical and aesthetic phases of Kantianism, Fichte unfolding those subtle phases of mental activity by which the mind determines itself as universal categories or forms of thought—Time, Space, Causality, and Substantiality— the fourfold form of reflection superinduced upon mere feeling or sensation. Schelling devoted his attention to the explanation of the world as a phenomenon of which the constitution of our mind is the noumenon. Here the pure Kantian movement begins to impinge upon the ancient view of the world—the classic world of Art and Philosophy. In the school of Schelling, Hegel first appeared. He is the first one of the post-Kantians to take up the Aristotelian philosophy and perceive its profound truth. He is the first one to draw parallels from the psychological, subjective basis of Kantianism to the vast objective, world-comprehending system of Aristotle. It is Hegel's advice that has been followed in Germany, now that in each university of that country there are from one to five courses on Aristotle's philosophy given each semester! Even the attacks against Hegelianism which have arisen in Germany come chiefly from the Aristotelian studies inaugurated by Hegel, and not a single new insight or great idea in Aristotle has been added by any one of Hegel's Aristotelian opponents to the list of those ideas and insights inventoried by Hegel himself in his *History of Philosophy*! Even Trendelenburg, who blamed Hegel for using *Bewegung*—(which we may in English translate by the word "activity")—in his logical treatment of the categories of "pure thought," and accused him of borrowing the idea from experience, and yet tried to establish *Bewegung* as a category of pure thought in his own system, has no acknowledgment to make for assistance obtained through Hegel's explanation of Aristotle, and often, indeed, fails himself to see

Aristotle's deep thoughts where they have been fully expounded!

Hegel's significance in the history of philosophy consists in the fact that he mastered the Greek philosophy, and did not, at the same time, recede from the Kantian.

Hegel ascends to a standpoint wherein are united the two antitheses which lead, respectively, the ancient and the modern worlds of thought—the antithesis of subjective *versus* objective, and the other antithesis of the universal *versus* particular. Hegel does not reconcile the two antitheses by omission or suppression; he finds that Kant maintains a subjective result simply through an inconsistent application of his own principles, by which he surreptitiously made objective use of his categories, while claiming for them subjective application exclusively. If made consistent throughout, and the Fichtean discovery of the deduction of the categories superadded, the Kantian system falls into perfect harmony with the system of ancient thought, and philosophy becomes doubly firm on its twofold foundation of psychology and ontology.

The insight into Aristotle's thought of the unity of all potentialities in the true actuality, the thought of the entelechies, makes for Hegel the great luminous principle to which he always returns for light to explain all problems. With it he newly defines the thought of *Begriff* (German word for what the English call the "notion," and we Americans "the logical concept," or simply "the concept") as the total of form of a thing or being. The "Begriff" is the complex of the entire round of potentialities, and signifies much the same as Aristotle's τὸ τί ἦν εἶναι. Having the *Begriff* as signifying the *Totality of Form*, he finds the highest category to be the self-determining Reason, which he calls *Idea* (German *Idee*). Here is Aristotle's νόησις νοήσεως, as Hegel himself tells us.

In other words, Hegel has discovered that Kant's Subjective constitution of the Mind is only hypothetically Subjective. In reality it is subjective, and objective too. For considering the wonderful character possessed by those categories which Kant inventories as the forms of the mind, it is almost impossible to regard Kant's claim of pure subjectivity for them as other than a deep piece of irony. As if he had said:

"Scepticism is right. We can never get at the Truth and know things as they really are—things-in-themselves.

"We can know only what is radically modified through our own subjective spectra; but look and behold what these subjective forms are, and learn to subtract them and find the remainder, which is the true Thing-in-itself.

"In the first place there are Time and Space: these are the forms of the Sensory, and are purely subjective. It is true that they are the logical conditions of the existence of what we call the World of Nature. They are more objective than the world of nature is, because they are its logical condition. That is the way we know Time and Space to be Subjective, and to belong to our mind only.

"This makes the science of mathematics possible. The world in-time-and-space, it seems, then, is subjective because the very logical condition of it is subjective. True, we have called it 'objective,' and have been satisfied if our subjectivity attained validity throughout all time and space. Nevertheless, if we are to make serious business of inventorying our subjective possessions, we must begin with writing down Time and Space at the head of the list.

"True enough, things-in-themselves, deprived of time and space, will never trouble us nor anybody else—for, you see, they cannot have extension nor change. Yes, it is worse off for them than that. They cannot have unity, nor plurality, nor totality, hence they cannot be spoken of as 'they'—it is a courtesy on our part to lend them our subjective category of 'plurality' to which they are not entitled. Nor can the thing in itself (singular or plural) have quality or existence for anything else—nor relation, nor mode of being either as possibility or necessity, or even as *Existence*. The 'thing-in-itself' cannot *exist* without borrowing one of our subjective categories (found under 'modality'). As for the objective, then, which is opposed to our subjectivity and unknowable by us, it cannot be found in the world of nature or in the world of man. It is a pure figment of the imagination, and cannot exist in any possible world without becoming 'subjective' at once."

In fact, Kant's subjective has taken up within it the entire antithesis of subjective and objective as understood by scepticism, and has become purely universal through the fact that its forms are universals. Such a subjective mind is Aristotle's νόησις νοήσεως and a Self-Knowing Being. Whether Kant intended it or not, his remarks on things-in-themselves and on the limits of our knowledge make no sense unless they are taken as ironical.

Hegel has treated again and again the system of Kant in the course of his works, praising its wonderful features and criticising its inconsistencies and its mechanical presumptions. In his history of Philosophy he does justice to the significance of the system in relation to preceding ones. In his large logic he discusses in appropriate places (a) Kant's idea of the construction of matter out of Attraction and Repulsion; (b) Kant's theory of Time, Space, and Matter as regards divisibility or indivisibility; (c) The application of degree, or intensive quantity to the soul; (d) The so-called "Synthetic judgments *a priori*"; (e) The limitation of the world in space; (f) Kant's "Thing-in-itself"; (g) Infinite divisibility or atomic nature of matter; (h) The beginning of the world in Time; (i) The paralogism involved in the proof of the nature of the soul. In his philosophy of Religion he discusses in full the Kantian refutation of St. Anselm's famous proof of the Existence of a God. Hegel's thought of the "Begriff" as the totality of potentialities, and of the *Idee*, as the absolute Totality, enables him to rescue St. Anselm's proof from the Kantian objections (which are not unlike the objections brought up by Gaunilo in the lifetime of St. Anselm himself).

For convenience, as it seems, Hegel has brought together his chief criticisms on Kant in the "Second Attitude of Thought towards the Objective World," contained in his Introduction to his Logic in the *Encyclopaedia*, and so admirably rendered into vernacular English by Mr. Wallace.*

The limits of my paper prevent me from quoting largely from Hegel's own writings, and from attempting to expound some of his more subtle polemics.

I must refer to one more thought of Hegel—and it is also a thought of Aristotle: it is that universality is always self-particularizing, for it is self-determination. He always condemns the indefinite, indeterminate Absolute as empty. Hence his thought does full justice to European, Christian philosophy as against all orientalism and pantheism.

With a general reference to the full details of Hegel's critique of Kant, found in Wallace's translation above referred to, I must close this paper without attempting more than this statement of Kant's significance in the struggle between ancient and modern thought, and of Hegel's position as the one who harmonizes Greek and German thought.

* William Wallace (1844–1897) was an Oxford philosopher and a leading authority on Hegel. In 1873 he translated Hegel's smaller "Logic" from Hegel's *Encyclopedia of Philosophical Sciences*. Wallace was killed in a bicycle accident on February 18, 1897. [Editor's note]

8

PSYCHOLOGY AND HEGEL

G. Stanley Hall

Though the psychologist G. Stanley Hall later repudiated Hegel's philosophy, during the early years of his career, while teaching at Antioch
College, he maintained close contact with the St. Louis Hegelians,
especially Harris. He had returned to America in 1871 after three years
of study in Germany, where Friedrich Trendelenburg, a disciple of
Aristotle and Hegel, had been his teacher, and where he had imbibed
deep draughts of German philosophy. The essay by Hall that follows
appeared in the *Journal of Speculative Philosophy* in 1878. It is entitled
"Notes on Hegel and His Critics," and while it indicates respect for the
whole anti-materialist resolve of Hegelian philosophy, it also harps on
the contradictions inherent in the tenets of the Hegelian "school." Hall
does not see the dialectical logic or the "concrete universal" as a genuine
way of relating mind to matter, but rather he views Hegel's philosophy
as the starting point for psychology, which will put "the same old question of philosophy in . . . new, tangible terms. . . ." Sympathetic as he
is to the rationalist outlook, and contemptuous as he is of crude Spen-
cerian materialism, Hall's position—his craving for laboratory experiment
and the physiological datum—inevitably led him to a newer and more
sophisticated materialist position, based nevertheless on the a priori
categories of time, space, and motion. For the sake of his argument,
Hall confuses Hegel with his followers and almost totally neglects Hegel's
own creative use of these concepts.

Hall took a Ph.D. at Harvard in 1878 and then went on to further
study in Germany, primarily with the psychologist Wilhelm Wundt in
Leipzig. In 1882, he established his famous laboratory of experimental
psychology at Johns Hopkins and by 1891 had become founder and first
president of the American Psychological Association. Most of his work
in psychology was concerned with children, adolescents, and education,
significantly paralleling the efforts of the St. Louis Hegelians whose
main interests came to center in these fields (as symbolized by Harris's
rise to the post of United States Commissioner of Education). After

1889, Hall also served as president of then newly founded Clark University in Worcester, Massachusetts. In 1909 he arranged to bring Freud to that university on his first visit to America.

G. Stanley Hall, "Notes on Hegel and His Critics," *JSP* 12 (1878): 93–103.

We cannot help believing in the reality of pure thought, Hegel argues, in the Encyclopaedia, no matter how thoroughly we may have schooled ourselves in the Cartesian scepticism. The *will* to think purely is all that is required of the beginner at the outset of the logic. Though it prove itself identical with being, pure thought is always the logical prius. Because it is first, and because, as any logical beginning must be, it is immediate, it is best represented as objective—as something given, to be observed or *speculated,* rather than controlled or comprehended. Here, as being and as essence, it is the most real of all realities; in short, it is substance itself, in its most self-subsistent nature.

In the logic of notion pure thought becomes its own equipollent subject, constituting the world in which consciousness lives and moves, and hence is the most ideal of all ideas—now not merely metaphysical, but transcendent. It is pure thought which is latent and determining abstract, in Hegel's sense, through all the stages of the Phenomenology, and which becomes articulate and explicit in the Logic. Thus, as the Neo-Platonists said of the relation between the Old and New Testaments, so we may say of the Phenomenology and the Logic: In the first the last lies concealed; in the last the first stands revealed.

There is no *jenseits* to the logician who has reached the perfect *entelecheia* of *für sich.* The picture *is* the curtain which seemed to hide it. Pure thought, then, which seemed so easy because it is so spontaneous and inevitable, proves in the end infinitely hard, because, as Michelet explains, not only are all the phenomenal stages of consciousness presupposed, but because the universal whole of thought is involved by the severest logical necessity in its simplest act. Pure thought, then, is not so much a dominant category in Hegel's system as the warp, which does not in itself contribute to form or color, although *through* it all the categories are woven with harmonious and determinate sequence into ideal patterns of things.

Does Hegel's system require us to conceive of thought as pure in an improbable sense? This has been a central question in all Hegelian discussions. It seems evident that "a presuppositionless beginning does not require us to forego the use of concrete predicates," or "metaphors of sense and understanding," in characterizing it, nor forbid us to recognize any of the previous determinations of thought as we proceed. Indeed, it is perhaps more necessary for the dialectic than for the deductive method that it pause and verify at every step. Even Rosenkranz insists that the logic needs modifications because this was not sufficiently done by Hegel. Indeed, this is necessary not merely for the didactic success of any system, but it is perhaps the highest philosophic motive, for no speculation was ever truly satisfying to the philosophical impulse, or even very convincing as a mere act of first intellection, before it was brought into manifold and harmonious relations to common thought and things. But, on the other hand, if what claims to be a pure geometry of thought is found to be merely description of particular objects of thought—if *idola fori*, or the *Zeitgeist*, or empirical science are found to have furnished centers about which thought has accreted, instead of crystallizing into its own free forms, then it is impure, in a sense fatal to many cherished results of Hegelism.

Space, in Hegel's system, is derived only in the philosophy of nature as the first result of the creative resolve of the absolute idea in its pure freedom to become objective to itself. It is thus the other-being of spirit, the external as such, and in itself, without farther determination. While later, space and time, by their own imminent dialectic, become, as sublated, matter. Before this, quantity and measure, and even attraction, repulsion, and mechanism, are all characterized in the logic as non-spacial. It is evident, without discussion, that Hegel is no mathematician, and that this description of the origin of space is inadequate to the most important of all logical transitions, viz., from the subjective-intensive to the objective-extensive. This will at least be admitted by those who realize the complexities in which this, the central question of all recent psychology, is involved.

Pure vacuous space—is it something or nothing? We may even say that this is at the same time a real and a logical question. Substituting the word "space," first, for "being," then, again, for "nothing" in the large logic, we have, without a single change in the phraseology or illustration, a discussion of the above question. Like being, space is undetermined; like only to itself, cannot be known by means of any determination or content which can be distinguished in it, or out of it. It is, in short, nothing which sense or understanding can apprehend. It is perfect emptiness, or self-determination, and thus neither more nor less than nothing; though we cannot add of space, as Hegel does of being = nothing, that it is empty perception or thought itself. This, especially if we were to accept Werder's interpretation that nothing is, as it were, the memory of the vanished being, and, therefore, something additional to it, simply shows how sublimated and impossible is the thought here postulated. Will it be said that space is merely an illustration of pure being? If so, as the above are all *the* attributes of being and nothing, and as they belong to space, have we not a perfect identity? Where are the *differentia*?

The grounds upon which space is identified with being are far more logical than those by which thought and being are identified. Hegel's reasoning may be put as follows: Pure being is indeterminate, simple, immediate. Pure thought is indeterminate, simple, immediate. Therefore, thought is being. This violates two principles of logic. Two negative premises are made to yield a conclusion; and, secondly, that conclusion is positive when it should be negative, because the syllogism is in the second figure. In other words, Hegel starts with two *tabulæ rasæ*, and, because they are alike in being *rasæ*, he infers that the two *tabulæ* are identical. While we insist that there is but one conceivable *tabula* which is absolutely *rasa* in the universe, and that that is simply space, which thought tries to apprehend—now positively, as a condition and *prius* of all things; now negatively, as the absence of all content or determination.

When we remember how the Eleatics denied the existence of not-being, or, as we should say, failing to see the dialectic nature of the notion of space, made it more real than its content; or how the Vedic consciousness, abstracting all sensuous content, hypostatized emotional factors as its content of unlimited potentiality, the great merit of Hegel's characterization must be admitted. We prefer to stand, however with C. H. Weise, who, in his metaphysics, breaks with Hegelism by arguing that everything that is real and necessary must submit to the categories of space.

If Hegel's being were the mere infinitive of the copula *is*, as Erdmann thought, not only would whatever copulative force it might retain still presuppose two terms to be connected, but it is impossible to empty the word of all notion of existence. Of course, the phrase *nothing is* must be purely negative here. The *is* has no shadow of substantive quality about it. It has manifestly even less meaning than in such a phrase as abracadabra, which has no sort of existence, is. The predicate of the phrase *being is*, on the other hand, has, in spite of us, a positive substantive meaning. In characterizing or thinking *being*, we cannot escape the subtle connotations of the predicative verb; while, in thinking *nothing*, all reference to even its copulative function is, by hypothesis, excluded. We cannot escape the conviction that, though no doubt Hegel understood this distinction well enough, he has unconsciously *punned* upon two words which really have nothing in common except form and grammatical function.

Again, we may substitute for being and nothing, in the Hegelian equation, space with any homogeneous content, and it "solves and proves" quite as well; for instance, ether—Lucretian atoms uniformly and infinitely diffused, undifferentiated nebulae—anything which will serve as a background for the cogitable universe, even if it be so only in terms of sight and touch, it does quite as well. Are, then, intension and extension convertible terms instead of dialectic opposites, or have we here only an artificial abstraction from sensation? Hegel is fond of showing us that no more could be seen in pure unbroken light than in darkness, but how shall we explain his denunciation of Newton as a barbarian, who might as well have said water was made of seven kinds of dirt, as light of seven colors? Surely it was not because Newton had marred a mere metaphor of the Hegelian logic.

Leibnitz was the first to say that all science that could be *proven* must be referred to spacial intuitions. Schopenhauer has shown that many qualitative relations of thought may be best expressed diagrammatically. J. H. Fichte argues that space depends on a peculiar feeling of extension "inseparable from self-consciousness and grounded in the objective nature of the soul." The mechanical logic of Boole, and even that of Ueberweg, are founded upon the idea that as inference becomes certain it is best formulated by quantitative symbols. F. A. Lange, however, has attempted to show at some length that, after excluding modality, a spacial formularization in thought is always necessary when we would assign a general validity to any particular logical form. Thus, all the true may be best distinguished from all the fallacious forms of the possible syllogism by means of the spacial inclusion or exclusion of circles. Although syntactical forms furnish the most striking and suggestive illustrations of the innateness of these spacial determinations, was it not upon such geometrical references, far more than upon grammatical relations, that even Aristotle was led to infer the apodictic nature of syllogistic reasoning?

One interpretation of pure being makes it the same as the simplest psychic process. This is precisely what Hegel attempts to describe at the beginning of the Phenomenology. "Mere being," we are there told, "is an immediate delivery of sensuous certainty, but as the first object of consciousness it is identical with the abstract *now* and *here*." This is precisely the view of recent psychology, and ac-

cords with the verdict of perhaps most post-Hegelian speculation.
"Thought," says Ueberweg, "must be free from the compulsions of
experience, but not void of experience." "Thought without presupposition," argues Ulrici, "reverses the possibility of things." "Pure
abstraction," says Schelling, "must always presuppose that from
which abstraction is made." "Reason," says Schopenhauer, "is of
feminine nature. She can give only what she has received. Her
conceptions are never immaculate." "No concept-form" (*Begriff*),
Hodgson urges, "can ever grasp the infinite, but can only reach the
conviction that there is something beyond its power to grasp, and
this something we call ontological, because, and so far as, we feel
that thought does *not* correspond to things." In other words, intension, as divorced from extension, is inconceivable. Schleier-
macher's argument is that dialectic reason must always rest upon
the double basis of inner and of outer perception, and Kuno Fischer,
in his Hegelian period, understood Hegel to mean that the shadows
of earlier perceptions might enter and determine the dialectic
process.

Our conclusion, then, is, not that pure thought is demonstrably
unknowable or unreal, but only that it was as unknown to Hegel
as it is to the rest of us thus far; that what he has characterized is
neither single, immediate, nor extraneously undetermined. The fact
that the Idomedian eye—which Reid supposed to exist by itself, and
to perceive the world as it would look if sight were absolutely unin-
structed by experience or by the sense of touch—was unreal, does
not forever disprove the possibility of something that we may poetize
about as pure vision. If we close the eye, we have a dim sense of
spacial extension, over which the retinal darkness is spread—something, as Hegel assumes, the mind, emptied of all the products of
sensation, has a consciousness of being and nothing; but the one
feeling as well as the other is a mere residuum of experience, and
not the undifferentiated substance out of which experience is made.
If color had no objective ground, but were, as Schopenhauer argues,
only a physiological phenomenon, dependent for hue on greater or
less quantitative activity of the retina, and for intensity on the
amount of its undivided residual energy, then we should have something in the world at least analogous to Hegel's pure logic of quality.
But even this is far more demonstrable.

Pure thought, then, in the sense required by Hegelism, we regard
as a postulate, or rather an hypothesis, of logic, and not as an established verity, and still less as demonstrably identical with being.

But even this is not the greatest difficulty with the first triad. Thus
far all is static, motionless. Pure being is as seductive to the rest-

seeking reason as *Nirvana* to a world-sick soul. But where comes the vital, moving, evolving principle? Such random categories as matter, space, substance, being, are members of a very different order from such as cause, force, becoming, and the like. Whether because these last are based upon time, as the first upon space, we will not here pause to ask. However this may be, it is certain that *esse* and *fieri*, *stasis* and *dynamis*, are, as it were, the two poles of all thinking. Whence, then, comes the last? Logic, at length, has come to adequately recognize Leibnitz's dynamic negative as a universal determinant. But we have still to urge that an absolute *nihil privitivum* is not the presence, but the denial, of all possible determination or predication. If universal being *is* in pure thought, or otherwise, then non-being is not, else being is relative and finite. However, whatever or so far as being is, non-being is not. This is purely logical negation, or the mere denial of what the first or affirmative notion arrested, without in any way implying anything else in its place. Opposition is here equivalent to diametrical contradiction, and the application of the method of the excluded middle is undoubted. Hegel cannot, then, have meant that being and nothing are logically opposed, or else becoming, as their synthesis, would be forever impossible. But if we define *real* opposition, with Trendelenburg, as the denial of an affirmative notion, by another affirmative notion, so far as they must be mutually related, what have we, then, but the obverse side of Mill's "associative impulse," or a new and somewhat quaint illustration of the doctrine of relativity. Nothing, like being, is positive only; it is in a new relation, and the dialectic process, instead of being in any sense genetic, is as capricious and arbitrary as the psychological factors of attention. In fact there is no contradiction whatever, save in the Herbartian sense of mere difference.

Trendelenburg's question is still more searching. How does thought get from its first affirmative term to its second denying affirmation? It can only be by reflection from sense or understanding. "The nothing is attained by comparing the pure being of thought with the *full* being of sense-perception."

But we must not forget that being and nothing are not affirmed to be absolutely identical. We are not required to say both yes and no to the same sense, else there were no possibility of becoming. If A equals A, it cannot become A in any real sense. Everything flows, said Heraclitus, because it is and is not at the same time. Only movement is and is not at the same point and moment, said Trendelenburg, and so movement, understood in the most generic sense, as common to thoughts and things, and not becoming, is what is motivated here. But motion is an original factor, of a new species. It is, even Trendelenburg admitted, the existing contradiction which formal reasoning easily proves impossible. Thus, contradictions *are* overcome, though all static logic is powerless to tell how.

If the problem of creation were absolutely indeterminate, if the atoms of the Lucretian rain had been infinitely diffused, or had not swerved from the straight equidistant lines of their course, "there could have been no law, even of gravity, for its existence depends on the distribution and collocation of matter." These would have eternally remained an infinite equation of possibilities, every element perfectly poised and balanced, an infinite here, an eternal now. In language less mathematical and more familiar, the homogeneous is unstable, and must differentiate itself. But why, if purely homogeneous, can it be unstable, and whence comes the *must*? Formal logic, which deals with ready-made ideas, can always prove development impossible, for every sort of creation must be regarded as the irruption of an extraneous power into the realm of its Saturnian repose.

Thus it is that the necessity of an empirical principle is demonstrated, which must be at the same time simple and universal. Now, psychological analysis and physiological investigation concur in designating motion as such a principle. Vierordt, and Exner, and others have shown some reason for believing that the perception of motion is the only immediate sensation, and, unlike other rudimentary psychic processes, not founded on unconscious inferences of any sort. The sense of motion, it is claimed, is the quickest, the most minute, most primitive sensation of animal life; out of it all the higher faculties of the soul are developed, and in many common delusions of muscular and other feeling we may still detect its original forms, uninterpreted—indeed, almost forgotten—by adult consciousness. The facts upon which these inferences rest are, it need hardly be said, far too few to warrant any positive conclusion of this sort.

But shall we then urge, with Trendelenburg, that movement, in a broader sense, is the only aspect common to both thought and being —is the *prius* and the medium of all experience? Because, he argues, the original activity of mind is best described as the counterpart of material motion, knowledge of the external world is possible and valid, though it is imperfect so far as this analogy fails.

Because of this common term ideal, *a priori* categories are possible and valid in experience. Time is the internal result, space the external condition, of movement. If we are asked to explain light, heat, electricity, chemical change, the laws of physics or astronomy, the mode in which mind acts on matter, or the essence of either, or even the way in which the idea of a line, a surface, or a sphere, or a logical conception, arises in the mind, we can only reply in terms of movement in time. Molar is explained by molecular, known by hypothetical motion. Yet movement, which explains all things, is itself unexplained and undefined. By it all things are known. It must be self-known. If we try to *derive* movement, or construe it into non-motive terms, we are like a blind optician, who does not realize that sight can be understood only by seeing.

Here we shall at once be met by the objection that movement in thought and physical motion have nothing in common but the name. We grant at once that succession in consciousness and objective sequence are two very different, and perhaps quite incommensurate, series, but as soon as one psychic term follows another in the same *order,* as the corresponding objective term follows its antecedent, we have, if not as Chauncy Wright argued, the very beginning of consciousness—at any rate, *pro hac vice,* the truest form of knowledge; for what is causation but the postulation of something in the bond that joins two things, that is common with the bond that joins two thoughts, or *vice versa?*

We quite agree with Hegel that we may be said to know a thing, even the mind itself, most truly when our thought has followed all its changes in time, or has traced all its processes above, but we insist that the dialectic method is in no real sense genetic.

It is easy to conceive the external world as real, or as ideal, but impossible to conceive the *order* of the terms which common consciousness ascribes to it as real, as the reverse of that ascribed to it as ideal. Philosophy may still find pleasant pastime in resolving the universe into all-object or all-subject, but has she not a higher destiny than to amuse herself with this see-saw of reality and ideality, in despair of ever getting out of the labyrinth in which the theory of knowledge has entombed her, remote from the common life of men and dead to the issues and impulses of science? May not pure idealism read a wholesome warning in the fate of the obsolescent materialisms of the past, infinitely superior as it is in every way to them? Are mind and matter mutually exclusive or contradictory? Must the world be all one or all the other, or is there much that is common to, yet more than, both, as yet known? These are the questions which psychology has made pertinent, though it is as yet by no means certain that it can ever answer them. Its suggestions thus far may be briefly epitomized.

The simplest elements of sensation that common consciousness recognizes, and which seem immediate and instantaneous, are yet resolvable into a series of yet more ultimate states. The simplest act of vision, for example, is a whole cosmos of such psychic elements. Each of these changes has at some point of the nervous system, as a counterpart or background, some demonstrable form of molecular or electrical change. Now, if pure sensations may be described as an immediate knowledge of physical states; if aesthetic feelings, or pleasure and pain, are conditioned at all by the nutritive state of nerve fibres; if the muscular sense is an *a priori* knowledge of relative position or motion of parts of the body; if organic sensation, or the feeling of general depression or elation; and, above all, if Wundt's hypothesis of the direct consciousness of innervation registering accurately every increase or expenditure of nerve force be allowed, then, surely, those elements are not *unconscious*, but are the most innate forms of self-consciousness—the mother-tongues of sensation—from which all the functions of sense-perception are developed, along with the form of sentient organism, by intricate processes of extradition and *intradition,* if the word be allowable. A primitive immediacy, or absolute identity of subject and object at some point back of all of individual experience, perhaps, is thus postulated. That mind and matter may even be proven identical to the understanding, will, of course, seem a forlorn hope. It is so; but is not the alternative for philosophy still more forlorn? Of course, to all who do not thoroughly prefer the pursuit to the possession of truth, the assurance of Hegel that the problem of things is essentially solved, or even the confessed nescience of Spencer or the new Kantean school will seem far more philosophical than such a mere programme of long investigations yet to be made—a programme that must itself, no doubt, be re-cast again and again with every new discovery. But does not psychology, as well as the history of philosophy, teach us that the outstanding questions of thought have always seemed settled in proportion as men's minds were shut, or as they confounded the limits of their own individual development of culture with the limits of possible knowledge? If the truth-loving reason is not to be satisfied with ever deeper insights, in a ratio corresponding to its own increasing power—if, as Tyndall intimates, its essential principles of science are all found out—nothing remains but to pigeon-hole all the details of knowledge.

The world in which thought lives and moves is but little better than a dead moon, and pessimism, the true devil-worship of philosophy, is inevitable. The apparent achievements of individuals were never less, but the real work done in philosophy was never greater or more promising than now. It is for her to ask questions, and rarely, indeed, is it permitted her to answer them, save by other questions, broader, more earnest and searching. Philosophy is no longer a guild, or even a profession, so much as a spirit of research inspiring many specialties. It is because physiological psychology, with true Socratic irony, dares to take the attitude of ignorance toward both a positive philosophy and a yet more positive science, while it puts the same old question of philosophy in such new, tangible terms, and with such a divine soul of curiosity, that we love its spirit, and hope much from its methods. Nothing, since the phenomenology, which seems to us to contain the immortal soul of Hegelism, is so fully inspired with the true philosophic motive.

In creating and using a technical language, Hegel is unsurpassed throughout the logic. He is a master of illustration and of clearness in detail. If the maxim, *bonus grammaticus, bonus theologus*, were true of the philosopher, there would be little left to desire. But the trouble lies far deeper than style. Numerous as his school has been, no two Hegelians understand their master alike. Gabler says Trendelenburg's misunderstanding of him is inconceivable; while Michelet says Trendelenburg understands him better than most of his followers, but that Zeller's misconceptions are "monstrous." Stirling describes Haym's ignorance of Hegel's meaning as strange and inconceivable. Michelet considers that the greatest error of Krause, Herbart, and Schopenhauer is in fancying that they are not true Hegelians, while in a recent pamphlet he says— in emulation, perhaps, of Hegel's assertion that only animals are not metaphysicians—that all who think must be Hegelians. Gans thinks the dialectic method is an instance of pure deduction. Gabler says the idea created being out of itself; while the young, or left, Hegelians assert that the idea is God immanent, not so much in the world-process, or the race-consciousness, as in the individual soul.

But it is not concerning the logic so much as the philosophy of rights, æsthetics, and especially of religion and nature, that Hegelians disagree. Yet the impulse he gave to thought in these fields was unprecedented. The philosophy of nature, for instance, of which Trendelenburg, more wittily than truly, said that it might claim to be a product of pure abstract thinking more justly than the logic, and which, when the first editions of his works were sold, was most in demand, gave an impulse to natural sciences none the less philosophical, because, in the ferment which followed, Hegel's views were soon outgrown, and his method forgotten. As a mental discipline, then, as a wholesome stimulant of every motive of philosophical culture, and as the best embodiment of the legitimate aspiration of the philosophical sentiment, we have gradually come to regard Hegel's system as unrivaled and unapproached; yet, at the same time, as fatal as a finality, almost valueless as a method.

9

"A COMPLETE SCIENCE OF KNOWLEDGE"

George Sylvester Morris

"The first thing which philosophy had to do," wrote George Sylvester Morris, "in order to . . . prove its right to resist absorption into physical science is, and was, to labor for the establishment of a complete science of knowledge. . . ." This statement accurately charts the direction of mid-century Hegelian idealism, of which Morris was the foremost American academic exponent. The Hegelian attack on materialism generated a vast philosophical "science" of its own, focused primarily, as Morris indicates, on the problem of knowledge. Dismissing facts as mere data, the Hegelians concentrated, as had Kant, on the questions—how does man know what he knows and what is the relationship of the process of his knowing to his very existence, his self-definition, his being? These were questions old as Descartes, but nevertheless of central importance to all modern philosophy.

Morris, who studied at Union Theological Seminary with Henry Boynton Smith, America's earliest translator of Hegel, also worked with Trendelenburg in Germany. Unlike the latter and G. Stanley Hall, however, Morris did not try to mediate between Hegel and the rest of German philosophy. He regarded Hegel as the master. During his years of teaching at Michigan and Johns Hopkins, Morris expounded the savant's ideas to many of the key thinkers of his generation, including Josiah Royce and John Dewey, who was for many years Morris's chief disciple.

George Sylvester Morris, "Philosophy and Its Specific Problems," *The Princeton Review*, 9, ser. 4 (1882): 221–30.

THE first thing which philosophy must do—the first thing which philosophy had to do—in order to vindicate the foregoing assertions and prove its right to resist absorption into physical science is, and was, to labor for the establishment of a complete science of knowledge or—which amounts to the same thing—of *conscious experience.* For the creation of this science much more was accomplished than is generally supposed in the philosophy of Plato and Aristotle. But the most extensive labors in this direction have been accomplished in modern times. More especially the whole strength of the brilliant philosophical movement represented in modern history by the names of Kant, Fichte, Schelling, and Hegel lay in that which was therein demonstratively accomplished toward the comprehension of knowledge, or of the nature, the process, and the objective content of man's immediate intelligent experience. And the history and results of this movement are particularly full of instruction for those of us who have been reared in the atmosphere of British physico-scientific or sensational "empiricism." Kant, the leader in it, was at one time under the well-nigh complete influence of British empiricism, especially as represented by Hume and the older British moralists. Kant's "Critique of Pure Reason" is simply a re-examination of the traditional British theory of sensible consciousness, with the result of showing that all consciousness is not merely sensible, but also intelligible. Man's conscious experience, Kant showed, is not merely passive sense, but also involves active intelligence. But Kant only went half-way in his exploration of conscious experience. Under the influence of early prejudice he was led to treat intelligence only as a logical or formal aspect of sense, which latter was held to be the dominant factor in consciousness and alone the determining factor of real knowledge. His successors demonstrated, not by far-fetched, roundabout ways of indirect "proof" or of merely plausible but fanciful hypothesis, but by a more complete and unprejudiced scientific examination of the facts of the case itself, that sense is rather only an aspect of intelligence; that intelligence, further, is not merely subjective, a purely formal mechanism of the intellect, but is also objective, and stretches out spiritual arms to embrace, not the dark phantom of the "unknowable" or of the inaccessible, because non-sensible, *Ding-an-sich,* but an intelligible, rational, self-illumining, and self-explaining world of living, present, and effective reality. And so (to express this substantially in the language of Prof. Otto Pfleiderer, "Religions-Philosophie," Berlin, 1878, p. vi.) it is to be considered as "the immortal merit of the speculation of Schelling and Hegel that it made its way out of the barren heath" of sensational metaphysics—which was "so taken up with reflection concerning the possibility and limits of knowledge" that it had no time for or could not find its way to, knowledge itself —"to the green pasture of objective reality, and, rescuing us from empty formulæ, brought us to the rich and concrete knowledge of ourselves and of the world."

Now no science can afford to swear blindly by any name, nor to regard itself as bound up and irrevocably fixed, beyond possibility of improvement or extension, in any "system" or set of historic books. To do this were no less senseless in philosophy than in mathematics or any other human science. But it were no less senseless for philosophy than for any other science to ignore its great historic names and not to recognize and profit by the positive scientific achievement of the past. *Philosophic knowledge, in kind, if not in absolute perfection, has an historic existence,* and it exists with form and substance other than, tho in no sense contradictory— the rather complementary—to physical science. Moreover, its grander outlines have been determined, and that, too, on the basis of rigorously experimental demonstration. And the only way in which an unphilosophical age, turning anew to philosophy, can find its bearings in the field of this science is resolutely to learn and understand what the masters in such knowledge have known and declared. And so the unusually extensive study of the history of philosophy which is going on in our day is one of the most auspicious signs for the future of philosophy.

The limits of this article will permit only a few final indications respecting the more concrete methods and results and the special problems of philosophy as revealed in the history of philosophy (especially in Greek and German philosophy), and evident, in our opinion, upon any independent, impartial, and complete examination of the nature of the case itself.

1. *Science of Knowledge.* Knowledge does indeed, as above indicated, involve the real distinction of object and subject. And according to *first,* or *sensible,* appearance the distinction is simply mechanical. Subject and object thus appear as merely and absolutely different, separate from each other, and unrelated in nature. And knowledge appears as the result of contact or impact. This is the true account of sensible knowledge, *qua* sensible, or of knowledge naïvely considered only in its first, or specifically sensible, aspect. But it is not the complete, nor the true, account of knowledge, considered as knowledge. As a proof of this, we have but to

remember that the sensational theory of knowledge, taken by itself, ends not in knowledge or an intelligible account of knowledge, but in the confession of mystery or the dogmatic assertion of necessary ignorance. Subject and object, which were assumed as the mechanical factors of knowledge, turn out to be something of which we know, and by the terms of the theory can know, nothing—the justification of our "belief" in which is a *meta*-physical, *meta*-sensible, and hence finally insoluble problem! Not the factors of knowledge or consciousness are known, but only their contact, and how or why this contact should assume the form of consciousness, and how this consciousness should be known to itself, or to us (provided we really exist!) is "inscrutable." Now, to clear up this confusion of outer darkness, we have not to theorize "in's Blaue hinein," nor to go in any way outside of the facts of the case, but simply to examine more narrowly and to admit and comprehend all the facts themselves. The distinction of subject and object is experimentally real; and it is within, not behind, the veil of consciousness. Subject and object really confront each other and meet together. They must be, and are in fact, different, and they must be, and are in fact in some sense identical, in order that knowledge may exist. The object in order to be an object at all—even a *conceivable* one—must be *my* object, my *conscious* object. It must through my consciousness become identified with me, otherwise I cannot be conscious of it. For I can be conscious only of myself, and consequently of objects only as they are a part of myself. On the other hand, what am I, as so-called conscious subject, without an object? In order to be subject, I must have an object. The process by which I take the object up into myself, or into my consciousness, may otherwise be described as the process by which I invest the object with myself, or project myself upon the object. It is only on condition that I thus project myself that I become known to myself. The subject of consciousness must merge, nay, "lose" itself in the object, before it can "find" itself. Now, all these are hard sayings, notwithstanding their agreement with the literal, obvious, and experimental facts of the case, so long as we understand the words employed in their mechanical or sensible signification. For is it not the fact, does not even sensational psychology find it to be true, that the *real* object and subject of *knowledge*—independently of the fancied subject and object of our *ignorance*—are somehow identical in consciousness? Obviously we are required by experimental fact to give to our words another than merely mechanical or sensible meaning. If, as is immediately obvious, object and subject must be both different and identical, this cannot possibly be so in a mechanical sense. It cannot be so, if subject and object are so many merely different space-occupying entities or "phenomena." Such entities, thus considered, can only be different, not identical. Such entities, in mechanical, superficial relation to each other, subject and object may indeed, in one aspect, be. But this is not enough. They must be, and they reveal themselves as, something more. The relation between them is organic, and this implies—in agreement with demonstrable fact of living experience—that they, the terms of the relation, have an ideal, spiritual, or "universal" nature. An organic relation is the relation of the one effectively present in the many. Such a relation can only be ideal. But it is not for this reason any the less real. Rather, it is the essence and foundation of all conscious, experimental reality. It is an *active*, concrete relation, not abstract, mechanical, and dead. In it is contained the open secret of life. In a living organism, the idea of the whole includes by necessary implication all of the parts, and, *vice versa*, each of the parts implies and reveals the idea of the whole. In the bone of an extinct animal the naturalist will read the structure of the whole animal. The bone is and is not a whole by itself. It is mechanically separable from the rest of the structure, and seems to form by itself, when sensibly considered, a complete object by itself. But ideally and truly considered it is, in its separate existence, no more than a clump of earth. Rather it truly appears not as a whole, but as part of a whole. It needs an "other" to its own completeness. In it, the other, and the whole which both constitute, are to the mind's eye visibly legible. Now suppose the bone restored to its original place in the whole and living organism, and then endowed with the capacity of consciousness. The range of its consciousness we will suppose bounded by the superficial limits of the whole organism. The bone will be the immediate, empirical subject of consciousness, and the rest of the organism will be the direct or empirical object. Can we, now, suppose the subject to have true and complete consciousness of itself, unless this consciousness include the consciousness not simply of itself as an individual bone, but of the whole organic structure which is implied and revealed in itself? Can the "subject" bone have real consciousness of itself, unless it see itself, not merely (to suppose the impossible) in itself, *qua* individual, but in its other, its so-called object, which, while numerically other than, is yet ideally and organically one with, or is the real completion of, the true self of the individual bone? Is self-consciousness possible for it on any other condition, than that it lose and so find itself in and through its objective consciousness—its consciousness of the "object?" And, on the other hand, can it have consciousness of the object, except through consciousness of itself, not simply as individual, but also as universal, or participant in that universal (the one ideal whole, the living organism) which includes both subject and object? In short, we must see that the true, or potential, or universal "self" of the bone includes both the subject and the object of its putative consciousness, and that while subject and object are mechanically different, yet they are organically, ideally one. So is it with all our conscious knowledge and experience. The "identity" of subject and object is organic identity or oneness of nature. Subject and object are parts of a whole, and each part at once implies and reveals the other. Or, more exactly expressed, individual subject and individual object are so many particulars, which are included under and illumined by the pervasive and effective and, for this very reason, ideal and spiritual light of one concrete, organic universal, in whose nature all participate and by whose living power all are sustained. The subject can be conscious of its different object, because the object is a part of its true and whole or universal self. The subject in knowledge, the true, whole, and undivided self, must be, and is revealed as, ideally or potentially coextensive with the really "objective" universe. This was perceived by Aristotle, who declared that "the soul," in order to know aught, "must in some sense be identical with all things." It is the lesson of this truth that philosophy reads in Kant's "discovery" of the subjectivity of time and space, the forms of our sensible consciousness. Philosophy has, indeed, to deny Kant's allegation that space and time are exclusively subjective. But to know that they are at once and equally objective and subjective is, *pro tanto*, to know that subject and object are not separated by a mechanical chasm, but joined by continuity, community, or universality of ideal nature. In Kant's doctrine of the "categories" of "pure physical science" is contained by like implication the same lesson, which in the works of his successors we may read, set forth in greatest amplitude of illustration and experimental demonstration.

The immediate lesson of the science of knowledge is that all true consciousness is self-consciousness, all knowledge self-knowledge, all experience self-experience. But then, in order to recognize the substantive, objective truth of this, we have to revise and enlarge the individualistic conception of "self" which is posited by the sensational theory of knowledge. We must revise and enlarge it, so that it may agree with the full content of actual experience. We must regard self as not only individual, but also universal or participating in—organically one with—the universal. In its latter aspect it includes the "object" of consciousness—not excludes it.

In this way the real unity and the real difference of subject and object are reconciled, and really objective knowledge is made possible.

2. *Science of Being.* If the foregoing meagre outline be true to fact—and it certainly agrees in spirit with the historic results of inquiry—it is obvious that important ontological conclusions are involved in it. These conclusions are drawn with substantial unanimity—the difference is only one of relatively unimportant detail —in all those grander movements of philosophical inquiry which have reached and expressed really positive results, and have not, on the basis of a partial, dogmatically limited theory of knowledge, ended in mere negations of scepticism or agnosticism, or (as in the case of Spinoza) simply hypostatized mechanical abstractions.

Knowing and Being are one. That is to say, they are organically inseparable and identical. One cannot be rightly known without knowing the other. We frame our conceptions of being according to our conceptions of knowledge. "Being" is simply the "object" of knowledge. The conception of absolute being as an inaccessible, unknowable, the vaguely imaginable object of knowledge is simply an artificial creation of an incomplete, viz. the sensational, theory of knowledge. It results only from the discovery that the absolute object cannot be in merely mechanical relation to the subject,—or that it cannot be *merely* "sensible,"—accompanied by a refusal to go further in the examination of conscious experience and discover that the object in question really stands in another, an organic and perfectly intelligible, relation to the subject, and is more than sensible.

Being is the object of knowledge. But, by the terms of the science of knowledge, as is the object so, in *essential kind*, is the subject, and *vice versa.* And the nature of both is revealed in the relation subsisting between them in the act of knowledge, or in the essential relations of human experience.

First, the science of knowledge rigorously estops us from adopting any materialistic conception of absolute being. If being, as such, were materialistic, it is the senses, surely, which must inform us thereof. But, as we have seen, the knights of sensible knowledge tell us that we have no sensible knowledge of absolute material substance, but only—precisely!—of sensible, conscious phenomena. Besides, if matter possess absolute substantive reality, it must exist in atomic fashion. But the contradictions which the logical intellect discovers in the conception of a material atom are both too well known to need repetition here, and are also so glaring that the physicist himself (independently of the just-cited psychological evidence of the unknowableness of a thing called matter *per se*) is deterred by them from employing the terms of the atomic theory in any other than a symbolical sense. Again, we have seen that knowledge implies identity of nature between subject and object. If the latter be material, the former must be the same. That is to say—looking aside from other difficulties—the relation between the two must be mechanical, and then, as we have seen above, in spite of their identity in definition, neither of them can enter into that relation of organic union which is realized in actual consciousness. Still again, knowledge is a self-conscious process, partly self-determined and partly determined *ab extra*. Whatever enters into this process, and so becomes known, must exert an activity, must possess a force. But matter, even if it could be conceived as possessing any other than sensible or phenomenal reality, could exert no force. The forces possessed by a material or sensible reality must themselves be sensible. But to sense, and consequently to pure physical science (as we have seen above), no forces are known or knowable, but only motions, or signs of motions. That is, a *sensible force* is a contradiction in terms. Accordingly, as matter of historic fact, philosophic materialism has no scientific standing in the history of speculation. Its basis has always been recognized as purely dogmatic. But this is not to say that within the sphere of physical analysis and description the materialistic conception has not its full symbolic significance and justification.

The subject of consciousness, entering into and actively maintaining relations which are so different from mechanical or sensible relations, is called a spirit. It knows itself as a force whose activity is its life, and whose life is "energy of intelligence." Its object, by the terms of the science of knowledge, must be, and is, in varying potencies and in diverse forms of manifestation, of like kind. The world is indeed a manifestation of "force" (as we are told), and force is indeed "inscrutable" to sense. But to intelligence, to the living experience of man, force is the consciously self-revealing reality of spirit. If, as Plato finds at one stage of his inquiries, "being is simply power"; if, consequently, there is no *being* where there is no *doing*, so that the sphere of the former is precisely coextensive with the sphere of the latter, then we are entitled to say that there is neither being, nor power, nor doing, where there is no present reality of spirit. But there is no such reality where there is no life. The universe of reality, therefore, whether subjective or objective, is for philosophy a universe of spiritual life. This is the reality, of which the "phenomena" of physical science, viz. configuration and motion, are in sensible consciousness the manifestation. It is the same reality which, through or in alliance with the mechanism of sensible phenomena, is more clearly manifested according to its true nature, as energy of spirit in the life of nature, and of man in society, art, and religion.

The "ideal" relation which the science of knowledge found existing between subject and object was, and is, not abstract, but living and efficient. It was a sign of the only sort of efficiency which is known or conceivable in human experience. Being ideal and organic, its law is a law of purpose, of being which reveals itself in consentient harmonies of realized intelligence, of goodness, and love. The "Absolute," then, is, to speak with Plato, the Good; or with Aristotle, Νοῦς; or with Christianity, Love; or with Hegel, Spirit. All of these definitions agree. In and through the Absolute thus described all things are and consist.

10

PRAGMATISM'S DEBT
TO HEGEL

John Dewey

In his formative years, John Dewey, one of the founders of pragmatic philosophy, had come under the influence of Hegel's ideas, chiefly through the teaching of G. S. Morris at Johns Hopkins. Some of his earliest articles appeared in the *Journal of Speculative Philosophy.* In the selection below, Dewey is chiefly concerned with the problem of knowledge and, in particular, with the function of Hegel's dialectic in resolving some of the questions implicit in the work of Kant, especially the problem of breaking down the separation of mind and matter so that thought could work in the everyday world rather than simply the philosopher's study. Though, as a pragmatist, Dewey came to repudiate much of German rationalism, calling it "the spectator theory of knowledge," he never quite abandoned his Hegelian orientation, especially the concept of knowledge as an ongoing process.

John Dewey, "Kant and Philosophic Method," *JSP* 18 (1884): 170–73.

. . . THE only conception adequate to experience as a whole is organism. What is involved in the notion of organism? Why, precisely the Idea which we had formerly reached of a Reason which is both analytic and synthetic, a Reason which differentiates itself that it may integrate itself into fuller riches, a Reason that denies itself that it may become itself. Such a Reason, and neither an analytic Thought, nor an analytic Experience, nor a Reason which is analytic in itself, and synthetic for something else, is the ultimate criterion of truth, and the theory of this Reason is the Philosophic Method.

The two defects which we found before in Kant's theory now vanish. The method is no longer one which can reach untruth only, nor is it a method which cannot be made out. The track which we were upon in following the course of the Transcendental Deduction was the right one. The criterion of experience is the system of categories in their organic unity in self-consciousness, and the method consists in determining this system and the part each plays in constituting it. The method takes the totality of experience to pieces, and brings before us its conditions in their entirety. The relations of its content, through which alone this content has character and meaning, whereby it becomes an intelligible, connected whole, must be made to appear.

It was the suggestion of this method, it was the suggestion of so many means for its execution, it was the actual carrying of it out in so many points that makes Kant's "Philosophy" the *critical* philosophy, and his work the *crisis*, the separating, dividing, turning-point of modern philosophy, and this hurried sketch would not be complete if we did not briefly point out what steps have been taken toward the fulfilling of the Ideal. This is found chiefly in Hegel and his "Logic." We can only discuss in the light of what has already been said why Hegel begins with Logic; why the negative plays so important a part in his philosophy, and what is the meaning of Dialectic.

(1) *Logic*. One of Hegel's repeated charges against Kant is that he examines the categories with reference to their *objective* character, and not to determine their own meaning and worth. At first it might seem as if this were the best way to determine their worth, but it ought now to be evident that such a procedure is both to presuppose that they are subjective in themselves, and that we have a ready-made conception of object by which to judge them— in short, it amounts to saying that these conceptions are purely analytic, and have meaning only in relation to an external material. Hence the method must examine the categories without any reference to subjective or objective existences; or, to speak properly, since we now see that there are no purely subjective or objective existences, without any relation to things and thoughts as two distinct spheres. The antithesis between them is not to be blinked out of sight, but it must be treated as one which exists within Reason, and not one with one term in and the other out. The categories which, for the individual, determine the nature of the object, and those which state how the object is brought into the subjective form of cognition, must be deduced from Reason alone. A theory performing this task is what Hegel calls Logic, and is needed not only to overcome Kant's defects, but is immediately suggested by his positive accomplishments. In our account of the Transcendental Deduc-

tion we saw that self-consciousness was the supreme condition of all the categories, and hence can be subject in itself to none of them. When it is made subject we have no longer the absolute self-consciousness, but the empirical ego, the object of the inner sense. In short, the categories constitute the individuals as an object of experience, just as much as they do the material known. Hence they are no more subjective than objective. We may call them indifferently neither or both. The truth is, they belong to a sphere where the antithesis between subject and object is still potential, or *an sich*. It is evident, therefore, that logic, in the Hegelian use, is just that criterion of truth which we thought at first to find in Kant's Transcendental Logic—it is an account of the conceptions or categories of Reason which constitute experience, internal and external, subjective and objective, and an account of them as a system, an organic unity in which each has its own place fixed. It is the completed Method of Philosophy.

(2) *The Negative in Hegel.* It ought now to be evident that any Philosophy which can pretend to be a Method of Truth must show Reason as both Analytic *and* Synthetic. If History can demonstrate anything, it has demonstrated this, both by its successes and its failures. Reason must be that which separates itself, which differentiates, goes forth into differences, that it may then grasp these differences into a unity of its own. It cannot unite unless there be difference; there can be no synthesis where there is not analysis. On the other hand, the differences must remain forever foreign to Reason unless it brings them together; there can be no analysis where there is not synthesis, or a unity to be dirempted. If there be no synthesis in Reason, we end in the impotence of the former school of intellectualism, or in the helpless scepticism of Hume; if Reason be synthetic only upon a foreign material, we end in the contradictions of Kant. If there is to be *knowledge,* Reason must include both elements within herself. It is Hegel's thorough recognition of this fact that causes him to lay such emphasis on the negative. Pure affirmation or identity reaches its summit in Spinoza, where all is lost in the infinite substance of infinite attributes, as waves in the sea. Yet even Spinoza was obliged to introduce the negative, the determinations, the modes, though he never could succeed in getting them by any means from his pure affirmation. In Hume we find pure difference or negation, the manifold particularization of sensations, but even he is obliged to introduce synthetic principles in the laws of association, though he never succeeds in legitimately deriving them from sensations, for a "consistent sensationalism is speechless." Kant had tried a compromise of the

principle, synthesis from within, difference from without. That, too, failed to give us knowledge or a criterion of Truth. Hegel comprehends the problem, and offers us Reason affirmative *and* negative, and affirmative only in and through its own negations, as the solution.

(3) *Dialectic*. We have now the notion of Dialectic before us in its essential features. We have seen that the desired object is a theory of the Conceptions of Reason in an organic system, and that Reason is itself both integrating and differentiating. Dialectic is the construction by Reason, through its successive differentiations and resumptions of these differences into higher unities, of just this system. If we take any single category of Reason—that is to say, some conception which we find involved in the system of experience —this is one specific form into which Reason has unified or "synthesized" itself. Reason itself is immanent in this category; but, since Reason is also differentiating or analytic, Reason must reveal itself as such in this category, which accordingly passes, or is reflected, or develops into its opposite, while the two conceptions are then resumed into the higher unity of a more concrete conception.

Since the system of knowledge is implicit in each of its members, each category must judge itself, or rather, Reason, in its successive forms, passes judgment on its own inadequacy until the adequate is reached—and this can be nothing but Reason no longer implicit, but developed into its completed system. Reason must everywhere, and in all its forms, propose itself as what it is, viz., absolute or adequate to the entire truth of experience; but, since at first its *form* is still inadequate, it must show what is absolutely implicit in it, viz., the entire system. That at first it does, by doing what it is the nature of the Reason which it manifests to do, by differencing itself, or passing into its opposite, its other; but, since Reason is also synthetic, grasping together, these differences must resolve themselves into a higher unity. Thus, Reason continues until it has developed itself into the conception which is in form equal to what itself is in content, or, until it has manifested all that it is implicitly. A twofold process has occurred. On the one hand, each special form of Reason or Category has been placed; that is, its degree of ability to state absolute truth fixed by its place in the whole organic system. On the other, the system itself has been developed; that is to say, as Reason goes on manifesting its own nature through successive differences and unities, each lower category is not destroyed, but retained—but retained at its proper value. Each, since it is Reason, has its relative *truth*; but each, since Reason is not yet adequately manifested, has only a *relative* truth. The Idea is the completed category, and this has for its meaning or content Reason made explicit or manifested; that is, all the stages or types of Reason employed in reaching it. "The categories are not errors, which one goes through on the way to the truth, but phases of truth. Their completed system in its organic wholeness is *the* Truth." And such a system is at once philosophic Method and Criterion; method, because it shows us not only the way to reach truth, but truth itself in construction; criterion, because it gives us the form of experience to which all the facts of experience as organic members must conform. . . .

III

HISTORY
AND POLITICAL
THEORY

Hegel believed that human history was the story of progressive self-determination, which he called freedom. Down through time, each historical epoch, each great stage of civilization, was more free than the last as the universal realized itself in specific and concrete acts at particular times and places. Progress was possible through the dialectic of human behavior whereby each significant human act brought forth its negative which defined it as an act. Then, through the mediation process between the two, both the act and its negative were transformed and progressed to a higher stage at which there obtained quantitatively greater self-definition. The end of human history in theory was the final unfolding of the mind of God, but since the mind of God was infinite, history was infinite, hence freedom was infinite.

Man realized his selfhood and thus his freedom only when he interacted with other men; consequently, freedom was achieved through institutions—the family, the school, the church, the work group, the state. Thus, in *Lectures on the Philosophy of History*, posthumously published in 1837, Hegel concentrated on world cultural history, which entailed a discussion of the emergence of social institutions, the focal points of mass behavior, rather than upon the narrow chronicles of political events and kings and queens so characteristic of generations past. In so doing, along with Johann Gottfried von Herder, he brought into being a new kind of cultural history appropriate to the new century of the masses.

Hegel's followers differed, however, as to which particular institutions promoted the cause of freedom (though Hegel would have said they all did in their own way). Left-wing Hegelians, notably Ludwig Feuerbach and later Karl Marx, placed primary emphasis on economic institutions and saw them in creative conflict with one another and with the repressive state. Their ultimate vision was a socialist state in which all the means of production were controlled by the workers and the state was simply their creature. This point of view was represented in America by a long line of left-Hegelians beginning with August Paul Willich and including Friedrich Sorge, Joseph Weydemeyer, Daniel DeLeon, and Joseph Dietzgen. These men tended to criticize Hegel not for his method, but for his justification of the autocratic Prussian State, and to move more and more in the direction of a dialectical materialism concerned with the progress of the masses. That is, they accepted Hegel's logic and theories of historical inevitability, but they rejected the spirit of the universal itself, especially insofar as it implied a passive acceptance of things as they were, in favor of activist-induced change and a concentration on the more immediate goals of the proletariat. Thus Hegel's thought, which had been directed against mindless materialism, was put to the service of a cause he originally sought to oppose.

Right-wing Hegelians tended, on the other hand, to believe that whatever took place was right and destined. They conformed to existing institutions and they accepted (though they criticized) the state as it was.

In America, for example, in thinking about the Civil War, they felt that both parties, as duly constituted states, were right and should be obeyed. (See Woerner, doc. 1, ch. VII of present volume.) And yet they felt that each side would eventually negate itself and out of this would surely come a higher synthesis. Most of them were disillusioned.

11

THE PROPER STUDY OF
THE UNIVERSAL IS MANKIND

Johann B. Stallo

In the selection that follows, Johann B. Stallo presents a sweeping survey of the Hegelian point of view concerning history, the nation, society, and law. Stallo's interpretation suggests his innate conservatism, though he was in great sympathy with the radical workingmen of Cincinnati and the cause of abolitionism.

Johann B. Stallo, *The Principles of the Philosophy of Nature* . . . (Boston: Crosby and Nichols, 1848), pp. 158–75, 515–18.

NATION, STATE, LAW—GENERAL RESPONSIBILITIES IN SOCIETY

§ 106. The spiritual nature of man, which is cultivated in the family as *morality*, is enounced in the form of a positive assertion by the voice of society as *law*. The law is nothing *extraneous*, nothing foreign to man; it is nothing more than the universal reason slumbering in every individual mind, which manifests itself in the collective evidences of the Spiritual through its separate impersonations. The incorporated authority of the law, the *state*, is nothing else than society organizing itself; it is not a *machine*, of which the individuals are the material. The assertion has frequently been made, and is daily repeated by the wiseacres of this country, "that the *form* of government is a matter of indifference, provided men live in perfect conformity to law." As if the law were nothing more than an outward rule, according to which men are to shape themselves! The beau-ideal of a government would then be found, if a state had been devised in which every thing was perfectly *moulded* according to certain presumed divine criteria. The forms there would be of external derivation, society standing as the brute mass, to be circumscribed and defined by them. But this "brute mass" is the bearer of universal spiritual life,—this "material" *lives* and *reasons*,—this society thinks and acts spontaneously and develops itself,—in a word, exists as a spiritual organism! It is inherently, necessarily, a unity, not only for physical, but especially for mental coöperation,—not because the lawgiver has by main force riveted the individuals together and bound them by the same command; nor even, as the theory of Rousseau has it, because the individuals accidentally *consented* so to constitute themselves, but because society is but *one* eternal spiritual life. The law, therefore, is the *expressed consciousness* of society,—the act of intelligence, in which society takes cognizance of its immanent universal reason, —the act of volition, by which it establishes the validity of the unfolded Spiritual as paramount to particular impulses and opinions and desires. In the law society writes its own thoughts, reads its spirituality, brings it to the consciousness of its constituent individuals, and proceeds to regenerate itself,—*to think itself anew*. The form is by no means *adventitious*; it is *essential. Whatever is organic,—lives,—can have but one form; the form is the thing, and born from the essence, not added to it.* And that society lives and is organic will not be disputed, I hope. Society is progressive,— a progression towards *itself*, towards the Spiritual, of which it is the representative.—I have stated and shown that it is the destiny of the individual to identify his private reason and will with universal reason and will; and, obviously, this can take place only if the latter, in the form of law, be in the consciousness of the individual, and reproduce themselves *in* and *from* him. The organization of society is, therefore, *essentially democratic.* The objects of government are by no means barely to secure tranquillity, formal justice, stability of affairs, &c., as we are told by the prevalent theories of government; the object of government is *to embody the life of society*. And how could it embody the life of society in proceeding from a few individuals only, or in being superinduced from without, —in a word, unless it were *democratic*? A government, offering the strongest guaranties for individual security, material prosperity, formal justice, &c., if it were not born from society, not the representative of the people's reason and will, would nevertheless be an abomination; for it would be a stronghold for the imprisonment of divinity in man. Government is not a *means* for any extraneous purpose at all; it is its own object and purpose, because it is a concrete form, in which the Spiritual exists. Whatever is life cannot be construed according to a table of means and ends. Of course, government, such as it ought to be, *democratic government*, will likewise fulfil all these purposes, and be the most powerful warrant of the peace, prosperity, and happiness of the individuals,—a thing quite easily proven. We have a number of irreflective pedants in this country who bode downfall and destruction to our republic, "because Greece and Rome have vanished before us." There is no greater illusion in the world than the inference of an identity of things from an identity of names. Was Greece a republic, when it branded all those not born within the confines of Hellas as barbarians? And was Rome free, when it shouted, "Long life to the Republic!" only after having put its foot on the neck of another slave? Or was France a democracy, at a moment when revenge and blood had drowned all consciousness? But there is annually a day with us, when the heart begins to thrill and the countenance to brighten for a life to come, at the solemn enouncement of the simple words, "All men are born *free* and equal," which, I am assured, will soon be *perfectly* a truth.

But what are the guaranties of a democratic government? Whoever knows why he is a republican will disdain every other answer but this: the eternal reason, the Spiritual in man, which lives its life in that government. There is nothing higher than the Spiritual; you cannot prop it, you can offer no other earnest of its prevalence, than its own infinite power, than the energy of its own life. Nothing material, no "balance of interests," nothing beyond this spiritual life, can give "bail" for the Spiritual. And to what do *you* trust, who come with a theory, that the will of the individual must be extinguished, and a set of external laws substituted for that will? Must not your laws be *adopted* by society? And ere they become effective, must they not agree with the will, and therefore proceed from the consciousness and be sanctioned by the *reason* of society? Have your laws, therefore, any other strength, and can they afford any other security, but that of *reason*, of the Spiritual in man? Is the confidence in the prevalence of your laws, then, based upon any thing else than the faith in the power of reason in man? *All governments, however despotic in appearance, are in reality democratic.* Even the despot is the creature of the people's will. If the slaves of a despot collectively will to be free, has the despot any superhuman power to restrain them in their fetters? *The only difference between democratic and other forms of government is, that in the former the will of the people is a conscious and rational will, in the latter unconscious and unreasonable; that in the former thought and action are based upon conviction, in the latter upon illusion* (to which belong irreflective, "canine" loyalty, slavish terror, &c.) *brought about by hypocrisy and craft and a systematic animalization of man; that in the former society dwells in the light of day, while in the latter it gropes in an artificial night;* THAT THE FORMER IS A TRUTH, THE LATTER A LIE. It is a truism to say that the universal tendency of society is towards democracy.

I have said that government, like every organic bearer of spiritual life, cannot be valued and defined by outward purposes. An instance of this is the ordinary assertion, "Democracy is unfavorable to the culture of the arts and sciences." No matter as to the falsehood of this; first let us see what are the arts and sciences. Nothing else than the flower of the life of society, the expression of healthy social vigor, of the energetic realization of the Spiritual in society. The arts and sciences are of no other value than this. Science must be a beam of intelligence from the eye of the social organism, art the flush of beauty on its cheek. Both must be at the same time the fruit and the germ of the *whole* organization; if they are not this, they are utterly worthless. The only thing we can do for the promotion of art and science among us is to foster the *life* of society. Cultivate the plant, and its blossoms will greet the eye. It is a despicable, narrow view, to consider mankind as a set of craftsmen, destined to daub so many yards of canvas, to write so many books, to strike off so many epics, to fulfil so many commandments, whose connection with the purposes of human nature is nowise discoverable, to body forth so many foreign, *extraneous laws. There is no purpose for man beyond* HIMSELF, i.e. his true spiritual life. As to the treasures of art, which in Europe accumulate in the halls of the rich, unseen by the eye of ninety-nine hundredths of society, they are just as important to mankind as the supposed treasures of gold at the earth's centre.—But to return.

The individual man, in obeying the universal will, simply obeys his own true will; he does not succumb to an external antagonist. He only meets in reality what was ideally prefigured in himself. His *own true being* already demanded *for* him and in his name what is exacted *from* him by the law. His rights, therefore, perfectly coincide with his duties, his true wishes with his obligations, his subjectivity with his objectivity,—he is *free*. The whole nature of man is *freedom*. It is superfluous to mention, that lawlessness, the indulgence of momentary caprice, is not freedom, but *slavery,*—because it is the subservience of the *real* nature of man, his *reason*, to his self-estrangement, his particularities and passions. There is, in a word, slavery only where there is subordination of *mind* to *matter*.

The inevitable and natural consequences of a government which is not the incorporation of the nation's will, and whose laws are not its expressed consciousness and reason,—of a government, therefore, which does not keep pace with the development of society,—are sudden, violent, and calamitous revolutions. Man is the eternally active spirit; his nature is reason, and therefore development. So long as society *lives*, it will be impossible to hem it in by everlasting forms, however perfect they seem.

It has been often enough insisted upon now, that, wherever there is *mind*, there can be question no longer of subservience of any kind. I repeat, whatever is mind is *absolutely egotistical*. The person is not a tool of the family or the state; he subordinates himself to both, because in so doing he fulfils his *own* being,—because, in losing his particular self in society, he recovers his true self. The whole, society, is not something antagonistic to the individual, by which the latter is to be crushed; the individual attains to his full pride and happiness *through* society. Just as much, then, as the end of the individual is the welfare of organized society, of the state, the end of the latter is the welfare of the individual. The state is consequently bound to provide for the *intellectual* and physical subsistence of the individuals. I could have saved myself this verbiage by simply repeating the axiom, that the purpose of all social organization is the *identification* of the individuals, so that the same blood circulates in all, because the same life animates them all.—The practical means—the legal foreclosure of encroaching wealth in the hands of individuals, the measures to be taken for preventing the separation of labor from its products, the establishment of institutions for the relief of physical and mental destitution, &c.—do not belong here.

A purposed opposition of the will of an individual to the universal will expressed in law constitutes *crime*. The active assertion of the supremacy of the law in such a case is *punishment*. Its object is obviously no other than to break this individual will, and to reduce it to conformity with its own truth, with the universal will,—*correction* therefore, not *revenge*. In this sense, the recent theory, that punishment is the self-defence of society, though true, when properly understood, is liable to misinterpretation. All punishment ought to be *educational*. Only when the hostile will is perfectly identified with the criminal's being, when there is no possibility of correction, capital punishment is justifiable.*

---

* I may be indulged in a remark respecting the recent system of solitary imprisonment, which to me seems to be directly at war with the object of all punishment. The individual is to be brought back to a conformity with society, by perfectly estranging him from it! You want to re-instil into him good-will to man, to a cheerful intercourse with his human kindred, and you make

To regard the state, or any phase in the organization of society (and of nature generally), as a mechanical contrivance for certain particular purposes, to make it therefore a thing dependent upon man's *making*, a mere question of *expediency*, is an atrocity. Man is as necessarily a member of organized society as he *lives*. The state is an incorporation of the Spiritual; in it the Spiritual realizes its eternal intentions, which indeed present themselves to the understanding as finite purposes, and which will, in the true state, be *ipso facto* fulfilled; but it does not follow, that the meaning, the sense and validity, of the state consist in these purposes. All the socialistic schemes, on that account, are materialistic and false,—because they are schemes. Again and again it is to be said, the forms which bind society can be nothing else than the expression of the *life* of society,—they must proceed from that life; and this, as is amply clear now, can take place only in a democracy. The socialists relapse into the old contrast between *form* and *material*. Whoever attempts to formalize the life of mankind *externally*, instead of removing the artificial obstacles which impede the life of society in *formalizing itself*, is—a despot. The more intelligent socialists admit that society is an organism. "But on that account," say they, "the members are but *parts* of the whole, and therefore entirely subordinate to it. The absolute power is society; therefore all individuality (expressed in property, &c.) disappears. The person, the family, &c., have no validity against the state." True, not *against* the state, nor without it, but *in* and *with* it. *In every organism all the inferior stages are preserved in their full validity, though with absolute reference to higher stages.* . . . Thus the person and family are an *essential* existence in society, though they absolutely relate to, and derive their higher authority from, the state. The members of society—persons and families—are not only *parts*, they are also the *whole*. If person and family are ministrative to the maintenance of the state, the state is equally ministrative to the maintenance of the person and family.—

---

him the prey of despair! You mean to prepare him again for healthy life in the social communion, and you do all in your power to deaden that life; you deprive him of every thing that can awaken a sympathy with mankind, of the means for expressing his feelings, and for listening to the kind response of his fellow. Is not the converse of man with man the principal condition for ennobling, and in this case correcting, the individual? What the consequences are we already know from experience: all mental, moral, and physical diseases, which result from a repression of the manifestations of life,—idiocy, insanity, or at least irretrievable despondency, deadly misanthropy, masturbation, &c. I state this on the authority of an excellent medical friend, whose numerous observations in this sphere are trustworthy.

Socialism is based upon so many absurdities, that it would be vain to attempt a complete refutation of them; one or two only I will endeavour to point out. The person, as every socialist will admit, is at first, *immediately*, an egotist of physical desire. He is to renounce this egotism in favor of society. Now over this immense chasm from physical individuality to mental universality the socialist wishes to bound at one leap. There is to be no cultivation of the feelings in the quiet home of the family, no development of fraternal and filial affection, no attachment to country; one *salto mortale* is to carry the individual from egotistical instinct to the abstraction of universality and reason. There is to be an all-embracing brotherhood in abstract reflection, but the *natural feeling*, the immediate *reality* of the relations of brother and sister are to be annulled! There is to be absolute love of humanity, but the eternal love which man bears to man is to become the mockery of—a moment's duration! The fire is to burn, but—the hearth is to be destroyed! In short, there are everywhere ends without means. I trust that the statement of this is its own refutation.

Socialism is a lie in the face of nature and history; but it is eventually harmless, and will die from the disease of its birth. There is this truth, however, in the appearance of socialism, that society is to be indeed a community, and that *all* are responsible for the sustenance of each one. Moreover, there are numerous artificial obstacles to the free evolution of society, which are to be removed; but not by removing also the *means*, or rather *stages*, of that evolution. I, for one, despise the man who thinks life with all its wealth and ease and enjoyment worth the having, after you have robbed him of the proud consciousness of being the guide of his own bark and the creator of his own fortune,—of the infinitude and eternity of love,—of the sacred affections of brotherly and sisterly, of parental and filial attachment,—of patriotism,—in short, of every thing that sheds its first hallowing light over the private feelings of the heart.

MANKIND—HISTORY

§ 107. The comprehensive mental realization of the universal Spiritual is *mankind*, and its history, to which states and nations are again related as individuals. The one principle, that the Spiritual is infinite, eternal, intensive activity, has led us to the inevitable consequence, that it exposes itself without rest or limit on a multitude of stages, and therefore under a variety of forms. We thus meet with the one divine idea in a host of nations, and in a countless succession of epochs. It is present, and present as *mind*, in each and all of them, engaged in the work of its self-production and its self-recognition: for it is eternal activity. And here again, in the immense organism of historical mankind, we find the verification of the law,—that the Spiritual preserves all the phases of its existence, from the lowest to the highest, during every period of its evolution. The Spiritual is, as it were, its own biography, headed by its full portrait in the panorama of nations. The epochs, that are *past* in the life of one nation, are *present* in that of another. The aspects succeeding each other in *time* spread themselves out before the eye in the extension of *space*. The historical cadences, which strike the ear of the thinker as the *melody* of the Spiritual, are simultaneously heard by him as recollectively present in *concertant harmony*.

The source of all dependency in life is necessary *coexistence* and necessary *succession*; thus in the life of mankind one epoch depends upon another and one nation upon another. The life of the Spiritual is inevitably succession and coexistence,—a revelation in time and space; and yet it is its eternal intention and purpose to reproduce itself as an absolute intensive unity. How is this reconciled? Very simply in this, that the Spiritual is a unital *activity*, and therefore essentially a *revelation*,—an unceasing reproduction of itself. The absolute endeavour of the Spiritual to evolve itself as an intensive but universal unity appears, then, externally in the progress of its life as the free play of these dependencies. *Free reciprocation of man with nature and with all mankind* is therefore the law of our spiritual vitality. Nations and states have for this reason as little right to isolate themselves as individual persons. Liberty of material and mental commerce is the true inscription on every nation's flag. It is the duty of nations, as well as of persons, to diffuse the light of mind and freedom.

It is a very common view, to regard the life of mankind as a web of chance and adventure,—its history as an incoherent tale,—the whole as a confusion of efforts and failures, of hopes and disappointments, whose final boon is despondency, and whose product misery and woe. The scene of history is considered as a gloomy ocean, lit up by no star but the flitting meteors of ambition and deceit, enlivened by no breeze but the storm of passion, strewn therefore with nothing but wrecks, no other hope being left to the individual mariner, than, regardless of the general fate, to grasp the first plank that presents itself.

Views such as the above admit of no other refutation here than the simple statement, that the events of history are the events of one connected life,—the life of the Spiritual. Usually this is not altogether denied (except by some materialists); a *providence* is admitted; but this providence is regarded as something *accruing* to the world and history, not *resident in it.* In a word, the world and its history are looked upon as a sphere of finitudes, altogether distinct from the Infinite, which latter only *deigns* to support the former. It is properly unnecessary here to rebut this assumption, as I have amply proved (in the "Grounds and Positions") that neither the Finite nor the Infinite is any thing by itself, but that they respectively exist *in* and *through* the other; that the Infinite, the Spiritual, *must*, from its nature, distinguish itself in itself, whence all the material differences in time and space arise, and that the Finite *must* resolve itself and revert to the absolute Spiritual. But I will dwell a moment still upon the palpable and irremovable contradictions of this separation of the Infinite from the Finite, of providence from history, of the Deity from the Universe. If the Finite exist as extraneous, accidental to the Infinite,—if the latter be complete and insular in itself,—then the Finite and Infinite are in every respect *two*; the one *begins* where the other *ends.* One, therefore, is then the *absolute limit* of the other; instead of an Infinite and Finite, you have consequently *two finitudes*; and on the other hand, taking it for granted, that the Finite *is* any thing but what it is *in* the Infinite, that it has any existence, however chaotic and lawless, but that *in virtue* of the Infinite,—but that *belonging to and being* the Infinite,—that it exists otherwise than *as* the Infinite, you have two existences in themselves, you make the Finite infinite, you have *two infinitudes!!* You therefore have, not one absolute principle, but *two*,—not one Deity, but two Deities, —you have absolute war, irreconcilable contradiction; the only unital Absolute you have is an absolute—absurdity.

It is evident from this, that the Deity is not a personage who now and then stretches his hand towards the car of history, and shifts it in another direction; nor an artisan, who amuses himself by carving a curious toy, which we afterwards call nature, and whose droll gyrations we term history; nor a quaint alchemist, who occasionally walks into his rusty laboratory, the Universe, and mumbles a formula, and conjures up a bubble; nor a despot, who condescends to say, "Car tel est notre plaisir";—the life, the being, the essence, the existence of the eternal Spiritual is its activity. No act, which is not essential to the Spiritual,—which the Spiritual *is* not. And you can conceive no existence which is not *in* the Spiritual, which is not a phase of its universal vitality.

*History is therefore the life of the absolute Spiritual, and its
events are the manifestations in which the Spiritual comes to the
knowledge, the identification, the absolute possession of itself, in
its eternal self-evolution or origination.* And all those who deny this
—who assert that nature or history has any other existence, and
that their minutest events have any other reality, than that of the
Spiritual—deny the Spiritual itself, and are guilty of atheism and
blasphemy, however pious their mien, and however religious their
garb.

From this the guiding principles in history readily flow. All life
is a progress; the absolute life in history, then, is absolute progress.
All life is a change of form, an origination and evanescence of
phases, in which, nevertheless, there is an ideal constant; the
Spiritual therefore bodies itself forth in varying phases, and
destroys them again;—but it, the Spiritual, remains, and in it the
phase, not merely as a relict adumbration, but as an ideality, with
which the Spiritual, as it were, enriches itself. All the phases of
life are prefigured in the origin, and every succeeding phase is
immediately contained in and produced by the preceding one;—
so in universal life.

It is not my object, and it is altogether above my ability, to
furnish even a faint sketch of the progress of history in accordance
with the foregoing principles. I shall attempt only to make a few
general suggestions.—The evolutions of the Spiritual in history are
in every respect those of the mind. The first immediate union of
the mind with its natural organism presents itself in history as an
immediate union of man with nature, where the Spiritual is yet,
so to speak, the *flower* of nature; as such we behold it on its acme
(I point out only the heights in each epoch) in Greece. Mental life
was there as yet sensual,—the powers of life were objects of direct
perception, the serene gods dwelling on Olympus. The Highest,
the object of all aspiration, the fulfilment of all truth, was immediately present to the Grecians in the form of the Beautiful, in
the forms of classic art, which represented the perfect identity of
the Divine with natural being,—the beau-ideal of the human form.
The Grecian knew no despondency, no longing, no sentimentality,
no opposition between the Individual and Universal; the same life
lived in all. Hence, since the Grecian epoch, we nowhere meet with
individualities so well balanced on their own centre of gravity, so
perfect (perfect as they could be in that inferior phase), so full of
equable enjoyment and happiness. But the *depths* of the Infinite,
of the Spiritual, were not there in actuality; they only hovered over
them, in their dark bodings, as the sinister form of fate, which be-

came the ruling power of their tragedies. These depths mastered their consciousness in philosophy, and reduced the Olympic divinities to a shadow. The destiny was consummated; the Grecians struggled, but they perished, and the beauty of Grecian life with them. Rome is nothing but the epoch of transition,—the ferment of the elements that had been scattered by the fall of Olympus. Beautiful, classic individuality is no longer the principle; the Grecian gods in Rome are only recollections and formulæ. The vitality of Rome is an abstraction,—*national power*, in which all individualities are lost. Christianity appeared, and the *internal* life of the Spiritual, the "Beyond" of immediate nature, became the soul of life. Happiness became an aspiration, enjoyment a longing, the delight of existence an infinite grief; for the truth of nature was beyond nature, not its present being. True existence became a mortification, unwearied asceticism. Nature was a stranger to divinity,—nothing but a *fabric*, ministering to the base wants of man.* For the Grecians nature (and all existences) had been an *unconscious growth*,—for the Christian it was a structure designed by consciousness for particular purposes; the truth is, of course, the unity of both views,—a self-organization depending upon the laws of mind and consciousness. Christianity evolved the whole significance of life; it revealed the immeasurable expanse of feeling, the boundless exaltation of thought, the infinite power of love, the eternal craving of spiritual redemption,—all the potentialities of the heart and mind; but it detached them from nature and life, —it cast them like shadows in the distance. It separated the activity from its reward, the struggle from its peace (which, from the nature of the Spiritual, is but *in* the struggle), the labor from the product. History presents nothing nobler, nothing greater, nothing *truer*, than Christianity. In the Christian epoch, *classic art, the actual presence of divinity in nature*, became *romantic art, the painful longing for divinity*. Grecian beauty was there, but with the expression of inadequacy to its internal consciousness, with the *grief* of its natural existence, with an infinite *craving*, on its countenance.

During the epochs when Christianity culminated,—during the Middle Ages,—the Spiritual was present only *in* and *for faith*,— not for *reason;* and it could not be present for this, for reason was then nothing more than the *understanding*, to which the Infinite is inaccessible.—The Middle Ages were *free*,—perfect equality

---

* I speak only of that which lies in the fundamental idea of the epoch; in every epoch the following one prepares itself, so that here we gradually find also the recognition of nature. But Christianity, as such, is the principle of *perfect secession* from material nature.

reigned at the beautiful time when the church was the state. The true being of man lay beyond this life, and there all differences were equalized. The serf, who saw his lord kneeling with him at the same altar and at the same confessional, who beheld him voluntarily doffing the knightly armor, and humbling himself to the lowest level in the monastery, felt that there was no *real* distinction. The greater the suffering here, the greater the enjoyment hereafter.

I have said that Christianity in the ages of faith was a truth, and the sublimest truth, which history offers; I say so again. Every earnest man is essentially a Christian,—this epoch of the mind lives within him. But as an actual epoch, the noble days of the Middle Ages, with their benevolence, their chivalry, their romance, are gone by, and cannot and will not again be summoned up. The Spiritual never retraces its steps. We may try to stem the torrent of advance,—it carries us onward. The boundless spiritual resources of the Middle Ages continue in the life of the Spiritual, but this formalizes itself anew. The Christian epoch was that of division, we have seen; creation and the Creator, the Spiritual and the Material, faith and the understanding, labor and thought, were utterly distinct. We see this in the contrast between the classes doomed to toil and those devoting themselves to silent contemplation and religious thought in perfect seclusion from the world. That in our times the reconciliation is preparing, if not effecting itself, cannot be doubted. Science and life, thought and action, are no longer distant from each other. The man of learning is not a recluse now, nor the man of labor a mere machine.—May in our times the infinite meaning of Christianity infuse itself into actuality, and verify and exhibit all its powers in life, reevoking the serene individualities of Greece with all their ancient classic perfection, but with superior, because *significant*, beauty! May the coming age bring us a *mental, humanitarian* eudæmonism, and *a universal* liberty rivalling the *sensual, national* eudæmonism of the Grecians with their limited freedom! The epoch of Oriental life, with its vague pantheism, bears the same relation to the Grecian epoch as Christianity to the era which is beginning to dawn upon us. Hence the affinity of symbolic art in the East to art in the Middle Ages, and the romantic elements in Oriental poetry, which have recently been so much explored by the German poets of the romantic school. —Protestantism is to Catholicity what Rome was to Greece.

Just as the peculiar self-consciousness of the Spiritual, at each of its epochs, pronounces itself in art, religion, and government, so it is transfigured in philosophy and science. These are but reflexes of the inner life, the religion, of the times, and therefore also present the rational development of the mind. I cannot refrain from adverting here to a very outrageous assertion of certain "philosophes," according to which the faith of former ages, with its forms and imaginings, was the artful device of a few imposters!—The universal consciousness of mankind never was a lie! Impositions have no doubt been practised; but they never determined the belief of mankind. Even at the present moment, the minds of the religious world are not held captive by an imposture. They are bound by the greatest, the holiest reality they can possess, by the infinitude of their being and destiny. Nor were mankind cheated by an illusion. The saints and martyrs did not live and die for an illusory shadow; they died for the divinity within them. "L'homme dupe" is a fit subject for comedy and derision; but "l'humanité dupe" has never existed.

An analogous assertion, which is not a jot the better, is, that all truths and mental boons were at times accidentally and externally communicated to mankind by a few chosen individuals, without the fortunate accident of whose appearance mankind would have continued to grovel in mist and misery. Certainly the spiritual sun of the world, at the break of each new historical day, gilds lofty eminences sooner than low valleys,—but only because it is on the point of rising above the general horizon; certainly the consciousness of every higher life will awaken first in genial minds, but precisely because this life has already filled the bosom of all. Such genial men—and poets especially are to be numbered among them —are but the foci in which the scattered rays of spiritual consciousness in mankind concentrate themselves, and are radiated forth again with increased brilliancy.—The spiritual life of mankind is not the mere *aggregate* of the mental acquirements of individuals, just as the work of history is not the mere sum of individual deeds. To maintain this would be the same as to maintain that a given quantity of lines and colors thrown together at random form a distinct painting. The Spiritual achieves its revelation in and by means of individuals; its great designs infuse themselves into the private purposes, its infinite aspirations into the passions, of men; but, as someone has well said, the eternal reason of the Spiritual is the *warp* of history, of which the particular acts and thoughts and passions of so-called historical persons are but the *woof.* . . .

SOCIAL MORALITY (POLITICS)

Social morality is the truth of the subjective and objective mind,
—the universal rational will, in which self-conscious freedom has
become the *nature* of the individual.—The substance which knows
itself as free has its reality in the spirit of a nation. The abstract
diremption of this spirit is its particularization in *persons*, of whose
independence it is the internal power and necessity. But the person
knows itself as essentially this substance, and looks upon the latter
as its absolute end and object, as prompting its activity, thus attaining to its freedom. The dependencies of the individual, in the relations into which the substance particularizes itself, constitute the
moral duties of the individual. The moral substance is

1. The immediate or natural mind—*the family;*
2. The relative totality of the relations of individuals as independent persons to a formal universality—*civil society;*
3. The self-conscious substance as the mind developed to an
organic reality—*the state.*

I The family

As immediate, the individual has its substantial existence in a
natural universality, founded upon the sexual relation, in the
family,—the unity of love and mutual confidence.

II Civil society

The substance which as mind particularizes itself into many *persons* (families or individuals) becomes a system of atomism, in
which it (the substance) remains merely the general mediating
connection between independent extremes and isolated, personal
interests; and as such it is *civil society*. It is founded upon mutual
wants, the necessary division of labor, the consequent distinctions
of rank, &c. The morality appears here as confidential honesty and
honor.—Hegel distinguishes three ranks in society, which he considers as permanently necessary; I shall be sufficiently understood
if I forego his phraseology and designate them as *proletarians,
ordinary citizens,* holding property, and the *higher classes* of society,
including the intellectual laborers.

III *The state*

The state is the self-conscious substance of morality, the union of the principles of the family and of civil society.

The state is (*a*) its internal organization—the *constitution,* the *internal law;* (*b*) a particular individual in its relation to other states—*external* (international) *law;* (*c*) these two as momenta in the development of the universal idea of the mind—*history.*

(a) CONSTITUTIONAL LAW.

The nature and essence of the state is the universality of the rational will, by which, on the one hand, the persons are maintained and promoted in their individuality, and, on the other, reduced to the life of the universal substance, and thus to annul the individuality. The laws are, first, limits, *bounds* for the individuals; secondly, they are *purposes* for the labor of the different classes; and, thirdly, the *substance* of the free will and morality of all. The constitution is the organization of the state power,—existing *justice* as the reality of *freedom* in the development of all its rational determinations.

The guaranties of a constitution are contained in the spirit and consciousness of the nation, and the conformity of the state organization to this.—The living totality of the state and its constitution is the government. In the government, as the organic totality, *subjectivity, the power of the prince,* is the pervading unity.* "In the perfect form of the state, in which all the momenta of the idea have their free existence, this subjectivity is not a so-called moral person, or a resolution of the majority,—forms, in which the unity of the resolving will has no real existence,—but a real individuality, the will of one resolving individual,—*monarchy.*" (!!!) The monarchical constitution is therefore the constitution of developed reason; all other constitutions belong to inferior stages of development.

It is without interest to expose the remainder of Hegel's disquisitions on this particular subject; they all hinge on the scheme of a very equivocal constitutional monarchy.

(b) INTERNATIONAL LAW.

A state of war endangers the independence of states, while, on

* As if the true subjectivity of a state, or of any thing organic, could be something extraneous,—which the power of the prince always is,—something else than a *reflex objectivity!* But Hegel wrote in Prussia.

the other hand, it leads to the mutual recognition of the different nations, which is established in *treaties of peace*.

(c) HISTORY.

The spirit of a nation is determined by geographic and climatic particularities; it exists in *time*, and necessarily percurs the development of a particular *principle*, and therewith the development of a particular consciousness and reality,—it has an internal *history*. As a limited spirit it is subordinate to *universal history*, whose events exhibit the dialectics of nations,—the *world's judgment*. This movement is that in which the spiritual substance liberates itself, in which the absolute purpose of the world is realized, and becomes the *spirit of the world*. This liberation and its labor is the supreme and absolute right. The self-consciousness of a particular nation is the bearer of a stage in the development of the universal spirit, and the objective reality, in which this *states* its will. Against this will that of the other nations is without right; but even this will is annulled and transcended. The individuals active in this appear as *instruments*, whose boon is *renown*.

12

"A REPUBLIC OF LABOR AND INTELLIGENCE"

August Willich

The leading left-Hegelian thinker in America was August Willich, who had come to the United States in 1853 after a stormy career as a German revolutionary associate of Karl Marx, Friedrich Engels, Friedrich Hecker, and Moses Hess. Born in East Prussia, not far from Königsberg (Kant's lifelong residence), Willich was reputed to be the illegitimate son of a Polish actress and a Hohenzollern prince. With malicious amusement, Marx and Engels always referred to him as "the Hohenzollern Knight" in their correspondence. Trained as a soldier in the Prussian Royal Military School, Willich, impressed by the philosophy of Hegel and the doctrines of Feuerbach, along with his own observations of proletarian misery in Germany, resigned his commission in the aristocratic army to become a carpenter and workers' leader in Cologne. In the 1848 struggle, he led the Workers' Legion into several battles, but the cause was always lost, despite his excellent leadership and that of his adjutant, Friedrich Engels. From 1849 to 1853, he lived among the poor in London and joined with Marx, Engels, and British and French proletarian leaders in forming a World Society of Revolutionary Communists. The first article of their charter, written by Willich, declared: "The aim of the Association is the overthrow of all privileged classes and their subjection to the dictatorship of the proletarians by maintaining the revolution in permanence up to the achievement of communism which is to be the ultimate organizational form of the human family." The World Society collapsed a few months later, however, and Willich split with Marx over the issue of immediate action versus long-run political agitation. "The Hohenzollern Knight" wished to organize German soldiers and workers in the Rhineland and revolutionaries in Paris and begin the revolution immediately. Marx viewed his ideas as quixotic. Enraged, Willich challenged Marx to a duel which he did not accept. One of Marx's friends took his place, and received a bullet in the head from Willich on a lonely beach in Belgium.

Such was the man Judge Johann B. Stallo met in Washington in 1858 and brought to Cincinnati to edit the Cincinnati *Republikaner* for that city's Workingman's League. For two and one-half years, Willich edited the paper with consummate skill and in so doing introduced the ideas of left-Hegelianism to western America. In addition, he constantly sided with workingmen's causes and fought violently for the abolition of slavery. During the Civil War, he rose from private to major general and distinguished himself in several of the war's major battles—most conspicuously at Shiloh, where he was promoted to general.

Willich's ideas derived from Hegel, but, following Feuerbach and Marx, he rejected the "Divine Idea" and saw the dialectic working out in terms of a conflict between workers and capitalists in a class struggle. He also rejected supernatural religion and instead was a pioneer exponent of "the religion of humanity," whereby man, not God, stood at the center of all things. Something of an original theoretician, Willich, analyzing the situation in the United States in 1859–60, anticipated the Paris Commune of 1871 by more than ten years, when he envisioned the fusion in America of republican methods with socialist ends leading to the formation of workers' unions (soviets) into a national assembly with representatives by occupations which would make the United States Congress, as then constituted, superfluous. He conceived of it as "a Republic of Labor and Intelligence" that would expand its methods on a worldwide scale. Marx, however, saw him as too much the visionary, too much suffused with lofty Hegelianisms, and so rejected his plan. Marx's followers did likewise. Only later, after Daniel DeLeon had revived the idea at the end of the nineteenth century, did communist theoreticians take seriously the practical possibility of a socialist republic of soviets.

The selections below are from the Cincinnati *Republikaner*, and include Willich's redefinition of religion and of the state, which he viewed as a "mutually based insurance association on a large scale."

Reprinted with permission from Loyd D. Easton, *Hegel's First American Followers* (Athens, Ohio: Ohio University Press, 1966), pp. 312–20.

WHY DO SO FEW RELIGIOUS WORKERS PARTICIPATE IN LABOR MOVEMENTS?
(February 5, 8, 10, 1859)

WE cannot completely explain this lack of participation as resulting from tendencies toward persecution and witch-hunting. In these movements there must necessarily be something lacking which represents a deeper need to the religious workingman than the immediate, apparent goals of the movement can satisfy. To ascertain this we should inquire as to what human need lies at the basis of religion. Then we shall come upon the key, that this need persists as essential to human nature even if all that is called religion disappears and that religion, insufficient by itself to enchain the human spirit, loses its power as this need is satisfied in a deeper and more real way. So long as we confuse religion with its external organization in the church we cannot understand it any more than we can understand human rights through law courts or humanity through the police department.

What need of human nature lies at the basis of religion? From what natural law does this need arise? It is the basic law of all life —and in nature everything is alive,—it is the *law of self-preservation*. The self-preservation drive is thus so much at one and inseparable from the life-urge that it can never be repressed and never be rejected—yes, so inseparable that it lies even at the basis of suicide, where we would least seek it. If, however, only this *single* drive of self-preservation lies at the basis of *all* life, why then do we thus have diverse religions and why are we able to dispense with them? The answer is difficult and easy. Difficult for anyone who has not yet learned to realize his most noble capacity, free thought, and easy for thinking men.

The human organism is the result and epitome [*Inbegriff*] of all the organic life of our earth, and in it all the powers of nature are united to a single creative, fundamental power—*Thought*. Whoever has not learned to recognize thought as the epitome and result of all the powers of nature—not only as the most mighty among them, but *as nature's power*—asks himself whether there is something besides *human thought* which, through our machines, masters the forces of nature, blind in themselves. Will he not discover an outcome of human thought in everything that surrounds him? Thus is thought *our* essence, the life-source of our existence. As far as our thought extends, as far as we strive to extend our existence and what we can think, that far do we will to *live*, to exist. Thought is infinite, *i.e.*, it is not limited in space and not limited in time. Hence our life-drive is infinite and our existence should be infinite since the human drive for self-preservation is the drive maintaining life as infinite.

Life as infinite has been given many names but man has never been able to renounce it without at the same time renouncing his true human essence. With his feeling and awareness of the infinity of life man has also lost power over life. He has split himself and become shallow. He has deprived political life of all deep significance and driven beauty from his social life. He has fallen into a wretched and superficial daily existence out of which are born the powder-puff and coiffure, the white collar, clerical robes and livery, the follies of artificial gentlemen and the crudeness of the rowdy, the upturned nose of the gossiping woman and the shamelessness of the streetwalker, the fighting of our legislators in congress, and the filibuster-politics of Buchanan. The form and name with which mankind most readily designates infinite life is *"immortality of the soul."*

We have acknowledged the indwelling life-force in the human organism as the epitome and unity of all the powers of nature. We have seen that thought as the power of infinity in man allows him no peace if he extricates himself from the total life of nature and humanity and wants to content himself with a small, fragmented, circumscribed place in life.

The power of thought drives him forth, but life, out of which thought comes as its substance, its concentrated ideal content, must win thought back again.

This life, however, is the infinite life of nature, of humanity. The fact that a particular man is at once an "individual" and on the other hand, as thinker, the universal nature or *the essence* of the universe—this is the basic cause of the opposition in human nature. World history unrolls before our eyes the battle which is and will become the transcendence and resolution of this contradiction. The general comprehension of world history as the battle to overcome this contradiction is only a result of modern times, though a similar depth may have been achieved by thinkers of the ancient world and expressed in particular aspects. Only in modern times has cultural history been identified with *history itself.*

The self-preservation drive in man appears to us as much in history as in our civic and social life, with every experience and every particular act we commit, corresponding, in double form, to the contradiction in the human organism. At several points of attention we will find man's self-preservation drive as individual (commonly called egoism) opposed to his self-preservation drive as an embodiment of the whole (commonly called reason, humanity) as much in the falling and rising of races and nations at war as in the buying and selling of a 5-cent article, voting, a few hours with a good book or listening to a lecture or with beer and a game of cards.

Where the self-preservation drive on one side of the opposition heavily contends with the self-preservation drive on the other, men exist either as representatives of humanity, as individuals in whom the mass of mankind sees itself personified and in whom it recognizes its own essence (the so-called great men of history) or as individuals who are thrust out of the community of mankind as criminals. There are periods in the history of peoples in which one or the other direction of the self-preservation drive comes to the fore. Where the former side predominates, we see the rich development of national life. All powers become alive. Agriculture, industry, trade, art, science bloom and the nation exerts a dominating and civilizing influence on the life of other nations. Ancient Greece with its Athens presents the most beautiful picture of such a development.

Where the other side is preponderant national life deteriorates. Crudeness, the drive for oppression, physical and moral degeneration become general and national life sinks into the healthier life-development of another nation. The Roman empire and its destruction by our forefathers shows us the terrible picture of this process. In any case, the more powerful both sides of this opposition are at the same time in the same political community, *as in this our republic*, so much stronger is the development-process and so much *greater* will be the *nation* and the *individual* resulting from it.

We shall next see how religion, art, science, politics, and economics originate in the self-preservation drive as we see how far and in what ways each of these enterprises of the human spirit is reconciled and in some cases absorbed in the self-preservation drive of the individual (called egoism). This will clarify the developmental stages of humanity and the individual for which religion was and is justified and show where the justification of religion yields and must yield to science.

We have seen that the history of mankind, essentially developmental history, is the cultural history of man, that the self-preservation drive of man presents itself as the thinking essence, the personal totality of the whole life of humanity and nature in a necessary opposition to the self-preservation drive as single in man and nature. In the first form, the self-preservation drive is concerned with man's maintenance as species, as universal individual, and thus with the preservation of the whole. In the second, it appears as the single man striving to maintain himself in the struggle for existence against other individuals and nature. This opposition in the nature of man was perceived in the earliest ages of mankind and in one way or another appears in the consciousness of men as the opposition between God and the devil, heaven and hell, good and evil, light and darkness, spirit and nature, truth and falsehood,

reason and sensibility, sacrifice and selfishness. There is no experience or thought of mankind which does not contain in itself
this opposition.

While both directions of the self-preservation drive appear
mutually exclusive, they are inseparable from one another for they
are united in one and the same man. One simple drive for self-
preservation is the source of both directions. As man seeks to
maintain himself as the whole or universal, as he seeks to maintain God and Reason as his essence, he also finds therein the other
side as Devil, as sensuality, etc. He has never created for himself a
god without a devil, the good without the evil, spirit without nature, or vice-versa. Every effort to realize fully one side of the
preservation-drive without the other ends in the self-destruction of
life-power. The life of the individual as well as humanity consists
only in working through both opposites to full harmony and unity.
This struggle of opposites to reach harmony is the life-process of
man, of humanity.

Rational man appears as a result of this struggle. Rational man
is nature become reason or mind become nature. In this result God
and Devil are recognized as creations of one and the same mind
and become simple thought-concepts to man, their creator. Man
needed these concepts in his development just like other concepts
of opposites such as light and darkness, the whole and its parts,
which also exist independently as particular thought-concepts but
in actuality belong to one and the same thing as the whole is
nothing but its parts, only the parts in their unity, etc. Man has
necessarily had these thought-concepts, we say, in order to recognize, find, and become harmony and unity in the infinite mani-
foldness of the universe and of life.

If we have recognized this briefly-developed opposition in man's
self-preservation drive and the necessary interpenetration and
unity of both of its directions, it will be easy to grasp the various
areas of man's spiritual and material activities and the basic views
related to them, their origination and necessity, as *developmental
stages* of mankind at which they were necessary and beneficial and
equally to recognize *where* this necessity and efficacy cease and
become detrimental. Thus we will acknowledge all religions in
their historical justification and likewise in their insufficiency to
satisfy the life-preservation-drive of mankind if the human spirit
as knower has looked more deeply into its own essence, if the
human spirit as immanent power over nature has penetrated more
deeply into its secrets, and if the human spirit as nature's creative
power self-consciously restores to human nature what seemed to be

blind power. It will become apparent how the same life-need out of which religion arose is also the source of the free philosophical work of the mind. We shall see that religion was deserted by the free mind only because the free mind fights for its life with more powerful weapons than religion can provide. We shall also recognize, however, that we can only achieve this life if we are able to struggle against and overcome mind-limiting prejudices and body-restricting political and social abuses with greater seriousness and energy than religion can muster. He who takes no part in this work takes no part in life.

THE STATE
(March 2, 1860)

Yesterday fourteen fathers of families among us were buried under a collapsed church wall—today their wives who were left behind are helpless widows and their children are given the sympathy reserved for orphans. Not many weeks ago hundreds of workers were buried under the debris of a factory whose state of delapidation was well known to the owners; the lives of these hundreds were deliberately bound to the quicker procurement of the dollar. What happened to those left behind? A collection was taken! Such large-scale butcherings on railroads and steamships have become regular, recurrent facts, and through the death of nearly every one sacrificed to the Moloch of profit another family is thrown into misery or into the arms of charity.

At this moment we see many thousands of men whose existence is based on a shoe factory engaged in a violent struggle with those who, through capital and credit, have in their hands control over this area of production. Why? Because in the present state of civilization, a 12–14 hour working day is no longer sufficient to secure a bare existence for their families from day to day, much less to get property with which to secure their old age so as not to be a burden on their families. As it is with these men, so is it with the overwhelming mass of citizens of the republic. They are overcome in a bitter fight being led against them. Through capital and credit, management has in its hands the factories and businesses necessary for the preservation of the whole. In the area of culture it is the same as in material products. The immense treasures of our knowledge are closed to the majority of citizens. They have an education today which they could have had for the last 1000 years. The great spirits of humanity have not lived for them.

Let us consider the area of law! We have only to look around to see the most shocking contradictions. Yesterday a girl stole an umbrella valued at 75 cents—she will be sentenced to 4 months in jail,—and you need not look far to find palaces or palatial houses whose owners have stolen from their fellow citizens many, many thousands of dollars through bankruptcy and other swindles. We do not want to go further into these contradictions. They can't all be enumerated, but the question immediately arises: is such a condition the characteristic of the state?

If we look back into history, we must answer this question *"Yes."*

If we take in hand the Constitution of our Republic, the Declaration of the Rights of Man, we will indignantly shout *"No."*

The Declaration of the Rights of Man and the Constitution have done nothing to produce the present situation. This condition appears as criminal when measured against them. If we examine the bases of the historical European states and our own republic, we find absolute opposition between the two. However, if we examine the conditions of the people living in both, this opposition disappears. There are even some aspects of life in the historical states which could be preferred to our own.

Where is the opposition between the basis of the historical state and the basis of the republic to be found?

All institutions of historical states were designed for the domination of individuals, several or one class, to organize and protect the remaining people, *i.e.*, to hold them in servitude. The basic principle of these states is that men, which with them means subjects, exist not for their own sake but only as means for the rulers. The whole tax system is nothing but a system of tribute developed scientifically, as much as possible by the subjects, to secure the domination of those ruling over them. The whole economy is only a science which makes the subjects more capable of paying taxes. The whole science of law has no other purpose than to demonstrate dependence or submission as a citizen's duty on the basis of apparently general principles. The whole religion of historical states is concentrated in the propositions, "The government is from God" (the legitimacy-principle which the *N.Y. Staatszeitung* claims for the republic in a recent article), "Render unto Caesar that which is Caesar's and to God what is God's," "Submit to the authorities," etc. This is the essence of the historical state which is founded on historical right in contrast to rational right.

What is the essence, the basis, of our republic?

No man has a real right of possession either of men or of the control of the state—men are born equal and remain equal in rights. No man is a means to another but is himself his own end. The free community, the republic, has no historical, no supernatural, no legitimacy-basis but is grounded on reason which in turn rests on free will. As the institutions of the historical state seek to safeguard the domination of individuals, the republic, as a state, is no more and no less than a *mutually based insurance association on a large scale.*

All of our institutions have no other meaning and no other purpose than the mutual assurance of life, of freedom, of education, of the free use of our capabilities, of the unrestricted enjoyment of the value of our labor, of the care of widows and orphans—in a word, all of human goods on which everyone in a free community equally depends and which, through the free cooperation of millions of men, must all be protected from accident and loss.

What more the free community, the republic, has than such mutual assurance it has derived from the historical state. What it has less is the robbery perpetrated by the few on the many. The free community is incorrectly called "state." The state is of a political nature, it has "political justice" and, therefore, also "special privileges" since the two are inseparable. In the republic we need no political authority, because we have no opposing political rights to adjust. Insofar as such rights remain, our republic is still not a republic. In a republic we need only an administrative organization. To make this concept still more meaningful, one could also refer to it as a partnership of the assembled citizens.

But how did our community get into its present circumstances? Simply because while on a republican basis, on the basis of human rights, a constitution was devised which might leave those rights subject to hostile interpretation, the religious, social, and legal institutions of historical states, the monarchies, were grafted onto human rights and eventually submerged them. But these rights alone are rooted in the earth, and if the European grafts can be snipped from their stem, then will their own fruit-bearing twigs branch forth.

In Europe a man is a rebel and a traitor who, on the basis of human rights, fights political and social injustice. In our republic, he is a bad citizen and a traitor if he does not, on the basis of human rights, fight everything opposing them.

13

AMERICA, THE SUPERIOR HEGELIAN STATE

Denton J. Snider

In the section that follows, Denton J. Snider analyzes Hegel's conceptions of the state and of freedom based on a Prussian model, which compares unfavorably with that of the United States in which, according to Snider, a higher stage of political development has been reached. America is a true confederacy of independent states under the higher law of the Union. Disputes among American states can thus be resolved by law (reason) rather than war, as was characteristic of contemporary European states. Patriotically, but still in the universal spirit of Hegel, Snider calls for a "United States of Europe."

Denton J. Snider, *The State* (St. Louis, Sigma Publ. Co.: 1902), pp. 485–96, 529–30, 554–56.

Hegel. His name has been already mentioned in connection with Rousseau, whom he in many respects, though not in all, transcended. In the present work there are numerous direct and indirect allusions to his views. It is Hegel who says that the State is "the actualization of Freedom," and also that it is the "Will actualized." The thought he doubtless derived from Rousseau whose "Universal Will" and "Particular Will" are also very often used by Hegel. The influence of Rousseau upon Kant was likewise great, and the French thinker may well be deemed one of the chief sources of modern German philosophy.

The development of the State is, however, much more complete in Hegel than in Rousseau. The German thinker had a concrete State (the Prussian) before him, while Rousseau saw little in the France of his day to correspond to his idea. Still he had had the experience of the City-State in Geneva, and underneath his whole political consciousness lay the little Swiss world, with its cantonal governments.

Hegel calls the State an organism, "that is, the development of the Idea to its divisions" (*Phil. des Rechts*, s. 324—this work we shall hereafter cite by its initials). Such divisions (*Unterschiede*) are "the different Powers of the State," by which he means in a general way the three Powers, which with him are the essence of the Constitution, making it rational, since this division shows the State dividing (or organizing) itself "according to the nature of the Conception (*Begriff*)" which determines itself within itself (P. R., s. 344–5).

So Hegel's State has the Three Powers unfolding themselves out of the Conception of the State, which Conception, we may here add, is not distinctly the Ego or Self, but is projected as a metaphysical entity producing the State. But what are the three powers?

1st. The Legislative Power.

2d. The Administrative Power. (*Regierungsgewalt.*)

3d. The Royal Power, "in which the different Powers are grasped together into an individual unity which is the beginning and culmination of the Whole—Constitutional Monarchy" (P. R., s. 348).

This is not our well-known distinction into legislative, executive and judicial Powers. In fact, the judicial Power is not a co-ordinate Power in Hegel's State, nor is it in any leading European State of to-day. It belongs to the administrative branch, along with the Police Power (P. R., s. 372). How different this is from the American conception of the judicial Power the reader can find out by comparing it with the third Article of the American Constitution, which places Justice co-equal with the executive or administrative branch, and not subordinate to it.

As to the order of the Three Powers (certainly an important matter for their true comprehension), Hegel is not consistent with himself. In the statement just given he places the legislative first and the royal last; but when he comes to the special exposition, he begins with the royal and ends with the legislative. This destroys the inner necessity of his deduction of the Three Powers of the State (P. R., s. 354). The proceeding is the more strange, since Hegel puts such great stress upon the order of the Conception (*Begriff*) that he rejects the threefold division into legislative, executive and judicial because "the judicial Power is not the third element of the Conception" (P. R., s. 347), which should be "individuality" and hence the monarch. But after insisting on the necessity of this order "of the Conception," he violates it on the next page (P. R., s. 348), by placing the royal Power first instead of third.

Hegel's monarch is not elected but is given by Nature, by birth, so that his constitutional monarchy cannot be altogether constitutional. Nor does the monarch need to have "any particular character," good or bad, small or great; "he has to say only yes, and to put the dot on the *i*" (P. R., s. 365).

The monarch is not personally responsible for his actions, yet he is given the power of selecting all his officials, so that he is the head of the bureaucracy which is well-nigh absolute, being responsible only to him. The Classes (nobility, etc.) are maintained and declared to be rational.

Hegel's developed State is far less creditable to him than his germinal thought of the State. In the latter he took Prussia for a model (and that too in a time of reaction, about 1820, when his book was published); in the former he followed Rousseau. He declares the end of the State to be the "actualization of freedom," but his developed State does not show freedom actualized in a very high degree. Hegel's State is still an absolutism essentially, though modified by certain English ideas. He seems unaware of the American Constitution, though it had been working over thirty years at the date of his book. For this he ought not to be blamed perhaps, as Europeans knew almost nothing of the American State till Tocqueville told them. Still Hegel put great stress upon the reality, declaring in his famous dictum that "the real is the rational"; one may wonder why he did not search a little for the latest reality in the unfolding of his World-Spirit. But after all is said, Hegel truly represented the German people; his conception of the State is substantially theirs, as time has shown. Fries bitterly said that Hegel's book did not grow "in the garden of science but on the dunghill of servility;" the saying, however, is not just, though we must confess that Hegel was not in advance of his time or country, but rather narrowly limited by both. The English or American reader of Hegel's work on the State has a criterion in mind which Hegel did not and could not very well know.

Such is Hegel's inner development of the State. We are next to consider his view of the State in its external relation to other States, particularly in the European Society of Nation-States. "The first fact of a State is its independence which it is to assert against other States." The Property and Person of the individual must be taken by the State according to its needs; this negative side it shows to its own citizens, who, however, will what the State wills in orderly times. Hegel defends war "out of which States come forth not only strengthened but with an inner peace before unknown" (P. R., s. 412). A standing army he calls for, with its military class, which must really rule the State. All this means the military State, like Prussia.

In the European Society of States there is an international law, they make contracts and treaties with one another, but there is no Supreme Court to interpret or enforce such a law or the treaties, which are kept or broken according to the caprice of the Single-State. Hence the only restraining power that is final in this Society of States is war, for which they all must be always ready. How the American Constitution eliminates this terribly negative element of the European State has been already unfolded. But for Hegel such a political condition seems the highest; he rejects the idea of a per-petual peace secured by a federation of States or Kings, which was proposed by Kant, who had gleams of a Federal Alliance as the solution of the European difficulty.

Hegel declares that the highest law for the Single-State is its own welfare in its own opinion. "The States in their independence are particular Wills against one another" (*P. R.*, s. 420), and each is to follow its own self-interest, not its sense of justice. Hegel declares that the principles of morality belong to the relation of individual to individual but not to the relation of State to State. Each Single-State in this European Society seeks to dominate its neighbor for its own advantage, which is the end of the State as here given. Each State for itself, and the Devil take the weakest, which Devil is its stronger neighbor.

No doubt Hegel philosophizes his State from the real European condition of his time, for "the real is the rational." Still we may note for the sake of comparison what he does not see, yet was to be seen already in his time as a reality: his particular European Nation-State is to be freed of its national caprice and is to be institutional-ized through a new Society of States forming one State or State of States, which secures the inner Selfhood of each State without its dominating other States or being dominated by them. But such a universal State or State of States lay outside the ken of Hegel. Still he recognizes that there is something above the Single-State, calling it into existence, upholding it in its great career, then destroying it.

This brings us to the Hegelian conception of the World-Spirit, which has been one of the most significant and fruitful thoughts ever uttered concerning History. This World-Spirit is greater than the Single-State, using the latter as its instrument, and thereby making it a world-historical State, such as Egypt, Greece, Rome were suc-cessively in antiquity, each of which had its period of rise, bloom, and decline, in accord with the decree or the Will of the World-Spirit.

It should be added that the individual man may likewise be the bearer of the World-Spirit and carry out its command against his State or the Religion of his time, like Socrates and Christ. In the political sphere it has also some mighty individual representative executing its behests in regard to the State, like Caesar and Napoleon.

Now the World-Spirit is essentially a judge, and the World's History is a world-judgment over the Nations, "whose Law is the highest of all Laws"; or, as it has been pithily uttered, "*Weltgeschicht' ist Weltgericht.*" In this tribunal of Peoples, then, the World-Spirit pronounces sentence, out of its own caprice, as far as we can see, or out of its own notion of right, if right can be here applied.

In the Society of States Hegel leaves each Single-State to its own caprice or arbitrary judgments. Says he: "In the relation of States to one another is seen the animated play of passions, purposes, talents and virtues, right and vices, in which play the ethical Whole, the independence of the State is exposed to external accident" (*P. R.*, s. 420). But behind this spirit of accident is the World-Spirit calling forth or possibly destroying the State.

Such is the outcome: the Single-State acting capriciously for its own welfare is rewarded or punished by the World-Spirit, which reward or punishment is also ultimately an act of world-historical caprice. Hegel's World-Spirit (see its evolution in *P. R.*, s. 422–6), is an absolutist in true German fashion, a kind of Kaiser (*Weltkaiser*) over all the Single-States, ruling, trouncing, rewarding or cashiering them, according to his own sense of duty, but with absolute arbitrariness, so that even the undoubted good which he brings is felt to be tyrannical. Herein Hegel was true to the European reality before him, namely, the Society of Nation-States, each with the imperial idea. Over this struggling mass of colliding nationalities Hegel places a new Emperor, the Emperor of all Emperors, the World-Spirit, confirming or destroying according to his own particular Will, and thus realizing himself in a series of world-historical States rising and falling.

So much for Hegel's ultimate development of the State. Now we are to see that the World-Spirit has transcended the philosopher's conception of it; no longer is it something outside or over but within the States, and is actually existent as the universal State creating them yet created through them. It is no longer a capricious World-Spirit which capriciously punishes the caprices of the Single-State, perhaps justly but still not institutionally and hence tyrannically. Hegel's mighty conception of the World-Spirit is to remain, it cannot be cast away; still it too is in the evolutionary process, it is to be transformed and transcended, passing from its European to its American manifestation. The World-Spirit has found out a better way, which is to organize all these conflicting Single-States into a World-State corresponding to itself, which will prevent the great violations committed by States against States, prevent the State from its own inner self-destruction. So it will watch over the birth of the new Single-State, determining the same by Constitution and Law. Now the World-Spirit embodies itself anew in a State-producing State, in an actually existent Institution, and thus gets rid of its caprice, largely though not yet entirely. It lays down its law beforehand, which is in essence that the Single-State must will actualized Will, not assail it or destroy it, and this law is uttered and enforced from the central Institution or from the State of States. In such fashion the capricious European World-Spirit of Hegel has unfolded into the American institutional World-Spirit.

Still in the latter case we must note the limitation. The American Union is likewise a particular State against other particular States; after institutionalizing the Single-States within its vast boundaries, it too becomes a Single-State taken as a Whole. Thus it has to drop back into the society of conflicting World-States, till its principle be made universal, which will happen only when there is a United-States of the World. Such a universal State appears to lie far away in the future, though the prophecy of its coming has long since been uttered, and its prototype would seem to be already in existence.

It may be here added that Hegel's State is in full correspondence with Hegel's Philosophy, which is not only absolute in name, but absolutist in spirit and also in form. That Conception (*Begriff*) of his, to which allusion has been repeatedly made in the preceding account, may be called the Emperor of Philosophy, determining all notions of things and philosophic categories. The individual Self (or Ego) has nothing to do but to look on and see it work and obey its behest, according to Hegel. Still it is just the individual Self which is functioning [in] this Conception, and really is this Conception. When Hegel evokes the Absolute Spirit as the creator of the world and of himself, he has given only half of the process, for he has left out his own creative part. In his Logic he shows the Logos (or universal Reason) unfolding and ordering the fundamental categories of all Thought, while he simply "looks on"; but while the Logos generates all Thought, he somehow forgets to include his own Thought generating anew just this Logos.

Here lies the undeveloped element in Hegel, in fact in all European philosophy from the beginning. It projects an absolute principle which is to dominate and even create man, yet what is omitted is that man has to re-create it in turn, else it would not be. This omitted element in philosophy, always present but unrecognized, is now to be fully recognized in its creative nature. Philosophy as a European discipline was imperial, and sometimes imperious; but it must be democratized with other disciplines, whereby it is no longer philosophy strictly but psychology. In America the State too is imperial and commands the People, who obey its law; but the People are also imperial and command the State, creating it anew if they so will. And the Single-State as we have often seen in the preceding exposition, has over it an absolute State (the Union) which creates it, yet it has to return and re-create continually that absolute State, its creator.

Strictly speaking, there can be no philosophy of the American State; the latter requires a new way of thinking for its adequate comprehension, a way of thinking not given by philosophy as a European formulation of human spirit. This does not mean that philosophy is to be cast to the winds, but that its process must be completed by psychology, which in its true form gives the total movement of Spirit both creating and created. The Occidental State is the realization of the Occidental system of Thought, which, though already active, has yet to be unfolded fully and formulated in its own right. . . .

Here is the proper place for considering that much-abused word, freedom, and its different meanings. They are all derived from the various contents of the Will. Just as there is a capricious Will, so there is a capricious freedom which springs from some emotion or some finite end of Intelligence. This kind of freedom is legitimate and necessary within its province, but the citizen of a State must be able to rise above it. For there is also a rational freedom which originates in the rational Will, which always regards the freedom of others, in general it is an individual Will whose content is Will in all its manifestations. Such a content is therefore given to it, on the one hand by itself and on the other hand by the real world; it is therefore necessary. The State and institutions already exist which the individual must will. There is no choice, caprice is cut off, man must be rational unless he chooses the opposite, namely, to be irrational; there is only one option remaining inside of reason.

Such is the highest thought of freedom, a thought which takes in the whole field of Will. It should be the underlying principle of action for every citizen of the Republic. He ought to rise above the narrow aims of the individual into an universal life; what rights he demands for himself, he should concede to all. Wherever he finds Will, especially in its highest realized forms in the Constitution and laws of the country and of each particular State, he should respect it with a religious awe. Let him once begin to tear down these sacred institutions with violence, and though the locality may not be his own neighborhood, soon it will be found that every blow at a distant part is only a thrust at his own vitals. He is thus logically destroying Will, a destruction which must ultimately sweep back and include his own State, his own community, himself. For he is uprooting in his own mind the very consciousness upon which the institutions of his country repose. He is hence not only preparing himself for the loss of liberty, but he is nursing to life the usurper by arming his rulers with such unwarrantable powers. The citizen of the United States must be truly universal in his thought and sympathy, he must know and feel the wrong done to a distant State with the same intensity as if an outrage had been perpetrated at his own door. It will be a degenerate age when an American can look with indifference on any species of injustice and oppression; but woe be to him when heated by the passions of war or inflamed by the zeal of party, he not only applauds but demands the destruction of the fundamental principles of his government. . . .

But the true solution of the European problem is the Constitutional Confederacy. This, as was attempted to be shown before, signifies a confederation of States under a constitution whose entire substance and content is the security of the individuality of the States. Thus International Law becomes truly Law; thus the recognition of individuality is no longer subjective, merely somebody's notion, but it is real, an active institution in the world and embodied in an instrument, the Constitution. Thus too the standing army becomes impossible, for its only end and its only pretext, the security of nationality, is realized and perfected by a wholly different means, the Constitutional Confederacy. Thus Peace enters the world through its only passage, through securing individuality to nations, for when the consciousness has arisen that every nation is secure not merely of its own individual existence, but also is determined to secure an individual existence, a free and untrammeled activity, to every other nation, how is war any longer possible, war which is the struggle of one State either to wholly absorb or to influence the destiny of other States? Thus too fear and distrust must cease, for mark the nature of this consciousness; how is it possible for Missouri to hate and distrust Illinois or Illinois Missouri if both are permeated with the thought of securing not merely for themselves but also for their neighbors a free unfettered state-existence, and moreover have realized that thought in a Constitution? To be sure, such a Constitution without that consciousness is the most helpless of all sublunary things, but resting upon the same, it is the mightiest of all instrumentalities.

Thus the Constitutional Confederacy is the noblest edifice yet reared by man to secure his will, his freedom. The whole tendency of history has been to bring it forth; in its infantile form it has now appeared in the world: it may be reasonably added that the intelligence of man will yet perfect it in the course of history. The United States of America are still finite, not merely in their internal structure, but above all in the fact that they constitute a nation against other nations. Thus the Confederacy has its boundaries also against other nations and Confederacies, and hence the old struggle between hostile individualities may be resumed, this time between individual confederacies. But it need not be said that thus they are untrue to their deepest principle, the absolute Recognition of the Individual. For it is equally a violation of that principle, whether the individual person, the individual State, or the individual Confederacy be assailed. The outcome however must be the same; as we had a unity of nations brought forth by their mutual conflicts and wars, so we would now have a unity of confederacies. For upon this basis the most intense individualities must unite, the securing of individuality. Thus they all have a point of union, and their very intensity must only make that union stronger. The more determined they are to maintain their individual nationality, the more powerful securities do they demand; hence the combination into Constitutional Confederacy. Thus we see that the nature of true individuality is to be universal; the mightiest contradiction of human spirit is solved; absolute difference is turned into absolute unity and harmony. Unity by itself, as destroying individuality or individuality by itself as destroying unity are the most terrific mistakes of mankind which they can only atone for by the sacrifice of individual existence both of persons and nations. The true insight is for peoples to make their very distinction the principle of unity.

How long it will take the world to realize this principle in its complete universality is a question which it were wild to attempt to answer. The United States of America are already here; the United States of Europe are in the thoughts of her intellects and in the aspirations of her people, and seem to be coming; and shall we refuse the seal of universality to our principle, and relegate to dream-land the United States of the World? It is true that, before such a result can be attained, there is a vast ocean to be crossed, an ocean of time and probably of blood; but the truth of logic, the demand of thought, the aspiration of the heart and the faith of mankind all point to such a consummation.

14

EDWARD BELLAMY'S
VISION

William Torrey Harris

In 1888, Edward Bellamy published *Looking Backward,* a utopian socialist novel that envisaged future America as one large business corporation run by managers and technicians. Bellamy's novel caught the enthusiasm of the times and sold hundreds of thousands of copies. Bellamy socialist clubs sprang up all over the United States in a massive middle-class ideological revolt against capitalism. Keenly feeling the philosophical competition from Bellamy, William Torrey Harris attacked the book from the right-Hegelian point of view in 1889.

William Torrey Harris, "Edward Bellamy's Vision," *Forum* 8 (1889): 199–208.

THE novel has been called the epic poetry of the prosaic middle class of society. As the epic itself may exhibit the grand collisions that affect the relation of one nation or people to another, so the prosaic epic treats the collisions that affect the fortunes of the individual, his family, his vocation, his problem of life. At first devoted to strange and thrilling adventures, and allied to the epic poem in this, by degrees the novel has come to treat of every-day life and its petty cares, perhaps ennobling it by reflecting on its surface the growth of character that is brought about in its heroes and heroines by reaction against these circumstances. Thus the prose epic has changed from the romance to the novel. The educative influence of the novel can scarcely be over-estimated. Its theme is of such a character that it admits of infinite variety; it may reflect any one or all of the relations of the individual to his social or material environment. The epic poem is strictly limited in its highest form to the great collisions by which the people of a race have inaugurated a new departure in history. There are few such epochs and fewer poets great enough to treat them. The novel finds no practical limit to its list of subjects; anything that furnishes an obstacle to the career of the individual and is of a general type or character will serve the purpose. Thus we may have the difficulties of the lover that prevent the attainment of his infinite desire; or the antipathies that arise to unsettle fixed relations; or a career of selfishness encountering the steadily-increasing stream of reaction from the social whole; the sorrows of the poor; the stifled aspirations of souls that are held down by a superincumbent weight of domestic duties; and so on without end. The individual is related to the family, the industrial community, the nation, the church, and to himself. His realized self has to do with his ideal self, and the problem of life is to know the true ideal and actualize it.

But we must not pursue these reflections. They may serve to introduce our subject, the social-science novel, and more especially that eminent example of it, Mr. Edward Bellamy's "Looking Backward." A few years since Mr. Henry George showed the world how to write about political economy in such a way as to interest the masses of readers. Mr. Bellamy has learned the lesson and improved on it. Those not able to follow Mr. George's earnest pages find themselves quite equal to undertaking the story of the new Rip Van Winkle, who sleeps for a century or more and awakes in a new world at the close of the twentieth century. The picture of a state of Socialism realized by the adoption of a national syndicate to manage all the various sorts of industries, excites a lively interest, especially just now after a generation of well-nigh fruitless experiment in the organization of charities. It was the novel that first aroused the present impulse to secular charity organization. Dickens is the founder of the movement. Mrs. Stowe, also through a novel, precipitated our civil war, furnishing to literature a remarkable example of a novel which produced a national movement of a truly epic character. Dickens has inaugurated the literature of social reform which will produce greater revolutions and perhaps also involve national collisions of an epic character. This species of literature draws attention first of all to the inequalities of fortune among individuals, and especially makes prominent the relations of labor to capital.

The first effect of the social-reform novel was to occasion widespread charity movements. Direct help to the poor in the various forms of money, food, clothing, houses, asylums has been tried. The experiments have resulted in a general conviction that most of the direct help from outside does little toward curing the evil, while it often aggravates it. Persons already too devoid of energy to meet the demands of our civilization, upon receiving outside assistance rapidly lose what little self-help they had. The remedy increases the disease. What the managers of charity are seeking is a sort of aid to the poor and unfortunate which will enable them to help themselves. Thus far there is no instrumentality discovered that will effect this desirable result except education, and this is available only for the young. In the reformatories of penal institutions, it is true that good results are obtained with adults by educating them in the trades. But the respect for the sacredness of personal rights does not permit the social reformer to think of imposing education on the adult citizen who has not forfeited his rights through the commission of crime. The need has been felt, however, for some form of compulsion. The indigent poor classes are those who lack intelligent skill, industry, economy, and self-control. Intemperance counts as the chief among the obstacles to the cure of unthrift. It is difficult to frame laws which will bridle the wild appetites of the intemperate and not at the same time fetter, in a useless and meddlesome manner, the self-direction of people not indigent and not addicted to vices. Under these circumstances, it is quite natural that the large body of intelligent people interested in these humane questions of social reform should turn over in their minds very radical means of cure. "The persistence of poverty amid advancing wealth" causes Mr. George to question the right of private ownership in land. It causes the Socialists to attack the principle of competition and offer various substitutes for it.

Mr. Bellamy speaks of "widespread industrial and social troubles, and underlying dissatisfaction of all classes with the inequalities of society and the general misery of mankind" as the prelude to the great change which he pictures as completed in the twentieth century. His national syndicate, which owns all the means of production, and governs all the industry, and distributes to each individual in the community an equal share in the total product, is proposed as a remedy for the evils named. He says: "The industry and commerce upon which the people's livelihood depends is essentially a public business. The necessity of mutual dependence should imply the duty and guarantee of mutual support; and that it did not in your day, constitutes the essential cruelty and unreason of your system."

Previously, governments existed to administer justice and guarantee to the individual his freedom of action; but under the new *régime* they shall take charge of and direct all action. Previously, government limited itself to securing to the citizen the results of his deed—to punish him if a negative deed, to bless him if a wise deed, or to bring discomfort to him if a deed of folly; but by the close of the twentieth century government will have discarded this function of preserving freedom; it will not secure the fruition of the deed to the doer but will do the deed for him: "The nation became the sole employer, and all the citizens by virtue of their citizenship became employees, to be distributed according to the needs of industry." "The nation guarantees the nurture, education, and comfortable maintenance of every citizen from the cradle to the grave."

It is interesting to consider the exact relation of this remedy to the disease which it proposes to cure. The disease is inequality, caused by thrifty habits in a portion of the community, opposed to unthrifty habits in the remaining portion. The old remedy proposed to correct the evil by curing the unthrifty and making them industrious, skillful, frugal, temperate. The new remedy proposes to abolish altogether the idea of thrift as a trait of character, by removing all occasion for its exercise. There shall be no individual production of property and no individual accumulation of it. It shall be produced by the state, and distributed by the state equally to all individuals, without any reference to their function in producing it, intellectually or physically.

All other remedies proposed are mere makeshifts compared with this, if this may be called a remedy. Perhaps rather one should say that others propose reforms, but Mr. Bellamy proposes revolution. They are like physicians who propose to cure the body, while he proposes to get rid of the body altogether. Free proprietorship and competition have incidental evils, therefore get rid of private property altogether. Empty the child out with the bath. Freedom brings with it incidental evils; abolish freedom and get rid of these evils. But one might propose also to get rid of all society because there are evils incidental to it. This view was actually held by the hermits of old. One might say that evils are incident to life, and therefore it is better not to live; and this is in fact the doctrine of the Buddhists, comprising a third of the human race.

There are two assumptions underlying this book and all books of its species. They furnish the major premise or fundamental reason which is to move the reader to adopt the principles of Socialism in place of the doctrine of individual ownership and free competition. The first of these takes for granted that under the principle of competition the rich grow richer and fewer, while the poor grow poorer and more numerous: "The wealth of the world had increased at a rate before undreamed of. To be sure, this vast increase had gone chiefly to make the rich richer, increasing the gap between them and the poor." The second assumption is that the few rich people are rich at the expense of the poor; that the poor, in short, create the wealth, while the rich have a faculty of depriving them of it, honestly or dishonestly, but under the protection of the law: " 'Your necessity is my opportunity.' The reward of any service depended, not upon its difficulty, danger, or hardship, for throughout the world it seems that the most perilous, severe, and repulsive labor was done by the worst-paid classes, but solely upon the strait of those who rendered the service."

The first of these assumptions is a product of imagination and not the result of inquiry into existing facts. It is the principle announced by Karl Marx (near the close of his work *"Das Kapital"*). It was evolved from the depths of his consciousness, but not supported by any reliable or pertinent statistics, although Marx lived in England over thirty years and might have learned the actual facts from the British income returns and the probate records. He industriously collected striking cases of poverty in contrast to wealth, and used them as illustrations of his *a priori* principle that capital is necessarily hostile to labor and always enslaves it, limiting wages always to the bare cost of living. The actual facts are undoubtedly quite the contrary to his theory, as shown by any general statistics. For instance, in Great Britain the average income of the poorest class rose from $265 per family in 1850 to $415 in 1880; the next class above, with annual incomes from $750 to $5,000, had increased in numbers so that in each million of the population there were, in 1880, two and one half times as many as in 1850; the moderately wealthy class, with incomes from $5,000 to $15,000 a year, had increased to double the number in each million. The statistics of the United States show the same results, as the reports of Carroll D. Wright and the investigations of Edward Atkinson have demonstrated. The true law of capital has been announced by Cary and Bastiat: "As capital increases it draws a smaller proportional amount from the product as its share, while labor gets a larger proportional amount."

The second assumption is also unfounded either in theory or in fact. The results of thrift and economy are such as to benefit the unthrifty and the prodigal as well as the rich. Wealth begins with self-denial which saves a surplus, and it is preserved and increased by sagacity in investment. The unthrifty invests in what is consumed as means of gratification and enjoyment; the thrifty denies himself and invests his money in the means of production, and thereby increases the total productive power of the community. He makes permanent improvements in the shape of substantial houses, good roads and bridges, lands brought under a high state of cultivation, machinery, etc. Of course, with the accumulation of capital invested in permanent improvements and instruments of production, the means of comfortable living are cheapened and made constantly accessible, and labor becomes able to secure constant employment at remunerative wages. The larger the production of articles of enduring usefulness, the greater the skill and productive capacity in those lines, and hence the easier it becomes for each inhabitant to accumulate such items of permanent wealth. Hence it is evident that one economical person benefits another, and the average producing and accumulating power of each individual in a thrifty community is greater than that of a thrifty individual in a community of indolent and improvident people.

If these assumptions are all imaginary, it is evident that writings based on them can have no healthy or enduring effect, except so far as to call public attention to the importance of the question and induce more careful thought on these subjects. If competition and the system of private property are working the amelioration of all classes, poor and rich, there is no occasion for us to make rash experiments with an entirely different system. We know by the history of civilization that freedom of ownership and contract, freedom of labor and capital, have resulted in the largest degree of individual development on the part of the people. The great Roman contribution to civilization concerns the rights of private property on the one side and the definition of corporate and political powers on the other. While the individual must devote his life and property to the state for its defense, on the other hand the state will secure him in the free control of his property after the dues to the state are paid. And here in the possession of private property the citizen has a perpetual field for the cultivation of his individuality. It is his "*dominium*," and he can by its means gain self-respect and self-knowledge. For he learns to know himself by realizing his will in the creation, transfer, and acquisition of property. He learns to conquer nature and to combine by contract with his fellowmen. In contract two or more wills unite, each preserving its equality and freedom. In dealing with the state or nation there is not this equality and freedom, but the relation as of substance to accident, which crushes the individuality unless its influence is counteracted by the rights of private property.

Mr. Bellamy has with great artistic skill covered up the real difficulties of his scheme, giving it all the appearance of freedom of choice and spontaneous coöperation. He has carefully avoided all collisions that might arise in the system through the centrifugal influences of appetites and passions. In fact, there can hardly be said to be a single touch of human nature in the book; it is all political economy with a world of shadowy men and women in the background standing and sitting like the dummies in shop windows. Real human beings have other needs than food, clothing, and shelter. Were these things provided, as it were by magic, the chief difficulty after all would remain to be overcome. The definition of the limits of individuality, or rather the attainment of the higher individuality, which recognizes and uses the social whole as its instrument for perfection, just as it uses nature for the supply of its material wants, is the chief object. Individual man has learned how to use the results of his fellows, how to live their lives by learning of their experience, how to see nature and comprehend it through the results of their sense-perceptions and reflections, how to know his own as yet unrealized possibilities by seeing human nature revealed in the countless varieties of individuals in the entire race. This higher individuality is realized in our present civilization with enormous strides of progress. It contains socialistic results that infinitely surpass the possibilities of "Nationalistic Socialism" or any other "coöperative commonwealth," for it preserves all the freedom of self-determination in the individual, and at the same time connects him with all the world through the free play of individuality engaged in industry and commerce, so that all climes and all nations contribute to supply his wants through the world's market.

The age in which we now live is proclaimed to be an age of individualism and personal freedom. We have just completed a hundred years of protest against all manner of restraints and impediments to individual liberty. We have demanded that each citizen shall have his chance for a career, and that each shall be allowed to shape for himself the niche that he is to fill. We have insisted that the slave shall be declared a freeman and permitted to choose his vocation, make contracts with employers, or work for himself if he prefers—or refrain from work altogether, provided that he can render an equivalent for what he demands and receives from his fellow-men. The highest individualism is the ideal of our civilization; we look forward to greater and greater possibilities for each person in the way of conquest over nature. At a less expenditure of power he shall provide himself with food, clothing, and shelter in greater abundance. In fact, at the present rate of increase of productive power we shall average over $2.50 per day for each man, woman, and child, by Mr. Bellamy's year 2000 A.D. With present methods of distribution, this would make the average poor family in A.D. 2000 as well off as Mr. Bellamy supposes to be the case under his nationalistic syndicate. But considering the law of capital according to Carey and Bastiat,* the common laborer would be still better off at that remote epoch.

If we doubt the validity of our principle of individualism, we may test it by the oracles of religion and science. The Christian ideal which has made our civilization says in substance that God is divine-human, or that man is in the divine image because God is a self-conscious Reason. He creates nature in order to afford a cradle and place of nurture for human souls. He wishes each of these souls to reflect him in his perfections; to reflect his intellect, which knows all things in each thing and each in all; to reflect his will in doing good and "educing thence the better, and better thence again in infinite progression." According to this ideal, the world is no place for arrested development and for beings that exist only in a social whole which they do not at the same time reflect by their own self-activity. It is for individuals who are to develop continually in intellect and will and character.

This ideal is not merely an "other-worldly" aspiration of non-scientific enthusiasts; it is the sober conviction of natural science as it is and as it is becoming. To quote the words of Huxley, science looks upon nature and sees a "great progression from the formless to the formed; from the inorganic to the organic; from blind force to conscious intellect and will." Thus science makes the production of individuality the ultimate purpose of the world. The highest form is that which is self-forming, as intellect and will.

In the presence of this trend of our own civilization and of other civilizations, explained and confirmed by religion and science, we pause in surprise before a movement so reactionary as this one of Nationalistic Socialism, which insists on giving up the freedom of private property and competition that we have but recently secured, even for the slave, as a priceless boon.

For this system of freedom it would substitute a strict military system, in which the government is the sole will. Such a system as Mr. Bellamy describes in his book would prove in fact more repressive to individual development than any despotism of which we have any knowledge in recent times. We must bear in mind that the competitive system is a perpetual education in individuality,

---

* Henry C. Carey (1793–1879) was an American political economist and Philadelphia publisher. He formulated a capital *and* labor theory of value that emphasized the contribution of each to the economy. Carey also argued that, in a productive economy, workers' wages should rise faster than prices. Claude Frédéric Bastiat (1801–1850) was a French economist and satirist. His main work was *Economic Sophisms.* [Editor's note]

while the nationalistic system would be entirely devoid of such educative influence, except so far as it provoked its subjects to revolt or revolution. Mr. Bellamy himself intimates this characteristic now and then, but does not dwell on the theme. He says: "As for actual neglect of work, positively bad work, or other overt remissness on the part of men incapable of generous motives, the discipline of the industrial army is far too strict to allow much of that. A man able to do duty and persistently refusing, is cut off from all human society."

According to our system of letting the individual measure himself by his own deed, the personality of each one is respected in its integrity. According to all forms of Socialism—the patriarchal family, the tribe, the village community, the coöperative commonwealth—the individual is to have his wants supplied without reference to his capacity for production or his actual exertion, and yet he is to be perpetually under the judgment of his fellows as to his results, his real capacity, and his disposition. A tribunal that judges motives and disposition, going behind the overt act to do this, is the most fearful of all despotisms recorded in history. In the "reign of terror" suspicion governed the state; the overt act was set aside and disposition was the sole consideration. Disposition can never be known except through the overt act; beyond this it is all opinion or suspicion. Private property and free competition constitute the simple device by which civilization has been able to isolate individuals from one another and develop a sense of the sacredness of personality. Without this province for the free exercise of his will, and without a surrounding wall of privacy, the individual becomes attached to the social whole so closely that he can have no freedom of thought or action. An imperious public opinion watches all that he does or refrains from doing, and suspects any individual departure from the communal standard as treasonable in its intent. Wantonly to throw away these instrumentalities of our freedom is to throw away all that the race has gained for eighteen hundred years.

IV

THE PANTHEISM
QUESTION

Since every event in nature, according to Hegel, represented an expression of "the Divine Idea" or the mind of God, it could be concluded that nature itself was God. Hegel, of course, saw nature and its laws as evidence for the presence of a Divine Mind. His philosophy in the broadest sense was intended to prove the existence of God behind or beyond the appearances of nature. Indeed, nature itself was impossible without mind and especially the sustaining mind of God.

At the same time, in American eyes, Hegel was considered a German historicist or "higher critic" of the Bible. He was lumped in with scholars like David Friedrich Strauss, whose *Das Leben Jesu* (1835–56) was an attempt to establish scientifically the historical reality of Jesus the man and to see him not as divine but as God's model man who was worthy of imitation by other men. New England transcendentalist scholars like Theodore Parker and George Ripley were steeped in German religious historicism and theories of Christ the good man. Parker, though disagreeing with Strauss on many points, nonetheless borrowed the latter's title and theological approach for his greatest sermon, "The Transient and the Permanent in Christianity." Moncure Conway, one of the most important of the Ohio Hegelians, was greatly influenced by Parker and Ripley as well as by the work of Strauss, who himself owed an intellectual debt to Hegel. As Conway delivered his countless sermons in Washington and Cincinnati, it was easy for rival clergymen to see in his doctrines a German-influenced drift towards iconoclasm, atheism, or pantheism. As Kantian transcendentalism had done in New England, Hegelian perfectionism in the West alarmed traditional clergymen, who perversely turned Hegel's ideas upside down and labeled all Hegelians pantheists. Thus, ironically, what had been a continuation of the revolt against materialism was interpreted by conventional Protestants and Catholics alike as the very epitome of materialism—the worship of nature for its own sake.

At first, the American Hegelians were unaware of any real problem concerning pantheism. But under repeated attack they became extremely concerned. The readings that follow indicate the ways in which they speculated about the implications of Hegel's philosophy for traditional religion.

15

THE TEMPLE OF TRUTH

Peter Kaufmann

One of the more preeminent Ohio Hegelians was Peter Kaufmann, of Canton, Ohio. An immigrant from Germany who had been a teacher in the Rappite Community in Pennsylvania; a friend of Robert Dale Owen; and the founder of his own short-lived Utopian colony, "The Society of United Germans at Teutonia," Kaufmann was in a sense the Benjamin Franklin of the Hegelian Movement. As editor of a German-language newspaper, he also published countless almanacs, many of them bilingual, which sold in the hundreds of thousands. In 1838, he produced the widely distributed *A Treatise on American Popular Education,* which argued for German bilingual teaching. He also was active in politics and served as leader of the Cincinnati Workingman's Union. His *magnum opus,* however, was *The Temple of Truth, or the Science of Ever-Progressive Knowledge,* which appeared in 1858. *The Temple of Truth* grew out of Kaufmann's studies of Kant and Hegel which he grafted onto, not only utopianism, but the conventional Christian perfectionism of his day—as exemplified, *inter alia,* by the doctrines of Charles Grandison Finney, the major revival preacher of the era, who became president of Oberlin College. Kaufmann's book—naive, crude and labored as it was—commanded great attention. Its significance in the present context is as an indicator of the way in which Hegelianism, at least for a time, seemed to reinforce traditional religious ideas. In the essay below, for example, Kaufmann alludes to his chapter on "Dialectics" and sees the opposition between reason and nature as culminating in religion which was the way to "Absolute Truth." Clearly, he saw no pantheistic implications in Hegel's ideas.

Peter Kaufmann, *The Temple of Truth, or the Science of Ever-Progressive Knowledge* (Cincinnati and Canton, Ohio: 1858), pp. iii–iv.

IN the within volume, we hereby present to our NUMEROUS friends and the *truthseeking* part of the world at large, the *condensed result* of our most earnest and active *research* after ABSOLUTE TRUTH, prosecuted during a period of *thinking existence,* and amidst an interior and exterior *experience,* infinitely copious and multiform in *variegation,* in extent, and amount, of nearly *half a century* in duration. We feel great gratification in the possession of the immovable conviction, that we have neither lived, suffered, nor labored *in vain,* but have at last, in their *fullness, found* the foundation, elements, and skeleton theory of a system of absolute and unassailable truth, requiring now only for its extraneous actualization the noble spirited action, of clear heads and strong hearts. We consider that herein we have furnished not only what Archimedes demanded: the fulcrum whereon to place his lever; but also the lever itself, by the application of which, the mind of the age, panting for an all-sided and enduring progress, may henceforth lift the sluggish state of the world from its hinges of stagnancy, as likewise out of the vicious circle of motion whereinto, as it were, by an infernal magic, its movements seem, until now, to have charmedly been chained up, and upon a higher platform, where, it may forever move and rise "onward and upward." In surveying the line of concatenated thought, running from the beginning, to the closing sentence of this volume, the reader will perceive, that analysis forms the leading and most prominent feature in the whole of the mental operations that constitute the work. And, as the process of analysis, wherever duly consummated, is known and acknowledged, by all competent thinkers, to be the very essence and substance of what is called proof or demonstration: every idea exhibited in the book, must carry the impress of its irresistible self-evidence along with itself, until shown, that the analysis in its case, was performed defectively.

In casting our ken upon the past and present destiny of the human race, we discover the same to be, and always to have been, one of a mixed nature, combined of good and evil ingredients; but suffering and misery, in frightful shapes, to preponderate vastly at all times and everywhere, over happiness and true prosperity. Now, as every thing, as an effect, has a cause that constitutes its origin, the intellect is necessitated to endeavor to discover this grand cause of the general mischief. In examining then, as we have done (in Chapter XXII, on Dialectics, etc., and elsewhere), the primary sources and conditions of all human knowledge and existence, we have found the same to be but three in number, namely: Nature, Reason, and Religion. In Nature man physically exists, and is surrounded by it on all sides; by and with reason, or his thinking intellect, he knows that, which he knows, of nature and himself, whatever the kind or amount of such knowledge may be; and as nature and the individualized reason of the single man, exist conjointly with all beings extant, in a physical (by space), and an intellectual infinity (by the First Cause's omnipresent and eternal mind): man's reason can only know its own, nature's, and all other beings' and things' true being, nature, and condition, when clearly perceiving the absolute relation of each, to all surrounding infinity, and the laws that constitute its eternal statutes. This knowledge of infinity of eternity, being the focus or center, where all individual reason and intellect converges, is called Religion, and constitutes the science or philosophy of eternity.

Having thus proven that nature, reason, and religion, are equally the voice, a revelation of, and an emanation from, God, their common source and origin; we also proved that their nature and character is one of pure benignity, like absolute goodness, their divine cause, itself. Now, we are forced to further press the inquiry, by asking ourselves the question: in what mode and manner does it happen, and how does man contrive, that from these three divinely benignant sources, he gathers a crop so immeasurably richer in misery and sufferings, than in true happiness and joy? A brief, analytical statement of man's past and present mode of existence, and manner and kind of pursuits, will, if not the full answer to the query itself, at least furnish us the requisite materials for framing it in a satisfactory form. Man, everywhere, at all times, and in all things, is absolutely dependent on truth, that is, on his knowledge of, or insight into, the same. He brings not one single ray of such knowledge with him, when, as a helpless babe, entering existence. He finds the race he belongs to, split into nations, peoples, tribes, clans, castes, etc., all more or less unfriendly toward one another, not unfrequently destroying each other like ferocious beasts. He finds these nations and peoples again split up into numberless parties, factions, and sects of a political, ecclesiastical, scientific, or mixed nature, with correspondingly organized machineries to preserve and perpetuate their existence, and extend and fortify their power; warring hardly less fiercely with one another, than nations engaged in hostile conflict. And, finally, this state of split interests and actual antagonism, prevails again, more or less, between all the families and individuals, composing each of these larger sects or parties. Now, as this state of things is radically and diametrically just as much opposed to pure nature and true reason as to real religion; which all teach and preach to man peace, union, and harmony with himself and all creation: nations, sects, families, and individuals are thereby actually, more or less, at war, with one, the other, or both, or all three, of these divine (their only) sources of knowledge and existence; and, as far as they surrender their inmost light to this state of chaotic anarchy, become incapable of perceiving and comprehending the higher light, streaming conjointly from these trinal divine fountains. Hence, neither nations nor even individuals have, until now, understood the infinitely high aim and purpose of their existence and destination, and have, therefore, as a general rule, each pursued such self-chosen ends and objects, as temporal interest, desire, whim, and chance threw in their way, or circumstances and unbending necessity forced upon them. As thereby they become necessarily estranged from nature, reason, and living religion, committing sins and transgressions against the laws of each; these infractions of divine and eternal institutions are punished by an amount of misery and suffering corresponding to the turpitude and amount of the criminal action. And thus we can comprehend how man, by an abuse and perversion of things, forces, and institutions originally good and divine, can, from ignorance, imbecility, and frivolity draw poison, pain, and death, where his wisdom finds only honey, joy, and life.

In Chapter XXIII, we demonstrate apodictically, that the conjoint voices of reason, nature, and religion, unanimously declare: "All-sided perfection, forevermore ascending 'onward and upward,' to be man's and humanity's paramount and supreme aim, purpose, or end of existence." As soon as he aspires after this aim, he enters into incipient harmony with reason, nature, and God; and the evils theretofore pressing upon him, begin to diminish and disappear. But aspiring only singly and by disunited endeavors, the high aim can be reached merely in a subordinate degree, as likewise, for want of power, in some few points and directions only; but not at all in all others. Hence men have left but one of two alternatives; they must either unite and strive with conjointly irresistible power after perfection and the heaven flowing from it; or remain in their present split-up condition, forever a prey to its weakness, pains, sufferings, and horrors, as inevitable effects of a state, not in harmony, and at war with, themselves and all things else.

16

THE FINITE
AND THE INFINITE

Francis A. Henry

One of the most striking applications of Hegelian thought to the subject of Christianity was made by a young man only 23 years old, Francis A. Henry. The son of an Episcopal clergyman, he had not yet entered Berkeley Divinity School at Yale and embarked on his own long career as a minister when he published "The Finite and the Infinite" in the *Journal of Speculative Philosophy* for 1870. His refutation of the charges of pantheism leveled against Hegelians is extremely sophisticated and indicates a mastery of Hegel's thought. The article also indicates that the East had its Hegelians as well as the West.

Francis A. Henry, "The Finite and the Infinite," JSP 4 (1870): 294–99.

. . . But, it may be exclaimed, this co-existence of the Finite and the Infinite makes the Finite eternal, and so overthrows the doctrine of the Creation. Not at all; it only requires us to understand that doctrine. If the Creation of the universe be regarded as an effect of a creative fiat in time—an eternity anterior to this is presupposed. Some persons who perceive this, and are reluctant to admit a God eternally inactive, and a universe eternally nonexistent, think to solve the difficulty by asserting that God is eternally creative—that He creates from eternity to eternity. But this only removes the difficulty by a single step. If Creation proceed from creative fiat, at some time or other that fiat must have been spoken, and the question recurs, How was it *before?* The attempt to answer this question brings up the Infinite Progress again. Back of the creative act lies an eternity; at the beginning of this eternity we set another creative act; but then there arises a new eternity, to be antedated by a new creative act, and so on *ad infinitum.* It is the same thing with the future as with the past. God "creative to eternity" is God creating in succession; not creating the universe in one act, but working from world to world; and because space and time are endless, He can go on doing so forever. The creation of the universe cannot, then, be an act in time, unless we are to suppose an eternity when the universe was not, and when God was alone in the infinite void. Such a God may answer for Buddhism, but such is not the God of Christianity. What, then, is Creation? It is the objectivation of God's thought to Himself. As such it is certainly "from eternity," but not in the sense that you cannot reach the time when it began; for I must repeat once more that Eternity does not mean endless time, but *no* time; not progress towards an unreachable future, but rest in a perpetual present. God the Creator is, in that as in every aspect, God the Spirit; and the act of a spirit is thought. God creates like an Artist, not like a stone-mason. In the rare old Greek tongue only the Artist is called Creator, for he alone creates that which is spiritual—which, as St. John says, "abideth forever." The creation of the universe is co-incident and co-eternal with God's thought, and as to creation of particulars that is an affair of time, and as such it is continuous, and was by no means finished up as regards this planet six thousand years ago. As then the waters were gathered together, and the dry land appeared; as the earth brought forth grass, and herb, and fruit-tree; as the waters brought forth the moving creature that hath life, and the air was filled with the fowls that fly above the earth, and the earth with cattle, and creeping things, and beasts,—just so it is now: the rocks go on forming day by day, the minerals concrete, the waters work new ways, the forests spring up and are cut down, and all living creatures continue to be born and die. This emerging from and sinking in the vast billows of an ever-flowing sea is the very story of exist-ence. So far, then, from the Finite being made eternal, it appears to be that which has no permanence, whose being is altogether in succession.

Here it may be objected that this is to make the Creation a matter of necessity, which view savors of Pantheism. But if by creation be understood God's thought, no one need hesitate about its necessity. With Spirit, to think is to be, and you can as little relieve it from this "necessity" as you can a quadruped from the necessity of having four feet. On the other hand, if you suppose Creation an accidental circumstance—an exertion of arbitrary volition—you tolerate the supposition that God might just as well have been entirely solitary and entirely inactive; and such a God is simply no God at all. To conceive that existence only *happens* to be, to conceive it all super-fluous, and that there might just as well have been nothing at all, is to overlook this fact: in that God created the world, He demonstrated that abstract self-identity was not alone what constituted Him. As to Pantheism, so far from considering creation necessary, Pantheism declares it impossible. For the Pantheist there is nothing but the abstract Absolute, and the world of time and sense is not its immanent "otherness," but a *Maya* or delusion of the brain. The fact is that just this making Creation an indifferent thing—this making God the First and one of the universe, sufficient to Himself without the universe—may seem like piety, but *is* the essential principle of Pantheism. To stand by the abstract Infinite, or by the abstract Finite—to stand by the *one* to the exclusion of the *other*—this, as Mr. Mansel* correctly describes it . . . , is the position taken by Pantheism and by Atheism. The Universal by itself, without particulars, is Pure Being, or the Universal void; and Particulars by themselves, without the including Universal, are only Dependents cut from what they depend upon, which shrivel up and perish in our hands. The truth as against Pantheism and Atheism is *neither* the one *nor* the other, separately, but *both* sublated in each other. The true Absolute-Infinite contains the finite and relative; it is the Universal, and it is in the very notion of the universal that it involves the particular; that it be the All, and therefore every Each. To such as may fancy that this "unity of the finite and infinite" savors of Pantheism, I will say that, as matter of fact, Pantheism never came near enough to catch the faintest glimpse of this thought, and, further, that this thought overthrows Pantheism and treads it underfoot forever. But does the reader still shake his head dubiously and say: "Your doctrine nevertheless looks Pantheistical, or Atheistical, to me, for you make the Universe—the unity of Finite and Infinite—a self-existent, sufficient to itself; and you take the Beginning—the first cause of the universe—to be abstract Being, which you say is convertible with pure Nothing"? The explanation is very simple. This cannot be Pantheism, nor Atheism, for in all this there is no question of God. The Universe has the *form* of God, it is not God; it is thought, not the thinker; it is IS, not I AM. God is not The Infinite, but the Infinite one; He is not self-existence in

---

* Henry L. Mansel (1820–1871) was an English metaphysician and Anglican priest who held the Waynflete professorship of moral and metaphysical philosophy at Oxford. He was a Kantian and wrote the article on metaphysics for the eighth edition of the *Encyclopedia Britannica*. [Editor's note]

general, but the self-existent Singular. The dialectical evolution of Being through Negation after bringing us to the abstract Universal —the Infinite and the Finite, or Self and its Other—leads beyond this to Spirit or Personality—the concrete Universal—as the absolute thought and fact. The Universe is the equality of the Finite and the Infinite: so far as there is definite Being there is Infinite Being; or, there is only one Reality, the singleness of self-existence. But this is rather a single manifold than a single one; the extension and intension are coincident, but just *from this coincidence and equality* it results that there is a self-identical Many rather than a self-identical One. What is present is, therefore, Otherness in general, or a universal Being-for-Other, which, because it is *a single* Being-for-Other, is more properly Being-for-One. That is, the Singleness of the determination sublates the Otherness. "The Universal is necessarily *for*-One, but it is not for-*Another;* the one for which it is, is only itself." That is, the One is *for-itself* just because that which is *for-it* is nothing other than itself. To try another statement, Thought, or Reason, is the *implicit* or In-Itself of Nature; or, if one chooses, Nature is the *explicit* or Out-of-Itself of Thought; for the Universal is just this Inward-and-Outward, and as much one as the other. Thought, then, is Existence *in-itself*, Nature is existence *for-itself*, or objectivated to Thought, and Spirit is the whole truth of existence, at once *in-itself* and *for-itself*. This is the way, and the only way, that Nature can lead to Nature's God. No so-called arguments from design to prove an intelligent Creator of the universe have been worth the paper they were written on. Impersonal thought is all that Nature evidences to the sense-understanding; and seed-thought is scarcely a higher principle than seed-matter. Abstract Idealism and abstract Materialism are only the two forms of Pantheism—that is, of direct and indirect Atheism. Now just as Nature is the Out-being of Thought, so the unity of these two—the absolute Universal—is the Out-being of the absolute Spirit, which is thus absolute Subject and absolute Object. This may be stated thus: the Ego is, *first*, self-relation, simple identity, or In-Itself; *secondly*, the Ego discerns itself, distinguishes itself, others itself; this Otherness is, as contrasted with the first phase, its being Out-of-Itself, and, since the Othering is a making itself an object to itself, it is also its being For-Itself; *thirdly*, the Ego returns from Otherness, returns from the distinction in which it was set as a For-Itself to be discerned, back to the In-Itself, the discerner; but it carries back with it and retains this explication of itself; it is now Identity *and* Diversity, the Universal *and* the Particular, at once *in* and *for* itself. This is, of course, only logical analysis of an immanent process. There is no such thing as an Ego which is first of all *in* itself, then *for* itself, and then *in and for* itself, but it is *always* in this last or complete state of being.*

As to the difficulty about the Beginning, Pure Being is merely the *logical prius* of the universe, not the *actual prius*. The Immediate is the first in the order of abstract thought, but the Self-mediating is the first in the order of reality. The true Beginning of the universe is the self-thinking of Spirit, and this is also the end, or, more truly, there is neither beginning nor ending to the eternal Thought of God, the eternal IS of the eternal I AM. If this be Pantheism, it is such as is taught by St. John. "In the beginning was the Word, and the Word was with God, and the Word was God. The same was in the beginning with God. All things were made by him, and without him was not anything made that was made." *In* the beginning was the Word; there never was even a beginning when the Word was not. That is, the absolute Voice was and is *always* a speaking Voice. And not only is the Word *with* the Voice, but the Word *is* the Voice. For what is a voice which does not utter itself? And what is the vocalization but the voice itself?

As I have said, the subject-matter of philosophy and of religion is the same; the sole question involved in each is that of the spiritual interests of man, and philosophy has value only as it clarifies our faith and strengthens our convictions in the truths of religion. That

---

* Thoroughly to think is to think God, for to think is to seek an explanation, and *the* explanation of all, however we name it, is God. Thus the history of philosophy is only a history of the explication of the Divine Idea. Descartes, Spinoza, Locke, are all concerned with the One, the absolute as such, Substantiality, or the In-Itself of Spirit; Hume considers the transition to Many, Causality, or the For-Itself of Spirit; Kant establishes the truth of this interrogative suggestion by adding the notion of Reciprocity to the other two; and lastly Hegel takes up this tritheism into the trinity-in-unity of Self-determination. This is the most general statement of Hegel's derivation from Kant. Kant altered the relative positions of Subject and Object by showing that the Subject is necessary to the Object, that the Objective is in fact conditioned by the Subjective—for this was Kant's notion of the Categories. The Category, then, the essential form of Thought, is the middle ground between Subject and Object, and the truth of these is their necessary relation. Hegel carries out and completes this view. It is an error, he says, to regard this reciprocity as a relation somehow external to the Subject and Object, a view which would leave these standing by themselves as separable and independent, for this relation is rather their organic movement, and in it alone they have their being. In fact, the distinction into Subject and Object is a purely logical or formal one. What we have to do with is not two separates and their relation—Subject, Object, Reciprocity—but One inseparable in its immanent distinction—Spirit, Self-determination.

is the spirit which searcheth all things, yea, the deep things of God. Nor is such achievement a small matter, or its value trifling. Christianity is the revelation of the Infinite and Divine, not as an abstract ideal but as the veritable concrete truth, the great and only reality. . . .

17

PANTHEISM, OR GOD
THE UNIVERSE

William Torrey Harris

The selection below is a reply by William Torrey Harris to Laurens P. Hickok, retired president of Union Theological Seminary and perhaps the foremost Kantian theologian of his day. Hickok, who perceived the power and validity of German rationalism at a time when most of his fellow Presbyterian theologians, such as James McCosh at Princeton and Noah Porter at Yale, were still arguing for "common sense" religion, skirted dangerously close to pantheism in many of his theological works. The book that drew forth Harris's rejoinder, *The Logic of Reason* (1875), was Hickok's last book. In it he clearly acknowledged the pantheistic risks of German rationalism as a warning to those theologians who would uncritically accept its assumptions and its logic. He also implied that the post-Kantian German philosophers had carried things too far in the direction of pantheism. Harris's rebuttal, therefore, is also a defense of Hegel and the post-Kantians as against a Kantian position, with pantheism as the specific example at issue.

William Torrey Harris, "Pantheism, or God the Universe," *JSP* 9 (1875): 328–334.

A CORRESPONDENT calls attention to our notice of "The Logic of Reason," by Dr. Hickok, in the last number of this journal, and supports the position taken in that work against "Transcendental Logic," including under that term logic as developed in the systems of Kant, Fichte, Schelling, and Hegel. He characterizes Transcendental Logic as resulting in a system whose highest principle is a "totality of all potentialities, things, and men," a totality which "is but an abstract generalization from experience," though known as the idea of the Universe and taken as self-determining thought-activity, and so a divine Ideal at the source and centre of the Universe in actual evolution is still found and put there in logical deduction from empirical observation. The "God of the Universe," he thinks, according to this view, would be "one with the universe, and our philosophy and theology must determine themselves accordingly. Our speculation is [i.e. would thus be] our thinking out God's thought in its process of universal development, and our theology is [would be] the thought of God as a logical process unfolding the universe as a becoming through perpetual beginnings *à parte ante,* and perpetual ceasings *à parte post.*"

"To be satisfactory to reason," he thinks, "we must find a God independent of the universe, intelligibly competent to begin and cease action in the known right and claim of what intrinsically he is, and so an originator of his own ideals, and a creator by expressing his ideals in steadfast, universal forces."

To assert that the Transcendental Logic, as conceived by either one of the thinkers above named, is "but an abstract generalization from experience," is, of course, the most direct repudiation of the claims that they one and all set up for their systems. It was Kant who taught us how to recognize *à priori* ideas by the criteria of *universality* and *necessity.* The *à priori* ideas of the mind are the logical conditions of experience, and hence cannot be derived *from* experience, but are rather the presuppositions of it. Upon this basis —established by Kant—Fichte, Schelling, and Hegel erected their systems and set up their claims to announce therein the logical conditions of experience, the conditioning laws of empirical existence in time and space. Indeed, the clear perception of the implication of universality and necessity in ideas constitutes the great merit of the system of Dr. Hickok. Such sweeping repudiation of the claims of those thinkers to found their systems on an *à priori* basis ought therefore to exhibit with some detail the grounds which justify it. We will not attempt to declare that these systems are not understood, by many readers, in the sense defined by our correspondent. No doubt, every thinker who has reached only the stand-point of the lower stages of reflection will see in all systems that he reads only an empirical connection. He will also find only arbitrary links between the premises and conclusions of Dr. Hickok, because his mind is incapable of making the synthesis or combination required to follow the thoughts of that thinker. The inability to see the necessary connection between the members of a system does not prove that such necessity is not there. Still less does it prove that it is there. But if the author claims to see it, and if his claim is verified by the ability of others to see it, the claim should be refuted by showing that there can be no such necessary connection as that claimed, because another and a different necessity prevails.

Of course, he who verifies the claim of the author, and finds necessity where the author asserts it, cannot be convinced except by demonstration to the contrary. He does not simply hold an *opinion*, but has an insight, or at least thinks that he has, and will be moved from it only by a clearer perception of a necessity annulling the former one.

But we apprehend that this charge against Transcendental Logic, that it reaches only an empirical universality, is based upon a misconception of the claims of the system. This, of course, we must say with due deference. It is simply a matter of individual interpretation. We ourselves confess to have found the systems of thought as established by Kant, Fichte, Schelling, and Hegel, something—we will not say *altogether*, but something *essentially* different from what Dr. Hickok makes of them. And yet we must accredit to his own system a genuine speculative basis.—Inasmuch as our correspondent differs from us in the interpretation which he gives to Hegel and the others—following Dr. Hickok in this—it will, perhaps, be most conducive to mutual understanding to state on our part what we hold, and what we believe those thinkers hold. It frequently happens that two persons hold the same views, but neither can recognize them in the technique of the other.

1. We hold (and believe Hegel to hold) that we possess universal and necessary ideas (and may possess them consciously), and that these universal and necessary ideas are the logical conditions of our experience, and also logical conditions of the existence of objects in time and space.

2. We hold (and conceive Hegel to have demonstrated) that each thought or idea is a product of the self-determination of mind, and that each thought or idea as determined implies other thoughts or ideas as its definition or limitation: hence that it is implied in each thought that the mind, being self-determined in this process, can go from any one thought to any or all others simply by tracing out the implied limitation or definition by means of other thoughts. Hence all thought is a system expressed or implied. The complete evolution of the necessary connection implied in ordinary thinking is pure science. If all definition or limitation of thought is through others coördinate with it, then the system of science must necessarily be incapable of being exhausted; the process is an indefinite one, and never can reach a first principle. On the other hand, if a thought or idea can be reached which involves no limitation or

determination by means of other thought—in other words, is above and beyond multiplicity—we shall have only an abstract unity cut off from all relation to other thoughts, and hence by its very terms impossible: for by supposition it was to have been reached by tracing out the implied relations or determinations of other thoughts, and thus was necessarily to contain the relations by which it was found.

3. An actual realization of this systematic thinking-out of implied determinations and relations of thought we hold (and Hegel seems to have consciously attempted this realization) will result, if applied first to our ordinary consciousness—our sensuous certitude—in discovering one by one the presuppositions of our civilization: the practical and theoretical wants and needs of each stage of consciousness will unfold à priori, but the wherewith these wants and needs have been historically supplied must be sought for and recognized in history itself. This process of unfolding and developing presuppositions and recognizing the same in the world of time and space is twofold, involving in its analysis universality and necessity, in its recognition only empirical verification. "Such a want or presupposition necessarily exists, thus and so it seems actually to have been supplied." This is intended as a description of the process of Hegel's "Phenomenology of Mind." It is a recognition of the necessity of Reason (and by Reason is not meant Intellect alone, but also Will) as the explanation of all phenomena in time and space. The world is finally seen to be not the Absolute, but essentially a Revelation; and now we are ready to investigate the problem, "Of what is the World a Revelation?" Here we come to a different science, if you will. Hegel calls it Logic. The universality and necessity of ideas themselves shall now be investigated, and not the real presuppositions of consciousness. Ideas shall be investigated to find what relations or implications they have among themselves. In this investigation we must begin with the simplest. If we do not, we shall soon come to the simplest, on account of the necessity of analysis to take an inventory of the determinations of each idea. Our system then will sooner or later find its beginning in the simplest idea and pursue a synthetical course, finding that the simple idea implies another for its definition or necessary limitation in thought; and having found this other, adding the same to the former as being necessary to the thought of that former—both being implied in the thinking of either. The synthesis here made is an explicit one, and will be found to have its name as a distinct thought or idea—the ordinary consciousness using it, unconscious either of its constituent determinations or of higher presuppositions which it will be found

to have in union with others. Here, therefore, even in Pure Science or Logic there is an empirical activity to be discovered. A synthesis of two thoughts having been discovered as *necessary*, it is requisite to consider empirically what name has been applied in language as a historical affair to a thought or idea corresponding to this definition. Empiricism in this sense is not to be denied; and were its denial possible, we should be obliged to confess that the science of pure thought thus established had, or at least showed, no relation whatever to the actual world of thought, to the ideas and scientific activity of the race. Such a confession would acknowledge the science of pure thought to be no science of thought as it actually exists, but something else of no possible interest to man, any more than the succession of notions in the mind of a lunatic.

4. The outcome of such science of pure thought we hold to be necessarily one result: (*a*) The discovery that all ideas of being or immediate existence are in synthesis with others or their *altera*, and the net result of this synthesis is to find that such beings or somewhats are sides of relations, and that Relation is the truth of them and their explanation. They exist only in transition, they are dependent beings, and mutual dependence is their essence. Here we come, therefore, to consider the idea of Relation. (*Note*, it may be remarked that the natural science of the day has come to this basis.) (*b*) Relative existence, that which is only in relation— called "reflected existence," because it is only the appearance or reflection of something else—investigated, proves to be insufficient by itself. All phases of relation—and these include matter and form, force and manifestation, as well as causal and substantial relations —presuppose as their logical condition a self-determining being. We learn by this investigation that all predicates of relation such as cause, or substance, or force, &c. &c., are inadequate when applied to the First Principle; but our investigation at this stage would not have discovered what the First Principle is, except that it is self-determined. (*c*) Investigation of the presuppositions of self-determined being: It is found that self-determined being involves duality (action upon itself by itself) and unity. It involves self-externality, but also recovery of itself from self-externality—otherwise it would be one of two sides, a positive *or* a negative, a *this* to some *that*. It must be its *own* other, its own *negative*, its *own* determination. But thus it implies life, cognition, and will. But these three as isolated and sundered are finite and inadequate: they can neither of them be the highest principle. A life which did not know itself would be implicit, and have presuppositions beyond itself both as regards motives and potentialities and as its energizing principle. These

must become actual in cognition and will in order that life may become explicit—its own object. Cognition by itself remains a dualism. Only in its highest potence is it self-determining absolutely, and then it is pure will. Will devoid of cognition sinks back to mere Life, and becomes the external impulse called instinct. Neither is the mere union of these in one person adequate. Man as individual unites these, but in a finite manner. These must be in absolute identity in order to be adequate, and in order that self-determination may be perfect. The Absolute Idea, the Highest Principle, or God, then, must be this union of life, knowledge, and will, each in its perfection and in such identity that each is the other; so that to know is to will and to will is to know, and so that the immediateness of life belongs to it. Now, of course, this is transcendental inasmuch as it cannot possibly be derived from experience; but it is a necessary result of the dialectical examination of ideas in search of one that is adequate for a first principle, or, in other words, to find an idea that does not presuppose something else upon which it depends. Herewith logic as pure science ends, for it has found the object of its search—it has found the adequate Idea, the Eternal Being.

Now, what relation has nature and finite spirit to the Absolute? They certainly cannot be confounded one with the other so long as one has in mind the proved inadequacy of all categories of nature and spirit when set up for first principles. It is manifest that in the Absolute Idea alone we are to find the sufficient reason for nature and man. In God, knowing and willing are one. Hence He is essentially Creator. But not from any external constraint; not from Necessity, or Fate; but solely through freedom and because of freedom. Were He in any way necessitated, were there other being independent and alien to Him, He could not be creative. His self-knowledge is therefore the creation of the world, and of man as an image, object, or reflection of Himself. The World or created Universe is not God, but his Image, his Reflection, his Creation. If we analytically separate any phase or element of the universe and consider it, still less is it God—it is not even his Image. The imperfect concept of freedom as the deliberative state wherein one can do or not do anything is to blame for this difficulty in thinking the Absolute freedom of God. Instead of adding anything to the perfection of God, to conceive him as capable of creating, or refusing to create, we annul his essential attributes. For, why should the person hesitate when he sees absolutely the one best way, and nothing hinders him from doing it? Will and cognition are separate in man because both are imperfect in him.

Again, the idea that God is a Becoming never could be a clear thought. For that which renders possible a becoming is the separation of the ideal and real. There must be something potential and not real in God if he is a Becoming. But time alone separates the potential from its realization. Now in the past there has been indefinite time, and more than sufficient for the realization of all that is potential. Hence the Absolute must have become all that it could, and that, too, long ago—even from eternity. But the world—creation—as His image or reflection, must exhibit progress and becoming. For out of Chaos He creates the semblance of eternal reason, and this He does eternally in order that He may behold a reflection of Himself in the place of Chaos. As a whole, it does not become; for all stages of its progress were realized from eternity. But any given phase or stage of existence exhibits a progress or struggle toward the more perfect realization of God's reflection. Thus the inorganic gives place to the organic, plant to animal, animal to man, man the savage to man the human. The final link of this progressive scale of the reflection of God is man as spirit; for man possesses the capacity of infinite progress through self-activity. He can make not only the external and temporal a sensuous reflection of God, but he can reflect God in his holy will and in his intellectual vision of truth. He can by self-activity come to union with God. This is a self-activity which involves abnegation of self—a yielding up of naturalness, and an assumption of the forms of truth and of the divine will in place of selfishness and finite knowing; hence it is called a process of divine grace, although it is the very acme of self-activity in the individual—his highest freedom, in fact.

Again, this highest reflection of God as it appears in the human spirit cannot by any possibility be confined to one epoch of time and to one globe in the universe. It is necessarily the goal of all creation, and must have been realized from all eternity, so that the stream of souls coming into time and attaining to immortal existence is perpetual and always has been. Herein is the realization in the world of the reflection of the mystery of the Trinity, that God, though one and absolute and the only, yet is personal and spiritual, and demands from eternity recognition of Himself in others; and hence exists as Three Persons, who are yet One God. Thus God's creative activity has the effect to continually produce independent immortal beings, who become more independent and self-active and free the more they realize Him in their lives and thus become one with Him.

This we believe to be Hegel's view of the relation of Creator and Creation, although very imperfectly and hastily stated. He makes God transcendent over Nature, and free and non-identical with aught in Nature except what comes by its own conscious activity (as man does) into concrete identity with Him. And yet Nature reflects, in various degrees, Him. Its lower phases reflect His mechanical power, force, &c. &c.; His self-determination is reflected in various degrees from the crystal up to the self-moving animal. His Will and Intellect and Heart are reflected in various degrees in human history. But all of these are as nought beside the actuality of Him. Their own inadequateness is the negative principle which destroys them and makes them evanescent. Each link, compared with the one next below, is a manifestation of creative Reason, causing the higher to rise from the lower; but compared with its ideal it is inadequate, and gives way to another. Man only because he possesses conscious will preserves his identity in this progress.

Man is not a "logical machine," nor a machine at all. A free machine is a self-contradictory concept. Man's highest ideal is to realize a cognition adequate to his will and life, and to realize the latter in the former. This ideal, when realized, will be free in the highest sense. In fact, the thought of absolute freedom involves this identity of will and cognition, and is not possible on any other terms.

A Life which is so full and perfect that it includes all possibilities is a necessary one (in the sense Kant speaks of Necessity as the union of reality and possibility), for there is nothing else possible to it. In this sense, God's life and cognition and will and freedom, and other attributes, are necessary. They realize the entire sphere of possibility. If water could be ice and liquid and vapor all at once, it would become less a contingent being. Ordinarily, two of its states are potential.

As in the above we have not attempted to give any account of the *à priori* dialectical process which we have asserted to exist in pure science, we may be permitted to refer to two articles upon this point already published in this Journal: "On Hegel's Philosophic Method" (January, 1874) and "Trendelenburg and Hegel" (January, 1875).

18

SCIENCE, PANTHEISM, AND IDEALISM

George Holmes Howison

The one professor in the St. Louis Movement was George Holmes Howison, a mathematician and teacher of political economy at Washington University in St. Louis. His close contact with the local Hegelians turned him toward a distinguished career in philosophy, climaxed by his twenty-five years as head of the Philosophy Department at the University of California. Though he eventually forged his own theories of personal idealism, Howison also brought Hegel to California. Having been originally educated for the ministry and then later as a teacher of mathematics, Howison had a professional interest in both religion and science. In the excerpts below, from a paper which he delivered at the Concord School of Philosophy in the summer of 1885, Howison deals methodically with fundamental questions in both science and religion from an essentially Hegelian point of departure. The lecture was entitled "Is Modern Science Pantheistic?" and it explored the overarching question of the Gilded Age—what hope was there for spiritual and moral values in an era dominated by science, technology, and materialism?

George Holmes Howison, "Is Modern Science Pantheistic?", JSP 19 (1885): 367–69, 375–84.

THE RELATION OF PANTHEISM TO
MATERIALISM AND IDEALISM

IT will aid us in a correct apprehension of pantheism if we appreciate its relations to other anti-theistic forms of philosophy, particularly to materialism, and to what is known as subjective idealism. It will become clear that it forms a higher synthesis of thought than either of these. Its conception of the world may be read out either in materialistic or idealistic terms; and this is true whether we take it in its atheistic or its acosmic form. Yet, on a first inspection, this hardly seems to be the case. On the contrary, one is at first quite inclined to identify its first form with materialism outright, and to recognize in its second form a species of exaggerated spiritualism; and hence to contrast the two forms as the materialistic and the idealistic. Further reflection does not entirely do away with this mistake, for the apparent identity of atheistic pantheism with materialism is very decided; and the only correction in our first judgment that we next feel impelled to make is to recognize the double character of acosmic pantheism. The one and only Universal Substance, in order to include an exhaustive summary of all the phenomena of experience, must be taken, no doubt, as both extending and being conscious. But is the Universal Substance an extended being that thinks? or is it a thinking being that apprehends itself under a peculiar mode of consciousness called extension? In other words, is the thinking of the one Eternal Substance grounded in and mediated by its extended being? or has its extension existence only in and through its thinking? Which attribute is primary and essential, and makes the other its derivative and function? Under the conception of the sole existence of the Absolute, the question is inevitable, irresistible, and irreducible. It thus becomes plain that, to say nothing of a third hypothesis of the mutually independent parallelism of the two attributes, acosmic pantheism may carry materialism as unquestionably as it carries idealism, though not, indeed, so naturally or coherently. And sharper inquiry at last makes it equally clear that atheistic pantheism will carry idealism as consistently as it carries materialism, if doubtless less naturally. For, although in the sum-total of the particular existences there must be recognized a gradation from such existences as are unconscious up to those that are completely conscious, and although it would be the more natural and obvious view to read the series as a development genetically upward from atoms to minds, still the incomprehensibility of the transit from the unconscious to the conscious cannot fail to suggest the counter-hypothesis, and the whole series may be conceived as originating ideally in the perceptive constitution and experience of the conscious members of it. There is, however, a marked distinction between the two orders of idealism given, respectively, by the acosmic pantheism and by the atheistic: the former, grounded in the consciousness of the Universal Substance, has naturally a universal and, in so far, an *objective* character; the latter has no warrant except the thought in a particular consciousness, and no valid means of raising this warrant even into a common or general character, much less into universality; it is accordingly particular and *subjective*. Pantheism, then, in both its forms, is not only a more comprehensive view of the world than either materialism or any one-sided idealism, whether abstractly universal or only subjective, inasmuch as it makes either of them possible; but it is also a deeper and more organic view, because it does bring in, at least in a symbolic fashion, the notion of a universal in some vague sense or other. This advantage, however, it does not secure with any fulness except in the acosmic form. Indeed, the atheistic form is so closely akin to the less organic theories of materialism and subjective idealism that we may almost say we do not come to pantheism proper until we pass out of the atheistic sort and find ourselves in the acosmic. An additional gain afforded by pantheism, and eminently by acosmic pantheism, is the conception of the intimate union of the First Principle with the world of particular phenomena; the creative cause is stated as spontaneously manifesting its own nature in the creation; it abides immanently in the latter, and is no longer conceived as separated from it and therefore itself specifically limited in space and in time, as it is conceived in the cruder dualistic and mechanical view of things, with which human efforts at theological theory so naturally begin. . . .

WHY SHOULD MODERN SCIENCE GIVE ALARM OF PANTHEISM?

It is urgent, then, to inquire if there is anything in the nature of modern science that really gives color to the pantheistic view. It is obvious enough that there are not wanting philosophers, or even schools of philosophy, who read pantheism in science as science appears to them. But the real question is: Is such a reading the authentic account of the teachings of science itself? Here we must not mistake the utterances of men of science for the unadulterated teachings of science; for, on this borderland of science and philosophy, it need not be surprising if men familiar with only that method of investigation which science pursues, and not at home in the complex and varied history of philosophical speculation, should sometimes, or even often, be inclined to a hasty inference when the borderland is reached, and, overlooking the fact that their science and its method have necessary limits, take that view in philosophy which the illegitimate extension of their method would indicate. Disregarding, then, the mere opinions of certain cultivators of science, we are here to ask the directer, more searching and more pertinent question, What is there—if, indeed, there be anything—in the nature of science itself, as science is now known—what are the elements in it and its method, that might be taken to point toward a pantheistic interpretation of the universe and its Source?

And to this it must in all candor be answered that, both in the method of modern science and in the two commanding principles that have legitimately resulted from that method, there is that which unquestionably *suggests* the pantheistic view. Nothing less than the most cautious discrimination, founded on a precise and comprehensive knowledge of the course of philosophical inquiry, can detect the exact reach, the limits, and the real significance of this suggestion, or expose the illegitimacy of following it without reserve. The trait to which I am now referring in the *method* of science is its rigorously experimental and observational character; indeed, its strictly empirical or tentative character. And the two commanding *results*, which now in turn play an organizing part in the subsidiary method of all the sciences, are (1) the principle of the conservation of energy, and (2) the principle of evolution manifesting itself in the concomitant phenomenon of natural selection—the struggle of each species with its environment for existence, and the survival of the fittest. The apparent implications of this method and of these two principles accordingly deserve, and must receive, our most careful present attention.

How, then, does the experimental, or, more accurately, the empirical, method of science suggest the doctrine of pantheism? By limiting our serious belief to the evidence of experience—exclusively to the evidence of the senses. The method of science demands that nothing shall receive the high credence accorded to science, except it is attested by the evidence of unquestionable presentation in sensible experience. All the refinements of scientific method—the cautions of repeated observation, the probing subtleties of experiment, the niceties in the use of instruments of precision, the principle of reduction to mean or average, the allowance for the "personal equation," the final casting out of the largest mean of possible errors in experiment or observation, by such methods, for instance, as that of least squares—all these refinements are for the single purpose of making it certain that our basis of evidence shall be confined to what has actually been present in the world of sense; we are to know beyond question that such and such conjunctions of events have *actually* been present to the senses, and precisely *what* it is that thus remains indisputable fact of sense, after all possible additions or misconstructions of our mere thought or imagination have been cancelled out. Such conjunctions in unquestionable sense-experience, isolated and purified from foreign admixture by carefully contrived experiment, we are then to raise by generalization into a tentative expectation of their continued recurrence in the future—*tentative* expectation, we say, because the rigor of the empirical method warns us that the act of generalization is a step beyond the evidence of experience, and must not be reckoned any part of science, except as it continues to be verified in subsequent experience of the particular event. Thus natural science climbs its slow and cautious way along the path of what it calls the laws of nature; but it gives this name only in the sense that there has been a constancy in the conjunctions of past experience, a verification of the tentative generalization suggested by this, and a consequent continuance of the same tentative expectancy, which, however, waits for renewed verification, and refrains from committing itself unreservedly to the absolute invariability of the law to which it refers. Unconditional universality, not to say necessity, of its ascertained conjunctions natural science neither claims nor admits.

Now, to a science which thus accepts the testimony of experience with this undoubting and instinctive confidence that never stops to inquire what the real grounds of the possibility of experience itself may be, or whence experience can possibly derive this infallibility of evidence, but assumes, on the contrary, that the latter is underived and immediate—to such a science it must seem that we have, and can have, no verifiable assurance of any existence but the Whole—the mere aggregate of sense-presented particulars hitherto actual or yet to become so. Thus the very method of natural science tends to obliterate the feeling of the transcendent, or at least to destroy its credit at the bar of disciplined judgment, and in this way to bring the votary of natural investigation to regard the Sum of Things as the only reality.

On this view, the outcome of the scientific method might seem to be restricted to that form of pantheism which I have named the atheistic. Most obviously, the inference would be to materialism, the lowest and most natural form of such pantheism; yet subtler reasoning, recognizing that in the last resort experience must be consciousness, sees, in the subjective idealism which states the Sum of Things as the aggregate of the perceptions of its conscious members, the truer fulfilment of the method that presupposes the sole and immediate validity of experience. But beyond even this juster idealistic construction of atheistic pantheism—beyond *either* form of atheistic pantheism, in fact—the mere method of natural science would appear to involve consequences which, even granting the legitimacy of belief in the transcendent, would render the transcendent God the sole reality—that is, would bring us to acosmic pantheism. For the empirical method, so far from vindicating either the freedom of the personal will or the immortality of the soul, withholds belief from both, as elements that can never come within the bounds of possible experience; so that the habit of regarding nothing but the empirically attested as part of science dismisses these two essential conditions of man's reality beyond the pale of true knowledge, and into the discredited limbo of unsupported assumptions.

It is, however, not until we pass from the bare method of natural science to its two great modern consequences, and take in their revolutionary effect as subsidiaries of method in every field of natural inquiry, that we feel the full force of the pantheistic strain which pulls with such a tension in many modern scientific minds. It is in the principle of the conservation of energy, and in that of evolution, particularly as viewed under its aspect of natural selection, that we encounter the full force of the pantheistic drift. And it seems, at the first encounter, irresistible. That all the changes in the universe of objective experience are resolvable into motions, either molar or molecular; that, in spite of the incalculable variety of these changes of motion, the sum-total of movement and the average direction of the motions is constant and unchangeable; that an unvarying correlation of all the various modes of motion exists, so that each is convertible into its correlate at a constant numerical rate, and so that each, having passed the entire circuit of correlated forms, returns again into its own form undiminished in amount: all this seems to point unmistakably to a primal energy—a ground-form of moving activity—one and unchangeable in itself, immanent in but not transcendent of its sum of correlated forms, while each instance of each form is only a transient and evanescent mode of the single reality. Nor, apparently, is this inference weakened by the later scholium upon the principle of the conservation of energy, known as the principle of the dissipation of energy. On the contrary, the pantheistic significance of the former principle seems to be greatly deepened by this. Instead of a constant whole of moving activity, exhibited in a system of correlated modes of motion, we now have a vaster correlation between the sum of actual energies and a vague but prodigious mass of potential energy—the "waste-heap," as the physicist Balfour Stewart has pertinently named it, of the power of the universe. Into this vast "waste-heap" all the active energies in the world of sense seem to be continually vanishing, and to be destined at last to vanish utterly: we shift, under the light of this principle of dissipation, from a primal energy, immanent, but not transcendent, to one immanent in the sum of correlated actual motions, and also transcendent of them. Very impressive is the view that here arises of a dread Source of Being that engulfs all beings; it is Brahm again, issuing forth through its triad Brahma, Vishnu, and Siva—creation, preservation, and annihilation—to return at last into its own void, gathering with it the sum of all its transitory modes. And let us not forget that the conceptions out of which this image of the One and All is spontaneously formed are the ascertained and settled results of the science of nature in its exactest empirical form.

When to this powerful impression of the principle of conservation, as modified by that of dissipation, we now add the proper effect of the principle of evolution, the pantheistic inference appears to gather an overpowering weight, in no way to be evaded. As registered in the terms of a rigorous empirical method, evolution presents the picture of a cosmic Whole, constituted of varying members descended from its own primitive form by differentiations so slight and gradual as not to suggest difference of origin or distinction in kind, but, on the contrary, to indicate clearly their kinship and community of origin. Still, these differentiations among the members, and the consequent differences in their adaptation to the Whole, involve a difference in their power to persist amid the mutual competition which their common presence in the Whole implies. In this silent and unconscious competition of tendencies to persist, which is called, by a somewhat exaggerated metaphor, the struggle for existence, the members of the least adaptation to the Whole must perish earliest, and only those of the highest adaptation will finally survive. So, by an exaggeration akin to that of the former metaphor, we may name the resulting persistence of the members most suited to the Whole the survival of the fittest; and as it is the Whole that determines the standard of adaptation, we may also, by figuratively personifying the Whole, call the process of antagonistic interaction through which the survivors persist a process of natural selection. Here, now, the points of determinative import for inference are these: that the "survival" is only of the *fittest to the Whole*; that it is the Whole alone that "selects"; that no "survival," as verified to the strictly empirical method, can be taken as permanent, but that even the latest must be reckoned as certified only to date, with a reservation, at best, of "tentative expectancy" for hope of continuance; that "natural selection," *as empirically verified*, is a process of cancellation, a selection only to death; and that the Whole alone has the possibility of final survival.

The "tentative expectation" founded on the entire sweep of the observed facts, and not extended beyond it, would be that the latest observed survivor, man, is destined, like his predecessors, to pass away, supplanted by some new variation of the Whole, of a higher fitness to it. And so on, endlessly.

This clear pointing, by an empirically established and empirically construed doctrine of evolution, toward the One-and-All that swallows all, seems to gain further clearness still when the principles of conservation and of evolution are considered, as they must be, in their inseparable connection. They work in and through each other. Conservation and correlation of energy, and their "rider" of dissipation, are in the secret of the mechanism of the process of natural selection, with its deaths and its survivals; evolution is the field, and its resulting forms of existence, more and more complex, are the outcome of the operations of the correlated, conserved, and dissipated energies; and, in its principle of struggle and survival, evolution works in its turn in the very process of the correlation, dissipation, and conservation of energy. It therefore seems but natural to identify the potential energy—the "waste-heap" of power —of correlation with the Whole of natural selection. And thus we appear to reach, by a cumulative argument, the One and Only in which all shall be absorbed.

If we now add to these several indications, both of the method and of the two organic results of modern science, the further weighty discredit that the principles of conservation and evolution appear to cast upon the belief in freedom and immortality, the pantheistic tone in modern science will sound out to the full. This discredit comes, for human free-agency, from the closer nexus that the correlation of forces seems plainly to establish between every possible human action and the antecedent or environing chain of events in nature out of which the web of its motives must be woven; and from the pitch and proclivity that must be transmitted, according to the principle of evolution, by the heredity inseparable from the process of descent. For immortality, the discredit comes, by way of the principle of evolution, through its indication, under the restrictions of the empirical method, of the transitoriness of all survivals, and through its necessary failure to supply any evidence whatever of even a *possible* survival beyond the sensible world, with which empirical evolution has alone to do; while, by way of the principle of the conservation and dissipation of energy, the discredit comes from the doom that manifestly seems to await all forms of actual energy, taken in connection with the general discredit of everything unattested by the senses, which the persistent culture of empiricism begets.

In short, while the empirical method ignores, and must ignore, any supersensible principle of existence whatever, thus tending to the identification of the Absolute with the Sum of Things, evolution and the principle of conservation have familiarized the modern mind with the continuity, the unity, and the uniformity of nature in an overwhelming degree. In the absence of the conviction, upon independent grounds, that the Principle of existence is personal and rational, the sciences of nature can hardly fail, even upon a some-what considerate and scrutinizing view, to convey the impression that the Source of things is a vast and shadowy Whole, which sweeps onward to an unknown destination, "regardless," as one of the leaders of modern science has said, "of consequences," and unconcerned as to the fate of man's world of effort and hope, apparently so circumscribed and insignificant in comparison.

MODERN SCIENCE IS, STRICTLY, NON-PANTHEISTIC

But now that we come to the closer question, whether this impression is really warranted, we stand in need of exact discrimination. With such discrimination we shall find that, decided as the inference to pantheism from the methods and principles just discussed seems to be, it is, after all, illegitimate.

Our first caution here must be to remember that it is not science in its entire compass that is concerned in the question we are discussing. It is only "modern science," popularly so called—that is, science taken to mean only the science of nature; and not only so, but further restricted to signify only what may fitly enough be described as the *natural* science of nature; that is, so much of the possible knowledge of nature as can be reached through the channels of the senses; so much, in short, as will yield itself to a method strictly observational and empirical.

Hence, the real question is, whether empirical science, confined to nature as its proper object, can legitimately assert the theory of pantheism. And with regard now, first, to the argument drawn with such apparent force from the mere method of natural science, it should be plain to a more scrutinizing reflection that shifting from the legitimate *disregard* of a supersensible principle, which is the right of the empirical method, to the deliberate assumption that there *is* no such principle, because there is and can be no sensible evidence of it, is an abuse of the method in question—an unwarrantable extension of its province to decisions lying by its own terms beyond its ken. This shifting is made upon the assumption that there can be no science founded on any other than empirical evidence. That there is, and can be, no science deserving the name, except that which follows the empirical method of mere *natural* science is a claim which men of science are prone to make, but which the profoundest thinkers the world has known—such minds as Plato, or Aristotle, or Hegel—have certainly pronounced a claim unfounded, and, indeed, a sheer assumption, contradicted by evidence the clearest, if oftentimes abstruse. When, instead of blindly following experience, we raise the question of the real nature and the sources of experience itself, and push it in earnest, it then appears that the very possibility of the experience that seems so rigorously to exclude supersensible principles, and particularly the rational personality of the First Principle, is itself dependent for its existence on such Principle and principles; that, in fact, these enter intellectually into its very constitution. But, in any case, this question of the nature of experience, of the limits of possible knowledge, and whether these last are identical with the limits of possible experience, is one in the taking up of which we abandon the field of nature and enter the very different field of the theory of cognition. In this, the pursuer of natural science, as such, has not a word to say. Here his method is altogether insufficient and unavailing; if the problem can be solved at all, it can only be by methods that transcend the bounds of merely empirical evidence.

So, again, in the inferences to pantheism from the conservation of energy and the principle of evolution. Strong as the evidence seems, it arises in both cases from violating the strict principles of the natural scientific method. All inferences to a whole of potential energy, or to a whole determinant of the survivals in a struggle for existence, are *really* inferences—passings beyond the region of the experimental and sensible *facts* into the empirically unknown, empirically unattested, empirically unwarranted region of supersensible *principles*. The exact scientific truth about all such inferences, and the supposed realities which they establish is that they are unwarranted by natural science; and that this refusal of warrant is only the expression by natural science of its incompetency to enter upon such questions.

Natural science may therefore be said to be silent on this question of pantheism; as indeed it is, and from the nature of the case must be, upon all theories of the supersensible whatever—whether theistic, deistic, or atheistic. Natural science has no proper concern with them. Science may well enough be said to be *non*-pantheistic, but so also is it non-theistic, non-deistic, non-atheistic. Its position, however, is not for that reason anti-pantheistic any more than it is anti-theistic, or anti-deistic, or anti-atheistic. It is rather *agnostic*, in the sense, that is, of declining to affect knowledge in the premises, because these are beyond its method and province. In short, its agnosticism is simply its *neutrality*, and does not in the least imply that agnosticism is the final view of things. The investigation of the final view, the search for the First Principle, science leaves to methods far other than her own of docile sense-experience— methods that philosophy is now prepared to vindicate as higher and far more trustworthy. Yet, when once the supersensible Principle is reached in some other way—the way of philosophy, as distinguished from that of natural science—science will then furnish the most abundant confirmations, the strongest corroborations; the more abundant and the stronger in proportion as the First Principle presented by philosophy ascends, evolution-wise, from materialism, through pantheism, to rational theism. For science *accords* most perfectly with the latter, although she is, in herself, wholly unable to attain the vision of it. But it must be a theism that subsumes into its conceptions of God and man all the irrefutable insights of materialism, of deism, and, eminently, of pantheism; of which, as I will hope this paper has shown, there are those of the greatest pertinence and reality, if also of the most undeniable insufficiency.

19

DR. ABBOT'S "WAY OUT
OF AGNOSTICISM"

Josiah Royce

Hegel's ideas had a way of emerging in curious places, where they became counters in struggles between religious points of view. In 1890, Francis Ellingwood Abbot, former minister of the Independent Church in Toledo, Ohio, and editor of the *Index*, a "free religion" journal, published a book entitled *Way Out of Agnosticism*. The volume had grown out of lectures he had delivered in the philosophy department at Harvard, where he substituted for Josiah Royce in the spring term of 1888. When he read Abbot's book, Royce was enraged at the author's pretentiousness and his blatant appropriation without acknowledgment of Hegel's ideas, a sloppy reformulation of which formed the work's entire basis. The essay which follows is Royce's scathing review, which was printed in the first issue of the *International Journal of Ethics*.

Abbot quickly wrote an abusive reply, "Dr. Royce's 'Professional Warning,'" but withdrew it when the journal decided to permit Royce a rebuttal. The controversy erupted in *The Nation* in the summer of 1891, and both Royce and Abbot employed legal counsel. Meanwhile, the latter took further steps to have Royce removed from the Harvard faculty. He wrote two pamphlets addressed to the Harvard Corporation, one "A Public Appeal for Redress . . ." and the other "A Public Remonstrance . . . ." Harvard refused to consider the case and Royce remained, only slightly disturbed, as the foremost idealist philosopher in America. His review reveals something of the general currency Hegel's ideas had achieved and the way in which they were understood or misunderstood in late nineteenth-century America. Abbot's reworking of Hegel demonstrates that he, for one, did not consider the Swabian philosopher a pantheist.

Josiah Royce, "Dr. Abbot's 'Way Out of Agnosticism,'" *International Journal of Ethics* 1 (1890): 98–113.

I

IN the brief compass of a little more than eighty pages of text,* and after a few pages of well-written introduction, Dr. Abbot has here attempted "to show that, in order to refute agnosticism and establish enlightened theism, nothing is now necessary but to philosophize that very scientific method which agnosticism barbarously misunderstands and misuses." Readers of the same writer's well-known "Scientific Theism" will find in the present volume a fashion of argument with which they are already in general acquainted. They will admire, meanwhile, the courage by virtue of which the author chooses to meet his adversaries, armed not with the numerous pages in which philosophers usually love to array themselves, but, as it were, with so few pages that they might almost seem by comparison, like David's five smooth stones from a brook. In an age of many words, students who are not without wordy sins on their consciences must therefore indeed envy Dr. Abbot his light equipment and his courageous willingness to enter upon so serious a task with so little external assistance. There is one kind of external assistance which our author, to be sure, does not disdain; his text fairly bristles with italics and small capitals, a device which possibly serves to set off what the author is pleased to consider the extremely "modern" character of his work, through the contrast with so antiquated and unfortunate a typography.

If we leave the manner of the book for the time and pass to the matter, we shall find, first of all, as a noteworthy feature, the author's sense of his personal originality as to method, and, in part, even as to result. In so far as the result is a monistic theism, Dr. Abbot, of course, can be under no illusions as to the widely-spread agreement among many ancient and modern thinkers concerning the substantial truth of this doctrine. In so far, however, as the statement of this doctrine involves technical formulas of a philosophical sort, Dr. Abbot is confident of the newness of many of his propositions; and, with more courage than sense of humor, he is even pleased to name what he thinks to be his philosophical discovery concerning "Universals," the "American Theory of Universals," as opposed to the "Greek" theory, which he finds "undeveloped," and the "German" theory, to which he attributes a "malign influence."

* The "Way Out of Agnosticism; or, the Philosophy of Free Religion," by Francis Ellingwood Abbot, Ph.D., late instructor in Philosophy in Harvard University. Boston: Little Brown & Co., 1890.

The "Greek" theory is essentially Aristotle's. By the "German" theory is meant conceptualism. As to Dr. Abbot's originality, we receive also yet other and numerous assurances. "By a wholly new line of reasoning," drawn from the sources of "science and philosophy," the work of this book is to be accomplished. So the opening "Note" informs us. And, again: "The first great task of philosophy is to lay deep and solid foundations for the expansion of human knowledge in a bold, new, and true theory of universals. For so-called modern philosophy rests complacently in a theory of universals which is thoroughly mediæval or antiquated" (p. 12). At the conclusion of the book we learn that we have been shown "the way out of agnosticism into the sunlight of the predestined Philosophy of Science." This "way," it is plain, might, according to its author's view, be called with some propriety the "American" way; and, in sum, Dr. Abbot's sense of the originality of his philosophical thought is such as to seem, in this age when the historical continuity of human thought is so constantly in our minds, fairly childlike in its confidence and in its simplicity. How well founded it is, we can only estimate after we have looked a little more closely at the doctrine.

II

"The necessary beginning-point of all philosophy, which deserves to be called scientific" is in this volume as in the author's previous one, the principle, here stated on p. 5, that "the universal results of the special sciences, including the method common to them all, are the only possible data of philosophy or universal science." "Universal Human Knowledge," however, as thus defined, is embodied in "Universal Literature," in so far as this is a record of the positive results of human thought (p. 10). Universal literature depends upon language as its means of expression, and language is impossible without universal terms, in which, "in the last analysis," all human knowledge is "contained" (p. 11). "The results of science must be permanently stored in this form, and can only be found in this form." How necessary, then, the comprehension of the nature and objective relations of "Universal Terms." The true theory of these terms, now, is that they express universal meanings or "Concepts," and that any one of these stands for "the universal *what-is-meant*" (p. 13),—*i.e.* for "the genus."

To understand the nature of knowledge, then, we must know

what is the truth behind this word "genus." All science, Dr. Abbot teaches, presupposes that, in so far as we possess verified acquaintance with nature at all, we do know *real*—not abstract or ideal, but *actual*—genera in nature. "Nothing is known by itself alone; it is known through its kind. The essential constitution of every genus is *that of many things in one kind, one kind in many things;* the unity and multiplicity are known inseparably together. Hence the genus is in no sense an abstraction, but the concrete totality of many realities in one reality" (p. 14). Hence, again, the genus has an "essentially organic constitution"; and "science itself may be defined as knowledge of the genus, that is, knowledge of the universe as the highest kind which includes all other kinds." It is, meanwhile, some genus in the foregoing sense which is known through any scientific concept or word; and the word or the concept reveals "never the independent, isolated, or unrelated thing, nor yet the common essence of many unrelated things as a mere abstraction, but always the concrete kind of many interrelated things as one self-related reality" (p. 18). A fair example of a genus (p. 24) is the "family" in human society; for a family in every case is "essentially and necessarily composed of several individual members" (p. 25), whose relations "in their totality make up the family constitution, and are precisely as real as the individuals related, inhering in the family *as such* and *as a whole,* and subsisting neither in any one individual member, nor in any outside observer." "Nay, more: no individual as such can exist except as a member of some family precisely as real as himself." Meanwhile, "all individuals compose the genus family. All families compose the genus society. All societies compose the genus mankind. All individuals = all families = all societies = all mankind." Again (p. 26), "in this union and interrelation of many in one and one in many, in this immanent relational constitution by which many individuals exist and are indissolubly united in one kind, lies the very essence of the family," which thereby exemplifies the genus as it is found everywhere in the "world-order." Another example of a genus is "mankind" (p. 40). "Mankind" may be, for the sake of precision, distinguished as a "concrete universal kind or genus, including all concrete individuals," from "Man" as the "Concrete Individual," and from "Humanity" as the "Abstract Class Essence," including only the universal nature which is common to all men as a class, and excluding all that is peculiar to each individual. "Humanity," in this sense,—viz., as "human nature,"—is then not the real genus, and has no "independent reality." "It is real, but only as existing in all real men," while the genus or "kind" is as real as the individuals, and in the case of mankind "has its generic peculiarities, such as heredity, bisexuality, gregariousness, and all other attributes which can exist only through the social correlation of many individuals in one kind." Other examples of the genus are "book," "house," "tree" (p. 33), and the "three categorical types of Real Being," which the author discusses in his closing sections,— viz., "Machine," "Organism," and "Person."

The genus is therefore, of course, distinct from the individual as such. It is also distinct from the "abstract class essence." The relations of the three are, however, that (omitting Dr. Abbot's small capitals, in which the words next following are printed by him) "the Individual Concrete Thing and the Universal Concrete Kind reveal each other through the Abstract Class Essence which is common to both."

I have used Dr. Abbot's words in stating the foregoing notions about "Universals," because he plainly makes much of these forms of expression himself, and has a right to his words in so far as they are his own. As to the use to which he puts this "new, bold, and true" theory, this "American theory of Universals," I have space only for an inadequate suggestion. "The Universe," namely (p. 45), as the "supreme Kind of Kinds," is the "real genus in itself," and we learn about *this* genus, as a whole, "by studying the constitution of its own finite parts. Each known part reveals one character of the whole." "The real essence of the individual thing, and the real essence of the universal kind more or less repeat, exemplify, and manifest each other" (p. 47). Hence we can and must judge of the character of the highest genus by virtue of an examination of the genera known to us. The principle of the reciprocal relation of thing and kind, extended to the universe, authorizes us to generalize from actual to possible experience. Upon this authorization all science depends; and we must be sure that "the essential constitution of the universe more or less repeats, reflects, and reveals itself in miniature in the constitution of the innumerable concrete kinds of which it is itself the absolute unity" (p. 44). "Real knowledge of any of these kinds is, just so far, real knowledge of the Universe as the supreme Kind of Kinds."

If this suggests the procedure of "scientific philosophy" in general, the detail of the procedure is more fully suggested when we observe that in the universe of science these are, according to Dr. Abbot, the three types of Being: the "Machine" (under which name Dr. Abbot includes all embodiments of natural processes *qua* mechanical), the "Organism," and the "Person." These, then, properly studied, will, as subordinate genera, reveal or manifest something of the nature of the highest genus itself,—*i.e.*, the Universe as Infinite Being. Otherwise the American theory of universals is vain, and we are yet in our sins. For while ordinary agnostics, when they observe "machines" or "organisms" or "persons," remain still with foolish heart darkened as to the nature of the "Supreme Kind of Kinds," those who have escaped into the sunlight of the predestined philosophy of science know that, as the American theory teaches, and as the malign "German" theory does not teach, the higher kind and the lower kind reciprocally "manifest each other," so that in knowing persons, and the rest, we already know something of the universe. But still further, a closer examination of the concept of a "Machine," reveals to Dr. Abbot that a machine without an Organism, which constructs the machine "as a causal means to some definite organic end of its own," is an "abstraction," and can have no true reality. The reasoning by which Dr. Abbot reaches this result is, of course, supposed by him to be in principle founded upon his doctrine of the reciprocal manifestation of thing and kind and so on the "American" theory. In fact and in detail, however, the argument as stated will appear to any reader, who is not altogether in love with Dr. Abbot's formulas, nor yet terrified by the italics and the small capitals, as naught but our familiar friend the design argument, in forms which were in use some time before the discovery of America. By the aid of the science of "anthropology," to which Dr. Abbot, as "scientific philosopher," appeals on p. 50, he learns that men use axes as tools, and accordingly he gives as "anthropological definition" of machine, "a causal means between man and some definite human end." A reference to honeycombs, spider-webs, and the like, suggests the further generalization that "the essence of the Real Machine is to mediate causally between an Organism and its End," and one is thus led to a conception of a machine as a "material whole constructed by an Organism as a causal means to some definite organic end of its own" (p. 52),—a concept which, just because it "contains all the essential elements of the physical and anthropological concepts, but is more comprehensive than either," thereby shows that the concepts of the Machine and the Organism (*i.e.*, of natural processes as mechanical, and of organic processes as teleological) are "universally, necessarily, and inseparably connected." This monstrous *non sequitur* is supplemented by a "discovery of supreme importance" (p. 53),—viz., that "the constitutions of the Machine and of the Organism involve each the other, and therefore are intelligible each through the other alone." The only further suggestion of a proof for this discovery is given in the illustrations on page 53, which show that, as guns and scythes, and the like, are used by men to "extend their organisms," the "Real

Machine is only an Artificial and Separable Organ for Self-Extension of the Organism. When not used it is only a functionless lump of matter."

I am far from discussing here the truth of Dr. Abbot's conclusions apart from his method of reaching them. I am only reporting the nature of his "way out," just as a way. On p. 55 this "way" leads through an argument, presumably in Dr. Abbot's judgment, "wholly new" when applied to philosophy, although he quotes text-books which have already formulated it in special science. This argument assures us that the "causal nexus" in mechanical nature would remain utterly mysterious unless we supposed it to be in essence one with our own "conscious effort." This gives us another indication of the inextricable linking of the two concepts of "efficient causality and finality." With the remainder of the discussion, which leads Dr. Abbot along well-trodden roads to the monistic theism of his closing pages, where (as Julian Schmidt once neatly said of certain passages in Fichte) *"Er in's Erbauliche uebergeht,"* I will not just here deal, except by way of remarking that capitals and the italics become none the less numerous as the topics under consideration become more exalted.

III

It is due to Dr. Abbot's position and past services as a writer and a leader of liberal investigation, in this country, to give at least as full an account as the foregoing of his latest work, and I should be glad if I had time for fuller quotations. It is due also to the extravagant pretensions which he frequently makes of late as to the originality and profundity of his still unpublished system of philosophy, to give the reader some hint of what so far appears to be the nature of our author's contributions to philosophical reflection. But now, as to the estimate of the book, I must, however, insist that no amount of agreement with Dr. Abbot's monistic and essentially idealistic conclusion—no such agreement, I repeat, as I myself feel with this outcome, and no sympathy, such as we shall all sincerely feel, with his desire to serve our careworn and doubting age—can blind or ought to blind any intelligent reader to the essentially vicious and injurious nature of Dr. Abbot's fashion of argument. Of novelty, good or bad, the book contains, indeed, despite its vast pretensions, hardly a sign. The agnostic, meanwhile, who should actually be led "out" by Dr. Abbot, would be of necessity a person of so unreflective a mind, so ignorant of the history of thought, so badly afraid of italics, so little grounded in his agnosticism, that, whatever humanity might dictate as to the value of any pious effort to benefit his soul, there may be grave doubts whether his philosophically self-critical powers were worth the trouble of saving. And I say this not because I have the least desire to be disrespectful to Dr. Abbot, whose sincerity and earnestness are throughout admirable, but because the book, as it stands, forces such a judgment upon one, and that for the following simple reasons:

For the first, it is useless for any thinker in our day to undertake to philosophize, without both the time and the coolness of judgment needed to form some clear consciousness as to his own historical relations; and Dr. Abbot is hopelessly unhistorical in his consciousness. His "American Theory of Universals" is so far from being either his own or a product of America that in this book he continually has to use, in expounding it, one of the most characteristic and familiar of Hegel's technical terms, namely, "concrete," in that sense to which it is applied to the objective and universal "genus" itself. Dr. Abbot's appropriation of Hegel's peculiar terminology comes ill indeed from one who talks of the "malign influence" of the "German" theory of universals, and who interprets this theory as teaching that, in the case of his own illustration of the "family," "the observer and the family are one, and the observer is that one." As applied to Hegel's theory of universals, which is certainly not to be called precisely an "American" theory, Dr. Abbot's description of the consequences of the "German" theory would be an intolerable slander. And this I say not to defend Hegel, for whose elaborate theory of universals I hold in no wise a brief, but simply in the cause of literary property-rights. When we plough with another man's heifer, however unconscious we are of our appropriation, however sincerely we seem to remember that we alone raised her from her earliest calfhood, it is yet in vain, after all, that we put our brand on her, or call her "American." Hegel himself never made any secret of his own historical dependence, but at all events it was Hegel who, as the outcome of his study of the history of thought, said, in speaking of the relation of the universal and the individual, "*der Begriff* (substantially one with Dr. Abbot's genus in so far as the latter is "one kind in many things and many things in one kind") *ist das schlechthin Konkrete.*" And Hegel's *Begriff*, I repeat, is *not* Dr. Abbot's merely subjective "concept," which the "German theory" shall put wholly "in the observer." On the contrary, as § 167 of the "Encyclopädie" has it, "To say that a judgment shall be merely subjective in sense, as if *I* attributed a predicate to a subject, contradicts the very form of expression of the judgment, which is objective: 'The rose *is* red,' 'Gold *is* a metal.' *It is not I who merely attribute something to them.*" Nor is this a chance word of Hegel's. His whole system depends on the assertion that there is an objective *Begriff*, a universal kind, manifested in the individuals, and at the same time, as universal a truth, as real, as they are, and making the individuals possible. For this reason—viz., *because* of this objectivity and reality of the *Begriff*—Hegel calls it "concrete," makes it organic, precisely as Dr. Abbot does, so far, at least, as concerns this initial definition, and then tries to demonstrate, in his own fashion, that his concrete and objective universal is a person. Now Hegel's whole theory may be false; but what is certain is that Dr. Abbot, who has all his life been working in an atmosphere where Hegelian ideas were more or less infectious, has derived his whole theory of universals, so far as he has yet revealed it with any coherency, from Hegelian sources, and even now cannot suggest any better terminology than Hegel's for an important portion of the doctrine. Yet in the volume before us we find all this pretentious speech of an "American" theory, and discover our author wholly unaware that he is sinning against the most obvious demands of literary property-rights.

Discussions about priority are indeed often of peculiar uselessness in philosophy, just because of our inevitable bondage to the history of thought, and to the common notions of our age. I should therefore owe the reader a hearty apology for the suggestion of the present discussion, were it not for the light that it throws upon Dr. Abbot's whole method of work. If we are unable to discover, after the most sincere and pious scrutiny, our own most obvious debts, is it not a little hopeless for us to undertake to straighten the world's accounts, and to lead all the agnostics of our generation out of their reflective embarrassments?

If the book is thus based upon an historical misjudgment, the main doctrines, regarded as Dr. Abbot's, are, in the second place, not a little confused in statement. So far, I have said, as Dr. Abbot actually defines his genus, his "concrete kind of many interrelated things as one self-related reality," his genus is nothing but Hegel's *objektiver Begriff*. Meanwhile, however, Dr. Abbot, as "scientific philosopher," disdains to give any argument for this doctrine of the genus but the bare *Versicherung*, as Hegel would have said, that *so it is, since so science assumes.* Beyond this assurance here, as in his previous book, Dr. Abbot, who has an especially keen hatred for sceptically critical reflection upon fundamental truths, has nothing to suggest to his agnostics, by way of leading them "out," save a certain lofty and stern abuse of their dreary scepticism, an abuse which has a well-known and somewhat clerical sound, and which may be left to one side here along with the rest *des Erbaulichen* of which the book, as I before said, contains a little. The edifying is indeed one of the most necessary and useful things of life; but it has as such no place in a philosophical argument about fundamental problems. We ought not to be enticed to accept a philosophical theory by the suggestion that it is "new and bold." We ought not to be warned away from a critical scrutiny of the bases of science by hearing that, "If popular agnosticism only had philosophy enough to understand the logic of its own denials, it would be a mad plunge into bottomless, shoreless, skyless ignorance,—the suicide of reason itself in a delirium of cowardice." This sort of thing, one may remind Dr. Abbot, is very much what the parson said of old to us in the country village: *nur mit ein bisschen andern Worten,* and with the further difference that the parson of old used, if I remember rightly, to warn us that just such evil consequences would follow from any doubt as to Jonah's precise relations with the whale. Agnostics of any experience are used to such speeches, and we shall in vain get them "out" after that fashion.

But if one looks a little further at Dr. Abbot's development of the doctrine of the genus, one finds indeed at least this about it which, if not precisely either novel or "American," is at all events not wholly due to Hegel. I refer to a certain unexplained confusion in his mind as to what his *genus* shall be or imply. A given "family" in human society, as would seem from his chosen example, is a genus as against its individual members. Meanwhile, "book" and "house" are just as truly genera. All these genera have an "organic" constitution, and are "units" of existence (p. 15). They exemplify the "concrete kind of many interrelated things as one self-related reality." Each of them, namely, has "an inherent system of relations or immanent relational constitution," and Dr. Abbot is never weary of pointing out that relations are as real and objective as are the related things. "Immanent in the very nature of being, this principle of the objectivity or reality of generic relations is the absolute condition of the possibility of a World-Order" (p. 26). The "relational constitution" of each genus is discovered by "classification" (p. 14), and this, as scientific and methodical procedure, depends upon "observation," which first discovers real genera, "hypothesis," which tentatively extends generalizations, and "experimental verification," which tests hypothesis (p. 36). Through the "immanent relational constitution" thus discovered, we find that "many individuals exist and are indissolubly united in one kind" (p. 26); and this "indissoluble" unity of the individuals in the kind is again apparently the same as Dr. Abbot's "organic" unity of the generic constitution of things.

Now, it needs no special ingenuity to suggest that this doctrine about the organic and "indissoluble" unity of things in their kind has very different values when applied to the "family" of Dr. Abbot's illustration, and when applied to such a "genus" as, say, corkscrew, or rat-trap, or rainbow, or pebble, or atom, or tiger, or constellation. All these last are unquestionably "genera" of some sort. And I should fully agree with Dr. Abbot that the relations among things which these various generic names imply are as real and objective as the things related. This objective "relational constitution" of things is to my mind a very certain truth, although I should not, like Dr. Abbot, refuse to inquire as to the philosophical basis of this truth before making it the basis of the rest of my philosophy. But granting that truth, it is the barest confusion to dump thus all the genera into one place, as it were, and talk of the "indissoluble" unity of many things in one kind as if it were characteristic of every genus. "Indissoluble" and "organic" relations subsist, after a fashion, between the members of a given family, because, should any members die or go away, just this family must cease to exist in its old form as a genus, and must, if it persists at all, become an altered genus. No *such* organic relations characterize, however, the rat-traps and the pebbles. Even the genus tiger is unaltered by the death of thousands of tigers. The pebbles resemble one another, and this resemblance is indeed an objective fact in nature, dependent upon no observer (save God). But to call the pebbles, and the rat-traps, and the corkscrews, and the tigers, and the rainbows, genera, each one of which is a "concrete kind" of many interrelated pebbles, or rat-traps, or corkscrews, or tigers, or rainbows, as one "self-related reality," and to illustrate this "organic relational constitution" by the further case of a family with its interrelated parents and children, brothers and sisters,—all this is but to confuse, surely not to clarify. Hegel, whose doctrine of the organic unity of thing and kind Dr. Abbot has unconsciously appropriated, was himself far too sly a bird to be caught by the chaff of such confusion. His *Begriff* is objective and organic, and it owns the whole universe; but the various corkscrews and the individual tigers and rainbows are still not by any implication suggested as "necessarily united." On the contrary, Hegel's ingenious system of graded categories, with its successive forms of Being,—viz., *Sein, Dasein, Existenz,* and *Wirklichkeit,*—gave a formula which enabled him to declare *das Wirkliche* through and through organic, while leaving room for all sorts of imperfect realizations of unity in the lower realms of *Dasein* and *Existenz*. I would not desire to recommend Hegel's devices to Dr. Abbot, for they might produce worse effects upon his agnostics than even his present account of things. I only wish to suggest that the actually true doctrine of the organic unity of the world requires of us more adroitness in its statement than is involved in simply declaring every possible genus an organic unity, and avoiding distinctions. The pebbles have "unity" because they resemble one another; the atoms because, in addition, they have, or may have, physical and chemical relations; the corkscrews or the rat-traps because of their community both of structure and of purposes. The "family," however, shows us a wholly different sort of organic or "indissoluble" relation among its members; while the constellation in the heavens is again a sort of "genus" in relation to the stars that compose it; but its unity, while indeed founded upon the "immanent relational constitution" of the world in space, has a yet widely different "organic" character from that suggested by the other "genera" mentioned. I use, indeed, examples which are my own; but Dr. Abbot has only himself to blame if, stating the "immanent relational constitution" of all genera in this direct and naïve way, without any distinctions, he forces upon a reader such reflections. In brief, as the foregoing reference to Hegel suggests, Dr. Abbot's doctrine is in so far "American" as it is Hegel with the subtlety of that crafty old fox left out. Hegel managed to make the *Begriff* organic, and yet leave room for the confused genera of ordinary observation. Dr. Abbot marks all genera with the same stripe, sees "indissoluble unity" in every case of objectively significant classification, and so makes indeed short work of "agnosticism," but unfortunately of the clearness of his whole thinking also.

For, of course, the whole use of this "American theory of universals" is to prove, by means of the reciprocal relation of thing and kind, that the universe as a whole has such unity as certain of its parts—to wit, "organisms" and "persons"—are already empirically known to possess. This is the whole question at issue between Dr. Abbot and his agnostics. No other line of investigation shall be "scientific" or "modern," except a study of empirical nature in the light of the "American theory." And this theory is, "Every genus is an organic unity of interrelated individuals in one self-related kind." Hence the kind of kinds, containing as it does persons and organisms, is at once in a fair way to appear as a person with an organism. Dr. Abbot's agnostics have, however, a right to ask how the organic unity of the universe, as the highest genus, differs from the organic unity of the rat-traps in the genus "rat-trap," or of the rainbows in the genus "rainbow," or of the tigers in the jungle, or of the stars in the constellation? Why is the human "family" a better case of the immanent relational constitution of the objective world than is the genus "corkscrew"? Upon the answer to such questions all must turn for these unhappy agnostic readers.

And Dr. Abbot indeed "more or less" feels, I apprehend, how the bare and undeveloped assertion, that science knows organic and unified genera, is not enough to make clear the peculiar unity which he attributes to the One Person. Hence the detailed discussion of machine, organism, and person, as scientific genera, in the concluding sections of the book. A more hopelessly "mediæval" discussion it would be hard to find. The design argument in all its dogmatic and animistic play with analogies is here repeated as if it were something wholly new. A "machine" needs a maker and a user. *Proof:* men make axes. Science discovers physical nature to be a machine. *Ergo:* science discovers the world of physical nature to need a maker and a user. This maker and user cannot be a part of nature, but must be the whole of it. Hence the world is one organism. A further proof of the same bold and new doctrine is found in the fact that (as M. Deschanel observes, in the revised sixth edition, by Everett, of his "Elementary Treatise on Natural Philosophy") "we obtain the idea of force through our own conscious exercise of muscular force" (p. 57 of Abbot). Several other persons have said the same thing. Hence (p. 64) "the universe is a real organism." As for the rest of the argument, it is short and easy. The universe as a whole has nothing outside of it. Hence, for the real organism which is the infinite, "self and not-self are numerically identical. But numerical identity of self and not-self, subject and object, constitutes the unity of self-consciousness in the person. Consequently the infinite universe cannot be a real organism without being a real person too."

And so, finally, after this somewhat detailed study of Dr. Abbot's little book, I feel constrained to repeat my judgment as above. Results in philosophy are one thing; a careful way of thinking is another. Babes and sucklings often get very magnificent results. It is not the office of philosophy to outdo the babes and sucklings at their own business of receiving revelations. It is the office of philosophy to undertake a serious scrutiny of the presuppositions of human belief. Hence the importance of the careful way of thinking in philosophy. But Dr. Abbot's way is not careful, is not novel, and, when thus set forth to the people as new and bold and American, it is likely to do precisely as much harm to careful inquiry as it gets influence over immature or imperfectly trained minds. I venture therefore to speak plainly, by way of a professional warning to the liberal-minded public concerning Dr. Abbot's philosophical pretensions. And my warning takes the form of saying that if people are to think in this confused way, unconsciously borrowing from a great speculator like Hegel, and then depriving the borrowed conception of the peculiar subtlety of statement that made it useful in its place,—and if we readers are for our part to accept such scholasticism as is found in Dr. Abbot's concluding sections as at all resembling philosophy,—then it were far better for the world that no reflective thinking whatever should be done. If we can't improve on what God has already put into the mouth of the babes and sucklings, let us at all events make some other use of our wisdom and prudence than in setting forth the "American theory" of what has been in large part hidden from us.

I speak plainly. Moreover, I give this work a treatment whose minuteness is wholly out of proportion to the value of the book criticised. Were I writing for expert students of philosophy, this paper would have been much briefer. But I write for the general reader, as well as for the expert. And, I repeat, nothing less than the foregoing fulness and plainness of speech is due to Dr. Abbot's rank as a public teacher, and to his well-earned reputation as a man who wants to advance the cause of sound religion. That cause, by his practical labors, as editor and counsellor, by his personal devotion to high ideals, by his heroic sacrifices in the service of duty, he has long indeed advanced; and I trust that he will very long continue to do so. But if we will philosophize in public, we must be content to be judged by formal criteria of a very impersonal sort. If not every one that saith Lord! Lord! is a good servant of the Lord, surely it is equally true that not every one who preaches a lofty creed and lives up to it can give even an American theory of why he holds it. And, in judging of the actual work of philosophical writers, we must lay friendly esteem aside in so far as it is necessary to do so for the cause of the "greater friend." In brief, in estimating these matters of the accuracy and fruitfulness of our reflective thought, we must show no mercy,—as we ask none.

V

SOCIETY AND ECONOMICS

The key to freedom or self-definition in Hegelian philosophy was to be found in the working-out of the concrete universal through societal institutions. Right- and left-Hegelians held conflicting views as to which specific institutions were most important and most crucial to true progress. Right-Hegelians promulgated a "concentric" theory of institutions that could be traced back to Aristotle. For them, an individual engaged in social relationships in an ever-widening circle, beginning with the family and continuing through religious, economic, and political groups, infinitely outward to all mankind. Moreover, they viewed the progression of institutional relationships historically, such that an individual was presumed to relate to institutions in a sequence paralleling the history of mankind from family to clan to tribe to nation, etc. Left-Hegelians characteristically focused on economic institutions, their interaction, and the clash between labor unions and the rest of society.

20

"TO MAKE ETHICAL THE SEXUAL INDIVIDUAL"

Denton J. Snider

In his exhaustive treatise *Social Institutions*, Denton J. Snider looked upon the family as the fundamental unit of society. The following selection examines the family's philosophical status according to the reasoning of a dyed-in-the-wool Hegelian.

Denton J. Snider, *Social Institutions* (St. Louis: Sigma Publ. Co., 1901), pp. 59–62.

THE FAMILY

THE Family has long been recognized in a general way as the first of man's Social Institutions, foundation and source of the rest. We may indeed call it supremely the creative Institution, in which takes place the genesis of both man and of his Institutions. It is the primordial genetic unit, out of which are born both the Person and the Institutional World, or the individual subjective Self and the universal objective Self (as Institution).

We must not, however, forget its immediate psychical starting-point, which is the Will, in the present case the Will as sexual desire, which drives man into the Family. But this Will as desire has as its ideal end freedom or Free-Will which actualizes itself in an Institution, primarily that of the Family, whose lower forms may be simply Will actualized, but whose destiny is to be Free-Will actualized, that is, an existent, objective Free-Will which secures Free-Will in all the members of the Family.

The Family is that Institution which brings a Free-Will into existence, not only physically but morally and intellectually; it, therefore, can be seen to be an actualized Free-Will itself, that is, a Free-Will existent, objective, whose end is to will Free-Will. This does not mean that such an end always lies consciously in the parent of every child, though it may in certain cases. But in general, the Family, being the primary Institution, has the institutional end as implicit, unconscious, potential; as instinct, as emotion, as love. The individual through love becomes a member of the domestic Institution, and surrenders himself to its end; yet in this self-surrender he wins his freedom.

The physical presupposition of the Family is the sexual individual, in whom is manifested Nature's deepest dualism, that of sex. At the same time the sexual individual longs to transcend his halfness and to become whole through one of the opposite sex. Thereby he shows himself as generic or generative—not merely individual but also species, reproducing himself as individual. Thus he is not merely a man, but ideally mankind. Upon this ideal element in sex the domestic Institution is built, and domestic love has in it the double ingredient, physical and institutional.

The end of the Family, then, as actualized Free-Will, is the reproduction of the human individual as a new Free-Will in the world. In and through the Family the child is to be begotten, to have nurture (both pre-natal and post-natal), and to receive its first education, till the Educative Institution can take it and carry forward its training. Through the Institution of the Family the child is not simply born, but is born into the world of Institutions, and begins its career as an institutional being.

The destiny of the child is to become an independent individual, specially independent of the Family which has reared him. Thus the Family, starting with the individual, has returned to the same, being the instrument of his re-creation. But this independent individual must in turn enter the Family and re-create that; therein he wills into existence that Institution which has willed him into existence. With such a content in his life he is truly ethical, possessing and practicing the primary institutional virtue.

Biologically the Family has a close correspondence with the plant, which starts with the seed, blooms and unfolds into stem, flower, fruit, and then returns to the seed, its starting-point. Such is the vegetable cycle of Reproduction, which bears such a striking analogy to the domestic cycle, beginning with the reproductive individual and returning to the same, not simply through Nature however, but through the Institution. If the Family corresponds to the plant, Society bears more resemblance to the animal, and the State has its likeness to the Ego, being the self-conscious Institution.

Thus the Family is to institutionalize or make ethical the sexual individual. Starting with desire, he is not to gratify it immediately, but through the Institution. He must inhibit sexual propensities till they be transformed by their institutional end in the Family. Sensuality destroys the Family on one side, celibacy destroys it also on the other; indulgence and prohibition can be equally negative to domestic life. . . .

21

THE MONOCRAT

Denton J. Snider

In discussing the distribution of property, Snider devised the "Monocrat," a person whose basic function was to allocate the world's goods equitably and intelligently according to society's will. As the passage below suggests, Snider saw the "Monocrat" already at work in the society of his time. He was the great captain of industry or monopolist—someone like Andrew Carnegie who wielded enormous power over the distribution of goods and services and who also upheld the doctrine of stewardship which was part of the Gilded Age Gospel of Wealth. Stewardship implied that the powerful capitalist held his wealth in trust for the masses. As an enlightened, successful man, he presumably knew what was best for society and made economic and philanthropic decisions on its behalf. Success and industrial know-how were the criteria for selection of the steward, rather than education and morality. Snider clearly realized the shortcomings of this selection process and probably would have agreed with Mr. Dooley that "ivry time Carnegie givs away a library he givs himself away." He saw the "Monocrat" inevitably evolving, however, into a publicly responsible figure somewhat like the technocratic managers in Edward Bellamy's utopian dream, *Looking Backward*. As Snider saw it, the advantage of selecting the "Monocrat" from within the ranks of the business community was the expertise and proven ability that he could bring to the role. He had prospered on a vast scale for himself in a complicated world—why could he not be made socially responsible for society? By the early twentieth century, the "Monocrat" had become a reality as a central figure in the Progressive Movement, in the city manager, in commission government, in the Federal Reserve Board, for example. A complex society could hardly do without him, but could it survive with him without practical means of checking his power? The question remained unanswered at mid-twentieth century.

Denton J. Snider, *Social Institutions*, pp. 330–35.

THERE is to be communal ownership, but it is realizing itself in a different way from that conceived by M. de Laveleye and Henry George. Still these men will always be remembered and honored for their services in the general cause of the Community's rights, even if the stream does not run in their channel.

Thus the grand movement of Society has completed its cycle, which, however, is not stationary, but in the perpetual process of development. Manifestly, we have come back to our starting-point which was Positive Society, whose evolution we have just traced, after witnessing its negative descent. But this does not mean that the circle is closed and that the movement stops. We reached the point in which the civil Community is calling for a new communal ownership, which is to be established, confirmed and secured by Law. But who, what makes the law? Here we have the call for the State, the next great secular Institution, whose special function is to secure the free-acting Will through Law. The social Will in every form must finally invoke the State as its protector, as that Institution which is to make it actual. Thus Society presupposes the State for its existence on the one hand, and on the other passes over into the State as the next higher form of institutional development.

Some Observations on Society. We have now seen that the three fundamental stages in the movement of Society are the Positive or normally existent, the Negative or descending, and the Evolutionary or ascending. We have also seen that they are not stages fixed and separate, but in a continual process with one another, which process is necessarily psychical, being that of the very Self which produces Society. This same order we have already found in the Family.

1. We may now look back and verify the statement made at the beginning of the present chapter, that Society turns upon *the willed Product* with its manifold development and transformation, culminating in the universal middleman (not yet quite universal but rapidly tending thitherwards). This willed Product, becoming more and more complicated, is finally the all-willed Product, which Society is to mediate both in its production and its distribution. With this mediation of the willed Product all the great social conflicts of the time are connected—round it move social revolution as well as social evolution. Its name leads us back to the Will as the source of the social order, whose scientific development should, accordingly, be psychological.

2. The willed Product is, in general, Property, the object into

which the Will has put itself, and through which it has its first real existence. Proudhon, the socialist, seeking to do away with the present form of Society, showed his perspicacity in centering his attack upon Property, that is, individual ownership of it. "Property is theft," is his famous declaration, which concentrates in one keen sentence the fundamental faith of socialism.

3. The man whom we have above designated as the social Monocrat is the most interesting figure in the civilized world to-day. The people of both continents are looking at him with a kind of awe, wondering what will develop out of him next. No President of a Republic, no King or Emperor attracts the gaze and provokes the speculation of mankind like our Monocrat. Three or four of them have attained colossal proportions which are beginning to reach around the globe. And the curious fact about this matter is that he is the product of Democracy, to which Monocracy seems to be the rising counterpart and fulfillment. One might think that the political Monarch and the social Monocrat belong together; not so, however. Socialism as such cannot evolve itself practically in the Social Whole; it has been, is, and will probably continue to be a doctrine, an ideal scheme. But Monocracy is here, and in possession, socially evolved and at work in the world, born doing while socialism is still talking.

4. It is the Monocrat who is forcing communal ownership as the counterpoise to himself, and is destroying the last vestige of the old doctrine of *laissez-faire*. He is compelling the State to be a positive Institution, to take hold actively and to secure Free-Will, and not to look on idly and let things run their own course. Unquestionably the Monocrat is a direct and legitimate product of social evolution, and so has supremely the right to be. Yet he may abuse his right and become a tyrant, establishing a social, if not a political, despotism. Here, then, is the loud call for the State to safeguard freedom against him; still it is not to destroy him, but rather to secure him on his positive side. The social Monocrat has come to stay, as he fulfills a legitimate social function, that of the universal unification of man as a social being, not through the revolution, but through the evolution of the Social Order.

5. As yet the social Monocrat is purely individual in his work, is seeking his own personal gain. Is this the end of him, or is he being evolved for another and higher social purpose? We think that he is in training for becoming the recognized institutional administrator of the Social Whole, which is finally to choose him in some way. At present he seizes his power through his talent and uses it for himself autocratically; but he is to rise out of this in-

dividualistic condition, and work for all socially, and not simply for himself. He will administer the social Institution, not from the outside, but from the inside, being an organic constituent thereof, and as such his end will be the ultimate end of all Institutions, the actualizing of freedom in the world. His authority will no longer be capricious or even patriarchal, but institutional, perchance constitutional, like the President of the United States. A federated social world might make him its chief. For such exalted service he would receive adequate compensation, which, however, is not to be altogether settled by himself for himself. It would seem that the coming communal ownership is already calling for him, and he is now in the process of preparation for his future institutional vocation.

6. Thus the Social Monocrat would be no longer dangerous to freedom, at least not more than any ruler. In fact, his supreme function would be to secure to the social individual a higher freedom than has ever been possible without him. Every man must obey the Social Whole, not as a slave, but as a freeman, who surrenders his arbitrary Will and receives through the Institution his own Free-Will sanctioned by all and not by himself alone. Such a Free-Will the Social Monocrat may be able to make more valid than ever it was before, since he is not necessarily contained by national limits, but can be in his way a kind of world-ruler.

7. The new movements and conflicts of the Social Whole have found and are finding decided expression of themselves in art and literature. The modern novel in particular has busied itself with the collisions in this sphere, and has repeatedly sought to portray a workman's Paradise, as well as his Inferno; we read too of the Temple of Labor and the Palace of Industry. But architecture has actually built the multiplicity of the social Product in these days into the so-called High Building, which is indeed the architectonic image of the Social Monocrat both in its external colossality and in its manifold internal divisions. Sculpture has come down from its Greek Olympus, and, instead of revealing a God, presents to us the stalwart form of the digger. Even more emphatically is Painting adjusting itself to the new social movement.

8. At present the social Monocrat is his own steward or administrator, not that of Society, at least not institutionally so. He may give or not, he may will freedom or not, quite as he pleases. Hence he must be put under the law of the State, first of all, then he with his social power and ability may well become an integral portion of the State, and can be brought to will Free-Will not subjectively according to caprice, but objectively through the Institution, in whose administration he will naturally take part.

22

"WE WILL MAKE OF HELL A WELL ORGANIZED UNIONFOUNDRY"

August Willich

August Willich was, of course, the best expounder of the Marxist system of political economy—in part because he helped to fashion its basic ideas. The examples below from Willich's editorials in the Cincinnati *Republikaner* present a Marxist view of economics and society that sharply contrasts with Snider's view just above. Also described, at least in outline, is Willich's idea of a national assembly of trade unions that would eventually replace the existing American government. The reader can readily perceive from the following Willich's own important role in the forging of the Communist Movement.

Reprinted with permission from Loyd Easton, *Hegel's First American Followers* (Athens, Ohio; Ohio University Press, 1956), pp. 320–30.

KARL MARX'S SYSTEM OF POLITICAL ECONOMY
(June 27, 1859)

WE urgently call our readers' attention to the work in political economy whose announcement we reprint in its entirety from *Das Volk* in London.

Knowledge of political economy is the essential prerequisite for the self-government and self-management of a free people. Where such knowledge is lacking, the republican form of government becomes in many respects a mere illusion as is the case with our republic, the United States. Where such knowledge is lacking in the masses, a republic differs from a monarchy only in that the political authority over and exploitation of the people, which in the latter is the hereditary property of certain aristocrats, becomes available as easy plunder to all those who are cunning and crafty enough to use the wants and good feelings of the people to achieve popularity so that through their official position they can get their fingers into the public treasury and even private pockets as well. Only where this knowledge of political economy is lacking is it possible that there can be material want, poor education, degradation of the youth—in a word, "misery"—in a republic.

Those of our readers who have the means should get this book for themselves; we will seek to acquaint the others generally with its main features. If, as we suspect and hope, this work marks a transition-period in political economy, the moment of its appearance is the more significant because it coincides with the time of transition from Europe's old political forms to new ones.

"Under the title 'Contribution to a Critique of Political Economy' the first volume of a writing on political economy by Karl Marx has been published by F. Duncker in Berlin, a writing through which the author's social perspective is for the first time brought into German science. The book is the result of such serious, prolonged, and extensive study that it must be studied deeply before we venture to pass judgment on it. For the present we welcome it as gratifying evidence that the men of *our* party at least did not waste their period of exile, and we take this opportunity to save the editors of German newspapers any further effort to find the name of the expert strategist and author of the pamphlet 'Po and Rhine' in the ranks of the Prussian generals. We hereby share it with them. It was Friedrich Engels who—as the papers of Zabel and Dumont, as well as Binke and other parliamentary greats who appealed to the authority of this strategist, will still recall—was formerly co-editor of the *Neue Rheinische Zeitung*."

From Marx's book we present only the preface, in part, since it contains an interesting sketch of the scientific development to which we owe the book before us: "I investigate the system of bourgeois economy in the following order: *capital, property in land, wage labor, the state, foreign trade, world market*. Under the first three headings I examine the conditions of the economic life of the three large classes which comprise modern bourgeois society; the relationship of the three remaining headings is immediately apparent." The first part of the book dealing with capital consists of the following chapters: 1) Commodities. 2) Money or simple circulation. 3) Capital in general. The first two chapters form the context of the present book. The entire material lies before me in the form of monographs, written at long intervals and for self-clarification, not publication, and their systematic elaboration on the plans above will depend on circumstances.

My specialized study was in jurisprudence which I pursued, however, only as subordinate to philosophy and history. In 1842–43, as editor of the "Rheinische Zeitung," I first found myself in difficulty when I had to take part in discussions concerning so-called material interests. The proceedings of the Rhine Diet in connection with wood-stealing and the division of landed property; the official controversy about the conditions of the Mosel peasants into which Herr v. Shaper, then president of the Rhine Province, entered with the "Rheinische Zeitung"; and finally the debates on free trade and protection, gave me the first impulse to concern myself with economic questions. At the same time a faint, philosophically-colored echo of French socialism and communism made itself heard in the "Rheinische Zeitung" in those days when the good will "to go ahead" greatly outweighed knowledge of the facts. I declared myself against such bungling but had to admit at once in a controversy with the "Allgemeine Augsburger Zeitung" that my previous studies did not permit me to hazard a judgment on the substance of the French tendencies. When, therefore, the supporters of the "Rheinische Zeitung" conceived the illusion that by a less aggressive policy the paper could be saved from the death sentence pronounced on it, I was happy to take the opportunity to retire from the public stage into my study.

The first work undertaken to resolve the doubt that troubled me was a critical revision of Hegel's philosophy of law; the introduction to that work appeared in the "Deutsch-Französische Jahrbücher" published in Paris in 1844. My investigation brought me to the conclusion that neither legal relations nor forms of the state could be understood by themselves or explained from the so-called general evolution of the human mind, but that they are rooted in the material conditions of life whose totality Hegel, following the English and French of the 18th century, summed up under the term "civil society," and the anatomy of civil society is to be sought in political economy. The study of the latter, which I had begun in Paris, I continued in Brussels whither I emigrated as a result of Herr Guizot's order of expulsion. The general conclusion at which I arrived and which, once achieved, became the leading thread in my studies, can be briefly summarized as follows: In the social production in which men live they enter into definite and necessary relations independent of their will, productive relations which correspond to a definite stage of the development of their material powers of production. The totality of these productive relations constitutes the economic structure of society, the real foundation on which rise legal and political superstructures and to which definite forms of social consciousness correspond. The mode of production in material life determines the general character of the social, political, and mental processes of life. It is not the consciousness of men that determines their existence, but, on the contrary, their social existence determines their consciousness. At a certain stage of their development the material forces of production in society come into conflict with existing relations of production, or— what is only a legal expression for the same thing—with the property relations within which they had previously moved. From forms of development of the forces of production these relations turn into their fetters. Then comes a period of social revolution. With the change of the economic foundation the entire immense superstructure is more or less rapidly altered.

In considering such transformations the distinction should always be made between the material transformation of the economic conditions of production which can be determined with the precision of natural science, and the legal, political, religious, aesthetic, or philosophical—in short, ideological forms in which men become aware of this conflict and fight it out. Just as our opinion of an individual is not based on what he thinks of himself, so can we not judge of such a period of transformation by its own consciousness; on the contrary, this consciousness must rather be explained from the contradictions of material life, from the existing conflict between the social forces of production and the relations of production. No social order ever disappears before all the productive forces, for which there is room in it, have been developed; and new higher relations of production never appear before the material conditions of their existence have matured in the womb of the old society. Therefore, mankind always takes up only such problems as it can solve; since, looking at the matter more closely, we shall always find that the problem itself arises only when the material conditions necessary for its solution already exist or are at least in the process of formation. In broad outlines we can designate the Asiatic, the ancient, the feudal, and the modern bourgeois methods of production as so many epochs in the progress of the economic formation of society. The bourgeois relations of production are the last antagonistic form of the social process of production—antagonistic not in the sense of individual antagonism, but of one arising from conditions surrounding the life of individuals in society. At the same time the productive forces developing in the womb of bourgeois society create the material conditions for the resolution of that antagonism. With this social formation, therefore, the prehistory of human society ends. . . .

Of the scattered writings in which Friedrich Engels and I collaborated to present one or another aspect of our views to the public, I mention here only the "Manifesto of the Communist Party" written by Engels and me together and a "Discourse on Free Trade" written by me. The leading points of our theory were first presented scientifically, though in a polemic form, in my "Poverty of Philosophy, etc.," directed against Proudhon, published in 1847. An essay on "Wage Labor," written by me in German, and in which I put together my lectures on the subject delivered before the German Workmen's Club at Brussels, was prevented from leaving the hands of the printer by the February revolution and my expulsion from Belgium which followed it as a consequence.

The publication of the "Neue Rheinische Zeitung" in 1848 and 1849, and the events which took place later on, interrupted my economic studies which I could not resume before 1850 in London. The enormous material on the history of political economy which is accumulated in the British Museum; the favorable view which London offers for the observation of bourgeois society; finally, the new stage of development upon which the latter seemed to have entered with the discovery of gold in California and Australia, led me to the decision to resume my studies from the very beginning and work up the new material critically. These studies partly led to what might seem side questions, over which I nevertheless had to stop for longer or shorter periods of time. Especially was the time at my disposal reduced by the imperative necessity of working for a living. My work as contributor to the leading Anglo-American newspaper, the "New York Tribune," at which I have now been engaged for eight years, has caused very great interruption in my studies, since I engage in newspaper work proper only occasionally. Yet articles on important economic events in England and on the continent have formed so large a part of my contributions that I have been obliged to make myself familiar with practical details which lie outside the proper sphere of political economy.

This sketch of the course of my studies in political economy is simply to prove that my views, whatever one may think of them, and no matter how little they agree with the interested prejudices of the ruling classes, are the result of many years of conscientious research. At the entrance to science, however, the same requirement must be put as at the entrance to Hell:

> Qui si convien lasciare ogni sospetto
> Ogni vilta convien che qui sia morta.
> [Here all misgiving must thy mind reject.
> Here cowardice must die and be no more. Dante]

ORGANIZATION OF LABOR
(*April 25, 1860*)

In a series of brief articles about the "9 hours strike" in England, we find the following position in the *Pionier:* "The workers should, may, and must unite and organize, *i.e.*, they must not unite temporarily, but construct a permanent, ordered organism. They must draw the capitalists themselves into this organism, not through threats but by way of persuasion."

Quite right! Such an organism, however, can come about only through organization by occupations; otherwise it ceases to be *organism* and becomes a mechanism like our present political arrangement. The majority of the other opinions expressed in the above-mentioned articles reveal the incorrectness of the basic view dominating the whole series. This basic view consists in accepting the position of the laborer as permanent and seeking all improvements only in the shortening of working hours and the increase of wages.

What does it mean, then, that our system of production presupposes the position of the laborer? It means nothing less than that the administration of our system of production forever excludes the application of republican principles. The laborer is not a free member of the producing community. He has no voice in the administration or other affairs of the factory. The only connection between him and that community consists in his bartering away his work, or rather himself, as expensively as possible, by day or week. The worker's relation in the area of economics is the same as that of a subject in the political sphere or that of forced conscience in the ecclesiastical. The principle of free citizenship, the principle of the republic, carried over into the area of economics becomes the principle of the free association of labor.

According to this principle, the unity at the basis of the community is no longer a heterogenous mass of interests of subordinate groups but the various employment associations or, as the Americans say, "Trades Unions" or "Unions of callings" of each city or county. They form an organic community whose essential purpose is protection against the disturbances and irregularities of productive life. No man, regardless of his calling—not even a newspaper writer—is excluded from this labor organization, and no man is hindered by it in his free movement, *i.e.*, any change he might want from one occupation to another. Further, the various associations of each particular occupation organize a general association throughout the republic which Americans call a "National Trades Union." Assembled, these link themselves into one great association, a "National Trades Assembly," which takes the place of the present political state. That would probably fulfill the intent of the words just cited from the *Pionier*.

Would the author of the articles in the *Pionier* agree and if not, what does he understand by a "permanent, ordered organism" of workers into which the capitalists should be admitted? Does the author not see that *"to admit capitalists into the organization,"* if it has a meaning at all, means only "to admit capital into the association, or rather, to convert it into the capital of the association?" His acceptance of the present position of the laborer throws a false light on all the rest of his well-intentioned ideas.

However, if the author asks how we would let capital be absorbed by the labor-association, then it appears that he does not know how to judge correctly the nature of the presently dominant, *so-called* capital. Real capital is the means of labor: machines, factories, conditions of employment, means of communication, and means of transportation, which with improvement have achieved greater capacity for production from the soil, more skillful and scientific means of production, etc., etc. The precious metals, whose value has been determined by their relative cost of production, are actual representatives of capital and as such may also be called capital.

If we now had these forms of capital or their actual representatives, then nothing could be complained about the dependence of labor upon capital, because this capital must be earned, created, and is completely sound. But the presently dominant, *so-called* capital is no actual capital. It is only apparent capital. Most paper money actually represents no capital because the capital does not exist. Similarly, credit certificates do not represent capital because the capital does not really exist. Both represent nothing more nor less than the monopoly given by the state to corporations to disrupt the regular exchange of actual values with illusory values, to raise taxes from employees and workers, and finally, as it happens in fact, not only to snatch away the real capital already produced but even the capital newly produced by labor.

These forms of legislation of the monopolists for the monopolists must be brought to an end. Hence is necessary, first and foremost, an organization of working and useful men according to occupation, an organization opposed to the immense swarm of economic, political, and religious plunderers who not only without any productive activity but even through destructive and poisonous activities have ruined a great part of our national wealth and have appropriated another part for themselves.

Or can the writer in the *Pionier* set forth another definite organizational form for labor? In his articles only impractical wishes are set forth, impractical because they contain a contradiction within themselves.

UNIONS
(July 30, 1860)

Gentlemen Mechanics! Fellow Workmen! As I am designated to speak in German to those members of the workingmen fraternity who are of German origin, I wish to expose to you the general idea of what I intend to say to them.

Since the beginning of human history the great masses have been oppressed by the few and have struggled for emancipation. This has been the same under despotical as well as under republican governments. In what consisted that oppression and by what means was it exercised? The oppression existed independently if it had the form of slavery; if that of daily hired labor, it consisted therein that the many were forced to work to the advantage of the few, that the many had no part in the administration of the national wealth they produced, that they were excluded as well from the intellectual as the economical capital of society, that they were only boarders on earth and the few were the landlords.

What were the means of oppression since the beginning of History? Were not the many stronger than the few? Those means consisted therein that the many were kept in a state of disunion by the few, and that in this state they oppressed each other to the benefit of the few, they kept each other in servitude under the few.

By what means did the few succeed to keep the many in disunion? By carefully cultivating prejudices amongst the many, which prejudices hindered them to learn that they all had the same interest in life. Those prejudices were of a religious, national, political, and social nature. Those prejudices created hatred amongst the hard-working masses. They killed and oppressed each other because they had different notions of the life after death, because they were proud of one kind of occupation or trade and despised the other. By what means can we therefore succeed in the emancipation of the masses, of the workingmen? First to take out of the hand of the oppressors the means to keep us in disunion, we must break down the ruling prejudices. The first step to conquer the prejudices is to defend our own interest, the interest of our families; to defend the value of our labor by forming the unions, the Trades Unions, and then to connect those unions with each other. Then we will be able to form legislatures, in which all the different callings are represented on which men rely for their living; then we will be able to form a Government by and for the producing and useful classes of society. Then we will be able to say to everyone: Make thyself useful, work, and then thou willst have a happy and independent home, thine children will receive as well as the children of any other man the best education society can give— thou does not want to be afraid of thine old age—thou shalt enjoy, when thou canst work no more.

Therefore fellow workingmen, let us first be unionmen before we are Catholics or Methodists or Philosophers. Let us first be unionmen before we are Americans, Irish, Germans, English, French. Let us first be unionmen before we are moulders, physicians, cabinetmakers, mathematicians, farmers, or teachers or anything else. And when we succeed to create as unionmen a happy life and we come to die, and come as unionmen to heaven, God lord will respect us the more for that and give us a fine and comfortable place. And when by chance we should come to Hell, and we come there as unionmen, I am sure the evil Spirit, the Devil, will be afraid of us. As unionmen we will turn to advantage the fires of hell, we will make of hell a well organized unionfoundry, and furnish heaven with all the ironwork they want there.

As trades unionmen nothing wrong will withstand us. We are strong enough to conquer all evils and to create all that is just, good, and beautiful. Therefore fellow workingmen let the word be amongst us, UNION FOREVER.

This I will explain in German to the workingmen fraternity who accidentally have been born on the other side of the Atlantic. And let us hope that the day will come when the tie of brotherhood of the producing-class will no more be interrupted either by the Atlantic or the Pacific.

VI

EDUCATION
AND DEMOCRACY

Since they believed so strongly that societal institutions were the key to freedom and self-expression, it is not surprising that the American Hegelians were keenly interested in schools and education. Virtually all of them were connected with education in some fashion. Harris, of course, was superintendent of public schools in St. Louis and he was succeeded in that office by Frank L. Soldan. Snider taught in a Christian Brothers' school and in the St. Louis public schools. Anna Brackett and Susan Blow, two female auxiliaries of the St. Louis group, were also schoolteachers. And even Brokmeyer spent the latter years of his career instructing the Indians around Muskogee, Oklahoma.

As educators, the Hegelians were, of course, concerned with using the school as a vehicle for molding the young according to their ideas. They were also genuinely conscientious about lifting the whole cultural level of the West and, indeed, of the country. This meant exposing children to far more than reading, writing, arithmetic, and a crude Protestant social morality. It implied the introduction of the finest elements of European culture from Shakespeare to Beethoven, and it also entailed stimulating the child or the adult student to be creative, or "self-determined," in his own right and hence comparatively a freer citizen. In encouraging such activity, the Hegelians were themselves most original. They imported pedagogical systems such as those of Rosenkranz and Froebel and in so doing established the Kindergarten Movement. They experimented with free universities and communal schools. And, under Harris's leadership as U.S. Commissioner of Education, they set up the graded school and broadened the curriculum to include the fine arts and modern world history.

At the same time, in the Hegelians' view, the school was meant to inculcate absolute or ideal values. Models and ideals of conduct were very important because though the Hegelians were innovative, they were not child-centered. Always before them lay the ideal of the Divine Universal and an absolute morality. Children and students of all kinds needed most of all to learn to conform to institutional order and the laws of reason, since only through such means could they be truly free. Only in response to order could they relate to others significantly and hence define themselves. Only through order and orderly institutions could they become part of the community which extended out from the local scene to the world scene. Thus, the main impulse of Hegelian pedagogics, which came to dominate nineteenth-century America, was controlled creativity—a fostering of the individual's identity exclusively through his relations to the community. It was a paradoxical stand, but a thoroughly Hegelian paradox.

23

THE PUBLIC SCHOOL AND
THE UNIVERSAL SCHOOL

Denton J. Snider

After taking his B.A. degree at Oberlin in 1862, Denton J. Snider acquired a vast experience in education of all kinds. He taught in public and private schools, at Hull House, and in Chautauqua. He conducted free universities for the workingmen of Milwaukee, seminars for socialists in the ghettos of St. Louis and lectures for the ladies of the Concord School of Philosophy. He also established what he liked to think of as a "universal school" for all mankind through the medium of his forty books, which ranged over every topic imaginable in the arts and sciences and which he frequently gave away to anyone who would read them. In all of this, Snider maintained a clear Hegelian idea of the purpose of education.

Denton J. Snider, *Social Institutions* (St. Louis: Sigma Publ. Co., 1901), pp. 504–512, 521–26.

THE PUBLIC SCHOOL

THIS is often called the Common School, being common to all as an Educative Institution, teaching the common branches, common to the community and necessary for social intercommunication. It takes the undeveloped self of the child and unfolds it out of the Family into the Community, the School being itself a Community, a kind of reproduction and re-enactment of the latter's life, whereby the immature but impressionable mind is brought to re-create this early stage of the institutional world.

The Community is the primordial unit or cell out of which Society is evolved. In some form it is compelled to have a School for the purpose of reproducing itself in the new-born person, who must in the course of time be its supporter. The primitive Village Community had some such training, though chiefly through myth and folk-lore transmitted by tradition. At present the Public or Communal School has to develop this social germ inherited by every infant. This School is, accordingly, the first stage of the Educative Institution which has to preserve the whole institutional world by recreating it in every new generation and thus propagating it in each oncoming Free-Will of the Community.

The Educative Institution is not directly to embody freedom, or to reproduce it completely, but is to reproduce the Institutions which reproduce freedom, making it actual in the world. So there is always an element of authority in the School, which has, however, freedom as its end, training the untrained mind in obedience to Law, whereby the human being becomes free. The School must always be governed, but it must always be moving toward self-government.

Very briefly we shall have to deal at present with the Public School, which has already become one of the most important Institutions. Merely a slight sketch of its idea or conception can be here given, this conception being the germinal process underlying not only the Public School, but all the Schools of the Educative Institution—being in fact the inner movement of Education itself.

Education may be taken as somewhat different from the Educative Institution, just as Religion is different from the Religious Institution. The one is the idea, the other is the actuality of the idea. Education is made actual in its Institution, is organized, endowed with a body as it were, and given to the people. Through the Educative Institution, Education, which otherwise is simply an idea and subjective, belonging to the few or even to the one, is imparted to all. Hence it is often said that Education, or rather its embodiment in the Public School, is the saving principle of popular government, which depends upon the intelligence of the people.

We may here consider the three fundamental stages of Education, which are constituents of its complete process, or of its Conception.

1. Education is Information. Such is the most immediate, manifest, and indeed general object of Education: to get knowledge. The learner, be he child or man, in the Public School or in the School of Life, is to take up and assimilate certain facts, more or less useful, which constitute a body of instruction or of information. This is the pursuit of knowledge, which is native to the aspiring human spirit. Education must, primarily, impart knowledge, which opens the world of culture to the growing Ego.

At the same time the acquisition of knowledge can become one-sided. It can be so emphasized by drill and otherwise, that it stunts or stops development. Thus Information contradicts its own name and nature: it no longer informs but deforms the mind. It is well known that some of the narrowest souls in the Republic of Letters have been men of the greatest erudition. Hence comes the loud call for an Education which does not simply pour in from the outside, but unfolds from the inside outwards. That is, along with the training of the Intellect or receptive principle of spirit, we must have a training of the Will or the active principle thereof. Such is the demand which is chiefly heard in these days in opposition to the so-called old method of learning—a demand which in its present form goes back to the last century, but which has its fountain-head in the old Greek world.

2. Education is Development. So we make a new start, on the inside, so to say, from the Ego itself, which is now to be unfolded and made real; the true Self, hitherto overwhelmed by acquisition from the outside, asserts its right and takes the initiative. The word *Education* is cited as having just this meaning, which is that of leading out and of developing.

With the rise of Education as Development comes the need of method, or at least of a decided change of method. The branches of Information must be taken not so much for the sake of Information as of Cultivation; moreover they must be taught or presented in such a way and in such an order as to call forth with the least outlay of time and energy the latent powers of the Ego, transforming all its potentialities into a complete well-rounded, actual person. The organization of the Educative Institution becomes the great object, and with this rises the conception of the Normal School, which is to train the trainer. Thus the Educative Institution also develops and completes itself in its various organic members.

But this stage of Education likewise reveals its decided limitation. We have indeed attained the culture of the individual, which, however, becomes individualistic. Self-activity is the grand doctrine, but this activity of the Self ends or may end in selfishness. We have let loose the Ego and bid it speed forth in all directions untrammeled, and thereby unfold its freedom; the result is it has unfolded its freedom into caprice, perchance into license, or is in danger of so doing.

Education is, therefore, beginning to place limits upon those favorite categories: self-activity, self-culture, self-development. It goes so far as to emphasize control, authority, even restraint and suppression, but the latter would signify the extreme of reaction.

There is no doubt, however, that the individualistic Education of the time must be transformed, without throwing away the thought of inner development, and of true freedom. How can the work be done? At this point we pass to the third stage of Education which seems in the present epoch to be dawning.

3. Education is institutional. The profoundest element of Education is just this, its determining ethical end; all its other elements become at last means for this supreme end. Education must now realize itself in an Institution whose chief object is to train to an institutional life. So we come to the Educative Institution, which is to impart Information, to give Development, and supremely to recreate in thought and conduct Institutions.

Through the School as an Educative Institution the child acquires the institutional habit, which is, in general, to will Free-Will. As a member of the organization he is ruled by law, as if he belonged to the State. For every free act of his he must will the free action of the whole School. He learns that he cannot be truly free all by himself, and this is his best lesson. Every act must be universal, must be what all can do, or what is lawful. Even if he speaks, it must be through the will of the whole embodied in the authority of the teacher and of the School. Otherwise his speaking may assail the Institution, and thereby violate the Free-Will of all.

In complete Education, then, these three ends are present: (1) knowledge, the appropriation of what is different or unknown, the outer world assimilated by the Ego; (2) the separation of the Ego within, and the unfolding and expressing of itself through Will, the making of the potential Ego real in a complete self-active center, the whole being the sphere of individual freedom; (3) the return to the outer world, which is not now that of mere knowledge, or the information about things more or less external, but the world of Institutions, existent and objective on the one hand, yet in and through the Ego on the other.

It is manifest that we behold in these three stages of Education not only so many separate isolated phases, but an inner connection which unites them in a process, yea, just the fundamental psychological process, the Psychosis. They all belong together, no Educative Institution can do without them all, and all at once. It is true that sometimes the stress is put on one and sometimes on the other, still all are present. But the deepest principle of the three, as well as the supreme end of Education is the third. Yet we must not forget that it could not be and act without the other two.

It is, therefore, a mistake to denounce the acquisition of knowledge as one purpose of the School. It could not exist without such an end, and knowledge has a right to be loved for its own sake. Certainly every aspiring pupil will take delight in learning on its own account. It means mastery of the external limit in some form and triumph of the spirit—a justifiable joy if there be any, since such a mastery is prophetic of freedom, which prophecy is fulfilled by the Institutional World.

Here we may note the fact that these three stages of the educational process are also stages of its history. Leaving out the ancient and medieval period for the present, we find that the Renascence put stress upon Learning, Information, Expression, in its strong yet one-sided attempt to recover and reproduce antiquity. This was the need of the age and its educators responded, but the time came when the right of inner Development was demanded by the chafing human Ego, which, accordingly, asserted the full, free unfolding of the Individual. Montaigne started the cry, which was taken up by Rousseau and made to re-echo through Europe; Pestalozzi and Froebel realized the thought in educational Institutions. At present we are turning to the Institution itself and looking into that; we are beginning to find that in it lies the deeper fact of the whole movement.

So much upon the Conception of the School, in which we shall always find the three stages which we may name the informational, the developmental, and the institutional—none ever absent and each in a process with the rest, yet the latter largely implicit hitherto in educational history. All three belong really to the general Educative Institution—the Institution which trains people small and great, young and old, into the Institutional World.

The School, then, in its Conception or creative Thought, must be informational, developmental and institutional, all three as distinct and yet in a process together, which is the veritable soul of the School, its creative Psychosis.

It is the third stage—the institutional—which is to become explicit in the American School System, as this must give the training to freedom, that is, institutional freedom. The Prussian School System is probably the best in the world for the first two stages— the informational and the developmental—but in the third it must be completely transformed to suit this country. We may well learn from Germany in regard to methods of imparting knowledge and of training the individual mind; but the German institutional world, and specially the State, is so different from the American that there must be a corresponding transformation of the School, which is ultimately to re-produce just the Nation's Institutions in the mind of the pupil. . . .

THE UNIVERSAL SCHOOL

IT is not easy to find a suitable term for the present chapter, which takes a wide sweep over a large domain embracing many different spiritual activities. We wish to keep before the reader that this is still an Institution, and an Educative Institution, amid all its divisions and diversities; it is a form of actualized Will whose purpose is to reproduce Free-Will in the soul of all, especially of the grown man pursuing his vocation.

In the heading above we call it the Universal School in order to suggest in the name its correlation with the other two Schools, Public and Special. Still its purport is wider than the ordinary School, and we shall often call it the Universal Educative Institution, or, for short, the Universal Institute, quite distinct from the University proper which has been considered in the previous chapter. Still we may sometimes designate it as the University of Civilization, to which all men belong and through which all have to pass in one way or other; thus it is truly universal, the School of Life, the World's Institute.

In a way it is a return to the Common or Public School, through which all ought to pass in order to possess the primary implements of Civilization. It is the final or absolute School for which the previous Schools have been a preparation, into which they move and out of which they are called forth. It is their creative source, their determining principle, and also their ultimate end. It is an Institution, but an Institution which is likewise to reveal man to hmself as the moulder and the moulded of Institutions.

The School of the World, then, we have before us; but who is the teacher? Ultimately the World-Spirit, the absolute Ego who is at the center of Civilization and is unfolding it into a colossal image of himself. Undoubtedly there are many other teachers, every grade in fact; but the World-Spirit is the chief pedagogue in the World-School.

Moreover he has been at work from the beginning. Secretly he had a hand in the Public School and organized it for his own behoof, training the youth of the land for his purpose, which is indeed their own highest purpose. Also he was at work in the University, preparing its inmates specially for the task of his School, which is verily the sum total of all Schools, and in which he is finally to reveal himself, and teach himself what he is.

Still this Institution, though the end of all other Institutions, is itself also a means for their end which is freedom, and this freedom thereby can only be institutional freedom. Thus they all come back to the individual and elevate him into the universal life, while he on the other hand must incessantly reproduce them, both knowing and willing them. The Institutions of Civilization mean the Institute of Civilization, the universal training-school of humanity unto the one great end, freedom as institutional.

We have called this the Universal Educative Institution, because it is all three—universal, educative, and institutional. It is universal: all must enter it, the training is universal, the teacher is the universal teacher, and the man is to become universal, is to lead the universal life. It is educative: it is the School whose end is that of all schooling, and which embraces a vast constituency of Egos receiving their discipline; it is the totality of the race being trained for the race's end. It is institutional: it is the actualized Will of man willing Free Will; it is an existent Institution whose object is to reproduce the institutional world in every human being both through Will and Intellect, through the experience of the Deed and through the instruction of the Word. To this Institution, therefore, belong Art, Literature, Science, Philosophy.

The Universal Educative Institution is thus the true University of Man, whose very purpose is to reveal and to teach the Universal Creative Ego eternally creating the world, especially the world of Institutions into whose process it unfolds itself and thereby reveals itself. In this School of Life you may take the lesson immediately and learn it through yourself, transforming all experience, sad and joyful, all suffering and all happiness into a means for your own enfranchisement. Likewise the events going on in the world you are to see leading the race along the path of freedom, in spite of all backstrokes of destiny.

Still interpretation is needed, the World-Spirit uttering itself at first in the events of the time must have a new utterance in Art, Literature, Science. Hence the new teacher appears, the interpreter of the World-Spirit as artist, poet, thinker; this new teacher is the creative genius who belongs peculiarly to the Universal Educative Institution, is in fact its leading Professor, usually a very different man from that other Professor in the University proper.

In the School of Life we may start with the instruction which comes from the Deed, that is, from our individual Self originating actions, which flow out from the Ego as a center and pass into the world of occurrences. Every person is such a center of concentric waves of influence moving outwards. But also they come back to him from other sources and determine him. Still the main fact is that his own Deed comes back to him in its consequences, having passed through the institutional world in some of its forms, which return to him his conduct as that of a free-acting individual. Thus every man is cited before a court, a World-tribunal, which metes out to him the counterpart of his Self in reward and penalty. Our World-School has not abolished punishment, not even corporeal punishment, in its administration. Through the pains and penalties flowing from the Deed the individual learns the Law, yea learns the Divine Order, in which he lives and moves and has his being. So much instruction he may acquire directly through his own action.

But, in order that man may get the experience of man, a record must be kept of the most significant deeds and events, which show forth the decree of the World-Spirit or the divinely creative Ego. This record is properly the work of the genius making his poem, picture, statue, or speaking his thought as one with that of the Supreme Thinker. We may call him the recording angel of the court of last resort, who records the decision of this final tribunal, and imparts it to man, that the latter may know the Judgment and the Law of the highest Justiciary.

This record in its various forms—Poetry, Art, Philosophy, etc. —is the fundamental branch in the Universal Institute, which must also have its text-books of instruction. Now the best text-books in the School of Civilization have always been and still are the Bibles of the race which are studied in the great Institute of Humanity for the purpose of revealing to man the Divine Order and the workings of the Divine Ego. They are to call forth in him the consciousness of the Universal Creative Spirit or Ego, and thus are religious in the profoundest sense. Still we shall find these Bibles dividing themselves into two kinds, religious and literary or secular. This distinction, however, we shall elaborate later; at present we put stress on the fact that both kinds develop in man the God-consciousness, and so reproduce in him the religious Institution.

The individual educator, while educating the youth in his little school, is often being educated by this supreme Power in His Great School. Pestalozzi at Yverdon was working away in his small Institute for boys, but he was at the same time under training by the World-Spirit in whose Universal Institute he was chief instructor for the people in all countries and all ages. The same is true of Froebel when he started his little kindergarten for the little child at Blankenburg; he was really an original teacher, not in a German University, but in the far greater University of Civilization.

Thus we seek to catch some outline or suggestion of that School over all Schools with its supreme Schoolmaster, from whom proceeds the New-Idea which is to be imparted to all mankind. . . .

24

EDUCATION AS A SCIENCE

Anna C. Brackett

One of the most fascinating but neglected figures in American history is Anna C. Brackett. Born in Boston in 1836, she graduated from the Framingham Normal School at age 20 and began a lifelong career as a teacher and philosopher of education. In 1860, upon moving to St. Louis from a teaching post in Charleston, South Carolina, she became the first female principal of an American normal school. During her St. Louis years, she participated informally in the St. Louis Movement, and by the time she returned east to New York in 1870 she was a confirmed Hegelian, principally through the medium of the works of Karl F. Rosenkranz, Hegel's disciple and a philosopher of education much admired by the St. Louis Hegelians. It was Anna Brackett who, at the urging of William Torrey Harris, translated and introduced Rosenkranz's systematic pedagogics to the United States.

Building upon Rosenkranz's ideas, Brackett then became interested in the special problems of urban education and even more so in women's education. At a time when woman's place was said to be "in the home" and her role delicate and deferential, Brackett preached the gospel of the creative, enlightened, intellectual woman. She reached thousands through her books, *The Education of American Girls* (1874) and *Women and Higher Education* (1893). Beyond that, she gained an even larger audience through her column in *Harper's Bazar*.

The selection below is Brackett's summary of Rosenkranz's *Pedagogics as a System*, which represents the basis of her own pedagogical philosophy. Her debt to Hegel is obvious.

Anna C. Brackett, "The Science of Education," JSP 12 (1878): 67–81.

§ 1. The science of Pedagogics may be called a secondary science, inasmuch as it derives its principles from others. In this respect it differs from Mathematics, which is independent. As it concerns the development of the human intelligence, it must wait upon Psychology for an understanding of that upon which it is to operate, and, as its means are to be sciences and arts, it must wait upon them for a knowledge of its materials. The science of Medicine, in like manner, is dependent on the sciences of Biology, Chemistry, Physics, etc. Moreover, as Medicine may have to deal with a healthy or unhealthy body, and may have it for its province to preserve or restore health, to assist a natural process (as in the case of a broken bone), or to destroy an unnatural one (as in the case of the removal of a tumor), the same variety of work is imposed upon Education.*

§ 2. Since the rules of Pedagogics must be extremely flexible, so that they may be adapted to the great variety of minds, and since an infinite variety of circumstances may arise in their application, we find, as we should expect, in all educational literature room for widely differing opinions and the wildest theories; these numerous theories, each of which may have a strong influence for a season, only to be overthrown and replaced by others.† It must be acknowledged that educational literature, as such, is not of a high order. It has its cant like religious literature. Many of its faults, however, are the result of honest effort, on the part of teachers, to remedy existing defects, and the authors are, therefore, not harshly to be blamed. It is also to be remembered that the habit of giving reproof and advice is one fastened in them by the daily necessity of their professional work.‡

§ 3. As the position of the teacher has ceased to be undervalued, there has been an additional impetus given to self-glorification on his part, and this also—in connection with the fact that schools are no longer isolated as of old, but subject to constant comparison and competition—leads to much careless theorizing among its teachers, especially in the literary field.

§ 4. Pedagogics, because it deals with the human spirit, belongs, in a general classification of the sciences, to the philosophy of spirit, and in the philosophy of spirit it must be classified under the practical, and not the merely theoretical, division. For its prob-

---

* The parallelism between these two sciences, Medicine and Education, is an obvious point, which every student will do well to consider.

† This will again remind the student of the theories of treatment in medicine in diseases which, in the seventeenth century, were treated only by bleeding and emetics, are now treated by nourishing food, and no medicines, etc.

‡ The teacher will do well to consider the probable result of the constant association with mental inferiors entailed by his work, and also to consider what counter-irritant is to be applied to balance, in his character, this unavoidable tendency.

lem is not merely to comprehend the nature of that with which it has to deal, the human spirit—its problem is not merely to influence one mind (that of the pupil) by another (that of the teacher) —but to influence it in such a way as to produce the mental freedom of the pupil. The problem is, therefore, not so much to obtain performed works as to excite mental activity. A creative process is required. The pupil is to be forced to go in certain beaten tracks, and yet he is to be so forced to go in these that he shall go of his own free will. All teaching which does not leave the mind of the pupil free is unworthy of the name. It is true that the teacher must understand the nature of mind, as he is to deal with mind, but when he has done this he has still his main principle of action unsolved; for the question is, knowing the nature of the mind, How shall he incite it to action, already predetermined in his own mind, without depriving the mind of the pupil of its own free action? How shall he restrain and guide, and yet not enslave?

If, in classifying all sciences, as suggested at the beginning of this section, we should subdivide the practical division of the Philosophy of Spirit, which might be called Ethics, one could find a place for Pedagogics under some one of the grades of Ethics. The education which the child receives through the influence of family life lies at the basis of all other teaching, and what the child learns of life, its duties, and possibilities, in its own home, forms the foundation for all after-work. On the life of the family, then, as a presupposition, all systems of Education must be built. In other words, the school must not attempt to initiate the child into the knowledge of the world—it must not assume the care of its first training; that it must leave to the family.* But the science of Pedagogics does not, as a science, properly concern itself with the family education, or with that point of the child's life which is dominated by the family influence. That is education, in a certain sense, without doubt, but it does not properly belong to a science of Pedagogics. But, on the other hand, it must be remembered that this science, as here expounded, presupposes a previous family life in the human being with whom it has to deal.

§ 5. Education as a science will present the necessary and universal principles on which it is based; Education as an art will consist in the practical realization of these in the teacher's work in special places, under special circumstances, and with special pupils. In the skillful application of the principles of the science to the ac-

---

* The age at which the child should be subject to the training of school life, or Education, properly so-called, must vary with different races, nations, and different children.

tual demands of the art lies the opportunity for the educator to prove himself a creative artist; and it is in the difficulty involved in this practical work that the interest and charm of the educator's work consists.

The teacher must thus adapt himself to the pupil. But, in doing so, he must have a care that he not carry this adaptation to such a degree as to imply that the pupil is not to change; and he must see to it, also, that the pupil shall always be worked upon by the matter which he is considering, and not too much by the personal influence of the teacher through whom he receives it.*

§ 6. The utmost care is necessary lest experiments which have proved successful in certain cases should be generalized into rules, and a formal, dead creed, so to speak, should be adopted. All professional experiences are valuable as material on which to base new conclusions and to make new plans, but only for that use. Unless the day's work is, every day, a new creation, a fatal error has been made.

§ 7. Pedagogics as a science must consider Education—
(a) In its general idea;
(b) In its different phases;
(c) In the special systems arising from this general idea, acting under special circumstances at special times.†

§ 8. With regard to the First Part, we remark that by Education, in its general idea, we do not mean any mere history of Pedagogics, nor can any history of Pedagogics be substituted for a systematic exposition of the underlying idea.

§ 9. The second division considers Education under three heads —as physical, intellectual, and moral—and forms, generally, the principal part of all pedagogical treatises.

In this part lies the greatest difficulty as to exact limitation. The ideas on these divisions are often undefined and apt to be confounded, and the detail of which they are capable is almost unlimited, for we might, under this head, speak of all kinds of special schools, such as those for war, art, mining, etc.

§ 10. In the Third Part we consider the different realizations of the one general idea of Pedagogics as it has developed itself under different circumstances and in different ages of the world.

The general idea is forced into different phases by the varying

---

* The best educator is he who makes his pupils independent of himself. This implies on the teacher's part an ability to lose himself in his work, and a desire for the real growth of the pupil, independent of any personal fame of his own—a disinterestedness which places education on a level with the noblest occupations of man.

† See analysis [beginning next page].

physical, intellectual, and moral conditions of men. The result is the different systems, as shown in the analysis. The general idea is one. The view of the end to be obtained determines in each case the actualization of this idea. Hence the different systems of Education are each determined by the stand-point from which the general ideal is viewed. Proceeding in this manner, it might be possible to construct a history of Pedagogics, *a priori*, without reference to actual history, since all the possible systems might be inferred from the possible definite number of points of view.

Each lower stand-point will lead to a higher, but it will not be lost in it. Thus, where Education for the sake of the nation* merges into the Education based on Christianity, the form is not thereby destroyed, but, rather, in the transition first attains its full realization. The systems of Education which were based on the idea of the nation had, in the fullness of time, outgrown their own limits, and needed a new form in order to contain their own true idea. The idea of the nation, as the highest principle, gives way for that of Christianity. A new life came to the old idea in what at first seemed to be its destruction. The idea of the nation was born again, and not destroyed, in Christianity.

§ 11. The final system, so far, is that of the present time, which thus is itself the fruit of all the past systems, as well as the seed of all systems that are to be. The science of Pedagogics, in the consideration of the system of the present, thus again finds embodied the general idea of education, and thus returns upon itself to the point from whence it set out. In the First and Second Parts there is already given the idea which dominates the system found thus necessarily existing in the present.

FIRST PART

The General Idea of Education

§ 12. A full treatment of Pedagogics must distinguish—
  (a) The nature of Education;
  (b) The form of Education;
  (c) The limits of Education.

(a) THE NATURE OF EDUCATION

§ 13. The nature of Education is determined by the nature of mind, the distinguishing mark of which is that it can be developed only from within, and by its own activity. Mind is essentially free—

---

* Asiatic systems of Education have this basis.

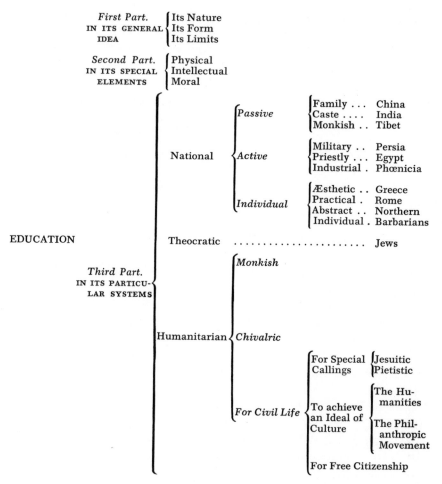

First Part. IN ITS GENERAL IDEA		Its Nature Its Form Its Limits			
Second Part. IN ITS SPECIAL ELEMENTS		Physical Intellectual Moral			
	National	*Passive*	Family ... Caste .... Monkish ..	China India Tibet	
		Active	Military .. Priestly ... Industrial .	Persia Egypt Phœnicia	
		Individual	Æsthetic .. Practical . Abstract .. Individual .	Greece Rome Northern Barbarians	

EDUCATION — Theocratic .... Jews

Third Part. IN ITS PARTICULAR SYSTEMS

Humanitarian:
- *Monkish*
- *Chivalric*
- *For Civil Life*
  - For Special Callings: Jesuitic, Pietistic
  - To achieve an Ideal of Culture: The Humanities, The Philanthropic Movement
  - For Free Citizenship

i.e., it has the capacity for freedom—but it cannot be said to possess freedom till it has obtained it by its own voluntary effort. Till then it cannot be truly said to be free. Education consists in enabling a human being to take possession of, and to develop himself by, his own efforts, and the work of the educator cannot be said to be done in any sense where this is not accomplished. In general, we may say that the work of education consists in leading to a full development of all the inherent powers of the mind, and that its work is done when, in this way, the mind has attained perfect freedom, or the state in which alone it can be said to be truly itself.*

The isolated human being can never become truly man. If such human beings (like the wild girl of the forest of Ardennes) have

---

* The definition of freedom here implied is this: Mind is free when it knows itself and wills its own laws.

been found, they have only proved to us that reciprocal action with our fellow beings is necessary for the development of our powers. Caspar Hauser, in his subterranean prison, will serve as an example of what man would be without men. One might say that this fact is typified by the first cry of the newly-born child. It is as if the first expression of its seemingly independent life were a cry for help from others. On the side of nature the human being is at first quite helpless.

§ 14. Man is, therefore, the only proper object of education. It is true that we speak of the education of plants and of animals, but we instinctively apply other terms when we do so, for we say "raising" plants, and "training" animals. When we "train" or "break" an animal, it is true that we do, by pain or pleasure, lead him into an exercise of a new activity. But the difference between this and Education consists in the fact that, though he possessed capacity, yet by no amount of association with his kind would he ever have acquired this new development. It is as if we impress upon his plastic nature the imprint of our loftier nature, which imprint he takes mechanically, and does not himself recognize it as his own internal nature. We train him for our recognition, not for his own. But, on the contrary, when we educate a human being, we only excite him to create for himself, and out of himself, that for which he would most earnestly strive had he any appreciation of it beforehand, and in proportion as he does appreciate it he recognizes it joyfully as a part of himself, as his own inheritance, which he appropriates with a knowledge that it is his, or, rather, is a part of his own nature. He who speaks of "raising" human beings uses language which belongs only to the slave-dealer, to whom human beings are only cattle for labor, and whose property increases in value with the number.

Are there no school-rooms where Education has ceased to have any meaning, and where physical pain is made to produce its only possible result—a mechanical, external repetition? The school-rooms where the creative word—the only thing which can influence the mind—has ceased to be used as the means are only plantations, where human beings are degraded to the position of lower animals.

§ 15. When we speak of the Education of the human race, we mean the gradual growth of the nations of the earth, as a whole, towards the realization of self-conscious freedom. Divine Providence is the teacher here. The means by which the development is effected are the various circumstances and actions of the different races of men, and the pupils are the nations. The unfolding of this great Education is generally treated of under the head of Philosophy of History.

§ 16. Education, however, in a more restricted sense, has to do with the shaping of the individual. Each one of us is to be educated by the laws of physical nature—by the relations into which we come with the national life, in its laws, customs, etc., and by the circumstances which daily surround us. By the force of these we find our arbitrary will hemmed in, modified, and forced to take new channels and forms. We are too often unmindful of the power with which these forces are daily and hourly educating us—*i.e.*, calling out our possibilities into real existence. If we set up our will in opposition to either of these; if we act in opposition to the laws of nature; if we seriously offend the laws, or even the customs, of the people among whom we live; or if we despise our individual lot, we do so only to find ourselves crushed in the encounter. We only learn the impotence of the individual against these mighty powers; and that discovery is, of itself, a part of our education. It is sometimes only by such severe means that God is revealed to the man who persistently misunderstands and defies His creation. All suffering brought on ourselves by our own violation of laws, whether natural, ethical, or divine, must be, however, thus recognized as the richest blessing. We do not mean to say that it is never allowable for a man, in obedience to the highest laws of his spiritual being, to break away from the fetters of nature—to offend the ethical sense of his own people, or to struggle against the might of destiny. Reformers and martyrs would be examples of such, and our remarks above do not apply to them, but to the perverse, the frivolous, and the conceited; to those who are seeking in their action, not the undoubted will of God, but their own individual will or caprice.

§ 17. But we generally use the word Education in a still narrower sense than either of these, for we mean by it the working of one individual mind upon or within another in some definite and premeditated way, so as to fit the pupil for life generally, or for some special pursuit. For this end the educator must be relatively finished in his own education, and the pupil must possess confidence in him, or docility. He must be teachable. That the work be successful demands the very highest degree of talent, knowledge, skill, and prudence; and any development is impossible if a well-founded authority be wanting in the educator, or docility on the part of the pupil.

Education, in this narrowest and technical sense, is an outgrowth of city or urban life. As long as men do not congregate in large cities, the three forces spoken of in § 16—*i.e.*, the forces of nature, national customs, and circumstances—will be left to perform most of the work of Education; but, in modern city life, the great complication of events, the uncertainty in the results—though careful forethought has been used—the immense development of individuality, and the pressing need of various information, break the power of custom, and render a different method necessary. The larger the city is, the more free is the individual in it from the restraints of customs, the less subjected to curious criticism, and the more able is he to give play to his own idiosyncrasies. This, however, is a freedom which needs the counterpoise of a more exact training in conventionalities, if we would not have it dangerous. Hence the rapid multiplication of educational institutions and systems in modern times (one chief characteristic of which is the development of urban life). The ideal Telemachus of Fénelon differs very much from the real Telemachus of history. Fénelon proposed an education which trained a youth to reflect, and to guide himself by reason. The Telemachus of the heroic age followed the customs ("use and wont") of his time and *naïve* obedience. The systems of Education once sufficient do not serve the needs of modern life, any more than the defenses once sufficient against hostile armies are sufficient against the new weapons adopted by modern warfare.

§ 18. The problem with which modern Education has to deal may be said, in general terms, to be the development in the individual soul of the indwelling Reason, both practical (as will) and theoretical (as intellect). To make a child good is only a part of Education; we have also to develop his intelligence. The sciences of Ethics and Education are not the same. Again, we must not forget that no pupil is simply a human being, like every other human being; he is also an individual, and thus differs from every other one of the race. This is a point which must never be lost sight of by the educator. Human beings may be—nay, must be—educated in company, but they cannot be educated simply in the mass.

§ 19. Education is to lead the pupil by a graded series of exercises, previously arranged and prescribed by the educator, to a definite end. But these exercises must take on a peculiar form for each particular pupil under the special circumstances present. Hasty and inconsiderate work *may*, by chance, accomplish much; but no work which is not *systematic* can advance and fashion him in conformity with his nature, and such alone is to be called Education; for Education implies both a comprehension of the end to be attained and of the means necessary to compass that end.

§ 20. Culture, however, means more and more every year; and, as the sum total of knowledge increases for mankind, it becomes necessary, in order to be a master in any one line, to devote one's self almost exclusively to that. Hence arises, for the teacher, the difficulty of preserving the unity and wholeness which are essential to a complete man. The principle of division of labor comes in. He who is a teacher by profession becomes one-sided in his views; and, as teaching divides and subdivides into specialities, this abnormal one-sidedness tends more and more to appear. Here we find a parallelism in the profession of Medicine, with a corresponding danger of narrowness; for that, too, is in a process of constant specialization, and the physician who treats nervous diseases is likely to be of the opinion that all trouble arises from that part of the organism, or, at least, that all remedies should be applied there. This tendency to one-sidedness is inseparable from the progress of civilization and that of science and arts. It contains, nevertheless, a danger of which no teacher should be unwarned. An illustration is furnished by the microscope or telescope; a higher power of the instrument implies a narrower field of view. To concentrate our observation upon one point implies the shutting out of others. This difficulty with the teacher creates one for the pupil.

In this view one might be inclined to judge that the life of the savage as compared with that of civilized man, or that of a member of a rural community as compared with that of an inhabitant of a city, were the more to be desired. The savage has his hut, his family, his cocoa-palm, his weapons, his passions; he fishes, hunts, amuses himself, adorns himself, and enjoys the consciousness that he is the center of a little world; while the denizen of a city must often acknowledge that he is, so to speak, only one wheel of a gigantic machine. Is the life of the savage, therefore, more favorable to human development? The characteristic idea of modern civilization is: The development of the individual as the end for which the State exists. The great empires of Persia, Egypt, and India, wherein the individual was of value only as he ministered to the strength of the State, have given way to the modern nations, where individual freedom is pushed so far that the State seems only an instrument for the good of the individual. From being the supreme end of the individual, the State has become the means for his advancement into freedom; and with this very exaltation of the value of the mere individual over the State, as such, there is inseparably connected the seeming destruction of the wholeness of the individual man. But the union of State and individual, which was in ancient times merely mechanical, has now become a living process, in which constant interaction gives rise to all the intellectual life of modern civilization.

§ 21. The work of Education being thus necessarily split up, we have the distinction between general and special schools. The work of the former is to give general development—what is considered essential for all men; that of the latter, to prepare for special callings. The former should furnish a basis for the latter—*i.e.*, the College should precede the Medical School, etc., and the High School the Normal. In the United States, owing to many causes, this is unfortunately not the case.

The difference between city and country life is important here. The teacher in a country school, and, still more, the private tutor or governess, must be able to teach many more things than the teacher in a graded school in the city, or the professor in a college or university. The danger on the one side is of superficiality, on the other of narrowness.

§ 22. The Education of any individual can be only relatively finished. His possibilities are infinite. His actual realization of those possibilities must always remain far behind. The latter can only approximate to the former. It can never reach them. The term "finishing an education" needs, therefore, some definition; for, as a technical term, it has undoubtedly a meaning. An immortal soul can never complete its development; for, in so doing, it would give the lie to its own nature. We cannot speak properly, however, of educating an idiot. Such an unfortunate has no power of generalization, and no conscious personality. We can train him mechanically, but we cannot educate him. This will help to illustrate the difference, spoken of in § 14, between Education and Mechanical training.

We obtain astonishing results, it is true, in our schools for idiots, and yet we cannot fail to perceive that, after all, we have only an external result. We produce a mechanical performance of duties, and yet there seems to be no actual mental growth. It is an exogenous, and not an endogenous, growth, to use the language of Botany.* Continual repetition, under the most gentle patience, renders the movements easy, but, after all, they are only automatic, or what the physicians call reflex.

We have the same result produced in a less degree when we attempt to teach an intelligent child something which is beyond his active comprehension. A child may be taught to do or say almost anything by patient training, but, if what he is to say is beyond the power of his mental comprehension, and hence of his active assimilation, we are only training him as we train an animal (§ 14), and not educating him. We call such recitations parrot recitations, and, by our use of the word, express exactly in what position the pupils are placed. An idiot is only a case of permanently arrested development. What in the intelligent child is a passing phase is for the idiot

---

* Perhaps, however slow the growth, there is real progress in liberating the imprisoned soul (?).

a fixed state. We have idiots of all grades, as we have children of all ages.

The above observations must not be taken to mean that children should never be taught to perform operations in arithmetic which they do not, in cant phrase, "perfectly understand," or to learn poetry whose whole meaning they cannot fathom. Into this error many teachers have fallen.

There can be no more profitable study for a teacher than to visit one of these numerous idiot schools. He finds the alphabet of his professional work there. As the philologist learns of the formation and growth of language by examining, not the perfectly formed languages, but the dialects of savage tribes, so with the teacher. In like manner more insight into the philosophy of teaching and of the nature of the mind can be acquired by teaching a class of children to read than in any other grade of work.

25

KINDERGARTEN CHATS

Susan E. Blow

Another outstanding woman associated with the St. Louis Movement was Susan E. Blow. A native of St. Louis, she came under the influence of Harris and the Hegelians. Like Snider and the others, she mastered the difficulties of post-Kantian philosophy at "the university Brokmeyer." But she soon developed a fascination with the educational theories of Friedrich Froebel and became an advocate of the Kindergarten Movement. In 1871, she went to New York to study Froebel's methods with Mme. Kraus-Boelte, who was Froebel's direct disciple and who had established the first training school for kindergarten teachers in America. When she returned to St. Louis in 1873, Susan Blow opened her own kindergarten and a training school for teachers as well.

An independent-minded person, Susan Blow did not slavishly follow Froebel in his mystical approach to learning. Instead, she infused his outlook with the systematics of Hegelian philosophy. The result was that, from her own writings on kindergarten education, one could gain a profound insight into Hegelian philosophy from a fresh point of view. The impact of Miss Blow's writings and of the systematized Kindergarten Movement is incalculable. In the Chicago School of Architecture alone, it is clear that the two giants of the day, Louis Sullivan and Frank Lloyd Wright, were greatly influenced by the Froebel kindergarten. And, as the selection below suggests, the whole Vorticist Movement in the arts, so enthusiastically spearheaded by the American Ezra Pound, may well have gained its meaning and vigor from Froebelian principles.

The following excerpts are taken from a late publication by Miss Blow and represent a matured version of her philosophy. By the date of its publication in 1909, the author had suffered a nervous collapse, as a result of which she came into contact with Dr. James Jackson Putnam, one of America's pioneering psychologists. Miss Blow's intellectual impact on Putnam was extremely important in the development of American psychiatry. Putnam's influence on Miss Blow was equally significant in that he introduced her to the ideas of Freud.

Susan E. Blow, *Educational Issues in the Kindergarten* (New York: D. Appleton & Co., 1909), pp. xi–xiv, 33–35, 37–38, 40–41, 42–45, 56–58, 67–68, 70–71, 73.

WITHIN the past thirty years all grades of education from the kindergarten to the university have been more or less influenced by the scientific doctrine of relativity as the controlling principle of the universe; by the working hypothesis of physiological psychology that "mental action may be uniformly and absolutely a function of brain action," and by the undue ascendancy of industrial aims over the mind of the American people.

The primary object of this book is to trace the results of these influences upon the kindergarten. The hope with which it has been written is that portrayal of their results within one small province of education may help to direct attention to the disasters they have caused and are causing in all provinces of education.

The plan of the book is a very simple one. Each of the above-mentioned modes of thought is concretely presented in the typical example of a kindergarten programme. Each programme is discussed with the purpose of throwing its creative principle into clear relief. Finally, some suggestion is given of the influence of this principle in other spheres of life and thought.

In addition to its general aim this book has a secondary and more specific purpose. It endeavors to set forth the theories of Froebel with regard to the education of little children.

The educational creed of Froebel contains four reciprocally dependent articles. The first is that man is a self-creative being; the second, that in virtue of this fact education shall encourage self-expression; the third, that encouragement shall be given only to those modes of self-expression which are related to the values of human life; fourth, that all great human values are revelations of the aboriginal self-determining energy which achieves its own ideal form in self-consciousness. This final article does not deny the influence of man's biologic and historic heredity, nor does it deny the influence of either his physical or his social environment. It does, however, insist both upon the priority and the primacy of self-determination.

The creators of concentric programmes either reject or ignore all

these articles of the Froebelian creed. The creators of free-play programmes accept the first and second, but either reject or ignore the
third and fourth. The creators of industrial programmes accept the
first three, but deny or ignore the fourth, and thereby are betrayed
into practical methods which violate the articles they theoretically
affirm.

It is due to readers of this book that I should explain my reason
for devoting its final chapter to a discussion of different philosophic
world-views.

The conflicting practice of kindergartners implies divergent conceptions of education. These divergent conceptions of education are
not mere eddies in the stream of thought, but correspond with different directions of its main current. In its jubilant sense of conformity with nature, and in its swift surrender to fatal impulse, the
free-play kindergarten repeats in its tiny circle the self-destructive
sweep of naturalism. In its tendency to conceive the child as shaped
and fashioned by the historic process; in its reaction from intellectualism to an exaggerated voluntarism, and in its practical emphasis
upon functional values, the industrial kindergarten betrays the influence of pragmatism. In its conception of the child, its symbolism
and its freightage of free activity with ideal values, the Froebelian
kindergarten reveals a lineage from the philosophy of idealism. A
study of educational issues in the kindergarten which should omit
consideration of these three world-views would therefore dismiss its
subject without any final explanation.

In the discussion of pragmatism I have restricted myself to that
form of the doctrine which has affected the practice of the kindergarten.

In my presentation of the philosophy which underlies the kindergarten I do not claim to have repeated exactly the conscious thought
of its founder. . . .

THE FROEBELIAN ANTITHESIS

THE Froebelian antithesis to concentric education is vortical education. The point of departure for vortical education is the typical fact.
What thought masses are to the Herbartian, typical facts are to the
Froebelian, and without clear comprehension of what is meant by a
typical fact it is impossible to understand the practice of the historic
kindergarten.

1. Let us approach the meaning of a typical fact by asking ourselves what we mean by any fact. Do we mean a single point of ex-

perience taken in detachment from the line it begins or ends? If so, we are thinking of something that does not exist. Each thing is what it is because of its relations to all other things. Therefore, to know any object or event apart from its relations is not to know it at all. To know it in some of its relations is to grasp it as a relative synthesis. To set it in the totality of its relations is to convert this partial synthesis into an absolute synthesis. We may see a mere point of fact; we may see an arc of fact; we may see a semicircumference, a circle, or a spiral of fact; we may see a vortical ascent and expansion of fact; or, finally, we may see a spherical totality of fact.

Thus far we have only discussed ascending definitions of a fact, and from our present point of view should relegate all adequate apprehension of facts to the period of maturity, leaving for childhood those detached unrealities which we know as sense objects and isolated events. We should hold that children must live in an atomic world and should deride the idea of quickening in infant minds any prescient sense of the ties by which objects are related and events bound together. But what if among the objects of sense-perception there are some which provoke surmises of relations and principles? What if life and literature offer types of character which reveal not mere points but arcs on the circle of rationality? What if the heart of childhood thrills with prophetic intimations of all master truths? What, above all, if the human mind ascends to insight, not through fusing many single sensations into those apperceptive masses we call sense objects, and forming from images of these objects the composite pictures we call general ideas, but by a series of effluxes of the mind itself and the imposition of its native forms upon the objective data of experience?

Dwelling in thought upon these possible alternatives, a new pedagogy begins to define itself, and the questions emerge whether the most universal truths have not always been first discerned under the disguise of concrete examples, and whether the one great object of early education should not be to select and present those visible embodiments of creative principles which may be approximately classified as typical facts, objects, actions, characters, relations, and processes. At the heart of each valid synthesis of facts works the force which, raying out in all directions, generates the spherical whole. A typical fact is one which stirs in the present imagination at least a vague awareness of this generative force.

---

3. Typical facts appeal to imagination, and through imagination to feeling and will. Froebel's insistence upon them declares his recognition of imagination as the predominant form of mental

activity between the ages of four and six. His genius, however, also divined a deeper truth, and he perceived that, in view of the young child's primary and persistent need for a self-expressive activity, typical facts must be presented in the guise of typical acts. Seizing, therefore, upon instinctive games, he charged them with ideal values, and by getting children to play with typical objects and represent typical characters, relations, and processes, he made the first complete educational conquest of that realm of phantasy in which all young souls dwell. His creative thought may be summed up in a very few sentences. Since children spend their lives in a waking dream, education must so influence them that their dreams shall be prophecies of truth. Since their waking dream is an active drama, the form through which prevenient imagination must seize upon truth is the typical deed. What a child does he tends to behold. What he plays he is, he tends to become. Through creating in play an ideal world he will be prepared for an ideal interpretation of the actual world. Representing in play an ideal self, he will be incited to that self-surrender and self-conquest whose goal is self-fulfillment.

---

4. . . . The spheres of the kindergarten are balls which children roll, bounce, toss, catch, whirl, and spin; the cubes are blocks with which they build; the squares, triangles, sticks, and rings are not geometric polygons and lines, but materials for making pictures. In a word all these type forms are primarily playthings, and Froebel's simple contention is that playing with them concentrates attention on them and thereby makes them prepotent in the selection and organization of experience. The selective interest of a baby brought up by hand singles out bottles from among all the objects of nature and art and devotes to them his absorbed attention. This is because bottles are intimately connected with his most appealing and engrossing experience. For precisely the same reason the kindergarten child whose balls and blocks are connected with plays which have given him keen enjoyment singles out of the confusion of sense presentation objects allied to these typical forms. And since, unlike bottles, geometric archetypes are really the keys to all form, the direction of attention to them means a valid classification of primary elements of experience.

---

5. . . . The archetypes of form have meanings of their own which we must learn to translate if we would understand what nature is trying to say to us. And as we learn to understand a foreign language through practice in speaking it, so we learn to translate the

language of form through its experimental and creative use. Will not children who have rolled balls and cylinders on level and inclined planes, who have tipped cubes and made them slide and who have whirled and spun spheres, cubes, cylinders, and cones be prepared for appreciation of those relations between form and motion which are fundamental facts of physics? Will not the axial divisions of spheres, cubes, cylinders, and cones made familiar through the building gifts, peas-work, and modeling, prepare for a more intelligent grasp of crystalline forms? Will not the kindergarten child enter more sympathetically than other children into nature's reason for giving flowers cylindrical stems and animals cylindrical legs? Will he not better appreciate "the appropriateness of cylindric forms for carriers of food and working supplies, for roots of trees and veins of animals, for drinking and breathing tubes throughout the animal and vegetable world?"* Will not the varied exercises throwing into relief the freedom of the sphere from bristling edges and pricking corners lead nascent thought to seal with intelligent approval nature's choice of spheroidal forms for the heads of men and animals, and for fruits, vegetables, flowers, and seed? Will not the twirling plays wherein all forms lose their angles and approximate to spheres give some clew to the activities through which pebbles are rounded and worlds shaped? In short, will not wisely directed play with archetypal forms gently lead little neophytes of thought out of the realm of nature's effects into the realm of her causative processes?

6. Passing from the scientific to the æsthetic interpretation of the world, let us remind ourselves that ideal art is never an external copy of nature, but a reaction of the mind against nature. It is an attempt to seize nature's living energies rather than their dead results, and its advance is marked by increasing ability to express generic ideals. It has been said that "the superiority of Japanese paintings of flowers is due to a perfect memory of certain flower shapes instantaneously flung upon paper and showing not the recollection of any individual blossom, but the perfect realization of a general law of form expression, perfectly mastered with all its moods, tenses, and inflections."† The Japanese artist has entered into nature's creative act, and through knowledge of and sympathy with certain generic forms of expression he produces individual examples of a common type superior to the individual

---

* *The Study of Type Forms and Its Value in Education,* John S. Clark (Boston and New York: Prang Educational Co., 1892).

† *Out of the East,* Lafcadio Hearn, p. 119.

examples of nature herself. Astir within him is the ideal toward which the Iris or Chrysanthemum or Lotus energy in nature aims, and therefore he is able to fling freely upon paper original images of this ideal. In like manner the eye of ancient Greece was fixed not upon the imperfect achievements, but upon the ideal striving of the man-making energy, and through her interior vision she was able to reveal to dwarfed and distorted humanity the grandeur and beauty to which it might dare aspire. Sublime Zeus and gracious Aphrodite, statues of heroic Ares and chaste Artemis defined great arcs on the circle of the ideal human and made men aware how divine is that spirit which is forever seeking incarnation in human form. In brief, the ideal reproduction of nature implies assimilation of various forms of creative energy.

---

11. I anticipate a question. Granting that acts of organizing will direct attention to organic wholes; that evolutionary exercises will awaken interest in evolutionary processes; and that the active mediation of antitheses will create a tendency to single out of the complex of experience mediatorial activities, what is the value of arousing these special forms of selective interest? The answer to this question admits us to the citadel of Froebel's thought. The goal of education is a true world-view and a conforming life. The key to a true world-view is the nature of mind. Mind is a generic and, therefore, self-creating energy. It is what it does, it does what it is, and it is aware of that active doing which is its being. Thought, feeling, and will are not independent faculties but related aspects of its indivisible energy. A completely realized mind must have completely objectified itself, and completely realized itself in this self-objectifying act. Every thought that mind can think must have uttered itself in a creative deed; the relations and processes of thought, no less than its detached distinctions must have been objectified; finally, the aboriginal self-determining energy must have duplicated itself as well as objectified its distinctions, relations, and processes. This completely self-objectified and self-duplicated mind is God. The cosmos is the boundless volume of His objectified ideas. The relations and processes of nature correspond to the relations and processes of eternal intellect. The evolutionary ascent of nature is the revealed path of an eternally realized ascent of mind. Man is the crown of nature, because in him is incarnate not God's thought, but His thinking, not God's deeds, but His doing or willing, not divine self-determinations, but divine self-determining. In virtue of this self-determining energy man is a free being; in virtue of the fact that self-determining energy is generic energy, he is intrin-

sically a social being, and must make himself actually what he is ideally through the corporate progress of history, and through those ascending forms of social organization which we know as the hierarchy of human institutions. In brief, nature is the becoming of mind; man is self-realizing mind; God is eternally self-realized mind. Hence, to know the structure of mind would be to know God, nature, and man, and to live in conscious and free conformity with the structure of mind would be to fulfill with joy the most compelling demands of the categorical imperative.

14. . . . The characters represented in kindergarten games must have three marks. They must be typical, elementary, and ideal. Children should not waste time dramatizing the merely capricious. They should not represent elementary types of evil. They should not represent complex types of either good or evil.

The duties of life arise out of its relationships, and the doing of duty creates ideal types of character. The good man is an affectionate son, a kind brother, a faithful husband, a protecting and tender father, a staunch friend, and a genial comrade. He is also an industrious member of the economic organization and a grateful recipient of its lavish bounty. He is a patriot ready to respond to the call of his country. He feels the appeal of a common humanity and is prompt to help the needy and succor the weak. He lives in sympathetic touch with the invisible source of life, and through the two great acts of religion, worship and sacrifice, perpetually renews the tie which binds him to the heavenly powers.

In view of this close connection between relationships, duties, and character, it is evident that if we desire to reveal the ideal to children, or better, if we wish to help them discover it for themselves, we should incite them to play that they are kind fathers, tender mothers, obedient sons and daughters, affectionate brothers and sisters, busy members of the working world, soldiers marching in defense of flag and fatherland, and worshipers old and young answering the call of the solemn bell and wending their way to the mysterious building whose spire, like a great finger, points to the sky. So obvious, indeed, is this method of revealing the ideal that it was instinctively adopted by unlearned peasant mothers in ages beyond the reach of our chronology. The kindergarten simply does with more conscious intent and clearer vision what maternal love has always tried to do.

---

16. In addition to the impersonation of typical characters, and the portrayal of typical relations, Froebel suggests the representation of typical processes, such as the series of activities through

which we get milk and bread; the process of house-building, and the making of a wheel. Games of this kind are so planned that they not only hint the dependence of the individual, but the interdependence of different industries. The baker depends upon the miller and farmer; the carpenter upon the woodman; and without the wheel the whole industrial world would fall to pieces. From the moral point of view it is not a matter of small moment whether children take food, shelter, clothing, and transportation as natural and inalienable rights, or whether they realize in some measure the conspiring activities which make possible these gifts of life. . . .

When adult humanity gets rid of types it will be time enough to ask how we may do without their indispensable assistance in the education of the young child. Until that impossible moment let us use without misgiving types of form, types of character and situation, types of relation and process, being sure in our own minds that a type is the concrete embodiment of a universal standard, the picture form in which all great ideals must be first revealed to the eye, the heart, and the imagination. . . .

26

HARRIS'S PEDAGOGICAL CREED

William Torrey Harris

William Torrey Harris wrote so extensively and emphatically on education that it is difficult to single out one work that completely sums up his philosophy. Perhaps his most comprehensive statement is embodied in the series of five lectures he gave at Johns Hopkins in 1893. An abstract of those lectures is printed below. Clearly, Harris rooted education in the broadest possible cultural and historical setting. Just as clearly, as late as 1893, he had not forgotten that Herbert Spencer and materialism were the enemy.

William Torrey Harris, "The Philosophy of Education," *The Johns Hopkins University Studies in Historical and Political Science* 11 (1893): 1–9.

THE PHILOSOPHY OF EDUCATION

By William T. Harris, LL.D.
U.S. Commissioner of Education

A course of five lectures on the Philosophy of Education was given to those members of the University who are engaged in teaching or who expect to become teachers, by William T. Harris, LL.D., Commissioner of Education, January 7–14, 1893. An abstract of the principal topics discussed is here given.

The following list of books is suggested as useful for reference in connection with the course:

1. Rosenkranz: Paedagogik als System (*English Translation, D. Appleton & Co., New York*). Third part, treating of the substantial contents of the national education—its sacred books, and the idea that the nation stands for in the history of the world. (Lecture 1.)

2. Karl Schmidt: Geschichte der Paedagogik; gives a much

fuller statement of the details of the culture systems of the several nations. (Lecture 1.)

3. R. H. Quick: Educational Reformers. (Lectures 2, 3, 4, and 5.)

4. Pestalozzi: Lienhard und Gertrud. (*English Translation, Boston.*) (Lecture 3.)

5. Herbart: Lehrbuch zur Psychologie. (*English translation, New York.*) (Lecture 3.)

6. Rousseau: Émile. (Lecture 4.)

7. Herbert Spencer: Essay on Education. (Lecture 5.)

LECTURE I—JANUARY 7TH, 1893

THE LITERATURE OF EDUCATION

The first and most important of all educational literature is that showing the ideals of a people—the literature on which they are brought up—generally the sacred books which reveal what the people regard as divine; consequently what is the highest ideal to be realized. China, for example, has Confucius and Mencius, showing the family as the type of the social whole. These writings furnish the contents of the mind of the Chinese—minute observances of etiquette; how to behave towards one's elders and superiors in rank; towards one's inferiors or juniors; towards one's equals. Chinese schools are almost exclusively devoted to filling the memory of the pupil with the ethical maxims of these sacred books, so that the mind shall be full of family etiquette. The aim of Chinese education was to teach the young how to behave; that of the Persians, how to ride, shoot, and speak the truth—a faculty not much thought of by the Hindus. The Persian differs from the Buddhist in that the latter wishes to get rid of the world, while the former attempts to conquer the real. The Phoenicians, again, furnish a contrast to Chinese education. Their object was to wean the child from the family; whereas the Chinese endeavor to educate the young so that they will become submerged in the family. The Phoenicians aimed to create a love of adventure. Their children were educated in myths. The stories in Homer's "Odyssey" must have been derived from the tales of the Phoenician sailors, which were calculated to engender a hunger and thirst for adventure, so that the young Phoenician would gladly get on board ship and go to the ends of the world in the interests of trade. The Greeks were imbued with the new world-principle of a spiritual and beautiful individuality. They thought more of the games which they practised in the evenings on the village green than of the tasks by which they earned their bread. They learned history and geography from the second book of

Homer's "Iliad." They thought not of commercial education, like the Phoenicians, but of that heroic individual who furnished a beautiful ideal. Later on, Greek education became more scientific and more reflective. The Roman concentrated his whole mind on the will. He went beyond the circle of his city, and studied to cause even foreigners to live under the same laws with himself. Freedom meant more to him than to any of the Asiatic nations. It meant the power of the individual to hold, alienate, and devise property. This was an enormous step upward in educational progress. Hitherto, property could only be held by the family. Contract is the supreme idea of the Roman. He even carries it into his religion. Thus he prays to one of his deities to help him in some extremity or to give him his desire, and he promises, in turn, to build the god a temple. The Roman wants to conquer all peoples and to make them free under the law. But the greatest educational lesson is derived from the Hebrew people. They teach the personality of the Divine apart from Nature. This Divine Person creates Nature in order that He shall have something to recognize Him. The Divine Being does not efface man simply, but is the embodiment of goodness and righteousness —the righteousness that breathes the spirit of loving kindness, holding his creatures responsible only in so far as they know the right, and returning their deeds upon them. Art education ranked first in the Greek mind, for he worshipped the beautiful. Then came science and philosophy. From the Greeks we get these elements of our educational curriculum. From the Romans we get the principle of organization. Whether or not a person is educated reflectingly into civilization, he finds himself in the great network of usages that go to make up civilization. Education is meant to give one an insight into the genesis of these things, so that he can detect an element of each in the threads of his civilization. Ninety-nine out of a hundred people in every civilized nation are automata, careful to walk in the prescribed paths, careful to follow prescribed custom. This is the result of substantial education, which, scientifically defined, is the subsumption of the individual under his species. The other educational principle is the emancipation from this subsumption. This is subordinate, and yet, in our time, we lay more stress upon it than the other. Look at the French Revolution. What a prodigious emancipation that was. It was predicted by Rousseau; but those who read him only superficially, without first studying his genesis, will find that their minds are poisoned by his doctrine of the supremacy of nature. Comenius taught the emancipation of the individual from the printed page. Spencer says that the modern school system is all wrong, and has a tendency to get away from science and cause students to waste time over the dead languages. Emancipation has now become the important side of the educational question. But the student of advanced education must first avail himself of the wisdom of the race, and learn how not to be limited by it. He cannot progress unless he is a free man, for he must not be so much subsumed that he cannot investigate scientifically, and with safety to himself, all problems that present themselves.

LECTURE II—JANUARY 14TH, 1893

PROBLEMS PECULIAR TO AMERICAN EDUCATION

There are two kinds of education. The first may be called substantial education—the education by means of the memory; the education which gives to the individual methods and habits and the fundamentals of knowledge. It is this education which the child begins to receive from its birth. This sort of education is education by authority—that is, the individual accepts the authority of the teacher for the truth of what he is told, and does not question it or seek to obtain insight into the reason for its being so. It is this education by authority—the education of the past—that the modern or second kind of education seeks to supersede. This second kind may be called individual or scientific education; it is the education of insight as opposed to that of authority. When this kind of education is acquired, it frees the individual from the authority of the other. Under the system of education by authority when told, for instance, that the sum of three angles of a triangle [is] equal to two right angles, this will be blindly believed only as long as authority sanctions this belief; but when an insight into the reason for this geometrical truth is obtained, no change of authority is able to make the individual doubt. But there is this danger in the system of education by insight, if begun too early, that the individual tends to become so self-conceited with what he considers knowledge gotten by his own personal thought and research, that he drifts toward empty agnosticism with the casting overboard of all authority. It is, therefore, necessary that this excessive conceit of self which this modern scientific method of education fosters be lessened by building on the safe foundations of what has been described as the education of authority. The problems of the reform movement centre, therefore, on the proper method of replacing this authoritative or passive method of education by education through self-activity.

There is another problem—that of the method of study. Germany advises us to teach by oral methods, by giving pieces of information and insight orally by word of mouth. But the American educators have blundered upon what may be defended as the correct method, namely, the text-book method. It was merely the outcome of an unconscious trend. The method is of course liable to very serious abuse, but the good points greatly outweigh the bad. It has the advantage of making one independent of his teacher; you can take your book wherever you please. You cannot do that with the great lecturer, neither can you question him as you can the book, nor can you select the time for hearing the great teacher talk as you can for reading the book. And it is true that nearly all the great teachers have embodied their ideas in books. The greatest danger of text-book education is verbatim, parrot-like recitation; but even then from the poorest text-book a great deal of knowledge can be gleaned. Then there is the alertness which in any large class will necessarily be engendered by an intelligent understanding and criticism of the results arrived at by different pupils in discussing a certain piece of work given in his own words. And then there is the advantage to be found in the fact that with the text-book the child can be busy by itself. Lastly, there is the problem of discipline. There should be very little corporal punishment; the milder forms of restraint should be used. The child that is brought up accustomed to the rod loses his self-respect, and may become the man who must have police surveillance. Silence, punctuality, regularity and industry are fundamental parts of a "substantial education" as much as the critical study of mathematics, literature, science and history is a part of the "education of insight." These two kinds of education, that of authority and that of self-activity, should be made complementary.

LECTURE III—JANUARY 21ST, 1893

OPPOSITION BETWEEN PESTALOZZI AND HERBART

AS EDUCATIONAL LEADERS

Pestalozzi laid great stress on sense-perception as the foundation of all school education. Herbart lays stress on the elaboration of sense-perception or rather upon the mental reaction against the impressions made on our senses. Thought goes back of the object to understand and explain its origin, how it came to be what it is, what purpose it is to serve. Thought sees objects in the perspective of their history. It studies causes and purposes. Thus thought is not, as the disciples of Pestalozzi hold, a continued and elevated sort of sense-perception, but rather a reaction against it. It is a discovery of the subordinate place held by objects in the world; they are seen to be mere steps in a process of manifestation—the manifestation of causal energies. A new perception is received into the mind by adjusting it to our previous knowledge; we explain it in terms of the old; we classify it, identify it; reconcile what is strange and unfamiliar in it with previous experience; we interpret the object and comprehend it; we translate the unknown into the known. This process of adjusting, explaining, classifying, identifying, reconciling, interpreting and translating, is called *apperception*. We must not only perceive, but we must apperceive; not only see and hear, but digest or assimilate what we hear and see. Herbart's "apperception" is far more important for education than Pestalozzi's "perception." At first the memory was the chief faculty cultivated in education; then Pestalozzi reformed it by making the culture of sense-perception the chief aim; now with Herbart the chief aim would be apperception or the mental digestion of what is received by perception or memory. Illustrations of the power of apperception to strengthen perception: Cuvier could reconstruct the entire skeleton from a single bone; Agassiz the entire fish from one of its scales; Winckelmann the entire statue from a fragment of the face; Lyell could see its history in a pebble; Asa Gray the history of a tree by a glance. Apperception adds to the perceived object its process of becoming. Noiré has illustrated apperception by showing the two series of ideas called up by the perception of a piece of bread. First the regressive series—dough, flour, rye; and the processes—baking, kneading, grinding, threshing, harvesting, planting, &c. Each one of these has collateral series, as for example, planting has plowing, plow, oxen, yoke, furrow, harrowing, sowing seeds, covering it, etc. The second series is progressive—bread suggests its uses and functions; food, eating, digesting, organic tissue, life, nourishing strength, supply of heat, bodily labor, &c. The course of study in schools must be arranged so as to prepare the mind for quick apperception of what is studied. The Pestalozzian makes form, number, and language the elements of all knowledge. He unfortunately omits causal ideas, which are the chief factors of apperception; we build our series on causality. Accidental association satisfies only the simple-minded and empty-headed.

LECTURE IV—JANUARY 28TH, 1893
ROUSSEAU AND THE RETURN TO NATURE;
REVOLUTIONARY PROTEST

The time of Louis XIV: the nobles attracted to Court and to a life of gayety, neglecting their estates and wasting the fruits of toil in riotous living; the laborers deprived of the advantage of the directive power of the nobility fail in power of production. The French Revolution is the result. Rousseau its prophet; he proclaims a return to nature. "Nature," a word of ambiguous meaning; human nature versus physical nature; human history the revelation of man's nature; it is realized in institutions and not by man as an isolated individual. Nature in time and space is under the dominion of necessity, everything constrained to be what it is by outside forces. Human nature is an ideal, and when realized it has the form of freedom and self-determination, each man a law unto himself and each one engaged in helping every other one, for by this each one helps himself. Rousseau appealed to nature in everything. What we call civilization was to him a mere artificial form. His plea was to be natural, come back to the point where nature leaves you. Rousseau came from Switzerland to France, and at an opportune time for him; for there was a great ferment of ideas at this epoch. He was struggling along in Paris, barely securing a livelihood, when there came the offer from the Academy of Dijon of a prize for an essay on the progress of the arts and sciences, whether it has tended towards the purification of morals and manners. The negative side suggested itself more forcibly to him, as he was better fitted for it by his mode of living and morals, and by his literary style, and he found himself at once a "censor of civilization." This essay was soon followed (1752) by one on the origin of the inequality among men. The great tension produced by the artificiality of the civilization of the Court life of the time had caused men to become anxious to get back to a simplicity of living, and Chateaubriand painted the charms of the forest life of the Indians. In this reaction the meaning of civilization is ignored. Man emancipates himself from drudgery and compels nature by the forces of his intellect to feed and clothe him. The "Social Contract" followed (1762) this with an attack on the authority of the State; and in the same year his *Émile* undermined the School and the Church; and so he attacked all the social institutions one after another—the family, civil society, the Church and State. He proposed to sweep all away by summoning them before the bar of his individual judgment and condemning all. In the opening paragraph of his *Émile* he declares that everything which comes from nature is good, while everything degenerates in the hands of man. The antithesis of civilization is savagery, and Voltaire wittily exposed the fallacy of Rousseau's teaching in his letter accepting the book. He said—"never has anyone employed so much genius to make us into beasts. When one reads your book he is seized at once with a desire to go down on all fours." External authority is a perennial necessity for man in his immaturity. An appeal to nature is always a piece of jugglery with words. In mere nature we have matter and force. Everything inorganic is made by some external influence. But organic nature is the opposite of inorganic. The plant has the power of assimilation, and the animal the further powers of locomotion and feeling, or ability to select or choose its surroundings. In man this is still further increased by recollection and memory, by which the mind makes over its impressions. To do his duty properly he must look to higher things, and in ethical ideas the human becomes transcendental. The moral man acts as though the sole being in the world is humanity. No natural instinct is admitted as having validity against the moral law. If we adopt the doctrines of material nature and yield to our feelings and impulses, we remain animals. But if we take nature in the sense of our ideal, divine possibility, and realize it by education, we attain to human nature properly so-called, which is not something given us without effort, but only the product of culture.

LECTURE V—FEBRUARY 4TH, 1893

HERBERT SPENCER AND WHAT KNOWLEDGE

IS OF MOST WORTH

In Herbert Spencer, the return to nature means the study of natural science, and this becomes the great thing. But natural science is only the instrument with which we conquer nature. Everybody becomes filled with the idea of progress by it, for we see that nature as it is, existing in time and space, is conquered by inventions and made to serve man. There was never a more unscientific book made than Spencer's essay on education; for while he praises science, he does not apply it to a study of education as it is and has been. To do this he ought to study the genesis of the course of study and explain its functions. The unscientific person takes things as they are, and cares not for their origin. To study things from a scientific standpoint means to take an inventory of them—to find the process in which they are being produced; to connect them with other things; to see things in their causal process. He does not understand the system of education as it exists, because he does not know the educational value of its branches. The education he proposes for us is for the purpose of complete living; but what is Spencer's definition of this complete living? Spencer does not take education as the genesis of man's spiritual life, but merely as something useful for showing how to care for the body and perform the lower social functions as the tool of life, the instrument by which life is preserved. Now suppose the definition of complete living to be, to elevate each individual so that he can take advantage of the life and experience of his race. Then he would find complete living to involve the initiation into the civilizations of the past that furnish the elements out of which our own civilization is formed. Spencer thinks that the first business of the child is to know physiology; the next is the selection of a vocation or trade, which leads to training for citizenship; and last of all he puts relaxation and amusement, in which he includes literature and art. Now, Aristotle characterized man as the symbol-making animal. Human nature has to be expressed by symbols. The poets of a people first paint the ideal, which makes civilization possible. Literature furnishes the most essential branch of education, so far as its function is to help the child into civilization. Man sits in the theatre of the world (as Plato tells us) and sees the shadows of men and events thrown on the curtain before him. Behind him and out of his sight is the Great Leader, who is making these shadows. From them he draws his ideals, but ideals are potentialities, not realities. Self-activity, the freedom of the soul, is made possible by the institutions of society, the family, civil society, State and Church. We must not confound the mere school with these other great institutions of civilization. In the family are learned the mother tongue, habits, and nurture. Civil society teaches him his vocation; the State, his duties as citizen; and the Church shows him his place in the divine plan of the universe. Spencer calls education the subject which involves all other subjects, and the one in which they should all culminate. But someone has better said that school education is the giving to man the possession of the instrumentalities of intelligence. By his school education he does not attain all education, but he gets the tools of thought by which to master the wisdom of the race. There are, then, three epochs of school education—elementary, secondary and higher. The first or elementary stage is the opening of the five windows of the soul. (1) Arithmetic is the foundation of our knowledge of nature, by which we measure and count all things inorganic. When its first principles are mastered the child begins to want to combine the organic with the inorganic, and then we come to another window, (2) that of elementary geography. The distribution of animal and plant life is learned, and the child begins to peep into the organization of things, the growth of plants, and the formation of the continents and the earth. Thirdly, he learns to read and write, and gets a glimpse into literature. The original colloquial vocabulary learned at home, variously estimated at from 300 or 400 to 3,000 or 4,000 words, deals only with commonplace things. But the school takes this colloquial vocabulary as a key and opens up the great reservoir of literature in books, initiating him into a higher class of words, expressive of fine shades of feeling and thought. Thus, to his own vocabulary are added those of great writers, who have seen nature from a different point of view, and presented their thoughts in gems of literary style. Literature lifts up the pupil into the realms of human nature and discloses the motives which govern the actions of men. Yet Spencer puts this last in his course of study. After learning all science has to give, after learning one's trade and the care of his body, he would then, if there is leisure, permit literature and art. But literature is the greatest educator we have. It has made possible newspapers and periodicals and books, with pictures of human life and of the motives governing our actions. The fourth window of the soul is grammar, wherein we have a glimpse of the logical structure of the intellect as revealed in language. The fifth window is history (that of his own country), wherein he sees revealed the aspirations of his countrymen, his own nature, written out in colossal letters; and these five studies should make the elementary education of the student. The secondary education takes up human learning and continues it along the same lines, namely: (1) inorganic nature; (2) organic nature; (3) literature (the heart); (4) grammar and logic (the intellect); and (5) history (the will). Algebra deals with general numbers, while Arithmetic has definite numbers to operate with. Geometry and physics continue inorganic nature, while natural history continues the study already commenced in geography. Then come Greek and Latin, and here is opened up a great field of study into the embryology of our civilization. In the dead languages we have the three great threads running through the history of human progress. The Greek, with its literature and aesthetic art and its philosophy, showing the higher forms of human freedom in contrast with the Egyptian, which showed only the struggle for freedom and never the man separated from the animal and the inorganic world. The Roman, with the continual gaze upon the will of man, seeks the true forms of contracts and treaties and corporations, whereby one man may combine with another, and it essays the conquering of men and reducing them to obedience to civil law, not only external conquest but internal conquest as well. The Hebrew thread is the religious one, which we recognize in the celebration of worship one day each week and in the various holy days. We acknowledge this the most essential thread of our civilization. So, with the secondary education we begin to get the embryology of our forms of life. The higher or collegiate education is the comparative step of education. Each branch is studied in the light of all the others. Natural science and sociology are investigated; logic and mental philosophy; ethics and rhetoric; as well as the philosophy of history and of literature, and the comparative sciences, which furnish the light for the whole method of higher education. The first, or elementary education, then, is but superficial, a mere inventory; the secondary insists on some reflection on what has been learned; and the third, or higher education, is the unity and comparison of all that has been learned, so that each is explained by the whole. Give the child possession of the embryology of civilization, and his insight into the evolution of civilization is insured. Educators have adopted the course of study as it exists, led by an unconscious or blind impulse. Herbert Spencer should have investigated and discovered its purpose, which is a far deeper one than he has thought out when he advocates its overthrow for the sake of knowledge that leads to direct self-preservation.

27

DEWEY'S PEDAGOGICAL CREED

John Dewey

Although he had started out as a Hegelian under the influence of G. S. Morris, by the turn of the century, John Dewey had arrived at a definition of the pragmatic philosophy that led him away from German rationalism. Nonetheless, certain Hegelian concepts remained in his matured pragmatism, notably the sense of philosophy as process, the stress on the community and institutions as values in their own right, and an emphasis on self-creativity or ego-development that he carried so far as to make the child's own desires the center of educational activity. By 1916, Dewey, along with G. Stanley Hall, had become the most important authority on education in the United States, symbolically, if not actually, replacing William Torrey Harris. His ideas of child-centered education, the practicality of learning by doing, and his notion of educational institutions as schools for citizenship struck the right notes in the Progressive Era. His books of the period, *Interest and Effort in Education* (1912), *School and Society* (1915), and *Democracy and Education* (1916) were landmarks in American educational thinking and appeared to usher in a new era.

When one examines Dewey's theories closely in comparison with those of Snider, Harris, and Blow—his bitterest enemy—they do not seem to really differ greatly from the Hegelian ideal. The generation of self-creativity was all-important to the Hegelians, and they utilized every device at their command to stimulate it, from broadening the curriculum to the use of Froebel's blocks, which influenced Frank Lloyd Wright. Moreover, the Hegelians heavily stressed the role of education as training for decision-making in the community of which the child was unavoidably a member. Only through reasoned participation in the community decision-making process could the individual ever be free; hence the American Hegelians linked their educational views directly to democratic government. Thus, to a large extent the goals and methods of the Hegelians and the Progressives were similar. They differed, however, in one important respect. Dewey demanded that the teacher "explore" the child in an attempt to discover his own innate interests and then that the teacher allow the child to express himself at random according to those interests. Only gradually, almost at random, or perhaps never at all, would the child discover his role in the community. To a certain degree, Dewey's method subtly concealed pedagogical pressures on the child, leading him to believe that he was free when actually he was not. In progressive education the child was guided, however indirectly, by current psychological theories, by the demands of his social context, and by the political values of his teachers. But the Hegelians were rationalists and insisted on a structured curriculum whereby progress and direction were made clear to the child and the reason for his participation in the educational process was rendered explicit.

The essay below is a concise though comprehensive statement of Dewey's "pedagogic creed" as of 1897. It is useful to compare it with the preceding statements by Snider, Brackett, Blow, and Harris.

John Dewey, *My Pedagogic Creed* (New York: E. L. Kellogg, 1897).

ARTICLE I. WHAT EDUCATION IS

I BELIEVE that all education proceeds by the participation of the individual in the social consciousness of the race. This process begins unconsciously almost at birth, and is continually shaping the individual's powers, saturating his consciousness, forming his habits, training his ideas, and arousing his feelings and emotions. Through this unconscious education the individual gradually comes to share in the intellectual and moral resources which humanity has succeeded in getting together. He becomes an inheritor of the funded capital of civilization. The most formal and technical education in the world cannot safely depart from this general process. It can only organize it; or differentiate it in some particular direction.

I believe that the only true education comes through the stimulation of the child's powers by the demands of the social situations in which he finds himself. Through these demands he is stimulated to act as a member of a unity, to emerge from his original narrowness of action and feeling, and to conceive of himself from the standpoint of the welfare of the group to which he belongs. Through the responses which others make to his own activities he comes to know what these mean in social terms. The value which they have is reflected back into them. For instance, through the response which is made to the child's instinctive babblings the child comes to know what those babblings mean; they are transformed into articulate language, and thus the child is introduced into the consolidated wealth of ideas and emotions which are now summed up in language.

I believe that this educational process has two sides—one psychological and one sociological; and that neither can be subordinated to the other or neglected without evil results following. Of these two sides, the psychological is the basis. The child's own instincts and powers furnish the material and give the starting-point for all education. Save as the efforts of the educator connect with some activity which the child is carrying on of his own initiative independent of the educator, education becomes reduced to a pressure from without. It may, indeed, give certain external results, but cannot truly be called educative. Without insight into the psychological structure and activities of the individual, the educative process will, therefore, be haphazard and arbitrary. If it chances to coincide with the child's activity it will get a leverage; if it does not, it will result in friction, or disintegration, or arrest of the child nature.

I believe that knowledge of social conditions, of the present state of civilization, is necessary in order properly to interpret the child's powers. The child has his own instincts and tendencies, but we do not know what these mean until we can translate them into their social equivalents. We must be able to carry them back into a social past and see them as the inheritance of previous race activities. We must also be able to project them into the future to see what their outcome and end will be. In the illustration just used, it is the ability to see in the child's babblings the promise and potency of a future social intercourse and conversation which enables one to deal in the proper way with that instinct.

I believe that the psychological and social sides are organically related, and that education cannot be regarded as a compromise between the two, or a superimposition of one upon the other. We are told that the psychological definition of education is barren and formal—that it gives us only the idea of a development of all the mental powers without giving us any idea of the use to which these powers are put. On the other hand, it is urged that the social definition of education, as getting adjusted to civilization, makes of it a forced and external process, and results in subordinating the freedom of the individual to a preconceived social and political status.

I believe each of these objections is true when urged against one side isolated from the other. In order to know what a power really is we must know what its end, use, or function is; and this we cannot know save as we conceive of the individual as active in social relationships. But, on the other hand, the only possible adjustment which we can give to the child under existing conditions is that which arises through putting him in complete possession of all his powers. With the advent of democracy and modern industrial conditions, it is impossible to foretell definitely just what civilization will be twenty years from now. Hence it is impossible to prepare the child for any precise set of conditions. To prepare him for the future life means to give him command of himself; it means so to train him that he will have the full and ready use of all his capacities; that his eye and ear and hand may be tools ready to command, that his judgment may be capable of grasping the conditions under which it has to work, and the executive forces be trained to act economically and efficiently. It is impossible to reach this sort of adjustment save as constant regard is had to the individual's own powers, tastes, and interests—save, that is, as education is continually converted into psychological terms.

In sum, I believe that the individual who is to be educated is a social individual, and that society is an organic union of individuals. If we eliminate the social factor from the child we are left only with an abstraction; if we eliminate the individual factor from society, we are left only with an inert and lifeless mass. Education, therefore, must begin with a psychological insight into the child's capacities, interests, and habits. It must be controlled at every point by reference to these same considerations. These powers, interests, and habits must be continually interpreted—we must know what they mean. They must be translated into terms of their social equivalents —into terms of what they are capable of in the way of social service.

ARTICLE II.   WHAT THE SCHOOL IS

I believe that the school is primarily a social institution. Education being a social process, the school is simply that form of community life in which all those agencies are concentrated that will be most effective in bringing the child to share in the inherited resources of the race, and to use his own powers for social ends.

I believe that education, therefore, is a process of living and not a preparation for future living.

I believe that the school must represent present life—life as real and vital to the child as that which he carries on in the home, in the neighborhood, or on the playground.

I believe that education which does not occur through forms of life, forms that are worth living for their own sake, is always a poor substitute for the genuine reality, and tends to cramp and to deaden.

I believe that the school, as an institution, should simplify existing social life; should reduce it, as it were, to an embryonic form. Existing life is so complex that the child cannot be brought into contact with it without either confusion or distraction; he is either overwhelmed by the multiplicity of activities which are going on, so that he loses his own power of orderly reaction, or he is so stimulated by these various activities that his powers are prematurely called into play and he becomes either unduly specialized or else disintegrated.

I believe that, as such simplified social life, the school life should grow gradually out of the home life; that it should take up and continue the activities with which the child is already familiar in the home.

I believe that it should exhibit these activities to the child, and reproduce them in such ways that the child will gradually learn the meaning of them, and be capable of playing his own part in relation to them.

I believe that this is a psychological necessity, because it is the only way of securing continuity in the child's growth, the only way of giving a background of past experience to the new ideas given in school.

I believe it is also a social necessity because the home is the form of social life in which the child has been nurtured and in connection with which he has had his moral training. It is the business of the school to deepen and extend his sense of the values bound up in his home life.

I believe that much of present education fails because it neglects this fundamental principle of the school as a form of community life. It conceives the school as a place where certain information is to be given, where certain lessons are to be learned, or where certain habits are to be formed. The value of these is conceived as lying largely in the remote future; the child must do these things for the sake of something else he is to do; they are mere preparations. As a result they do not become a part of the life experience of the child and so are not truly educative.

I believe that the moral education centers upon this conception of the school as a mode of social life, that the best and deepest moral training is precisely that which one gets through having to enter into proper relations with others in a unity of work and thought. The present educational systems, so far as they destroy or neglect this unity, render it difficult or impossible to get any genuine, regular moral training.

I believe that the child should be stimulated and controlled in his work through the life of the community.

I believe that under existing conditions far too much of the stimulus and control proceeds from the teacher, because of neglect of the idea of the school as a form of social life.

I believe that the teacher's place and work in the school are to be interpreted from this same basis. The teacher is not in the school to impose certain ideas or to form certain habits in the child, but is there as a member of the community to select the influences which shall affect the child and to assist him in properly responding to these influences.

I believe that the discipline of the school should proceed from the life of the school as a whole and not directly from the teacher.

I believe that the teacher's business is simply to determine, on the basis of larger experience and riper wisdom, how the discipline of life shall come to the child.

I believe that all questions of the grading of the child and his promotion should be determined by reference to the same standard. Examinations are of use only so far as they test the child's fitness for social life and reveal the place in which he can be of the most service and where he can receive the most help.

I believe once more that history is of educative value in so far as it presents phases of social life and growth. It must be controlled by reference to social life. When taken simply as history it is thrown into the distant past and becomes dead and inert. Taken as the record of man's social life and progress it becomes full of meaning. I believe, however, that it cannot be so taken excepting as the child is also introduced directly into social life.

I believe accordingly that the primary basis of education is in the child's powers at work along the same general constructive lines as those which have brought civilization into being.

I believe that the only way to make the child conscious of his social heritage is to enable him to perform those fundamental types of activity which make civilization what it is.

I believe, therefore, in the so-called expressive or constructive activities as the center of correlation.

I believe that this gives the standard for the place of cooking, sewing, manual training, etc., in the school.

I believe that they are not special studies which are to be introduced over and above a lot of others in the way of relaxation or relief, or as additional accomplishments. I believe rather that they represent, as types, fundamental forms of social activity; and that it is possible and desirable that the child's introduction into the more formal subjects of the curriculum be through the medium of these activities.

I believe that the study of science is educational in so far as it brings out the materials and processes which make social life what it is.

I believe that one of the greatest difficulties in the present teaching of science is that the material is presented in purely objective form, or is treated as a new peculiar kind of experience which the child can add to that which he has already had. In reality, science is of value because it gives the ability to interpret and control the experience already had. It should be introduced, not as so much new subject-matter, but as showing the factors already involved in previous experience and as furnishing tools by which that experience can be more easily and effectively regulated.

I believe that at present we lose much of the value of literature and language studies because of our elimination of the social element. Language is almost always treated in the books of pedagogy simply as the expression of thought. It is true that language is a logical instrument, but it is fundamentally and primarily a social instrument. Language is the device for communication; it is the tool through which one individual comes to share the ideas and feelings of others. When treated simply as a way of getting individual information, or as a means of showing off what one has learned, it loses its social motive and end.

I believe that there is, therefore, no succession of studies in the ideal school curriculum. If education is life, all life has, from the outset, a scientific aspect; an aspect of art and culture and an aspect of communication. It cannot, therefore, be true that the proper studies for one grade are mere reading and writing, and that at a later grade, reading, or literature, or science, may be introduced. The progress is not in the succession of studies, but in the development of new attitudes towards, and new interests in, experience.

I believe, finally, that education must be conceived as a continuing reconstruction of experience; that the process and the goal of education are one and the same thing.

I believe that to set up any end outside of education, as furnishing its goal and standard, is to deprive the educational process of much of its meaning, and tends to make us rely upon false and external stimuli in dealing with the child.

ARTICLE III.   THE NATURE OF METHOD

I believe that the question of method is ultimately reducible to the question of the order of development of the child's powers and interests. The law for presenting and treating material is the law implicit within the child's own nature. Because this is so I believe the following statements are of supreme importance as determining the spirit in which education is carried on:

1. I believe that the active side precedes the passive in the development of the child-nature; that expression comes before conscious impression; that the muscular development precedes the sensory; that movements come before conscious sensations; I believe that consciousness is essentially motor or impulsive; that conscious states tend to project themselves in action.

I believe that the neglect of this principle is the cause of a large part of the waste of time and strength in school work. The child is thrown into a passive, receptive, or absorbing attitude. The conditions are such that he is not permitted to follow the law of his nature; the result is friction and waste.

I believe that ideas (intellectual and rational processes) also result from action and devolve for the sake of the better control of action. What we term reason is primarily the law of orderly or effective action. To attempt to develop the reasoning powers, the powers of judgment, without reference to the selection and arrangement of means in action, is the fundamental fallacy in our present methods of dealing with this matter. As a result we present the child with arbitrary symbols. Symbols are a necessity in mental development, but they have their place as tools for economizing effort; presented by themselves they are a mass of meaningless and arbitrary ideas imposed from without.

2. I believe that the image is the great instrument of instruction. What a child gets out of any subject presented to him is simply the images which he himself forms with regard to it.

I believe that if nine-tenths of the energy at present directed towards making the child learn certain things were spent in seeing to it that the child was forming proper images, the work of instruction would be indefinitely facilitated.

I believe that much of the time and attention now given to the preparation and presentation of lessons might be more wisely and profitably expended in training the child's power of imagery and in seeing to it that he was continually forming definite, vivid, and growing images of the various subjects with which he comes in contact in his experience.

3. I believe that interests are the signs and symptoms of growing power. I believe that they represent dawning capacities. Accordingly the constant and careful observation of interests is of the utmost importance for the educator.

I believe that these interests are to be observed as showing the state of development which the child has reached.

I believe that they prophesy the stage upon which he is about to enter.

I believe that only through the continual and sympathetic observation of childhood's interests can the adult enter into the child's life and see what it is ready for, and upon what material it could work most readily and fruitfully.

I believe that these interests are neither to be humored nor repressed. To repress interest is to substitute the adult for the child, and so to weaken intellectual curiosity and alertness, to suppress initiative, and to deaden interest. To humor the interests is to substitute the transient for the permanent. The interest is always the sign of some power below; the important thing is to discover this power. To humor the interest is to fail to penetrate below the surface, and its sure result is to substitute caprice and whim for genuine interest.

4. I believe that the emotions are the reflex of actions.

I believe that to endeavor to stimulate or arouse the emotions apart from their corresponding activities is to introduce an unhealthy and morbid state of mind.

I believe that if we can only secure right habits of action and thought, with reference to the good, the true, and the beautiful, the emotions will for the most part take care of themselves.

I believe that next to deadness and dullness, formalism and routine, our education is threatened with no greater evil than sentimentalism.

I believe that this sentimentalism is the necessary result of the attempt to divorce feeling from action.

ARTICLE IV.   THE SCHOOL AND SOCIAL PROGRESS

I believe that education is the fundamental method of social progress and reform.

I believe that all reforms which rest simply upon the enactment of law, or the threatening of certain penalties, or upon changes in mechanical or outward arrangements, are transitory and futile.

I believe that education is a regulation of the process of coming to share in the social consciousness; and that the adjustment of individual activity on the basis of this social consciousness is the only sure method of social reconstruction.

I believe that this conception has due regard for both the individualistic and socialistic ideals. It is duly individual because it recognizes the formation of a certain character as the only genuine basis of right living. It is socialistic because it recognizes that this right character is not to be formed by merely individual precept, example, or exhortation, but rather by the influence of a certain form of institutional or community life upon the individual, and that the social organism through the school, as its organ, may determine ethical results.

I believe that in the ideal school we have the reconciliation of the individualistic and the institutional ideals.

I believe that the community's duty to education is, therefore, its paramount moral duty. By law and punishment, by social agitation and discussion, society can regulate and form itself in a more or less haphazard and chance way. But through education society can formulate its own purposes, can organize its own means and resources, and thus shape itself with definiteness and economy in the direction in which it wishes to move.

I believe that when society once recognizes the possibilities in this direction, and the obligations which these possibilities impose, it is impossible to conceive of the resources of time, attention, and money which will be put at the disposal of the educator.

I believe it is the business of everyone interested in education to insist upon the school as the primary and most effective interest of social progress and reform in order that society may be awakened to realize what the school stands for, and aroused to the necessity of endowing the educator with sufficient equipment properly to perform his task.

I believe that education thus conceived marks the most perfect and intimate union of science and art conceivable in human experience.

I believe that the art of thus giving shape to human powers and adapting them to social service is the supreme art; one calling into its service the best of artists; that no insight, sympathy, tact, executive power is too great for such service.

I believe that with the growth of psychological service, giving added insight into individual structure and laws of growth; and with

growth of social science, adding to our knowledge of the right organization of individuals, all scientific resources can be utilized for
the purposes of education.

I believe that when science and art thus join hands the most
commanding motive for human action will be reached; the most
genuine springs of human conduct aroused, and the best service
that human nature is capable of guaranteed.

I believe, finally, that the teacher is engaged, not simply in the
training of individuals, but in the formation of the proper social life.

I believe that every teacher should realize the dignity of his calling; that he is a social servant set apart for the maintenance of
proper social order and the securing of the right social growth.

I believe that in this way the teacher always is the prophet of the
true God and the usherer in of the true kingdom of God.

VII

AESTHETICS AND
INSTITUTIONS

The fine arts occupied a central place in the Hegelians' thoughts because
they were considered to be the highest expression of "the Divine Ideal."
A great work of art was itself an ideal or model of the universal order
that governed the cosmos. And, since it was a model, art was thus meant
to instruct by example. But in order to teach the highest truths, only the

best art should be studied and admired; consequently, the Hegelians' approach to art and literature tended to be selective. They singled out the established masterpieces, rather than the purely innovative. Thus, in the broadest sense, their approach was classical. Their perception of the intimate relationship between the arts and the institutions of civilization and their penchant for a high degree of selectivity in which they deliberately chose a pantheon of greats foreshadowed the later philosophical criticism of another St. Louis citizen, T. S. Eliot, whose early years were spent under the tutelage of the city school system dominated by Hegelians.

Though the *Journal of Speculative Philosophy* was to a very large extent devoted to highly technical philosophy, nearly 16 percent of its pages (through the entire series) dealt with the fine arts, again with emphasis restricted to a relatively few artists whom the Hegelians considered immortal. Homer, Shakespeare, Dante, and Goethe among the writers; Michelangelo and Raphael among the sculptors and painters; Herman Grimm among the critics; and Beethoven among the composers, commanded the greatest attention. Brokmeyer's interminable "Letters on Faust," Snider's frequent papers on Shakespeare, and Harris's treatises on music as an art form were among the Hegelians' most prominent aesthetic writings, though Snider among his forty books covered all the major writers of the classical world, published all his lectures on Shakespeare's plays, and properly canonized the greatest of the German romantic writers.

In all their artistic criticism, the Hegelians tended to apply the dialectic, or rather to see it implicit in the work of any given artist, no matter what his time or place. For example, Harris writing in the *Journal of Speculative Philosophy* professed to see a "dialectical unity in Emerson's prose," while Snider in his book on Emerson saw the Sage of Concord as "the Institutionalized Emerson." For Brokmeyer, Goethe's *Faust* was a perfect example of the dialectic. Snider even carried the critical approach into architecture, as the article below indicates. And when as in Snider's novel, *The Freeburghers*, or Woerner's *The Rebel's Daughter*, they attempted creative writing of their own, the dialectical structure always prevailed. Thus the Hegelian approach to aesthetics in some ways foreshadowed the canons of modern Soviet "socialist realism" or true proletarian art in all countries from the Chinese State Ballet to the American Depression novels of Tillie Lerner. At its worst, the universal prevailed over the concrete. At its best, the concrete served to make the universal convincing and moving.

The whole range of Hegelian aesthetic endeavor is too vast and certainly too tedious for inclusion in this volume. The two selections included here represent, in the editor's view, a sampling of the most interesting aesthetic work accomplished by the Hegelians. Woerner's novel, a very lengthy tome, redeems itself by its sense of the "felt life" of the common people of the Civil War era and by its keen insights into every phase of the workings of American democracy. Snider's architectural criticism astutely focuses on the Chicago skyscraper as the aesthetic climax of the period and makes it culturally significant at a time when Eastern architects still dominated American taste. But Snider's perceptivity is understandable because, as he himself said, long ago he had "gone to school to the Eads Bridge."

28

AN AMERICAN WAR
AND PEACE

John Gabriel Woerner

John Gabriel Woerner, the author of *The Rebel's Daughter: A Story of Love, Politics and War,* an excerpt from which is reprinted below, was still another immigrant German patriot. Though he had come to America in 1833 and had worked his way upward from a baker to a newspaperman, Woerner sympathized strongly with the German revolts of 1848 and went to Germany as a correspondent for the New York *Herald* in support of the workers' cause.

Eventually, he became owner of the St. Louis *Tribune,* a Democrat, and a supporter of Thomas Hart Benton. He served through the Civil War as a lieutenant colonel of the Union Volunteer Militia. Later, he was for 25 years probate judge of St. Louis. A prodigious worker and scholar, he produced two legal classics on probate law, *A Treatise on the American Law of Administration* (1889) and *A Treatise on the American Law of Guardianship* (1897). While engaged in the busy life of a practicing politician and judge, Woerner also became one of the founders of the St. Louis Movement and contributed not only to the *Journal of Speculative Philosophy* but also to the many heated discussions of the Philosophical Society. He was, in short, the Oliver Wendell Holmes, Jr., of the St. Louis Movement.

The Rebel's Daughter was published in 1899, the year before Woerner died. Clearly autobiographical, the novel focused on the great American Civil War which fascinated the Germans who believed it to be a "world-historical event." In overall structure (as well as in episodic detail) the book is dialectical, with the main opposition being the Union versus the Southern States, as might be expected. The plot turns on the conversion of the rebel's daughter from a fiery Southern states' rights proselytizer to an adherent to higher unity and loyalty. Woerner's book outwardly, then, is very much like John W. DeForest's earlier novel, *Miss Ravenel's Conversion from Secession to Loyalty* (1867). But what gives

Woerner's novel its special significance is the fact that the panoramic events of the Civil War are observed largely through the naive eyes of Victor Waldhorst, a German immigrant youth. As the observer, Victor is fascinated by virtually every institution, pageant, and political process in Civil War America. He thus becomes the vehicle for Woerner's shrewd immigrant observations of the American scene in which he is able to see things both within and without the German community that a native American, like DeForest, could never notice or would normally ignore. *The Rebel's Daughter* is hence a cultural historian's gold mine as well as a moving and reasonably well-crafted work of fiction.

In addition to setting down his general observations of Civil War America, Woerner also attempted to capture the vivid personalities of his fellow founders of the St. Louis Movement. The chapter below is a set piece from the novel—a tea at which the principals of the St. Louis Movement are present and engaged in their usual animated dialectical discussion. The voices of Brokmeyer as the irascible Professor Rauhenfels, of Snider as the mellifluous Dr. Taylor, and Harris as Professor Altrue emerge clearly and vividly out of the past, just as they were— or at least as Judge J. Gabriel Woerner remembered them all his life.

J. Gabriel Woerner, *The Rebel's Daughter: A Story of Love, Politics and War* (Boston: Little, Brown & Co., 1899), pp. 420–30.

PHILOSOPHERS AT TEA

THE meal passed off pleasantly. The distribution, by the young ladies, of the pretty posies, had put the gentlemen in good humor, and started the conversation in a merry mood. Like a babbling brooklet the stream of talk flowed on,—smoothly now, now breaking into purling ripples of sparkling repartee; not deep, but gliding briskly over the well-worn pebbles of generalities, moving over such topics as educed from each guest some pleasant remark. Doctor Taylor, for instance, said something pretty about the affinity between the bloom of flowers and the bloom of the maidens dispensing them; Professor Rauhenfels indulged in some punning on the names of May and Waldhorst, which latter he explained as meaning a nest in the forest; he was in turn corrected by Professor Altrue, who asserted that the word "horst" meant not a nest, but the place where birds of prey build their nests, the exact equivalent of our "aerie," or, as the word is spelled in our editions of Shakespeare, 'eyry." Then Woldemar Auf dem Busch had his fling at Professor Rauhenfels, wherein he was seconded by Miss May, who said some sharp things about German names, but was glad, in the end, that the professor's barbed shafts of cutting retort were aimed rather at the young merchant than at her. Pauline spoke but little. By a judicious remark, now and then, she suggested a pleasant subject, upon which others dilated. Colonel May noted, with silent approval, the unpretending efficiency with which she assisted the hostess. Both he and Mrs. May were highly amused by the curious English in which Auf dem Busch Senior served up the few remarks in which he indulged,—furnishing to the lady proof indubitable of the correctness of her estimate of his low origin.

But a remark made by the host himself presently turned the conversation into a deeper channel. "Go you straightway home from here with your madam and daughter," he inquired, "or go you first to the State capital?"

"Our route home passes very closely by the capital, so that we shall not lose much time by a visit there," was the colonel's answer. "I shall be detained a few days in the city; but then we shall start for home. If we find it necessary on reaching the capital, we shall remain there until the convening of the General Assembly. Otherwise I may take the ladies home first, and then return to the capital."

"But you will let me stay in the capital, papa?" said Miss May, in a tone that was at once precatory and confident. "I have never attended at a governor's reception yet, and this is too good an opportunity to be neglected." Then, with a sly look at Victor, she added: "And I wish to have a dance with the Honorable Victor Waldhorst at the governor's reception."

"May I take you at your word, Miss Nellie?" said Victor, flushing deeply.

"Of course, Miss May will be at the governor's reception," Professor Rauhenfels spoke up. "I take it for granted, that you wish to be elected to the United States Senate, Colonel May; and even if it should not be your wish, you owe it to these gentlemen here, most of whom have been pretty active in your behalf, to make the best race you know how. And if you do not suspect it yourself, these gentlemen here—Mr. Waldhorst not excepted—are satisfied, that Miss May's presence at the capital next week will put your election out of doubt, whatever your chances otherwise may be."

"The professor has right, like always," Mr. Auf dem Busch Senior proclaimed. "If the colo-nell is prudent, then Miss May shall be in the capital. The colo-nell's election is may be sure; but double-stitched holds better."

"*A propos* of the election," said Woldemar, thereby cutting off whatever reply might have been intended to Miss May's suggestion, "is the outlook quite so clear as the present company seem to wish?

To me it seems, that Lincoln's election has so complicated the slavery question, that political combinations are uncertain."

"One thing, however, *is* certain," the colonel observed, amid profound silence of the others. "If this Union is to be preserved, as I devoutly hope and trust it shall be, it will be upon condition that one-half of the people shall not be robbed of their property by the other half."

"Robbed?" said Woldemar. "Is not that a stronger term than you meant to use?"

"It is not too strong a term!" Victor almost shouted in his eagerness. "It is just the right term. If a lot of pharisaical hypocrites should demand of you to turn loose your horses and cattle, because they are God's creatures as well as you,—would you do it? And if you were made to do it by force, would not that be robbery?"

"Horses and cattle are not human beings," said Woldemar confidently. "Nor is it proposed, so far as I understand, to liberate the slaves by force, or at all."

"Call it liberation or not as you please," said Leslie May. "You deprive us of our property, if you interfere with us in its use. And mark me, sir, the South will not tamely submit to such monstrous spoliation, as the abolition of slavery would involve. If it be attempted under color of law, it will be such law as the highwayman imposes upon his victim, with the knife at his throat."

"The South will never yield to force!" Nellie added, with flashing eyes. "If it comes to that, the Yankees will find that two can play at the game. I hope—no, I don't hope for war. But if war ever comes, let the Yankees beware!"

"Peace, children!" the colonel demanded. "You talk as though it were proposed to fight. The danger does not lie there. There will be no fighting; but there may be disruption of the country. It is very clear, that if the abolitionists carry out their fanatical program, the constitution will be violated—broken, in fact,—and what will there be then to hold the country together?"

"There will be a new constitution," Doctor Taylor now spoke. "Our present constitution seems too narrow for the vigorous people to which we have grown. Our nation has been expanding in every direction,—in territorial extent, in population, in power and wealth, and,—may I add?—in moral tone. But our constitution which fitted us very well just after the Revolution, is now the same as it was then. Fixed and rigid in its inflexible written form, it could not, like for instance the British constitution, grow with the growth of the nation—"

"You forget, sir, the chief characteristic of the American constitution," the colonel threw in, "which is precisely the quality that your statement denies it,—its capacity to conform to the changing views and needs of the people."

"By means of constitutional amendments, do you mean, sir?"

"Exactly."

"But if what I say is true,—if the growth of the constitution has not kept pace with the growth of the people, then its amendability has been of little avail, so far. Nor is the prospect promising, that the slavery quarrel will be settled by that means. Your son has just now stated,—and I believe that he fairly voices the Southern sentiment in this particular—that the South will *not* submit to what he calls—justly, let us admit—being robbed of their slaves. Mr. Auf dem Busch—the young man, I mean—inclines to the view that the abolition of slavery is demanded by public opinion, at least by a sufficient majority of the people to put it into the shape of a law. Thus you will have a breach of the constitution: for interference with the right of slaveholders in the States, in any manner other than by an amendment of the constitution, is, I take it, indubitably a breach of that instrument."

"I beg that you will not misunderstand my statement," young Auf dem Busch protested. "I distinctly disavow any intention that Congress shall interfere with slavery in the States. I simply desire that it shall be confined to the States in which it now exists."

"Well," said Victor, rather warmly, "do you not intend thereby to eventually exterminate slavery? For, whether you confess it or not, is it not perfectly evident, that your policy will prevent any new slave State from being added to the Union? And do you not thereby deprive those States, whose interest requires the recognition of slavery, of their due share of influence in the councils of the nation? And will not that lead to the abolition of slavery as inevitably as direct abolition would?"

"It strikes me that my young friend has fairly and accurately stated the case," Colonel May remarked. "Whether it be the conscious policy of the free soil party to enhance the prosperity of one section of the country at the cost of the ruin and beggary of the prosperous citizens of the other, or not,—that is certainly the prospect before us, if Lincoln should side with the radical wing of the party that elected him. I am happy to say, that I do not believe be will."

"There is an element of profound truth in what our friend, Doctor Taylor, has suggested, that deserves, I believe, closer attention."

It was Professor Altrue that spoke, in a low, melodious voice, that, however, made itself distinctly heard. "He has pointed out the impossibility that a written constitution should accurately or truly represent the consciousness of a nation. Sir, I dare say, that if you will abstract from the political bearing of the question, you will readily see that this constitution, which you, very properly, so strongly defend as the safeguard of your rights, does not reflect the conviction which you yourself entertain on the morality of slavery."

"Whether I see this or not, you will readily grant me," said the colonel, "that an individual cannot be permitted to set up his own opinion as the standard of right and wrong."

"Clearly not for others," Professor Altrue assented. "Else no one's rights could be protected—"

"Then," the colonel interrupted, "let me say, that the constitution is good enough for me, and that I do not propose to sit in judgment on its morality."

"That is a thing that you cannot help doing, sir," said the Dominie amid the breathless attention of the others. "For while your own opinion has no binding force for others, it is the voice of God to yourself, and this very constitution that you set up as your standard demands of you that you judge it by that divine criterion."

"Why must I judge it at all?"

"By judging I do not mean, necessarily condemning. But you do decide (for yourself, and so far as your influence goes) whether the constitution adequately performs its functions. The humblest citizen does this every time he performs his duty at the polls: how much more yourself, who are called on, as an illustrious statesman, to guide the ship of State. You certainly know it to be your duty to actively assist in amending the constitution so as to purify it from any defect that has become apparent to you. Is not that a judgment against its adequacy? Or you may oppose any suggested amendment, or simply remain inactive. Is not that a judgment in its favor? In this way every human being that owes allegiance to our government continually passes judgment on the sufficiency of the constitution."

"And in doing so," Doctor Taylor interjected, "they have no higher criterion than their conscience."

"Precisely," the Dominie assented. "Now, what I wished to comment on is, as Doctor Taylor happily pointed out, the necessarily unequal development of the people and their constitution. Grant that a law, when enacted, represents the clear judgment of a majority of the people. That is the theory upon which we recognize its binding validity. To-morrow, changing circumstances, or it might be, the riper judgment of the people, may have changed the views of some of them, so that the law no longer represents the opinion of the majority. Such changes are of daily occurrence; and it is obvious, that until such law can be amended or repealed, there is a tension between the will of the people and the law which, theoretically, expresses it. Ordinarily, such amendment or repeal follows as soon as this tension has made itself felt by the majority. But how, when the amendment requires more than a majority? Such substantially unanimous concurrence of opinion, for instance, as is conditioned by a majority of two-thirds of each House of Congress, to be ratified by a majority of every one of three-fourths of the State legislatures? It is evident, that a determined minority— it may be of less than one-tenth of the people—may defeat the will of the other nine-tenths, provided that they constitute the majority in one more than one-fourth of the States, though they be of the smallest. If the majority, then, is as determined as the minority, the tension will become so great, that a rupture, such as is dreaded by Colonel May, would not be surprising; nor, as Doctor Taylor suggests, that a new constitution—even several new constitutions—should result, if the old one, instead of being amended, should be fractured by the tension."

"Which may God hinder!" the old merchant exclaimed. "Professor Rauhenfels, you have said us nothing over this point. We might hear an opinion of you."

"Why do you want another opinion?" the professor responded, looking around at all the company, and then addressing the host with an amiable face. "Opinions are cheap, and worth about what they cost. Every man has, or ought to have, one of his own, worth more to him, probably, than to anyone else. Does anyone expect to change his opinion on hearing someone else's? I can give a shrewd guess, that Colonel May still wishes to preserve the Union, slavery and all, although he may not be able to refute the argument of Doctor Taylor that it is superannuated and needs overhauling; or the reasoning of our friend, the Dominie, that written constitutions are like a tightly-fitting garment on a fast growing youth, that must presently be rent asunder, unless replaced by one of ampler dimensions. And so, I suspect, our young friend Auf dem Busch will still insist that it is the duty of a Christian government to abolish slavery, although Mr. Waldhorst indignantly proves this to be highway-robbery, and young Mr. May shows us that if it is done, it must be done by sheer force, the which Miss May is equally sure, will be met with like force."

"But will you not favor us with your views on the subject?" Colonel May inquired. "I will confess that I am very eager to hear from you, after what Leslie has written and spoken to me of your part in the election."

"Do, Professor," said the Dominie. "I am sure the whole company are anxious to hear your views."

There was general assent to this statement.

"My views as to what?" said the professor. "Do you wish to know, why I am in favor of Colonel May for the United States Senate? I will tell you: Because, by his course in Congress, he has given ample proof of his devotion to the American principle,—which demands Liberty through Law, and Law in Liberty. He knows, that there can be no liberty without law, and therefore demands the strict and literal compliance with our written constitution, as the only safeguard of our rights. And yet I agree with the Dominie and Doctor Taylor, that a written constitution does not grow with the body politic, like the bark of a tree, which expands as the tree grows. But I see just in the tension which these gentlemen emphasize, as a possible consequence of the fluctuation, in public sentiment, the Magna Charta of individual liberty,—since it operates as a check upon the caprice of the people. For no tyranny is more oppressive and galling than the despotism of unbridled majorities. Colonel May recognizes in the conservative element of our government the sheet-anchor of Freedom and Right. So do I. He has evaded the question put to him by the Dominie, as to his view on the morality of slavery: I care not what it is; under the present condition of things it is of far greater importance to humanity,—to the cause of freedom—that our government remain intact, than that the normal condition of the slaves be changed. As Doctor Taylor once neatly expressed it,—

> ' 'Tis not the outward bond that makes the slave,—
> But the base craven thought within the man.'

Slaves are such upon their own compliance. No freeman, loving liberty above life or ease, was ever yet made a slave. To the slave, then, manumission is of no benefit. The vice of slavery consists in its degradation to the master, because slavery is incompatible with his own freedom. Its recognition in the constitution is a monstrous contradiction of the principle of our government, and of the solemn declaration upon which we achieved independence. In depriving a human being of his liberty (for though this cannot be done with[out] the slave's consent, neither can it be done without the master's act) he destroys the divine quality wherein man is the image of God. This is the sin that will bring upon us retributive punishment as surely as effect follows cause. But the forcible abolition of slavery would be no remedy: It would be a new crime. Not only sinning against the constitutional rights of the slave-owner, but adding the base perfidy of violating our own solemn covenant. Colonel May, whether abhorring slavery or not, abhors the treachery involved of robbing the South of the property solemnly guaranteed to them by the constitution. To this extent he truly represents my political conviction."

"It is your conviction, then, that slavery cannot be abolished under the constitution?" This question was put by Victor.

"Only by the spontaneous co-operation of the States," the professor answered, with impressive emphasis.

"So!" said Woldemar Auf dem Busch, a perceptible touch of sneering sarcasm in voice and mien. "That means, that under the constitution human freedom is at a discount,—good only for one class, wicked in another. How glorious the 'land of the free, and the home of the brave'!"

"That means," the professor repeated, closely imitating the young man's sneering voice and manner, "that in this 'land of the free and home of the brave' neither covert theft nor open robbery are reckoned, as yet, among the virtues to be cultivated." Then, laying down his knife and fork, and fixing his opponent with a look of fierce contempt, he added, his voice pitched to the deepest bass, the impassioned earnestness of which impressed his audience with the solemn gravity of the subject: "Sir, you have probably studied Mrs. Stowe's 'Uncle Tom's Cabin,' and learned from her soul-stirring pictures of Life among the Lowly how easily Eva St. Clair would have settled this question that is agitating the country. Romantic sentiment makes short work of problems, such as these, that sorely try the wit of the anxious statesmen, philanthropists and philosophers. It is so easy to follow the dictates of the heart if you can only stifle the skeptical protests of the head,—most easy to those who are least oppressed with brains. What a glorious task is that of the poet, or even of a poetess, or one who is reckoned so, to divide mankind into two classes,—the wicked, who, like Shylock, stand on their bond, in this case the constitution, and the pious, the good, who insist that their neighbors shall liberate their slaves, constitution or no constitution—taking the latter to the place where little Eva and Uncle Tom are supposed to have gone, while providing for the former a warmer reception elsewhere. Is this, sir, what your wisdom comes to? Out upon such hypocritical cant! Such nursery-room morality, such St. Crispin virtue! You will not solve the eternal conflict between conscience and law by imposing your conscience as law upon others. Liberate your slaves, if you have any, and appease *your* conscience; but let your neighbor liberate or keep his, as *his* conscience may demand. That, sir, is the law of the land. Let no one violate it, pleading a higher law of God. Be warned by the fate of Antigone: She obeyed what she felt to be the law written in her breast by the gods themselves in preference to the king's decree, and perished, because Institutions are valid, though individuals deem them cruel or absurd. So shall they perish, who lay sacrilegious hands on the constitution, come they from the North, or come they from the South!"

29

THE HIGH BUILDING

Denton J. Snider

In *Architecture, As a Branch of Aesthetic Psychologically Treated*, Snider, as early as 1905, completely understood the cultural significance of the Chicago Movement in skyscraper architecture. True, he forced it into an Hegelian mold, but that mold in retrospect appears to have had as much if not more significance than the naive "form follows function" interpretation that a whole generation of architectural critics has passed on to American readers. Snider caught the essence of the technological achievement involved in steel skeletal construction and the passing of the load-bearing wall. But he also discerned the spiritual significance of the buildings which transcended mere practical function and which, for example, justified much of Louis Sullivan's symbolism and apparently nonfunctional ornamentation. Very early, Snider realized that buildings of all kinds must be psychologically as well as practically functional and must symbolize something to masses of people, however unconsciously. His insight was gained, of course, through placing the "high building" in the context of the world-historical development of architecture as an expression of the chronological stages of culture. That is, he simply applied Hegel's philosophy of history to the history of building.

Denton J. Snider, *Architecture, As a Branch of Aesthetic Psychologically Treated* (St. Louis: Sigma Publ. Co., 1905), pp. 8–15.

. . . Toward the close of the Century the modern High Building, usually called the American after the place of its origin, began to raise itself from the Earth, in which act we may conceive Architecture herself leaping up from her previous outstretched condition. Out of this new appearance came a fresh creative breath which at once swept through and began to rejuvenate the whole Art. Here indeed is something hitherto unknown; no such construction was ever before possible. Not simply another style is this, not merely another variation of the old tune; far deeper is the significance of the phenomenon, since a new principle of building has come to light, along with new materials and new constructive methods. Distinctly does the American High Building proclaim itself to be not European, not Oriental, though it is evolved out of both and shows affinities to both as its ancestors. It is Occidental, representing a new world not merely of Space but of Spirit, not only of men but also of institutions, being not simply a new Style of Architecture but a new Type of the Art.

This is not saying that all people or even a majority are enraptured with the High Building. The connoisseurs of Art are in the main against it, the architects as a body have not been friendly to it, the very builders of these structures seem unable to defend their work in any adequate manner. Still such buildings continue to increase in number and have been also growing in height. From their two starting-points, Chicago and New York, they are rapidly passing to all the lesser American cities. They are crossing the Atlantic back to Europe, through a tempest of scorn and protest; they have gone forward over the Pacific to the most enterprising nation of the Orient, Japan. The High Building begins already to span the globe, and gives a promise of becoming the universal Building, the world-edifice. All other Architectures have been epochal or national, limited in time and in place; Egyptian, Greek, Roman, Gothic they are named even when they overflowed into other peoples besides their originators. The High Building is to-day the architectural loadstone of the globe, attracting architects from abroad to study its principles and their significance. It is the only object of Art that draws students and observers to America from Europe. In all the rest of the Fine Arts the stream is the other way, running to the East, not to the West.

What is it that gives to this edifice such a power of overriding all opposition, even the strongest? Some secret energy it possesses which laughs at criticism, even that of the profession; something it has within it mightier than any antecedent form of Architecture or possibly mightier than all of these forms put together. The Spirit of the Age has taken up its abode in the High Building and renders it impregnable against any attack. The critic is indeed weak compared with such an antagonist; the whole army of opponents cannot possibly prevail over a power of that kind. So the High Building goes its own triumphant way through the very hisses of the multitude of its foes. The majority may and do vote against it, still it has that mighty hand with it which puts down the majority till they learn its significance and are whipped into voting aright.

Hence the first and fundamental task of a thinker on Architecture to-day is to interrogate the High Building and to make it tell if possible the secret of its being—tell why it has risen up before us so mightily and so surprisingly just now and not hitherto, just here and not elsewhere, with such a triumphant, gigantic defiance of the well-established and long-transmitted canons of Art.

I. The basic fact of the High Building is that it has a skeleton within itself which supports the outer enclosing members of the architectural body. This skeleton is usually made of steel, sometimes of iron, being carefully jointed together into a lofty framework which is separate from what it supports. It holds itself up first, and then it upholds the outer material of stone or brick, in which are wrought the old architectural forms handed down by time. These are still a part of the wall, but they and the whole wall with them are now borne aloft into the air by this new inner power which has suddenly developed in the structure.

If we note carefully the fact just presented, we see what may be called the architectural separation of the ages, the separation in the Enclosure between the supporting and the supported, between the upholding and the upheld, between the burden-bearer and the burden borne. In all previous Architecture, in so far as it was of a permanent material, the encompassing wall had to do double duty: to enclose the space of the building, and to support the weight of the roof and its own pressure upon itself. But now the wall divides within, it cracks in its own growth wide open lengthwise, we may say; it frees itself almost wholly of its oppressive, burden-bearing task, and devotes itself exclusively to its space-enclosing duty, which is its primal architectural function. This epoch-making liberation of the Enclosure is the work of the steel skeleton, and means a vast new freedom of development for Architecture, which has been moving from its commencement far back in Egypt just toward the enfranchisement seen in the High Building. Thus Architecture reflects the unfolding of man himself toward a completer freedom, and becomes truly an Art mirroring in its advance the advance of humanity. Nor should we here forget to add that the nation with the freest spirit and the freest institutions will produce the freest Architecture. Not without good reason did the High Building originate in America, and it would seem in the freest, most enterprising portion thereof, the West.

The liberation of the Enclosure, hitherto enslaved to its burden-bearing task, is, then, the supreme work of the High Building. Within it lies ensconced the steel skeleton hidden to the vision of men, yet always performing its function, upholding the encompassing wall which is visible, and hence presents or may present to sight all the architectural ornamentation descended from the past. These two elements, the space-enclosing and the burden-bearing, thus become the outer and the inner, the seen and the unseen; previously in the wall of stone or brick they were united immediately, the flesh and the skeleton of the architectural organism were one, grown together as it were, till the distinction between them evolved itself, somewhat as the same differentiation took place in the evolution of the animal body. Stone and brick (with glass and other materials) are now reduced to a casing or covering, which is simply supported by the secreted giant standing upright; their former additional labor of support has been taken away and handed over to a far mightier power. This division, then, is also a division of labor; the enclosing wall has only to enclose and not to bear the weight of the building; in which fact Architecture is seen developing like the society of which it is the home.

Still there is a time when all may observe this hidden skeleton in the very process of formation. It is that part of the structure which is first set up by the architect; not now is stone laid upon stone, brick upon brick, one after the other in monotonous succession. The steel framework rears itself with its posts, girders, rods, stretching skyward in lofty outline; it looks as if Architecture herself were getting to her feet and preparing to put on her clothes, really erect for the first time in all her long existence. The old wall of temple or cathedral has no such skeleton except what lies within it sleeping the sleep of stone itself. But now we may see that ideal framework of the ancient edifice separate itself from its heavy incumbrance and rise up to a gigantic height, almost in a day, for the whole thing is carefully calculated and made ready for adjustment beforehand. A very striking and suggestive object is the High Building while in the course of erection, manifesting the separation and birth of a new Architecture in the World's History, the very process of its parturition. The slender lines of network against the blue Heaven are the thews of our new infant Hercules, made of the most tenacious and elastic material known on our earth. True it is that every High Building in its construction must re-create the architectural movement of the ages, and take up into itself essentially all the structural forms of the past.

Thus we begin to penetrate to the meaning of the High Building in its primal constructive principle. We find in it an architectural liberation which has a counterpart in the liberated man who reared it, mirroring what had transpired in his own soul. This is not a liberation from work or duty, but from an outside subjection to a task not its own. Behold the Enclosure of the High Building; with ease, with an airy lightness and a new joy does it rise or perchance fly upward on many a line to the eaves, being relieved of its alien service of struggling under external burdens laid upon it, such as roof and ceiling, yea relieved of even holding up its own weight as a whole. It can now confine itself to its native task, that of enclosing and of expressing the same in various forms, new and transmitted. All architecture is Enclosure, making the same an institutional abode of some kind; but when Architecture becomes a liberated Enclosure hitherto subjected or enslaved to tasks other than its own, surely a new architectural epoch has dawned.

We are not to rest till we see and express for ourselves that Architecture and all Art and even Machinery are profoundly connected with the social Institutions of a country, from which indeed they take their origin and character. To some people it may seem forced to join together the new liberation of Architecture with the new liberation of Man through a new institutional world. The great end of the race is freedom, and that end with its striving can be read in Architecture as well as in Literature. . . .

VIII

EPILOGUE

As the nineteenth century passed into the twentieth, the American Hegelian movement waned and was gradually superseded by pragmatism, progressivism, relativism, and modernism. The United States joined the Great War which made everything German seem anathema. The St. Louis Movement was long forgotten by the time its last surviving member, Denton J. Snider, was buried in Belle Fontaine Cemetery in St. Louis in 1925. And yet the Hegelian Movement, in reality, was no time-bound phenomenon. Rather, it was a variety of intellectual energy that diffused itself through American culture and continued to re-emerge in various modified forms down to the present. Hegel himself would have seen this as the natural progression of his ideas—one more instance of the unfolding of the "concrete universal."

At its zenith, the Hegelian Movement probably had its greatest impact on American education—through the work of Harris as Commissioner of Education and through the kindergarten schools. In introducing the highly technical post-Kantian philosophies into America, the Hegelian Movement also did much to bring about the professionalization of philosophy and the social sciences in this country. Naive, moralistic, college president–common sense philosophy gave way to departments of philosophy with specially trained professors—men who had studied in Germany. Harvard, under the leadership of the Hegelian George Herbert Palmer, assembled one of the great departments in the world. The 'eighties and 'nineties knew the golden age of philosophy at that institution. And the conceptual questions raised by Hegel led also to departments and laboratories of psychology as an intensive era of the study of the mind began. Hegel's insistence upon the relational definition of all phenomena laid the groundwork for the general acceptance of relativity and all aspects of cultural relativism. A new "great chain of being" was in the making, one in which the heuristic, the abstract, the unempirical, and the non-common-sense modes of thinking that post-Kantianism had espoused were soon to become dominant, but where there were no longer any fixed absolutes, not even the "concrete universal."

More specifically, however, the Hegelian Movement dissolved into ever-larger concerns. In 1880, Harris moved east and helped form the Concord School of Philosophy, which lasted for ten years. He saw this as a larger stage for his ideas, as indeed it was, and himself as the logical successor to Emerson as the national sage, which indeed he was not. Stallo in his brilliant book of 1881, *The Concepts and Theories of Modern Physics*, specifically recanted his earlier Hegelian work and yet built upon Hegel's assumptions in an attempt to define the concepts of modern science. John Dewey turned to pragmatism, G. Stanley Hall to psychology, and George Holmes Howison to personal idealism. Brokmeyer simply went on struggling along with his abortive translation of Hegel's *Larger Logic*. The most dramatic impact of Hegel's thought, however, was upon the socialist movement. Here, men like Daniel DeLeon, Eugene Debs, and Joseph Dietzgen fully accepted the dialectic and used it as a powerful organizational tool to command the allegiance of the workers. They abandoned spirituality, however, in favor of Marx's dialectical materialism and a philosophy of the here and now so that the Hegelian revolt against materialism had come full circle. In a sense, it had succumbed to the science it had sought to subsume. Its spiritual unities had collapsed before the practical complexities of the modern world.

30

THE WEST MOVES EAST

Denton J. Snider

The best account of the break-up of the St. Louis Movement was Denton J. Snider's elegaic tale of the trek to Concord. His shrewd analysis of Harris's motives for moving east and his description of the foibles of the Concord School testify better than anything else to the way in which the promise of St. Louis was never fulfilled.

Denton J. Snider, *The St. Louis Movement* (St. Louis: Sigma Publishing Company, 1920), pp. 262–77.

THE CONCORD PHILOSOPHICAL SCHOOL

ANOTHER step it was in the Great Departure of the time, when the St. Louis Movement itself departed or began to depart from St. Louis, its original home, and to settle elsewhere in a sort of spiritual estrangement. Our philosophic President Brockmeyer had departed from us into a voluntary exile among the unphilosophic savages; but he cannot be forgotten by this history—he the massive but increate and uncreative potentiality underlying the entire St. Louis Movement. Our Secretary Harris, the tireless propagandist, had departed from us in the other direction, toward the highly tutored New Englanders, whom he would still further tutor and inoculate with the philosophic world-view of Hegel. Here we may be allowed to mention the third man of the original triad, none other than private Snider who was still holding the fort at St. Louis with the loyal assistance of other privates. But he too was getting ready to straddle, that is, both to stay and to depart, seeking if possible, to unite the two sides in some new reconciling combination. Each of these three diverse actions doubtless sprang from the deepest instinct of their respective doers, and mirrored their individual characters, re-acting on the common cause, which we still shall name the St. Louis Movement.

Taking up now this third person and making him the first, at least

345

grammatically, I may announce concerning myself, with modesty I hope, that I received not long after my return to St. Louis an invitation to give a course of lectures on Shakespeare at the Concord School of Philosophy during the summer session of 1880. To me, the St. Louis schoolmaster, with small ability for self-pushing and seemingly smaller for any public function, this seemed a surprising advancement. Moreover it has remained an influential turn in my life. How did it come about? And what is this new School of Philosophy which has risen to light during my absence overseas on my European Journey?

I think it was in September, 1879, as I was sauntering around Lafayette Park, rather listless and uncertain of the future, that I saw Harris, recognizing me, leap out of his buggy and approach me with a hearty smile and salute, which I warmly requited, as I had not seen him since I had come back from abroad, for he had been out of town. He told me that he had been giving some lectures at Concord, Massachusetts, during the summer, that a School of Philosophy had been established there to be held every summer, and that I had been appointed one of the lecturers. He furthermore informed me that he had just given his first course at the Orchard House, the old well-laureled mansion of Mr. A. Bronson Alcott and daughters, that the attendance, beyond all expectation, had overflowed parlor and hall and even windows, and that next year the School was to have a new commodious building, known as the Hillside Chapel, the generous gift of a New York lady philanthropist, Mrs. Elizabeth Thompson.

It was evident that Harris felt very buoyant in his new elevation (so he held it), and he radiated over me and into me his glowing prospects. He said he had calculated upon my help, and at once asked what theme I would like to take on the program: philosophic or literary, Hegel or Shakespeare? I answered that I was not in the mood for philosophy, not even for Hegel, and that he was well able to cover the field himself, but that I would come to his aid in the discussions, whenever I could serve him. "Very well," he replied, "I shall put you down for Shakespeare; your book has made you known; you are recognized as"—and so forth and so forth—all of which had better here be expurgated. Finally looking around to see if anybody were near, and then bowing his face close to mine, he spoke in a whisper: "When this scholastic year is up, I intend to resign as Superintendent of the St. Louis Public Schools, and move permanently to Concord, where I shall occupy with my family the Orchard House of Mr. Alcott, who is going to live downtown in the old Thoreau residence. Just across the street from me, you know, is

the home of Emerson." It was evident that Harris smiled much
elated over his establishment among the eminent Concord Worthies,
whose coming successor he might with some self-appreciation regard himself. Fleeting traces of this ambition I had long forefelt in
him at St. Louis.

Still my surprise hit me hard, indeed I became quite speechless
at this strange new throw of fate's dice-box. Meanwhile he had
turned away, and with the parting words, "Enough for this time,
come to see me as soon as you can," he leaped into his buggy, nod-
ding to me a flash of felicity as he whisked around a corner. He left
me quizzing: Well what does this sudden fresh intervention of the
Powers mean again? For it was evident that here had arrived some
decisive crisis or node in the St. Louis Movement, of which Harris had
been hitherto the most efficient and the most distinguished propagandist. And he was going to quit his own well-tilled field, abandon
the world he had built during his whole youthful two decades of
years in St. Louis. He touched now forty-four, and had poured forth
an enormous energy in a number of directions. But is his creative
power still at high flood?

I paced the Park in slow deliberation about what I should do with
myself in the emergency. It seemed indeed a new allotment, but also
a new opportunity, and the trend of it looked toward the scattering
of the St. Louis group and of their Movement. The oracle appeared
foretelling to us our dispersion, or, to employ the capital term already used, our Departure. My trip abroad lay ensconced in the same
general plan. This Concord project signified at least a separation into
two lines, possibly a transfer from West to East. Did Harris, who had
in him ever the lurking Yankee, intend such removal? I did not fail
to notice that the glow of his talk with me illumined especially the
famous men of Concord headed by Emerson, to whom he was now
to be the next neighbor.

Harris had at this time the outlook upon a modest but sufficient
competence for the future, as I understood from several of his allusions. He had saved something from his salary, he received fair
royalties from his publishers, his articles and lectures produced quite
a little income—once and only once, as far as I know, he took home
to Concord from a six weeks' course of lectures in St. Louis some
fifteen hundred dollars—which he thought pretty good, and so did
I even more emphatically, for it summed up considerably above all
that I could scrape together in a year through my class-work. Moreover his living expenses needed not to be so very high in a New
England country-town. Thus Harris was going to Concord in company with that first and best freedom, condition of all other kinds

of freedom, namely economic freedom. If he chose, he was now in a condition to write unremunerative books and to do free labor in honor of his dearest Philosophy, and for the sake of his love alone to defy the three primordial fates of human existence—food, raiment, and shelter. In other words he could now give himself up wholly to his Super-vocation, to which indeed he had already shown himself consecrated at St. Louis.

In this seemingly sudden and cardinal change, which included vocation, career, and locality, Harris had his unspoken motive deeper than the spoken. I had noticed that underneath all his enthusiasm for the West lay in the bottom of his heart an exile's longing for his native New England. Now there has come the opportunity in his homeland for a new succession in philosophy after Transcendentalism, whose very fortress he wished to capture and reconstruct. Emerson, though still alive, was mentally gone; Alcott had turned eighty, and was creatively closed out, but he could yet be active enough to form an excellent bridge from the old into the present. But he, not very long after the School had well begun, went to pieces, still living. And Sanborn, the unparalleled man of publicity and doubtless the School's chief practical organizer, was even eager to start a new order for a number of reasons, some of them with me conjectural. In his own town I once heard him berated as the Yankee renegade for his part in foisting the Western set of philosophers upon Emerson's Concord. And I had kept wondering in St. Louis why Harris should so often bring to us the aged Alcott to say over again and again what the repeating sayer of the said had already better said, and why he should be so assiduous in admiration of what he had often already sufficiently admired. He was preparing the time and manner of his great Departure from the St. Louis Public Schools to a new career purely philosophical. In 1879 he went to Concord and made his opening trial; he found the transition begging him to seize it at the right psychologic moment. I saw him while still in the furnace white-heat of his first resolution. Certainly a justifiable goal for him or any man; but will he be able to do the deed against all the learned jealousies of Harvard and the other Academies elsewhere in New England? It was Emerson's old fight to be fought over again without his chances. So the question has often come up to me, Was it the part of wisdom in Harris to make this change, and never to unmake it afterward when he had found out?

He probably proposed to hitch the two horses, Concord and St. Louis, to his philosophic chariot, and to keep them in the race from his Eastern home. This he succeeded in doing for a time. Then he had here able and devoted lieutenants, especially one cleverest woman, who would obey him to the letter. For when Harris quit us, he easily held the cultural primacy of St. Louis, and he knew it. He dominated more than any other man or institution the intellectual character of our city. Undoubtedly he had opposition, and at times much worry even in his official administration. Still his influence was central, and radiated through the whole community.

As for me, my attitude was that of independent co-operation. I followed a somewhat different line, but in the same St. Louis Movement. I had to develop and then to express myself in my own right. I may say here that I also harnessed those two steeds, St. Louis and Concord, to my little wain, not the philosophical but the literary, and kept them prancing together for several years. But my goal remained in the West, even when I was compelled to quit St. Louis; I had no Mayflower tradition to chain me to Plymouth Rock or any other piece of stone.

Accordingly, in the summer of 1880, I again turned my face Eastward, sped across the Mississippi, over the Alleghenies, to the ancient Bay State, and in due time stepped off the railroad train at Concord. It was a new sensation to find myself and the St. Louis Movement steaming across the mountains and over the rivers toward the Atlantic seacoast, and entering an old colonial Commonwealth, just the most highly educated and self-appreciative in the whole country. It was an adventure, however, in which I was not alone.

Evening had come, I had taken my repast, and was seated on a little veranda at the Hotel Middlesex, gazing towards Thoreau's Musketaquid, and listening still to that famous Emersonian shot heard round the world and also down time, when three men came up to me in the twilight. I soon recognized the first of them to be Harris, who introduced me to the others. One of the two was Mr. S. H. Emery, Director of the School, who, a born New-Englander, had early in life come to the West, made his fortune in business at Quincy, Ill., and especially had become inoculated with Hegel through Harris's Journal of Speculative Philosophy. He was still in middle life, had given up a profitable partnership, and had settled at Concord for the purpose of devoting himself to Philosophy, as I then understood him, for the rest of his days. Can he hold out? The fact, however, of his doing such a deed at once gave him a high standing in my eyes. The second stranger was Mr. F. B. Sanborn, officially called the Secretary, the chief journalistic spirit of the enterprise. He was tall and spare, with keen-edged features in the center of which would play a little drama of winsome smiles; I might call them honeyed from the bee, for there is no doubt that his mellifluous mouth concealed a stinger which he knew how to flash upon occasion. In a few days I found that out and somewhat more. Just now he bantered me pleasantly by flinging at me the name of Elpinike, the Greek maiden of my *Delphic Days*, which book he had in some way unknown to me gotten hold of, and out of which he had at least fished that one word for future use, whose moment had now arrived. I want to say that just on account of this character I took a decided liking for Mr. Sanborn; we could antagonize, even get a little angry, and still remain friends. His last letter to me I received only a few months before his death during the past year (1918), and it remains to me a precious heart-stirring token. Just now I have taken his letter out of its corner and read it anew as a memorial of the man. He was still, though very old, on the look-out to do a service, as usual, without request. Though we often took a tilt at each other in the course of the School's discussions, and once at a private house in the town, with mutual satisfaction of triumph, I think, I would plant now upon his new-made grave in Sleepy Hollow this little flower plucked from my own experience: Among all the men whom I have ever seen tested he stands first in his love of secretly extending anonymous help to those who might, in his opinion, have need of it, and who would never let such need be known.

The course of my Shakespeare's lectures started and plodded along rather uneventfully, as far as I now remember, with the usual amount of criticism and of defence. I should conjecture fifty people were the average of attendance; among them was Miss Blow, whom I had not seen before, but she soon made herself known. Indeed there was quite a delegation from St. Louis in the audience, who were especially friends of Harris, and in consequence strong supporters of the St. Louis Movement. I think Emerson appeared once to hear me, and Mr. Alcott presided. Men of distinction dropped in to see what was going on, since the public press was making a great noise by extended reports, and by comments serious and comic. One day a stately gentleman having a look of eminence passed the door with his lady, and took a seat near the front row; I recall the crinkles in the rim of his furled Panama hat, as he lifted it off his head and laid it down beside him with judicial dignity. When I had finished my lecture, in which Hamlet received his tragic doom, Emery, who sat near, leaned over to me and whispered: "That is Judge Alphonso Taft, ex-Attorney-General of the United States." I had heard a good deal some years before about Judge Taft of the Superior Court when I lived at

Cincinnati, though I had never seen him; and Harris (William Torrey) told me once, with the only gleam of family pride I ever knew him to shoot, that he was related to Mrs. Taft through the famous New England Torreys. Judge Taft now twisted a little in his seat, and started to cross-examine me on the question of Hamlet's madness, as was his right, when I laid down the law, at least my law, in the case: "Hamlet is never so mad as not to be responsible; hence our poetic Judge Shakespeare condemns him to his tragic death at the end of the play; and this Superior Court now sitting here in the Concord School of Philosophy affirms the judgment of the poet." Somehow thus, not precisely perhaps, was worded the rather legalized decision in honor of the distinguished guests. The audience stared with vacant face-long gravity, nobody seemed to understand the nub, being deemed possibly some deep metaphysical subtlety, such as is expected of philosophers. Only Mrs. Taft turned to her husband and smiled against him (I think) so exuberantly that she raised her fan to her lips to check or at least to hide their perhaps too informal overflow. The Judge murmured a word which I did not then understand, but which I dare now conjecture to have been "overruled." This ended the discussion, when Harris ran down from the rostrum in front of me to salute his illustrious kinsfolk.

But the real episode of the course took place at the last lecture, which I concluded to make practical and to apply directly to Concord. I had found in my studies an entire group of Shakespeare's comedies in which there is a flight from civilized life to the woods and to a primitive existence, whereof an example is seen in "As You Like It." Then, after due experience there is a return of the fugitive to civilization and its institutions. Now the poet makes such flight and return the setting of his comic action in no less than eight plays, according to my count. Herein lay the point of comparison: Concord in her famous individuals had passed through a very similar phase of human experience, had fled in protest from the existent social order, had remained out for a while in the new sylvan or rural paradise, but had at last come back in a sort of penitent disillusion. Thus Concord had actually lived through a great human comedy of the Shakespearian model, which was thus verified in the town's history. Alcott had taken his flight to Brook Farm, Thoreau to Walden, Emerson longed to flee to Berkshire Hills, even to Canada, as we see by his Journal, but he never could quite break loose from his family and from his revenues. These men were the great Concordites of the past and representatives of their town and time; and with them were other, even if lesser, ex-

amples of the same tendency, making a comic era which Shakespeare had already observed more than two centuries before, and
had put into a dramatic structure.

The special play of Flight and Return which I took up for local
application was *Love's Labour's Lost,* in which the King and his
three Lords retire from the world, and especially from the presence
of woman, for the purpose of studying philosophy, making the court
"into a little Academe," named and patterned after the Athenian
home of Plato. Herein lay a striking similarity to the Concord
School of Philosophy, which also had its Platonic course of lectures
with devoted followers, and had even called itself the modern
Academe. But now enters the trouble; love, the old enemy of con-
templative philosophy, appears in the persons of four ladies who
storm the whole celibate Academe and carry off the four philosophers as their captives. Such was the outcome of the Shakespearian
School of Philosophy as portrayed in the poet's famous comedy, a
far-off foreshow of our present School, and now held up as a kind of
mirror before Concord. Three-fourths or more of the audience were
ladies, who smiled appreciation if not approval of the solution of
the great master's dramatic collision between Love and Philosophy.
And it so happened that this was the main theme which the joke-
smith of newspaper and even of magazine delighted to set forth in
the supposed dialect of the School, when it discussed "the What-
ness of the Howsoever," or "the Thingness of the Why," though I
never heard such talk there. One of these squibs crossed me several
times in its travels round town, running thus: Two philosophers, a
young lady and a young gentleman (both of them not so very
young) were promenading in the Walden woods, and had become
deeply entangled in a warm philosophic discussion, when the
woman was heard to exclaim: "Pshaw! you are no philosopher, else
you would understand the Yesness of my No!" In a shoemaker's
shop whither I had gone to get my foot-gear cobbled, and where
I heard the tale told with new variations, I was asked by the artist
point-blank: Were you that philosopher?

But the worst scrimmage I ever saw in the School, with angry
flashes and hot words, I happened to be the means of bringing on
quite unintentionally at the close of my last lecture. I was talking
about Thoreau's flight to Walden hardly a mile distant from his best
friend's door and from the town itself, and I rather made light of
such a minute separation from society. I know that I was thinking
of, but I did not mention, the far more spacious and defiant with-
drawal of Brockmeyer to a hunter's life in the primitive forests of
Warren County, Missouri, from which, however, he also had to

come back to civilization and earn money for his gunpowder and some apparel, and finally to win a wife. When I had finished, Sanborn jumping up scowled at me in a sort of pale tremble, and declared that he was there to defend the good name of his friend Thoreau who was no longer on this side to defend himself. Thereupon he launched into a sharp damnatory criticism of my whole Shakespearian course, and especially my attempt to make fun of his townspeople. I felt inclined merely to smile at him, for in his ire he hardly grazed the mark; but I noticed that Harris began to get white about the lips, which I knew of old to be his native warpaint; then he started a warm defence of my views, of course without their teaseful banter. Sanborn replied and Harris retorted. It looked squally for a moment when the two chief promoters of the School began to knock their heads together in hot disputation. Then the aged reverend form of Mr. Alcott rose from his presidential chair, and with his calm rather sepulchral voice and words allayed the tempest, saying that he had in his life fled thrice from the established social order, and had thrice returned, and that he still thought himself young enough to play once more at least the same Shakespearian Comedy of flight and return before he passed over into Sleepy Hollow. Whereat we all rippled into a smile at the old man's Yankee humor and philosophic serenity, in spite of the somewhat funereal close of his talk. The session broke up in a love-feast; still I rather thought that this last speech of mine would be my last at Concord.

Here I may remark concerning the conversational frequency of Sleepy Hollow in Concord, that this beautiful cemetery seems to be inwoven into the very life and speech of the citizenry. I never knew an American town whose graveyard was such a vital, intimate even artistic part of its daily existence. Dead Concord in a way appears more alive than living Concord. I suppose that Egypt with its mummied cities must have been somewhat similar, and perhaps China is, with its worship of ancestors. At times there came over me in certain places of Concord the uncanny feeling with which I wandered through the old Etruscan tombs of Italy—all that is at present left of a great people, of its glory and its civilization. Concord's own folks are now saying, as I have been told, in grim self-criticism, that Sleepy Hollow has become their chief civic asset.

31

THE SECRET
OF HENRY BROKMEYER

Henry C. Brokmeyer

One of the reasons for the decline of the St. Louis Hegelians, in addition to Harris's defection to the East, was Henry Brokmeyer's failure ever to complete a satisfactory translation of the Hegelians' "Book of Fate" —the master's *Larger Logic*. This prevented Hegel at his best from reaching a larger English-speaking audience and denied the St. Louis philosopher the chance of attaining an international reputation of the sort gained by the British philosopher J. H. Stirling, when he published in 1865 *The Secret of Hegel*, a widely read general guide to Hegel's thought. Stirling's book had a marked impact, for example, on both Emerson and Whitman, whereas Brokmeyer never did, except when he insulted Emerson on one of the latter's speaking engagements in St. Louis.

Rescued by Harris from death by fever in his Warren County hut in 1859, Brokmeyer set to work on his translation of the *Larger Logic* that same year, in a rooming house in St. Louis. By the end of 1860 he had finished it, but in such badly garbled form that it was promptly rejected by publishers. Subsequently the Civil War, and a political career leading to the governorship of Missouri, intervened for Brokmeyer, and then a long period of service as a railroad lawyer and teacher of the Creek Indians in Muskogee, Oklahoma. During all this time, down to 1896, he worked intermittently on his translation. Meanwhile, handwritten copies were made of his original effort and circulated among the various Hegelian societies of the Middle West. Finally, during the last ten years of his life, Brokmeyer completely redid his translation; but, even with the help of editors, this version, too, proved disastrously unsuccessful. By 1906, the year of his death, he had lost all interest, and his manuscript lay consigned to the corner of an attic. A copy survived, however, and was deposited with the Missouri Historical Society in St. Louis, where it now resides.

The excerpt below is a sample of Brokmeyer's final manuscript—published at last for the first time. It is from Hegel's brilliant "Introduction" to the *Larger Logic* in which he describes how philosophy has arrived at a point where abstract logic and concrete matter—form and content—are seen never to meet; hence thinking becomes unfortunately separated from reality. In the second part of the extract, Hegel suggests how his dialectical method offers a way out of this philosophical predicament.

All this is somewhat difficult to grasp from Brokmeyer's translation. Small words and strange neologisms, rather than large meanings, seem to get in his way. Nothing testifies so eloquently to the reasons for the failure of the great leader of the St. Louis Movement, and for his apparent inclination to be distracted into any other career but that of philosopher and writer. Brokmeyer simply could not adequately translate the beloved *Larger Logic*. He never succeeded in "making Hegel talk English."

Selection published through the courtesy of the Missouri Historical Society, Jefferson Memorial, St. Louis, Missouri. Subsequent attempts at correcting and editing Brokmeyer's original words have been deleted from this text.

INTRODUCTION

General Comprehension of Logic

By no science is the necessity realized so clearly, to begin with the subject matter itself, without precursory reflections, than by the science of logic. In every other, the object which it treats of, and the scientific method employed, are distinct from each other; nor does the content make an absolute beginning, but depends upon other comprehensions, and is connected with other material in every direction. It is therefore, permissable for these sciences, to speak of their foundation and its connections, together with the method, lemmatically, to apply without farther ado, the forms of definitions and the like, which are assumed as well known, and accepted, and to avail themselves of the usual modes of reasoning, for the establishment of their general comprehension and fundamental determinations.

Logic, on the contrary, can pre-suppose none of these forms of reflection, or rules and laws of thought, for they constitute a part of its content, and are first to be founded within the science itself. Not merely the statement of the scientific method, however, but the comprehension itself of science in general, belongs to its content, and indeed, constitutes its final result; what the science is, it can therefore, not say in advance, but, its entire exposition first brings this knowing-of-itself, into existence, as its final completion. Its object, too, the thinking, or, more definitely, the comprehending-thinking is essentially discussed within the science; the comprehension of the same begets itself in the course thereof, and can thus, not be adduced in advance. What is stated, therefore, in this introduction, does not have the purpose to found the comprehension of logic, or to justify, scientifically, in advance, either the content or the method of the same, but to bring the point of view from which this science is to be considered, nearer to conception by means of some explanations and reflections in a discoursive historical sense.

When logic is assumed as the science of thought, in general, this is understood to mean, that the thinking constitutes the mere form of knowledge; that logic abstracts from all content, and that the second constituent part, which belongs to knowledge, the matter, is to be given from some other source; that logic, thus, of which this matter is entirely independent, only adduces the formal conditions of true knowledge, but does not contain real truth itself, nor yet, that it can be the road to real knowledge, since, precisely, the essential of truth, the content, lies outside of it.

But, in the first place, it is already inapt to say that logic abstracts from all content, that it only teaches the rules of thinking, without affecting that which is thought, and without being able to consider the nature of the same. For, since the thinking, and the rules of the thinking are to be its object, it has in them, its peculiar content; it has in them also, that second constituent part, for a knowledge, a matter, about whose nature it concerns itself.

Secondly, the conceptions, however, upon which logic has hitherto rested, have, partly, crumbled away already, and it is high time, that the rest should vanish entirely, in order that it may be apprehended from a higher point of view, and the science obtain an entire new form.

The hitherto prevailing comprehension of logic rested upon the separation, once for all, pre-supposed by the common consciousness, between the content and the form of knowledge, or between truth and certitude. It is, in the first place, pre-supposed, that the material of knowing is in-and-by-itself subsisting, as a complete world, that the thinking, by-itself, is empty, that it, as an external form, steps up to that material, fills itself with it, obtains through this, a content, and in this manner, becomes a real knowing.

In the next place, these two constituent parts—(for they are to have the relation of constituent parts, and the knowing is compounded out of them in a mechanical, or, at farthest, chemical manner), stand in the hierarchical order, that the object is supposed to be, by-itself, complete and finished, which can dispense with the thinking for its reality entirely, while on the contrary, the thinking is supposed to be something defective, which has to perfect itself, first, on a material, and that too as a yielding form, that has to accommodate itself to its material. Truth is the correspondence of the thinking, with the object, and, in order that this correspondence may be produced—for it is not in-and-by-itself subsisting—the thinking must accommodate itself to the object.

Thirdly, while the difference between the matter, between the object and the thinking, is not left in this hazy undeterminateness, but, apprehended more definatly, each becomes a separate sphere, distinct from the other. The thinking, therefore, does not get beyond its own self in its receiving and forming of the material, its receiving and accommodating itself, remains a modification of-itself, it does not become, through this, another; and, the self-conscious determining belongs only to it anyway; hence, in its relation even to the subject matter, it does not get out-of-itself to the object, the latter remains as a thing-in-itself, directly a beyond of the thinking.

These views concerning the relation, of the subject and the object, to each other, express the determinations which constitute the nature of our common, the appearing consciousness; but these prejudices transplanted into reason, as if, in it, the same relation subsisted, as if this relation possessed truth, in-and-by-itself, they become the erroneous opinions, whose refutation throughout every part of the spiritual and natural universe, constitutes philosophy, or, rather, since they obstruct the entrance into philosophy, they are to be laid aside before the study thereof is attempted.

The older metaphysics entertain a higher comprehension of the thinking, than what has obtained currency in recent times; it laid down as fundamental, that that which is cognized by the thinking of the things, constitutes their real truth; thus, not in their immediateness, but, as elevated first into thought, as things that are thought. This metaphysics, therefore, held, that the thinking and determinations of the thinking, are not something foreign to the objects, but, rather, their essence, or, that the things, and the thinking of the same, (just as our language expresses a relationship between them) correspond in-and-by-themselves, that the thinking, in its imminent determinations, and the true nature of things, are one and the same content. But, the reflective understanding took possession of philosophy. It will be sufficient, to mention here, what this expression is intended to mean, which has become a kind of partisan cry of the day; what is meant by it is the abstracting and separating understanding, which adheres to its abstraction. Turned against reason, it conducts itself as the common sence of mankind, and makes its opinion valid, that truth rests upon sensuous reality, that thoughts are merely thoughts, in the sense, that it is sensuous observation first, that gives them content and reality; that reason, in so far that it remains in-and-by-itself, only begets mental vagaries. In this renounciation of reason by-itself, the comprehension of truth is lost, it (reason) is limited to the cognizing of subjective truth only, of appearances, of something to which the nature of the subject-matter does not correspond; the knowing has fallen back to opinion.

This turn, however, which the knowing takes, and which appears as a loss and retrogression, has at bottom something deeper, and, upon which the elevation of reason, into the higher spirit of the more recent philosophy is based. The ground, namely, for the mentioned conception that has become general, is to be sought for in the necessity of the contradictory character of the determinations of the understanding. The already mentioned reflection is this, that the understanding goes beyond the concrete immediate, and determines and analyzes the same. But, it is compelled, likewise, to go beyond these its determinations, obtained from the analysis, and, first of all, to relate them. Upon the standpoint of this relating, their contradictory character becomes apparent. The relating, by reflection, belongs in-itself, to reason; the rising above these determinations, which reaches the in-sight of their contradictory character, is the great negative step towards the true comprehension of reason. But, the partial insight falls into the misapprehension, as if it were reason that entangles itself in contradiction; it does not recognize that the contradiction is precisely the elevation of reason above the limitations of the understanding, and the solution of the contradictions. Instead of taking the last step upwards, the knowing has fled from the unsatisfactoriness of the determinations of the understanding, back to sensuous existence in the persuasion, that it possesses in that the unified and permanent. But, upon the other side, this knowing knows itself as a knowing of appearances only, its unsatisfactoriness is conceded, but, at the same time, the assumption is made, that, although the things cannot be known in-themselves, still, in the sphere of appearance, they are correctly known; just as if it were only the kind of object that made the difference, as if the one kind, the things in-themselves, did not, but appearances did fall in the knowing. Just as if a correct insight were attributed to a man, with the addition, that he was incapable, however, of seeing anything true, but only the untrue. As absurd as the latter is, just so absurd is a true knowledge, which does not know the subject-matter as it is in-itself.

The critique of the forms of the understanding has had the quoted result, that these forms have no application to the things in-themselves. This can have no other meaning than that these forms are by-themselves, something untrue. Since, however, they are left, as valid for subjective reason, and for experience, this criticism has wrought no change in them themselves, but leaves them in the same form for the subject, in which they were formerly valid for the object. But, if they are insufficient for the thing in-itself, still less ought the understanding to which they are said to belong, be willing to be satisfied with them. If they cannot be determinations of the thing in-itself, much less can they be determinations of the understanding, to which, at least, the honor of being a thing in-itself should be attributed. The determinations of the finite and infinite are as contradictory, whether they are applied to time and space, to the world, or, they are left as determinations within the spirit; just as well as black and white produce a gray, whether they are mixed upon a wall or upon the palette; if our world-conception destroys itself, when the determinations of the finite and the infinite are applied to it, then the spirit itself, which contains both of them, is still more a self-contradictory, a self-destroying existence. It is not the nature of the matter, or, of the object, to which they may be applied, or in which they might be found that can make a difference; for the object has the contradiction to it, only through and in these determinations.

The mentioned critique, therefore, has only removed the forms of objective thinking from the thing, but left them in the subject as it found them. It has, namely, not considered these forms, in-and-by-themselves, according to their peculiar content, but has assumed them lemmatically from subjective logic, directly; so that there was no thought of a deduction of them by themselves, or, even a deduction of them as subjective logical forms, much less of a dialectical consideration of them. The more consequently elaborated transcendental idealism, has recognized the nugatoriness of the phantom of a thing in-itself, this abstract shade, devoid of all content, left by the critical philosophy, and has had the purpose to destroy it completely. This philosophy also made the beginning, to permit reason to present its determinations itself. But, the subjective leaning of this attempt, did not permit it to reach completion. After that, this leaning, and with it, the development of the pure science has been abandoned.

But, what is usually understood by logic, is considered entirely without any reference to any metaphysical signification. This science, in the condition in which it is still extant, has, of course, no content of the kind that is valid as a reality, and as a true subject-matter, for the ordinary consciousness. But, upon this ground, it is not a formal science destitute of a veritable content. In that material, which is missed in logic to the want of which it is usual to attribute its unsatisfactoriness, the province of truth is not to be looked for anyway. On the contrary, the content-lessness of the logical forms, lies entirely in the manner in which they are considered and treated. While they fall asunder as permanent determinations, and, are not held together in an organic unity, they are dead forms, and have not the spirit dwelling within them which is the vital concrete unity. With this, however, they are wanting in a sterling content, which would be of intrinsic worth by itself. The content which is missed on these logical forms, is nothing less than a solid foundation, and concretion of these abstract determinations; and such a substantial essence is usually sought for them outside. But, the logical reason itself is the substantial or the real, which holds together within itself, all abstract determinations, and is their sterling absolute concrete unity. Hence, it was not necessary to look far off for what is usually called a matter; it is not the fault of the subject-matter of logic, if it is regarded as destitute of content, but only of the mode and manner in which that subject-matter is apprehended.

This reflection lends to the statement of the standpoint, from which logic is to be considered, in how far it distinguishes itself from the hitherto prevailing mode of treatment of the science, and, in how far it is the only true standpoint upon which it is to be placed in time to come.

In the phenomenology of spirit, I have presented the consciousness in its progressive dialectical movement, from the first immediate opposition, between it and the object, up to the absolute knowing. In the course of this treatment, all the forms of the relation of consciousness to the object have been passed in review, and the comprehension of science is its result. This comprehension, therefore, needs no justification here (the fact that it originates within logic, not taken into account), for the reason that it has received it there; and it is incapable of any other justification than this, its begetting by consciousness, all of whose forms dissolve themselves in this comprehension, as in their final truth. A discoursive founding or explaining of the comprehension of the science, can, at farthest, accomplish this, that it is brought before conception, and that a historical knowledge of it be furnished; but, a definition of science, or, more definitely of logic, has its proof alone in the necessity of the course of thought through which it originates. A definition with which a science makes an absolute beginning, can contain nothing but the definite and correct expression of that which is the well known, and acknowledged conception of the object and aim of the science. That just this is understood by it, is an historical assurance, in regard to which one can only appeal to this or that as well established, or, in reality, add requestingly that this or that may be regarded as the acknowledged understanding. It never happens but someone from this, another from that side produces a case or instance, according to which something more and something else is understood by this or that expression, in whose definition, therefore, there ought to be included a more definite or more general determination, and the science be arranged accordingly. It next depends upon discoursive reasoning, what is to be included and to what limit and extent it is to be drawn into, or excluded; but, this reasoning itself, has open before it an unlimited field of assumptions, in which, caprice alone can reach a solid conclusion at last. In connection with this mode of proceedure, to begin a science with its definition, the question is never asked as to the necessity of its object, and thus of the science itself.

The comprehension of pure science, and its deduction, is, therefore, pre-supposed in the present exposition, as the phenomenology of spirit is nothing else than the deduction of that comprehension. The absolute knowing is the truth of all modes of consciousness, since, that development of the same has produced it; it is only in the absolute knowing that the separation of the subject matter from its certitude of-itself, has completely resolved itself, and the truth has become equal to this certitude no less than this certitude to proof.

The pure science, therefore, pre-supposes the liberation from the opposition of consciousness. It contains the thought, in so far as it is, just as well, the nature of things, or, the nature of things, in so far as they are just as well, the pure thought. As science, truth is the self-consciousness developing itself purely from within, and has the form of selfhood, that the in-and-for-itself existing, is the known comprehension, and the known comprehension is the in-and-for-itself existing. This objective thinking, is the content of pure science. It is, therefore, so little formal, it is so far from wanting a matter, for a real and true knowledge, that its content is rather, the only absolutely true, or, if one saw fit to still employ the word matter, the veritable matter—but, a matter to which the form is not external, since this matter is the pure thought, hence, the absolute form itself. Logic is thus to be apprehended as the system of pure reason, as the realm of pure thought. This realm is the truth, as it is, without obscuration, in-and-by-itself. One may express one's self thus, that this content is the exposition of God, as He is in His eternal essence, before the creation of nature, and of a finite spirit. . . .

. . . Up to recently, philosophy had not discovered its method; it considered the systematic structure of mathematics with envy, and borrowed it as stated, or managed to get along with the methods of sciences which are only a compound of given material, propositions of experience and thoughts or, it resorted to the barbaric casting aside of all method. But, the exposition of that which alone can be the true method of philosophical sciences, falls within the exposition of logic itself, for the method is the consciousness concerning the form of the internal self-movement of its content. I have adduced, in the phenomenology of spirit, an example of this method, on a concrete object, on consciousness. We have there forms of consciousness, each one of which destroys itself in its realization, has for its result, its own negation—and thus has passed over into a higher form. The one thing that is necessary, in order to gain the scientific proceedure, and for the entirely simple insight of which earnest effort should be made, is a knowledge of the logical principle that the negative is just as well positive, or, that the self-contradictory does not resolve itself into zero, into abstract nothing, but essentially only into the negation of its particular content, or, that such a negation is not all negation of its particular content; or, that such a negation is not all negation, but the negation of a definite subject-matter, which destroys itself, hence, determined negation; that, therefore, there is contained in the result, that from which it results;—which is really a tautology, for otherwise it would be an immediate, not a result. Inasmuch as the resulting, the negation is determined negation, it has a content. It is a new comprehension, but a higher, a richer comprehension than the preceding one; for it has become enriched to the extent of the negation of that, to the extent of the opposite of that preceding one; it contains that comprehension, therefore, but also more than it, and is the unity of that and its opposite.— In this manner, the system of comprehensions, in general, has to construct and complete itself with a pure uninterrupted progress, taking up nothing from without.

How could I entertain the opinion that the method which I have followed—or rather, which the system has followed of its own accord—is not capable of many improvements, as regards perfection of detail, but, I know, at the same time, that it is the only true one. This is at once evident from the fact that it is not something separate and apart from its subject matter and content;—for it is the content itself, the dialectic which it has to it, that moves the content along. It is evident that no exposition can be regarded as scientific which does not follow the way of this method, and is not in harmony with its simple rithm, for it is the way of the subject-matter itself. . . .

32

THE ERRORS OF
METAPHYSICS

Johann B. Stallo

Johann B. Stallo, as suggested above, had recanted his youthful Hegelian indiscretions by 1881. In *Concepts and Theories of Modern Physics* (1881), he attempted to work much more closely with science than he had previously and to inquire into the basis of scientific knowledge. The burden of the book was to cast aside all the earlier metaphysical assumptions of science, particularly the mechanical evolutionism of Spencer, and to portray the relational aspects of science as a mental activity. He did not, of course, go far enough, for he chose to reject Georg Riemann's conceptual logic, an example of what he was really arguing for, and a primary tool in the construction of Einstein's theory of relativity. He also failed to realize that the true basis for this conceptual approach to science rested in the work of Kant and Hegel. Stallo never really escaped them.

Johann B. Stallo, *Concepts and Theories of Modern Physics,* The International Scientific Series, Vol. XLII, English Edition (London: Kegan Paul, Trench & Co., 1882), pp. 133–139, 158–159, 295–296.

I DEEM it important to have it understood, at the outset, that this treatise is in no sense a further exposition of the doctrines of a book (*The Philosophy of Nature,* Boston, Crosby & Nichols, 1848) which I published more than a third of a century ago. That book was written while I was under the spell of Hegel's ontological reveries—at a time when I was barely of age and still seriously affected with the metaphysical malady which seems to be one of the unavoidable disorders of intellectual infancy. The labor expended in writing it was not, perhaps, wholly wasted, and there are things in it of which I am not ashamed, even at this day; but I sincerely regret its publication, which is in some degree atoned for, I hope, by the contents of the present volume. . . .

Now, in any discussion of the operations of thought, it is of the utmost importance to bear in mind the following irrefragable truths, some of which—although all of them seem to be obvious— have not been clearly apprehended until very recent times:

1. Thought deals, not with things as they are, or are supposed to be, in themselves, but with our mental representations of them. Its elements are, not pure objects, but their intellectual counterparts. What is present in the mind in the act of thought is never a thing, but always a state or states of consciousness. However much, and in whatever sense, it may be contended that the intellect and its object are both real and distinct entities, it can not for a moment be denied that the object, of which the intellect has cognizance, is a synthesis of objective and subjective elements, and is thus primarily, in the very act of its apprehension and to the full extent of its cognizable existence, affected by the determinations of the cognizing faculty. Whenever, therefore, we speak of a thing, or a property of a thing, it must be understood that we mean a product of two factors neither of which is capable of being apprehended by itself. In this sense all knowledge is said to be relative.

2. Objects are known only through their relations to other objects. They have, and can have, no properties, and their concepts can include no attributes, save these relations, or rather, our mental representations of them. Indeed, an object can not be known or conceived otherwise than as a complex of such relations. In mathematical phrase: things and their properties are known only as functions of other things and properties. In this sense, also, relativity is a necessary predicate of all objects of cognition.

3. A particular operation of thought never involves the entire complement of the known or knowable properties of a given object, but only such of them as belong to a definite class of relations. In mechanics, for instance, a body is considered simply as a mass of determinate weight and volume (and in some cases figure), without reference to its other physical or chemical properties. In like manner each of the several other departments of knowledge effects a classification of objects upon its own peculiar principles, thereby giving rise to different series of concepts in which each concept represents that attribute or group of attributes—that aspect of the object—which it is necessary, in view of the question in hand, to bring into view. Our thoughts of things are thus, in the language of

Leibnitz, adopted by Sir William Hamilton, and after him by Herbert Spencer, *symbolical*, not (or, at least, not only) because a complete mental representation of the properties of an object is precluded by their number and the incapacity of the mind to hold them in simultaneous grasp, but because many (and in most cases the greater part) of them are irrelevant to the mental operation in progress.

Again: the attributes comprised in the concept of an object being the representations of its relations to other objects, and the number of these objects being unlimited, it follows that the number of attributes is also unlimited, and that, consequently, there is no concept of an object in which its cognizable properties are exhaustively exhibited. In this connection it is worthy of mention that the ordinary doctrinal statement of the relation of concepts to judgments is liable to serious objection. A judgment is said to be "a comparison of two notions (concepts), with a resulting declaration of their agreement or disagreement" (Whately), or "a recognition of the relation of congruence or confliction between two concepts" (Hamilton). Here it is assumed that the concepts preëxist to the act of judgment, and that this act simply determines the fact or degree of their congruence or confliction. But the truth is that every concept is the result of a judgment, or of a series of judgments, the initial judgment being the recognition of a relation between two data of experience. In most cases, indeed, a judgment is a collation of two concepts; but every synthetic judgment (i.e., every judgment in which the predicate is more than a mere display of one or more of the attributes connoted by the subject) transforms both concepts which it brings into relation, by either amplifying or restricting their respective implicatons. When a boy learns that "a whale is a mammal," his notions, both of a whale and of a mammal, undergo a material change. From the judgment of Thomas Graham that "hydrogen is a metal," both the term "hydrogen" and the term "metal" emerged with new meanings. The announcement by Sterry Hunt, that "just as solution is chemical combination so chemical combination is mutual solution," extended the concept "solution" as well as the concept "chemical combination."

It is apparent, from these considerations, that the concepts of a given object are terms or links in numberless series or chains of abstractions varying in kind and diverging in direction with the comparisons instituted between it and other objects; that the import and scope of any one of these concepts are dependent, not only on the number, but also on the nature of the relations with reference to which the classification of objects is effected; and that for this reason, too, all thoughts of things are fragmentary and symbolic representations of realities whose thorough comprehension in any single mental act, or series of acts, is impossible. And this is true, *a fortiori,* because the relations of which any object of cognition is the entirety, besides being endless in number, are also variable—because, in the language of Herakleitos, all things are in a perpetual flux.

All metaphysical or ontological speculation is based upon a disregard of some or all of the truths here set forth. Metaphysical thinking is an attempt to deduce the true nature of things from our concepts of them. Whatever diversity may exist between metaphysical systems, they are all founded upon the express or implied supposition that there is a fixed correspondence between concepts and their filiations on the one hand and things and their modes of interdependence on the other. This fundamental error is, in great part, due to a delusory view of the function of language as an aid to the formation and fixation of concepts. Roughly stated, concepts are the meanings of words; and the circumstance that words primarily designate things, or at least objects of sensation and their sensible interactions, has given rise to certain fallacious assumptions which, unlike the ordinary infractions of the laws of logic, are in a sense natural outgrowths of the evolution of thought (not without analogy to the organic diseases incident to bodily life) and may be termed structural fallacies of the intellect. These assumptions are:

1. That every concept is the counterpart of a distinct objective reality, and that hence there are as many things, or natural classes of things, as there are concepts or notions.

2. That the more general or extensive concepts and the realities corresponding to them preëxist to the less general, less comprehensive concepts and their corresponding realities; and that the latter concepts and realities are derived from the former, either by a successive addition of attributes or properties, or by a process of evolution, the attributes or properties of the former being taken as implications of those of the latter.

3. That the order of the genesis of concepts is identical with the order of the genesis of things.

4. That things exist independently of and antecedently to their relations; that all relations are between absolute terms; and that, therefore, whatever reality belongs to the properties of things is distinct from that of the things themselves.

By the aid of these preliminaries I hope to be able to assign to the mechanical theory its true character and position in the history of the evolution of thought. Before I proceed to this, however, it may not be without interest, in connection with the preceding inquiry into the relation between concepts and their corresponding objects, to consider the question which has long been the subject of eager debate, whether and to what extent conceivability is a test of possible reality. It is contended by J. S. Mill and his followers, that our incapacity of conceiving a thing is no proof of its impossibility; while Whewell and Herbert Spencer maintain (though not strictly in the same sense and on the same grounds) that what is inconceivable can not be real or true. A trustworthy judgment on the merits of this controversy can only be formed after a careful determination of the conditions of conceivability as indicated by the nature of the process of conception which I have attempted to describe.

It has been shown that all true conception consists in the establishment of relations of partial or total identity between the fact to be conceived and other known facts of experience. The first condition of conceivability, therefore, is that the thing or phenomenon in question be susceptible of classification, i.e., of total or partial identification with objects or phenomena previously observed.

A second and very obvious condition of conceivability is the consistency of the elements of the concept to be formed with each other. It is clear that two attributes, one of which is the negation of the other, can not simultaneously belong to the same subject and thus be parts of the same concept.

These two are the only conditions which are directly deducible from the theory of conception, and may, therefore, with some propriety be termed theoretical conditions. But there is a third, practical condition: the consistency of the new concept with previously-formed concepts bearing upon the same subject-matter. As I have said, this is a practical condition—not so much a condition of conceivability as of ready conceivability. For the old concepts may be defective or erroneous; the very concept with which they conflict may supplement or supplant, rectify or destroy them. . . .

The errors of evolutionism in its confessedly metaphysical forms (exhibited in numerous hylozoic and pantheistic doctrines) are more glaring, it is true, than those of materialistic evolutionism. It is characteristic of many of the most prominent metaphysical systems that the *summa genera* which serve as the basis of evolution are reached by leaps into vacuity beyond the boundaries of legitimate generalization. Thus Hegel evolves all things from pure *Being*, which, as he himself says, is wholly devoid of attributes—a mere logical phantom conjured up by a forced rejection of the last attributes that can be constitutive of the *summum genus* of any classification of phenomena whatever.* This phantom, as Hegel expressly declares, is not to be distinguished from, and is therefore identical with, pure *Nothing;* and for this reason some of Hegel's intellectual descendants—Dellingshausen, Rohmer, Werder, George and others—have boldly undertaken to deduce the phenomenal world from the alleged concept *Nothing* or *Zero.* The same attempt is made by other metaphysicians in whose systems the initial blank appears under various disguises—by Schopenhauer and Hartmann, for instance, whose germinal principle is an impersonal will, a concept whose attributes are contradictory of each other, and which is, therefore, as void as the pseudo-concept Nothing. The most imposing among the disguises of the substantial Nothing as the fountain and origin of all phenomenal existence are *The Absolute* and *The Thing per se,* both of which are denials in terms of all possible relation, and thus negations of all possible attributes, inasmuch as every attribute is essentially a relation. But, although such concepts as *matter* and *force* are somewhat less hollow than the pseudo-concepts of current metaphysical speculations, they are not less unavailable as starting-points for the evolution of concrete physical realities. . . .

It may be said that physical action is utterly indeterminable except on the supposition of the atomic or molecular construction of matter. This is true only in the sense that we are unable to deal with forms of physical action otherwise than by considering them as modes of interaction between distinct physical terms. Physical action can not be subjected to quantitative determination without a logical insulation of the conceptual elements of matter, and without ultimate reference to conceptual constants of mass and energy. All discursive reasoning depends upon the formation of concepts, upon the intellectual segregation and grouping of attributes—in other words, upon the consideration of phenomena under particular as-

---

* Strictly speaking, the foundation of Hegel's "dialectic process" is not even a phantom of reality. "Being *per se*" is not so much as the mere locus of a vanished attribute. The copula between subject and predicate is nothing more than the formal expression of the fact that the relation of identity, inclusion or coexistence subsists between an attribute and a group of attributes. It is a mere abstract line (or pair of lines) pointing from the generic to the differential constituents of a concept. "Pure Being" is simply the specter of the copula between an extinct subject and a departed predicate. It is a sign of predication which "lags superfluous on the stage" after both the predicate and that whereof it was predicated have disappeared.

pects. In this sense the steps to scientific as well as other knowledge consist in a series of logical fictions which are as legitimate as they are indispensable in the operations of thought, but whose relations to the phenomena whereof they are the partial and not unfrequently merely symbolical representations must never be lost sight of. . . .

33

SCIENTIFIC SOCIALISM

Joseph Dietzgen

Joseph Dietzgen emigrated to America three times during the nineteenth century, the last time in 1884. He eventually became editor of the *Chicagoer Arbeiterzeitung* when its regular editors were arrested during the "Red scare" that followed the Haymarket bombing of 1886. For most of his life Dietzgen lived in the German Rhineland fighting for and philosophizing about the workers' cause. He was a friend of Marx and Engels and was introduced by Marx at the Communist Hague International Congress of 1872 as "our philosopher." He was also a close associate of Frederick Sorge, whom his son called "the Nestor of the American socialist movement." Dietzgen considered himself the theoretician of the Marxist movement and he published many articles and several books that were more speculative in nature than much of the writings of Marx's followers.

The selection below is an article he wrote for a socialist newspaper, the *Volksstaat*, in Leipzig in 1873. Strictly speaking, it is not an "American" document. But "Scientific Socialism" not only represents the kind of ideas Dietzgen brought to America, but is also the most cogent statement by an American Marxist of just what the Communist movement owed to Hegel. Despite his acceptance of dialectical materialism, Dietzgen realized quite clearly that Communism rested on the foundations of Hegelian thought. Dietzgen's essay also indicates what happened to Hegelianism when it became transformed by Marx and moved on into the twentieth century.

Eugene and Joseph Dietzgen, Jr., eds., *Some of the Philosophical Essays on Socialism and Science, Religion, Ethics, Critique of Reason and the World at Large by Joseph Dietzgen* (Chicago: Charles H. Kerr & Co., Cooperative, 1906), pp. 79–89.

SCIENTIFIC SOCIALISM

A CONSIDERABLE number of readers of the *Volksstaat* are opposed to elaborate and searching essays in these columns. I doubted therefore whether the following would be suitable for publication. Let the editor decide. Yet I beg to consider whether it is not as valuable to engage the more advanced minds and to gain qualified thoroughgoing comrades as to strive for great numbers by publishing popular articles. Both these aims, I think, should be kept in view. If the party is really of opinion that the emancipation from misery cannot be accomplished by mending particular evils but by a fundamental revolution of society, it necessarily follows that an agitation on the surface is inadequate and that it is moreover our duty to undertake an enquiry into the very basis of social life. Let us now proceed:

Contemporary socialism is communistic. Socialism and communism are now so near each other that there is hardly any difference between them. In the past they differed from each other as does liberalism from democracy, the latter being in both cases the consistent and radical application of the former. From all other political theories communistic socialism is distinguished by its principle that the people can only be free when they free themselves from poverty, when their struggle for freedom is fought out on the social, i.e., on the economic, field. There is this difference between the modern and the older socialistic and communistic theories: in the past it was the feeling, the unconscious rebellion, against the unjust distribution of wealth, which constituted the basis of socialism; to-day it is based on knowledge, on the clear recognition of our historic development. In the past socialists and communists were able only to find out the deficiencies and evils of existing society. Their schemes for social reconstruction were fantastic. Their views were evolved not from the world of realities, not from the concrete conditions surrounding them, but from their mental speculations, and were therefore whimsical and sentimental. Modern socialism, on the other hand, is scientific. Just as scientists arrive at their generalizations not by mere speculation, but by observing the phenomena of the material world, so are the socialistic and communistic theories not idle schemes, but generalizations drawn from economic facts. We see for instance that the communistic mode of work is being more and more organized by the bourgeoisie itself. Only the distribution still proceeds on the old lines and the product is withheld from the people. The small production is disappearing while production on a large scale takes its place.

Those are facts resulting from the economic development of history and not from any conspiracy of communistic socialists. If we define *work* as an industrial undertaking whose products the worker uses for his own consumption, and an *industrial undertaking* as the work whose products go to the market, then it is not difficult to perceive how the development of industry must finally result in an organization of productive work. On the material organization of society scientific socialism is based.

Scientific socialists apply the inductive method. They stick to facts. They live in the real world and not in the spiritualist regions of scholasticism. The society we are striving for differs from the present but by formal modifications. Indeed, the society of the future is contained in the present society as the young bird is in the egg. Modern socialism is as yet more of a scientific doctrine than of a political party creed, though we are also rapidly approaching this stage. And strange to say, the *International* is of purely national descent: it proceeds from the German philosophy. If there be a grain of truth in the prating of "German" science, then the scientific German can only be found in his philosophic speculation. This speculation is on the whole an adventurous journey, yet at the same time a voyage of discovery. As the clumsy musket of our forefathers represents a necessary stage to the Prussian needle gun of the present time, so the metaphysical speculations of a Leibnitz, Kant, Fichte, Hegel are the inevitable paths leading up to the scientific proposition, that the idea, the conception, the logic or the thinking are not the premise, but the result of material phenomena. The interminable discussions between idealism and materialism, between nominalists and spiritualists on the one hand, and the realists or sensualists on the other hand, as to whether the idea was produced by the world or the world by the idea, and which of the two was the cause or the effect—this discussion, I say, forms the essence of philosophy. Its mission was to solve the antithesis between thought and being, between the idea and the material. A proof of this view I find in the fortnightly review *Unsere Zeit* for the second half of January, 1873, in an essay on intoxicating articles of consumption, as wine, tobacco, coffee, brandy, opium, etc. The author, after having stated that the use of intoxicants was to be found among all nations, at all times and under all conditions of human society, proceeds to declare that the cause of that fact must be looked for there, "where the cause of all religion and philosophy lies, in the antithesis of our being, in the partly divine, partly animal nature of man." This antagonism between divinity and animality in human nature is in other words the antithesis between the ideal and the material. Religion and philosophy work towards a reconciliation of those conflicting principles. Philosophy proceeded from religion and began to rebel against its conception of life. In religion the idea is the primary element which creates and regulates matter. Philosophy, the daughter of religion, naturally inherited a good deal of her mother's blood. She needed ages of growth to generate the anti-religious, scientific result, the apodictically safe proposition, that the world is not the attribute of spirit, but, on the contrary, that spirit, thought, idea is only one of the attributes of matter. Hegel, it is true, did not carry science to that height, yet so near was he to it that two of his followers, Feuerbach and Marx, scaled the summit. The clearing up of speculation helped Feuerbach to give us his wonderful analysis of religion, and enabled Marx to penetrate the deepest recesses of law, politics and history. When we see, however, Herbart, Schopenhauer, Hartmann, etc., still going on speculating and philosophizing, we cannot regard them as more than stragglers, lost in the phantastic depth of their own thoughts, lagging behind in the back-woods and not knowing that the speculative fire has been overcome in the front. On the other hand, Marx, the leader of scientific socialism, is achieving splendid success by applying inductive logic to branches of knowledge which have hitherto been maltreated by speculation. As far back as the year 1620 Francis Bacon declared in his "Novum Organon" the inductive method as the savior from unfruitful scholasticism and as the rock on which modern science was to be built.

Indeed, where we have to deal with concrete phenomena, or, as it were, with palpable things, the method of materialism has long since reigned supremely. Yet, it needed more than practical success: it needed the theoretical working-out in all its details in order to completely rout its enemy, the scholastic speculation or deduction. In his famous "History of Civilization in England" Thomas Buckle speaks at great length of the difference between the deductive and inductive mind, without, as it seems, having grasped the essence of the matter; he but proves what he admits himself in the introduction to his work that, though having made German philosophy a serious study, he did not *fully* penetrate it. If this happens to ripe and ingenious scholarship, what shall become of immature and superficial general knowledge which deals not with specialties but with the general results of science? In order to indicate clearly the scientific basis of socialism, I venture to enter more fully into the general result of philosophy, into the solution of the antithesis between the deductive and inductive method. But I fear lest the result of metaphysics, so ostentatiously announced, may appear to the reader as somewhat insignificant and commonplace. I beg, therefore, to remind you of Columbus who by means of an egg once for all furnished the proof that great discoveries resolve themselves into an ingenious, yet simple, idea.

When we retire to the solitude of our cell to search there in deep contemplation, or, as it were, in the innermost of our brains, for the right way we want to follow the next morning, we must remember that our mental effort can be successful only because of our previous, if involuntary, experiences and adventures which we, by help of our memory, have taken along into our cell.

That tells the whole story of philosophic speculation or deduction. These philosophers imagine they have drawn their theories, not from concrete material, but from the innermost of their brains, while, as a matter of fact, they have but performed an unconscious induction, a process of thought, of argument not without material, but with indefinite and therefore, confused material. Conversely, the inductive method is distinguished only by this, that its deduction is done consciously. Scientific "laws" are deductions drawn by human thinking from empiric material. The spiritist needs material just as the materialist needs spirit. This thesis, when brought out with mathematical precision, is the result of philosophic speculation.

That may appear simple enough, yet even a cursory examination of any of our reviews will teach us how little familiar that truth is not only to our journalists and writers but also to our historians and statesmen who are untiring in their attempts to evolve views and theses not from the existing conditions but from their heads, hearts, consciences, categorical imperatives or from some other unreal, mystical and spiritual corner. The concrete questions of the day are, as a rule, solved by, or with the help of, given material. But in the discussion with Bismarck whether might goes before right or conversely; in the squabbles of theology whether the gods are made by the world or the world by the gods; whether catechisms or natural sciences enlighten the mind; whether history moves upward to a higher stage or goes down to its Day of Judgment; in political and economic questions: whether capital or labor creates value, whether aristocracy or democracy is the right form of government, whether we have to work on conservative, liberal or revolutionary lines: in short, in abstract categories, in matters of philosophy, religion, politics and social life, our leaders of science find themselves in the most unscientific confusion. They test human institutions by such principles or ideas as the idea of justice, of liberty, of truth, etc. "We," says Friedrich Engels, "describe things as they are. Proudhon, on the other hand, wants our present society to arrange itself, not according to the laws of its economic development, but in conformity with the precepts of justice." Proudhon is in this respect the prototype of all unscientific doctrinairism.

A far superior guide in all such questions is modern socialism. Owing to its philosophical foundation it stands out prominently as a unanimous, firm and compact method amidst the endless and shifting dissensions of its political opponents of every shade and opinion. What the dogma is to the religious belief, material facts are to the science of inductive socialism, while the views of liberalism are as whimsical and elusive as the ideal conceptions, as the ideas of eternal justice or liberty on which the liberals believe to be safely based.

The fundamental proposition of inductive socialism may be thus formulated: there is no eternal principle or an *a priori* idea of the divine, just and free; there is no revelation or a chosen people, but there are material factors which govern human society.

Far from bewailing that fact, we acknowledge it as absolutely necessary and reasonable, as something which may be denied by power of imagination, but which cannot be altered, nor, indeed, ought it to be altered. By granting that society is dominated by material interests we do not deny the power of the ideals of the heart, mind, science and art. For we have no more to deal with the absolute antithesis between idealism and materialism, but with their higher synthesis which has been found in the knowledge that the ideal depends on the material, that divine justice and liberty depend on the production and distribution of earthly goods. In the wide range of human needs the bodily ones are the most indispensable; our physical needs must first be satisfied before we are able even to think of our mental ones and those of our heart, eye and ear. The same holds good in the life of nations and parties. Their abstract conceptions depend on the way they make their living. Tribes living by warfare and booty have not the same heaven, the same sense of justice or of liberty as our patriarchs are supposed to have had who, as is well known, were living on cattle-breeding. Knights and monks had notions of righteousness, of virtue and honour which were decidedly illiberal and *anti-bourgeois*, because their means of life were not supplied by factory labor and financial transactions.

Of course, the defenders of Christianity strongly object to those views. In order to prove the independence of spirit from matter and of philosophy from economics they make the assertion that the same Christian truth is invariably taught to all sorts and conditions of men, and under all climes. They forget, however, how they trimmed the sails to the wind. They forget likewise that the love preached by the apostles and churchfathers—the love which gave away the second coat—is no more the many-coated love under the overcoat which strips the poor to the skin—of course, rightfully. To the diverse modes of property and trade correspond diverse Christianities. The institution of slavery in [the] U.S.A. was Christian, and Christianity was slave-holding there. The religious reformation of the sixteenth century was not the cause, but the effect, of the social reformation that followed upon the shifting of the economic center from the manor to the city. And that was preceded by the rise of navigation and the discovery of the New World and new trade-routes, which indicate the rise of manufacture. Industrial life having no use for ascetic bodies introduced the protestant doctrine of grace that abolished religious exercises in favor of stern industrial work.

That the materialist conception of history is scientific induction and not idle speculation manifests itself even more clearly when we apply it to political party problems. With its help the tangled mass of party struggles can be easily unravelled into a clear, running thread. The squire is enthusiastic over the absolute monarchy because the absolute monarchy cared for the squirearchy. Manufacturers, merchants, bankers, in short, capitalists are liberal or constitutional, for constitutionalism is the political expression of capitalism, which liberalizes trade and commerce, supplies the factories with free labor, promotes banking and financial transactions, and, in general, takes care of the interests of industrial life. Philistines, shopkeepers, small tradesmen and peasants join alternately one party or the other according to the promises made with regard to the promotion of their well-being and to the relief from the effects of competition with big capital.

The familiar accusation of political hypocrisy which the Parliamentary parties throw at each other was suggested to Bismarck by one of the renegades of our camp whom he likes to employ. That accusation is based on the recognition that the aristocratic and middle class consciousness was formed by the material requirements of the landed and manufacturing and trading classes, and that behind their idealistic watchwords of religion, patriotism, freedom and progress lurks the concrete interest as the motor power. I cannot deny that many of their followers are not conscious of their real motives, and that they sincerely believe their political work to be purely idealistic. But I should like to remark that it is with recognitions as with epidemics, they are in the air and people feel them somehow. Indeed, the political hypocrisy of our time is half conscious, half unconscious. There are many people who take the ideological phrases as gospel truth, but also the artful are by no means rare who want them to be taken as such. The matter can be easily explained. Different classes, distinguished by their different material conditions, succeed each other to political power. The interests of the ruling class are always for a certain time in harmony with the interests of the community, that is with the progressive forces of civilization. And it is that harmony which justifies the ruling class in regarding itself as the spring of social welfare. However, the onward march of history changes everything, also the justification for ruling power. When the economic interests of the ruling class cease to be in harmony with the general welfare, when the ruling class loses its functions and falls into decay, then its leaders can only save their predominant position by hypocrisy; their phraseology has been emptied of all reality. It is no doubt true that some individuals rise above class interests and join the new social power which represents the interest of the community. So did Abbé Sieyès and Count de Mirabeau in the French Revolution, who, though belonging to the ruling classes, became the advocates of the third Estate. Still, these are exceptions proving only the inductive rule that, in social as in natural science, the material precedes the ideal.

It may appear rather contradictory to make the Hegelian system of philosophy with its pronounced idealism the starting point of the materialist conception of history. Yet, the Hegelian "Idea" is striving for realization; it is indeed a materialism in disguise. Conversely, the Hegelian reality appears in the mask of the "Idea," or of the logical conception. In one of the latest issues of *Blätter für Unterhaltung* Herr J. Volkelt makes the following remark: "Our modern thinkers have to submit to the crucial test of empiricism. The Hegelian principle has no reason to be afraid of such a test. Consistently followed up it means that the spirit of history can only be conceived through the existing material." Gleams of truth like these we can find now here and there in the periodical literature, but for a consistent and systematic application of the theory we must go to scientific socialism. The inductive method draws its mental conclusion from concrete facts. Scientific socialism considers our views dependent upon our material needs, and our political standpoint dependent upon the economic position of the class we belong to. Moreover, this conception corresponds with the aspirations of the masses whose needs are in the first place material, while the ruling class must necessarily base itself on the deductive principle, on the preconceived unscientific notion that the spiritual salvation and the mental training of the masses are to precede the solution of the social question.

34

FROM ABSOLUTISM
TO EXPERIMENTALISM

John Dewey

Perhaps the best palimpsest of the thought of the whole period and the
role of Hegelianism in it is John Dewey's autobiographical article "From
Absolutism to Experimentalism." A towering figure in American philosophy, Dewey had passed through nearly every phase of American
thought in the late nineteenth century, beginning with Kantianism. In
this backward glance over his distinguished career, the foremost American pragmatist acknowledges with some precision his abiding debt to
Hegel and the American Hegelians.

John Dewey, "From Absolutism to Experimentalism," in George P.
Adams and William P. Montague, *Contemporary American Philosophy*
(New York: Russell and Russell, 1962), vol. 2, pp. 13–27. Reprinted by
permission of the editors and publishers.

IN the late 'seventies, when I was an undergraduate, "electives"
were still unknown in the smaller New England colleges. But in
the one I attended, the University of Vermont, the tradition of a
"senior-year course" still subsisted. This course was regarded as a
kind of intellectual coping to the structure erected in earlier years,
or, at least, as an insertion of the key-stone of the arch. It included
courses in political economy, international law, history of civilization (Guizot), psychology, ethics, philosophy of religion (Butler's
Analogy), logic, etc., not history of philosophy, save incidentally.
The enumeration of these titles may not serve the purpose for
which it is made; but the idea was that after three years of somewhat specialized study in languages and sciences, the last year was
reserved for an introduction into serious intellectual topics of wide
and deep significance—an introduction into the world of ideas. I

doubt if in many cases it served its alleged end; however, it fell in with my own inclinations, and I have always been grateful for that year of my schooling. There was, however, one course in the previous year that had excited a taste that in retrospect may be called philosophical. That was a rather short course, without laboratory work, in Physiology, a book of Huxley's being the text. It is difficult to speak with exactitude about what happened to me intellectually so many years ago, but I have an impression that there was derived from that study a sense of interdependence and interrelated unity that gave form to intellectual stirrings that had been previously inchoate, and created a kind of type or model of a view of things to which material in any field ought to conform. Subconsciously, at least, I was led to desire a world and a life that would have the same properties as had the human organism in the picture of it derived from study of Huxley's treatment. At all events, I got great stimulation from the study, more than from anything I had had contact with before; and as no desire was awakened in me to continue that particular branch of learning, I date from this time the awakening of a distinctive philosophic interest.

The University of Vermont rather prided itself upon its tradition in philosophy. One of its earlier teachers, Dr. [James] Marsh, was almost the first person in the United States to venture upon the speculative and dubiously orthodox seas of German thinking—that of Kant, Schelling, and Hegel. The venture, to be sure, was made largely by way of Coleridge; Marsh edited an American edition of Coleridge's *Aids to Reflection.* Even this degree of speculative generalization, in its somewhat obvious tendency to rationalize the body of Christian theological doctrines, created a flutter in ecclesiastical dovecots. In particular, a controversy was carried on between the Germanizing rationalizers and the orthodox representatives of the Scottish school of thought through the representatives of the latter at Princeton. I imagine—although it is a very long time since I have had any contact with this material—that the controversy still provides data for a section, if not a chapter, in the history of thought in this country.

Although the University retained pride in its pioneer work, and its atmosphere was for those days theologically "liberal"—of the Congregational type—the teaching of philosophy had become more restrained in tone, more influenced by the still dominant Scotch school. Its professor, Mr. H. A. P. Torrey, was a man of genuinely sensitive and cultivated mind, with marked esthetic interest and taste, which, in a more congenial atmosphere than that of northern New England in those days, would have achieved something significant. He was, however, constitutionally timid, and never really let his mind go. I recall that, in a conversation I had with him a few years after graduation, he said: "Undoubtedly pantheism is the most satisfactory form of metaphysics intellectually, but it goes counter to religious faith." I fancy that remark told of an inner conflict that prevented his native capacity from coming to full fruition. His interest in philosophy, however, was genuine, not perfunctory; he was an excellent teacher, and I owe to him a double debt, that of turning my thoughts definitely to the study of philosophy as a life-pursuit, and of a generous gift of time to me during a year devoted privately under his direction to a reading of classics in the history of philosophy and learning to read philosophic German. In our walks and talks during this year, after three years on my part of high-school teaching, he let his mind go much more freely than in the class-room, and revealed potentialities that might have placed him among the leaders in the development of a freer American philosophy—but the time for the latter had not yet come.

Teachers of philosophy were at that time, almost to a man, clergymen; the supposed requirements of religion, or theology, dominated the teaching of philosophy in most colleges. Just how and why Scotch philosophy lent itself so well to the exigencies of religion I cannot say; probably the causes were more extrinsic than intrinsic; but at all events there was a firm alliance established between religion and the cause of "intuition." It is probably impossible to recover at this date the almost sacrosanct air that enveloped the idea of intuitions; but somehow the cause of all holy and valuable things was supposed to stand or fall with the validity of intuitionalism; the only vital issue was that between intuitionalism and a sensational empiricism that explained away the reality of all higher objects. The story of this almost forgotten debate, once so urgent, is probably a factor in developing in me a certain scepticism about the depth and range of purely contemporary issues; it is likely that many of those which seem highly important to-day will also in a generation have receded to the status of the local and provincial. It also aided in generating a sense of the value of the history of philosophy; some of the claims made for this as a sole avenue of approach to the study of philosophic problems seem to me misdirected and injurious. But its value in giving perspective and a sense of proportion in relation to immediate contemporary issues can hardly be over-estimated.

I do not mention this theological and intuitional phase because it had any lasting influence upon my own development, except negatively. I learned the terminology of an intuitional philosophy, but it did not go deep, and in no way did it satisfy what I was dimly reaching for. I was brought up in a conventionally evangelical atmosphere of the more "liberal" sort; and the struggles that later arose between acceptance of that faith and the discarding of traditional and institutional creeds came from personal experiences and not from the effects of philosophical teaching. It was not, in other words, in this respect that philosophy either appealed to me or influenced me—though I am not sure that Butler's *Analogy,* with its cold logic and acute analysis, was not, in a reversed way, a factor in developing "scepticism."

During the year of private study, of which mention has been made, I decided to make philosophy my life-study, and accordingly went to Johns Hopkins the next year (1884) to enter upon that new thing, "graduate work." It was something of a risk; the work offered there was almost the only indication that there were likely to be any self-supporting jobs in the field of philosophy for others than clergymen. Aside from the effect of my study with Professor Torrey, another influence moved me to undertake the risk. During the years after graduation I had kept up philosophical readings and I had even written a few articles which I sent to Dr. W. T. Harris, the well-known Hegelian, and the editor of the *Journal of Speculative Philosophy,* the only philosophic journal in the country at that time, as he and his group formed almost the only group of laymen devoted to philosophy for non-theological reasons. In sending an article I asked Dr. Harris for advice as to the possibility of my successfully prosecuting philosophic studies. His reply was so encouraging that it was a distinct factor in deciding me to try philosophy as a professional career.

The articles sent were, as I recall them, highly schematic and formal; they were couched in the language of intuitionalism; of Hegel I was then ignorant. My deeper interests had not as yet been met, and in the absence of subject-matter that would correspond to them, the only topics at my command were such as were capable of merely formal treatment. I imagine that my development has been controlled largely by a struggle between a native inclination toward the schematic and formally logical, and those incidents of personal experience that compelled me to take account of actual material. Probably there is in the consciously articulated ideas of every thinker an over-weighting of just those things that are contrary to his natural tendencies, an emphasis upon those things that are contrary to his intrinsic bent, and which, therefore, he has to struggle to bring to expression, while the native bent, on the other hand, can take care of itself. Anyway, a case might be made out for the proposition that the emphasis upon the concrete, empirical, and "practical" in my later writings is partly due to considerations of this nature. It was a reaction against what was more natural, and it served as a protest and protection against something in myself which, in the pressure of the weight of actual experiences, I knew to be a weakness. It is, I suppose, becoming a commonplace that when anyone is unduly concerned with controversy, the remarks that seem to be directed against others are really concerned with a struggle that is going on inside himself. The marks, the stigmata, of the struggle to weld together the characteristics of a formal, theoretic interest and the material of a maturing experience of contacts with realities also showed themselves, naturally, in style of writing and manner of presentation. During the time when the schematic interest predominated, writing was comparatively easy; there were even compliments upon the clearness of my style. Since then thinking and writing have been hard work. It is easy to give way to the dialectic development of a theme; the pressure of concrete experiences was, however, sufficiently heavy, so that a sense of intellectual honesty prevented a surrender to that course. But, on the other hand, the formal interest persisted, so that there was an inner demand for an intellectual technique that would be consistent and yet capable of flexible adaptation to the concrete diversity of experienced things. It is hardly necessary to say that I have not been among those to whom the union of abilities to satisfy these two opposed requirements, the formal and the material, came easily. For that very reason I have been acutely aware, too much so, doubtless, of a tendency of other thinkers and writers to achieve a specious lucidity and simplicity by the mere process of ignoring considerations which a greater respect for concrete materials of experience would have forced upon them.

It is a commonplace of educational history that the opening of Johns Hopkins University marked a new epoch in higher education in the United States. We are probably not in a condition as yet to estimate the extent to which its foundation and the development of graduate schools in other universities, following its example, mark a turn in our American culture. The 'eighties and 'nineties seem to mark the definitive close of our pioneer period, and the turn from the Civil War era into the new industrialized and commercial age. In philosophy, at least, the influence of Johns Hopkins was not due to the size of the provision that was made. There was a half-year of lecturing and seminar work given by Professor George Sylvester Morris, of the University of Michigan; belief in the "demonstrated" (a favourite word of his) truth of the substance of German idealism, and of belief in its competency to give direction to a life of aspiring thought, emotion, and action. I have never known a more single-hearted and whole-souled man—a man of a single piece all the way through; while I long since deviated from his philosophic faith, I should be happy to believe that the influence of the spirit of his teaching has been an enduring influence.

While it was impossible that a young and impressionable student, unacquainted with any system of thought that satisfied his head and heart, should not have been deeply affected, to the point of at least a temporary conversion, by the enthusiastic and scholarly devotion of Mr. Morris, this effect was far from being the only source of my own "Hegelianism." The 'eighties and 'nineties were a time of new ferment in English thought; the reaction against atomic individualism and sensationalistic empiricism was in full swing. It was the time of Thomas Hill Green, of the two Cairds, of Wallace, of the appearance of the *Essays in Philosophical Criticism,* co-operatively produced by a younger group under the leadership of the late Lord Haldane. This movement was at the time the vital and constructive one in philosophy. Naturally its influence fell in with and reinforced that of Professor Morris. There was but one marked difference, and that, I think, was in favour of Mr. Morris. He came to Kant through Hegel instead of to Hegel by way of Kant, so that his attitude toward Kant was the critical one expressed by Hegel himself. Moreover, he retained something of his early Scotch philosophical training in a common-sense belief in the existence of the external world. He used to make merry over those who thought the *existence* of this world and of matter were things to be proved by philosophy. To him the only philosophical question was as to the *meaning* of this existence; his idealism was wholly of the objective type. Like his contemporary, Professor John Watson, of Kingston, he combined a logical and idealistic metaphysics with a realistic epistemology. Through his teacher at Berlin, Trendelenburg, he had acquired a great reverence for Aristotle, and he had no difficulty in uniting Aristotelianism with Hegelianism.

There were, however, also "subjective" reasons for the appeal that Hegel's thought made to me; it supplied a demand for unification that was doubtless an intense emotional craving, and yet was a hunger that only an intellectualized subject-matter could satisfy. It is more than difficult, it is impossible, to recover that early mood. But the sense of divisions and separations that were, I suppose, borne in upon me as a consequence of a heritage of New England culture, divisions by way of isolation of self from the world, of soul from body, of nature from God, brought a painful oppression—or, rather, they were an inward laceration. My earlier philosophic study had been an intellectual gymnastic. Hegel's synthesis of subject and object, matter and spirit, the divine and the human, was, however, no mere intellectual formula; it operated as an immense release, a liberation. Hegel's treatment of human culture, of institutions and the arts, involved the same dissolution of hard-and-fast dividing walls, and had a special attraction for me.

As I have already intimated, while the conflict of traditional religious beliefs with opinions that I could myself honestly entertain was the source of a trying personal crisis, it did not at any time constitute a leading philosophical problem. This might look as if the two things were kept apart; in reality it was due to a feeling that any genuinely sound religious experience could and should adapt itself to whatever beliefs one found oneself intellectually entitled to hold—a half unconscious sense at first, but one which ensuing years have deepened into a fundamental conviction. In consequence, while I have, I hope, a due degree of personal sympathy with individuals who are undergoing the throes of a personal change of attitude, I have not been able to attach much importance to religion as a philosophic problem; for the effect of that attachment seems to be in the end a subordination of candid philosophic thinking to the alleged but factitious needs of some special set of convictions. I have enough faith in the depth of the religious tendencies of men to believe that they will adapt themselves to any required intellectual change, and that it is futile (and likely to be dishonest) to forecast prematurely just what forms the religious interest will take as a final consequence of the great intellectual transformation that is going on. As I have been frequently criticized for undue reticence about the problems of religion, I insert this explanation: it seems to me that the great solicitude of many persons, professing belief in the universality of the need for religion, about the present and future of religion proves that in fact they are moved more by partisan interest in a particular religion than by interest in religious experience.

The chief reason, however, for inserting these remarks at this point is to bring out a contrast effect. Social interests and problems from an early period had to me the intellectual appeal and provided the intellectual sustenance the many seem to have found primarily in religious questions. In undergraduate days I had run across, in the college library, Harriet Martineau's exposition of Comte. I cannot remember that his law of "the three stages" affected me particularly; but his idea of the disorganized character of Western modern culture, due to a disintegrative "individualism," and his idea of a synthesis of science that should be a regulative method of an organized social life, impressed me deeply. I found, as I thought, the same criticisms combined with a deeper and more far-reaching integration in Hegel. I did not, in those days when I read Francis Bacon, detect the origin of the Comtean idea in him, and I had not made acquaintance with Condorcet, the connecting link.

I drifted away from Hegelianism in the next fifteen years; the word "drifting" expresses the slow and, for a long time, imperceptible character of the movement, though it does not convey the impression that there was an adequate cause for the change. Nevertheless I should never think of ignoring, much less denying, what an astute critic occasionally refers to as a novel discovery—that acquaintance with Hegel has left a permanent deposit in my thinking. The form, the schematism, of his system now seems to me artificial to the last degree. But in the content of his ideas there is often an extraordinary depth; in many of his analyses, taken out of their mechanical dialectical setting, an extraordinary acuteness. Were it possible for me to be a devotee of any system, I still should believe that there is greater richness and greater variety of insight in Hegel than in any other single systematic philosopher—though when I say this I exclude Plato, who still provides my favourite philosophic reading. For I am unable to find in him that all-comprehensive and overriding system which later interpretation has, as it seems to me, conferred upon him as a dubious boon. The ancient sceptics overworked another aspect of Plato's thought when they treated him as their spiritual father, but they were nearer the truth, I think, than those who force him into the frame of a rigidly systematized doctrine. Although I have not the aversion to system as such that is sometimes attributed to me, I am dubious of my own ability to reach inclusive systematic unity, and in consequence, perhaps, of that fact also dubious about my contemporaries. Nothing could be more helpful to present philosophizing than a "Back to Plato" movement; but it would have to be back to the dramatic, restless, co-operatively inquiring Plato of the Dialogues, trying one mode of attack after another to see what it might yield; back to the Plato whose highest flight of metaphysics always terminated with a social and practical turn, and not to the artificial Plato constructed by unimaginative commentators who treat him as the original university professor.

The rest of the story of my intellectual development I am unable to record without more faking than I care to indulge in. What I have so far related is so far removed in time that I can talk about myself as another person; and much has faded, so that a few points stand out without my having to force them into the foreground. The philosopher, if I may apply that word to myself, that I became as I moved away from German idealism, is too much the self that I still am and is still too much in process of change to lend itself to record. I envy, up to a certain point, those who can write their intellectual biography in a unified pattern, woven out of a few distinctly discernible strands of interest and influence. By contrast, I seem to be unstable, chameleon-like, yielding one after another to many diverse and even incompatible influences; struggling to assimilate something from each and yet striving to carry it forward in a way that is logically consistent with what has been learned from its predecessors. Upon the whole, the forces that have influenced me have come from persons and from situations more than from books—not that I have not, I hope, learned a great deal from philosophical writings, but that what I have learned from them has been technical in comparison with what I have been forced to think upon and about because of some experience in which I found myself entangled. It is for this reason that I cannot say with candour that I envy completely, or envy beyond a certain point, those to whom I have referred. I like to think, though it may be a defence reaction, that with all the inconveniences of the road I have been forced to travel, it has the compensatory advantage of not inducing an immunity of thought to experiences—which perhaps, after all, should not be treated even by a philosopher as the germ of a disease to which he needs to develop resistance.

While I cannot write an account of intellectual development without giving it the semblance of a continuity that it does not in fact own, there are four special points that seem to stand out. One is the importance that the practice and theory of education have had for me: especially the education of the young, for I have never been able to feel much optimism regarding the possibilities of "higher" education when it is built upon warped and weak foundations. This interest fused with and brought together what might otherwise have been separate interests—that in psychology and that in social institutions and social life. I can recall but one critic who has suggested that my thinking has been too much permeated by interest in education. Although a book called *Democracy and Education* was for many years that in which my philosophy, such as it is, was most fully expounded, I do not know that philosophic critics, as distinct from teachers, have ever had recourse to it. I have wondered whether such facts signified that philosophers in general, although they are themselves usually teachers, have not taken education with sufficient seriousness for it to occur to them that any rational person could actually think it possible that philosophizing should focus about education as the supreme human interest in which, moreover, other problems, cosmological, moral, logical, come to a head. At all events, this handle is offered to any subsequent critic who may wish to lay hold of it.

A second point is that as my study and thinking progressed, I became more and more troubled by the intellectual scandal that seemed to me involved in the current (and traditional) dualism in logical standpoint and method between something called "science" on the one hand and something called "morals" on the other. I have long felt that the construction of a logic, that is, a method of effective inquiry, which would apply without abrupt breach of continuity to the fields designated by both of these words, is at once our needed theoretical solvent and the supply of our greatest practical want. This belief has had much more to do with the development of what I termed, for lack of a better word, "instrumentalism," than have most of the reasons that have been assigned.

The third point forms the great exception to what was said about no very fundamental vital influence issuing from books; it concerns the influence of William James. As far as I can discover one specifiable philosophic factor which entered into my thinking so as to give it a new direction and quality, it is this one. To say that it proceeded from his *Psychology* rather than from the essays collected in the volume called *Will to Believe*, his *Pluralistic Universe*, or *Pragmatism*, is to say something that needs explanation. For there are, I think, two unreconciled strains in the *Psychology*. One is found in the adoption of the subjective tenor of prior psychological tradition; even when the special tenets of that tradition are radically criticized, an underlying subjectivism is retained, at least in vocabulary—and the difficulty in finding a vocabulary which will intelligibly convey a genuinely new idea is perhaps the obstacle that most retards the easy progress of philosophy. I may cite as an illustration the substitution of the "stream of consciousness" for discrete elementary states: the advance made was enormous. Nevertheless the point of view remained that of a realm of consciousness set off by itself. The other strain is objective, having its roots in a return to the earlier biological conception of the *psyche*, but a return possessed of a new force and value due to the immense progress made by biology since the time of Aristotle. I doubt if we have as yet begun to realize all that is due to William James for the introduction and use of this idea; as I have already intimated, I do not think that he fully and consistently realized it himself. Anyway, it worked its way more and more into all my ideas and acted as a ferment to transform old beliefs.

If this biological conception and mode of approach had been prematurely hardened by James, its effect might have been merely to substitute one schematism for another. But it is not tautology to say that James's sense of life was itself vital. He had a profound sense, in origin artistic and moral, perhaps, rather than "scientific," of the difference between the categories of the living and of the mechanical; some time, I think, someone may write an essay that will show how the most distinctive factors in his general philosophic view, pluralism, novelty, freedom, individuality, are all connected with his feeling for the qualities and traits of that which lives. Many philosophers have had much to say about the idea of organism; but they have taken it structurally and hence statically. It was reserved for James to think of life in terms of life in action. This point, and that about the objective biological factor in James's conception of thought (discrimination, abstraction, conception, generalization), is fundamental when the rôle of psychology in philosophy comes under consideration. It is true that the effect of its introduction into philosophy has often, usually, been to dilute and distort the latter. But that is because the psychology was bad psychology.

I do not mean that I think that in the end the connection of psychology with philosophy is, in the abstract, closer than is that of other branches of science. Logically it stands on the same plane with them. But historically and at the present juncture the revolution introduced by James had, and still has, a peculiar significance. On the negative side it is important, for it is indispensable as a purge of the heavy charge of bad psychology that is so embedded in the philosophical tradition that it is not generally recognized to be psychology at all. As an example, I would say that the problem of "sense data," which occupies such a great bulk in recent British thinking, has to my mind no significance other than as a survival of an old and outworn psychological doctrine—although those who deal with the problem are for the most part among those who stoutly assert the complete irrelevance of psychology to philosophy. On the positive side we have the obverse of this situation. The newer objective psychology supplies the easiest way, pedagogically if not in the abstract, by which to reach a fruitful conception of thought and its work, and thus to better our logical theories— provided thought and logic have anything to do with one another. And in the present state of men's minds the linking of philosophy to the significant issues of actual experience is facilitated by constant interaction with the methods and conclusions of psychology. The more abstract sciences, mathematics and physics, for example, have left their impress deep upon traditional philosophy. The former, in connection with an exaggerated anxiety about formal certainty, has more than once operated to divorce philosophic thinking from connection with questions that have a source in existence. The remoteness of psychology from such abstractions, its nearness to what is distinctively human, gives it an emphatic claim for a sympathetic hearing at the present time.

In connection with an increasing recognition of this human aspect, there developed the influence which forms the fourth heading of this recital. The objective biological approach of the Jamesian psychology led straight to the perception of the importance of distinctive social categories, especially communication and participation. It is my conviction that a great deal of our philosophizing needs to be done over again from this point of view, and that there will ultimately result an integrated synthesis in a philosophy congruous with modern science and related to actual needs in education, morals, and religion. One has to take a broad survey in detachment from immediate prepossessions to realize the extent to which the characteristic traits of the science of to-day are connected with the development of social subjects—anthropology, history, politics, economics, language and literature, social and abnormal psychology, and so on. The movement is both so new, in an intellectual sense, and we are so much of it and it so much of us, that it escapes definite notice. Technically the influence of mathematics upon philosophy is more obvious; the great change that has taken place in recent years in the ruling ideas and methods of the physical sciences attracts attention much more easily than does the growth of the social subjects, just because it is farther away from impact upon us. Intellectual prophecy is dangerous; but if I read the cultural signs of the times aright, the next synthetic movement in philosophy will emerge when the significance of the social sciences and arts has become an object of reflective attention in the same way that mathematical and physical sciences have been made the objects of thought in the past, and when their full import is grasped. If I read these signs wrongly, nevertheless the statement may stand as a token of a factor significant in my own intellectual development.

In any case, I think it shows a deplorable deadness of imagination to suppose that philosophy will indefinitely revolve within the scope of the problems and systems that two thousand years of

European history have bequeathed to us. Seen in the long perspective of the future, the whole of western European history is a provincial episode. I do not expect to see in my day a genuine as distinct from a forced and artificial, integration of thought. But a mind that is not too egotistically impatient can have faith that this unification will issue in its season. Meantime a chief task of those who call themselves philosophers is to help get rid of the useless lumber that blocks our highways of thought, and strive to make straight and open the paths that lead to the future. Forty years spent in wandering in a wilderness like that of the present is not a sad fate—unless one attempts to make himself believe that the wilderness is after all itself the promised land.

SUGGESTIONS FOR
FURTHER READING

GENERAL STUDIES

THE principal general histories of philosophy in America are: Herbert W. Schneider, *A History of American Philosophy* (New York: Columbia University Press, 1946), still the standard reference text; H. G. Townsend, *Philosophical Ideas in the United States* (New York: American Book Company, 1934); W. H. Werkmeister, *A History of Philosophical Ideas in America* (New York: The Ronald Press Company, 1949). These are good general analyses of the central issues and developments in American philosophy, concentrating on the classic figures. The *Journal of Speculative Philosophy* is possibly the best extant introduction to the history of American philosophy during the second half of the nineteenth century, John M. Muirhead, *The Platonic Tradition in Anglo-Saxon Philosophy: Studies in the History of Idealism in England and America* (London: G. Allen and Unwin, Ltd., 1931) and G. Watts Cunningham, *The Idealistic Argument in Recent British and American Philosophy* (New York & London: The Century Co., 1933) remain the best technical works on idealistic thought during the period.

Historical accounts of the emergence of pragmatism out of the idealistic tradition are beginning to appear. H. S. Thayer, *Meaning and Action: A Critical History of Pragmatism* (Indianapolis & New York: Bobbs-Merrill, 1968), is an interpretive work that clearly indicates the historical relations between the two schools of thought. John Dewey, "The Development of American Pragmatism," *Studies in the History of Ideas*, vol. 2, (New York: Columbia University Press, 1925), 353–77, is a brief version of the themes enlarged upon by Thayer. Murray G. Murphey, "Kant's Children: The Cambridge Pragmatists," *Transactions of the Charles S. Peirce Society* 4 (1968): 3–33, also emphasizes the importance of understanding pragmatism in relation to the historical context of idealism from which it acquired a great deal of its form. For an introduction to Hegel's thought, the most accessible volume is Carl J. Friedrich, ed., *The Philosophy of Hegel* (New York: The Modern Library, 1953, 54).

GERMAN CULTURE IN AMERICA

There are available some very helpful bibliographic and reference guides to the subject of German culture in America: Henry A. Pochmann, *A Bibliographic Guide to German Culture in America to 1940* (Madison, Wis.: University of Wisconsin Press, 1953) and *German Culture in America: Philosophical and Literary Influence, 1600–1900* (Madison, Wis.: University of Wisconsin Press, 1957); Scott H. Goodnight, *German Literature in American Magazines Prior to 1846* (Madison, Wis.: University of Wisconsin Press, 1907); and Martin H. Haertel, *German Literature in American Magazines 1846–1880* (Madison, Wis.: University of Wisconsin Press, 1902). All are outstanding. The bibliographies by Goodnight and Haertel are annotated, chronological listings of most of the periodical articles on German subjects. Haertel's study centers more on specifically literary subjects than does Goodnight's. Bayard Q. Morgan, *A Bibliography of German Literature in English Translation* (Madison, Wis.: University of Wisconsin Press, 1922) is also useful.

MARXISM AND SOCIALISM

On the subject of Marxism in America, David Herreshoff, *American Disciples of Marx from the Age of Jackson to the Progressive Era* (Detroit: Wayne State University Press, 1967), is one of the most complete studies of the early Marxists. Stow Persons and Donald D. Egbert, eds., *Socialism and American Life*, 2 vols. (Princeton, N.J.: Princeton University Press, 1952), is the standard work. The second volume is an especially good bibliography.

TRANSCENDENTALISM

Two convenient anthologies of American transcendentalism containing some suggestive leads regarding connections with German thought are: Perry Miller, ed., *The Transcendentalists* (Cambridge, Mass.: Harvard University Press, 1950), which has valuable headnotes; and George Hochfield, ed., *Selected Writings of the American Transcendentalists* (New York & Toronto: New American Library, 1966). Ronald V. Wells, *Three Christian Transcendentalists* (New York: Columbia University Press, 1943), deals with C. S. Henry, F. H. Hedge, and James Marsh. It also provides a good bibliography.

PHILOSOPHICAL MOVEMENTS AND CLUBS IN EARLY AMERICA

Historical accounts of early nineteenth century American philosophical movements and clubs are not numerous and the few that do exist are often superficial, with factual errors or contradictions between the different reports being far from rare. Pochmann's works are the best sources to consult for basic information. Loyd D. Easton, *Hegel's First American Followers, The Ohio Hegelians: J. B. Stallo, Peter Kaufmann, Moncure Conway, August Willich* (Athens, Ohio: Ohio University Press, 1966), is primarily an intellectual history with a good introductory background and an appendix including selections from rare books by the subjects. Paul R. Anderson, *Platonism in the Midwest* (New York: Columbia University Press, 1963) is a well-researched account of Hiram K. Jones's Platonist movement in Jacksonville, Illinois. Henry A. Pochmann, *New England Transcendentalism and St. Louis Hegelianism* (Philadelphia: Carl Schurz Memorial Foundation, 1948), is an imaginative reconstruction of the confrontations between the transcendentalists and the boisterous frontier Hegelians. Denton J. Snider, *The St. Louis Movement in Philosophy, Literature, Education and Psychology, with Chapters of Autobiography* (St. Louis: Sigma Publishing Company, 1920), contains a retrospective account of the cultural charm of St. Louis and its eccentric Teutonic sages. D. H. Harris, ed., *The St. Louis Movement in Psychology, Literature, Art and Education* (St. Louis: [privately printed] 1922), offers a valuable collection of retrospective essays by individuals who knew the Hegelians. Charles M. Perry, *The St. Louis Movement in Philosophy* (Norman, Okla.: University of Oklahoma Press, 1930), contains a complete bibliography of works by all the members of the St. Louis Movement and a scattered collection of interesting source material. Allen Forbes, "The St. Louis School of Thought," *Missouri Historical Review*, 25 & 26 (1930–31): 83–101, 289–305, 461–73, 609–622, & 68–77, is a good history of the movement. Frances B. Harmon, *The Social Philosophy of the St. Louis Hegelians* (New York: Columbia University Press, 1943) places most of its emphasis on Snider's social philosophy. Austin Warren, "The Concord School of Philosophy," *New England Quarterly* 2 (1929): 199–233, remains the most comprehensive historical account of the Concord School.

EARLY AMERICAN WRITERS ON GERMAN THOUGHT

F. A. Rauch, *Psychology; Or, A View of the Human Soul; Including Anthropology* (New York: M. W. Dodd, 1840) is one of the earliest Hegelian works in America. H. J. Ziegler, *Frederick Augustus Rauch, American Hegelian* (Lancaster, Pa.: Franklin and Marshall College Press, 1953), is a study which awards Rauch the honor of being the first American Hegelian. F. H. Hedge, *Prose Writers of Germany* (Philadelphia: Carey and Hart, 1847) influenced most of the early American Hegelians.

WORKS OF THE OHIO HEGELIANS

Some of the more notable books by the Ohio Hegelians are: J. B. Stallo, *General Principles of the Philosophy of Nature, with an Outline of Some of Its Recent Developments Among the Germans, Embracing the Philosophical Systems of Schelling and Hegel, and Oken's System of Nature* (Boston: Wm. Crosby and H. P. Nichols, 1848); J. B. Stallo (Percy W. Bridgman, ed.), *The Concepts and Theories of Modern Physics* (Cambridge, Mass.: Harvard University Press, 1960; first published in New York by D. Appleton Co. in 1881 and in London by Kegan Paul, Trench & Co. in 1882 as vol. XLII of the International Scientific Series; Moncure D. Conway, *Autobiography, Memories and Experiences*, 2 vols. (New York: Houghton Mifflin, 1904); and Peter Kaufmann, *The Temple of Truth* (Canton, Ohio: By the Author, 1858).

SELECTED WORKS OF THE ST. LOUIS HEGELIANS

Significant works by members of the St. Louis Movement are: Susan Blow, *Educational Issues in the Kindergarten* (New York: D. Appleton and Company, 1908), *Symbolic Education* (New York: D. Appleton and Company, 1894), and *Letters to a Mother on the Philosophy of Froebel* (New York: D. Appleton and Company, 1899); Anna C. Brackett, *The Education of American Girls* (New York: D. Appleton and Company, 1874), *The Philosophy of Education* by Karl F. Rosenkranz, translated by A. C. Brackett (New York: D. Appleton and Company, 1904), and *Women and Higher Education* (New York: Harper & Brothers, 1893); Henry C. Brokmeyer, *A Mechanic's Diary* (Washington, D.C.: E. C. Brokmeyer, 1910); William T. Harris, *Hegel's Logic* (Chicago: S. C. Griggs and Co., 1895), Marietta Kies, ed., *Introduction to the*

Study of Philosophy (New York: D. Appleton and Company, 1890); E. L. Schaub, ed., *William Torrey Harris* (Chicago: Open Court Publishing Company, 1936); Kurt F. Leidecker, *Yankee Teacher: The Life and Letters of William Torrey Harris* (New York: Philosophical Library, 1946); George Holmes Howison, *The Limits of Evolution, and Other Essays Illustrating the Metaphysical Theory of Personal Idealism* (New York & London: Macmillan, 1901); John Buckham and G. Stratton eds., *George Holmes Howison, Philosopher and Teacher: A Selection from His Writings with a Biographical Sketch* (Berkeley, Calif.: University of California Press, 1934); Denton J. Snider, *Social Institutions in Their Origins, Growth, and Inter-Connection. Psychologically Treated* (St. Louis: Sigma Publishing Co., 1901), *A Writer of Books in His Genesis* (St. Louis: Sigma Publishing Co., 1910), and *The St. Louis Movement* (St. Louis: Sigma Publishing Company, 1920) (a few of the more than forty publications by Snider); and J. Gabriel Woerner, *The Rebel's Daughter: A Story of Love, Politics, and War* (Boston: Little, Brown & Co., 1899).

OTHER MAJOR PHILOSOPHERS OF THE PERIOD

Some helpful works dealing with other American philosophers of the day who were touched by idealism are: Paul A. Schilpp, ed., *The Philosophy of John Dewey*, 2nd ed. (New York: Tudor Publishing Co., 1951), a convenient anthology accompanied by the most complete bibliography of Dewey's writings; Joseph Ratner, ed., *Intelligence in the Modern World* (New York: Modern Library, 1939); Sidney Hook, *John Dewey: An Intellectual Portrait* (New York: John Day Co., 1939); G. Stanley Hall, *Recreations of a Psychologist* (New York and London: D. Appleton and Company, 1920), and *Life and Confessions of a Psychologist* (New York and London: D. Appleton and Company, 1923), his autobiography; Lorine Pruette, *G. Stanley Hall* (New York & London: D. Appleton and Company, 1926); Marc E. Jones, *George Sylvester Morris: His Philosophical Career and Theistic Idealism* (Philadelphia: D. McKay Co., 1948), which contains a complete bibliography; John J. McDermott, ed., *The Basic Writings of Josiah Royce*, 2 vols. (Chicago & London: University of Chicago Press, 1969), which includes an annotated bibliography of Royce's publications by Ignas K. Skrapskelis; John Clendenning, ed., *The Letters of Josiah Royce* (Chicago & London, University of Chicago Press, 1970); Frank M. Oppenheim, "A Critical Annotated Bibliography of the Published Works of Josiah Royce," *Modern Schoolman*, 41 (1964): 339–65; and James H. Cotton, *Royce on the Human Self* (Cambridge, Mass.: Harvard University Press, 1954).

WILLIAM H. GOETZMANN was born in 1930 in Washington, D.C., and attended Yale University, where he received his B.A. in 1952 and his Ph.D. in 1957. He taught history and American studies at Yale from 1955 to 1964, and in September 1964 he became Director of the American Studies Program at the University of Texas, where he is Stiles Professor of American Studies and Professor of History. Mr. Goetzmann was awarded the John Addison Porter Prize of Yale University for his doctoral dissertation, which was later published by Yale University Press as *Army Exploration in the American West*. His *Exploration and Empire: The Explorer and the Scientist in the Winning of the American West* won the Pulitzer Prize in history in 1967.

A NOTE ON THE TYPE

THE TEXT of this book was set in a typeface called Primer,
designed by Rudolph Ruzicka for the Mergenthaler Linotype Company and first made available in 1949. Primer,
a modified modern face based on Century broadface, has
the virtue of great legibility and was designed especially
for today's methods of composition and printing.

Primer is Ruzicka's third typeface. In 1940 he designed
Fairfield, and in 1947 Fairfield Medium, both for the
Mergenthaler Linotype Company.

Ruzicka was born in Bohemia in 1883 and came to the
United States at the age of eleven. He attended public
schools in Chicago and later the Chicago Art Institute. During his long career he has been a wood engraver, etcher,
cartographer, and book designer. For many years he was
associated with Daniel Berkeley Updike and produced the
annual keepsakes for The Merrymount Press from 1911
until 1941.

This book was composed, printed, and bound by the
Haddon Craftsmen, Inc., Scranton, Pa.